DIEDRICH KNICKERBOCKER'S

A

HISTORY OF NEW-YORK

BY

WASHINGTON IRVING

WITH AN INTRODUCTION BY ANDREW B. MYERS

ILLUSTRATED BY F.O.C. DARLEY

SLEEPY HOLLOW PRESS

A FACSIMILE EDITION

Library of Congress Cataloguing in Publication Data

Irving, Washington, 1783-1859.
  Diedrich Knickerbocker's A history of New York.

  Reprint. Originally published: A history of New York / by Diedrich
Knickerbocker. Authors's rev. ed. New York : Putnam, 1854. With
new introd.
    1. New York (State)–Social life and customs–Colonial period,
ca. 1600–1775. 2. New York (State)–History–Colonial period,
ca. 1600–1775. 3. Dutch Americans–New York (State)–Social life
and customs. I. Myers, Andrew B. II. Title. III. Title.: History of
New York.
F122.1.18374 1981 974.7'02 81-9131
ISBN 0-912882-46-8   AACR2

Introduction Copyright © 1981 by Sleepy Hollow
Restorations, Inc.

For information, address the publisher:

SLEEPY HOLLOW PRESS
150 White Plains Road
Tarrytown, New York 10591

ISBN 0-912882-46-8

Library of Congress Catalogue Card Number: 81-9131

First Printing

Manufactured in the United States of America

INTRODUCTION

"Once upon a time" is a hoary opening gambit for the striving storyteller, and an especially fitting one if there is a never-never land quality to the tale that follows. The *History of New-York* before you begins otherwise, though its real author was a gifted yarnspinner. The imaginary "Diedrich Knickerbocker," whose chronicles of old New Amsterdam young Washington Irving (1783–1859) fashioned for fun in 1809, testily pretended more to serious scholarship than to lightminded storytelling, so another kind of start was called for.

Still, from the beginning, there was an unmistakably once-upon-a-time air to his Chapter after Chapter, in Book after Book. And old Diedrich's largely make-believe 17th-century Dutch men, and women, of his "beloved island of Manna-hata" quickly took on a life of their own and became the stuff of which folklore and legend are made. Indeed, Irving wrought better than he could ever have dreamed of doing as a brash amateur of letters in the miniscule metropolis of his native New York in that far-off year of the first edition — 1809. But he proved to have created a unique, book-length, droll epic which has become an American classic with a vitality that has carried it close to a second century of comic appeal.

By design the present volume is not a facsimile of the linsey-woolsey, homespun original, but a carefully crafted replica of the Author's Revised Edition (ARE), Irving's 1848 final *History* as decorated two years later by the premier American book illustrator, Felix Octavius Carr Darley (1822–1888).[1] The whole was under the aegis of George Palmer Putnam (1814–1872), the shrewd, ambitious, if also lucky, Manhattan publisher who was the catalytic agent that produced that extensive and successful Author's Revised Edition.

But, just as the quixotic Diedrich turned all the way back to the creation of the world for openers, I move too far ahead this early on. Irving's own emerging career as a writer – to say tenuous vocation might make more sense – was a very sometime thing. Looked back on now, *his* history has its own fairytale qualities. For he came first, a distinction that has more than chronological merit even granted our culture's often indiscriminate fascination with "firsts." There is a praiseworthy pioneering element in his emergence as a native author – this *History* is much a case in point – that rightly commands respect. To make this clearer now, as the 200th anniversary of Irving's birth nears, let us turn back to American life in the land of his birth and rearing – the land, place, and time.

The thoughtful reader hardly needs to puzzle over why the youngest Irving family child was christened Washington. Born in lower Manhattan in 1783, the year in which redcoats and tars long stationed in the vital port of New York finally took ship for home, this sibling was patriotically named for the greatest hero of the vividly remembered Revolution. Washington Irving grew up to see the first United States flags fly over what would be, however briefly, the victorious nation's first capital, New York. Each school term of his childhood, history was being made around him in a truly tiny community which nevertheless figured on the world's maps as a key American port of entry, a mart for commerce, and a city of growing international significance.

For all his inherited chauvinism, the youngest Irving must have felt a sense of communion still with the British colonial inheritance shared by all the new thirteen seaboard states. At the same time, he could hardly have ignored the remaining signs of an earlier Dutch colonial past that still impinged on the present. Hardly surprising, then, that when his eventual choice was made of writing as a way of life, he would think of history and literature as boon companions, not competitors.

In making that choice he knew there was as yet no unmistakably American literature in the sense of a profitable trade or respected profession. It was simply too soon for that. Great Britain's fashions in books continued to be each season's rage as the *quondam* parent culture, defeated on the battlefield, was still triumphant in American library, printshop and schoolroom. Overseas, the disciplined Neo-Classicism of the Age of Pope and Swift was now experiencing a crucial shift in artistic sensibilities. A sanguine freedom of expression, particularly of strong feeling, was growing into what came to be called Romanticism. Irving grew as man and artist as this sweeping transformation occurred, here all the more slowly as a result of the time lag forced by oceanic distances and the inevitable distractions for an infant culture learning to stand steady on its own feet.

Irving's first quasi-literary efforts reflect the unsettled nature of this youthful culture. The *Salmagundi* issues he contributed to over 1807–1808 in a periodical directly descended in form and content from the *Tatler* and *Spectator* of Addison and Steele was in purpose, at least, a similarly idealistic scrutinizer of mores in town and country. Matters of sophistication and style aside, the essential difference between the two was the thinness of the Yankee Doodle vein of ore in which the Salmagundians as satirists could dig as social history. By contrast, London's Augustans had a mother lode to mine.

When a decade and a half later Irving's "Geoffrey Crayon" put together the miscellany that was the *Sketch Book* (1819–1820), it was obvious on both sides of the Atlantic that the author, *nom de plume* and all, had a consciousness of both British and American history, current and accumulated, that gave him as sure an appreciation of shared Anglo-Saxon shrines like Stratford-on-Avon and Westminster Abbey as of the deeply rooted Dutch-American contribution to the Hudson River Valley which helped him give literary immortality to fictitious Van Tassels and Van Winkles.

These New World lessons he had to learn as much by open air observation as by closeted study for, as the several old prefaces that follow make clear, there was appallingly little available to him in books and manuscripts to teach much about 17th-century New Netherland. That remained in his nonage "almost a *terra incognita.*"

When in 1860 his equally venerable contemporary William Cullen Bryant came to eulogize Irving, he spoke of this learning-by-experience:

> The town at that time (1783, *seq.*) contained a mingled population, drawn from different countries; but the descendants of the old Dutch settlers formed a large proportion of the inhabitants, and these preserved many of their peculiar customs, and had not ceased to use the speech of their ancestors at their firesides. Many of them lived in quaint old houses, built of small yellow bricks from Holland, with their notched gable-ends on the streets, which have since been swept away with the language of those who built them....

INTRODUCTION

In the surrounding country, along its rivers and besides its harbors, and in many parts far inland the original character of the Dutch settlements was still less changed. Here they read their Bibles and said their prayers and listened to sermons in the ancestral tongue. Remains of this language yet linger in a few neighborhoods; but in most, the common schools, and the irruptions of the Yankee race, and the growth of a population derived from Europe, have stifled the ancient utterances of New Amsterdam. I remember twenty years since the market people of Bergen chattered Dutch in the steamers which brought them in the early morning to New York.[2]

How much Irving ever learned of this Low Dutch tongue is less than certain but his familiarity with such scenes and sounds as these is, in a settlement that before 1800 was really built up only from the Battery to Wall Street and became countryside and farmland beyond. His schoolboy rambles crisscrossed all of this. Diedrich's crusty ruminations would be one result. Their genesis is jocularly explained in the author's 1848 "Apology." In 1809 the results added up to:

> ...among other things, a lampoon on European histories, European epics, American politics, American windiness and braggadocio, New England tricksters, and New York torpor. It is also a history of New York, faithful to what was known in 1809 of the general outline of events in the Dutch province of New Netherland discovered by Henry Hudson in 1609 and surrendered to the British by Peter Stuyvesant in 1664. Nevertheless, the author freely and frequently invents anecdotes, characters, and events because he lacked historical data, or because he wanted to make New Amsterdam a seventeenth-century version of the New York of 1809, or because he wanted to show his skill as a writer.[3]

Appearing locally and not at all coincidentally on December 6, the age-old feast of St. Nicholas (Diedrich's paeans for whom must have conditioned our later Yuletide thinking) and in the year of bicentennial remembrances of Hudson's discovery, this whole mock-heroic admixture was a sensation. The way for this triumph was prepared by one of the cleverest, yet simple, prepublication advertising gimmicks in all our literary history – Seth Handaside's missing person bulletins. In reading them one can imagine why a schoolboy acquaintance of Irving long remembered joining, as a result of the hoax, rubberneckers in Mulberry Street where the lost scribe's odd manuscript was supposedly found.

As for the book, most readers responded to the satire with open delight, including some knowing grins at slightly salty passages. But if some fellow citizens enjoyed without reservation the author's broad but not slapdash parodies, and pointed ironies, stoutly clannish Dutch descendants in the area tended to take offense at Diedrich's really harmless imaginings. One proper Albany lady was so incensed at seeming insults to hallowed ancestors, she spoke of horsewhipping the villainous concocter if discovered. After sharing a transatlantic gift copy, Walter Scott wrote from Abbotsford in 1813 that "our sides have been absolutely sore with laughing."[4] European editions followed in time and by 1831, when Irving received an honorary D.C.L. degree from Oxford, undergraduates boisterously greeted him with customary outcries – in his case "Ichabod Crane!", "Rip Van Winkle!", and also "Diedrich Knickerbocker!" A decade before, young Ralph Waldo Emerson had been displeased with Knickerbocker's "deplorable Dutch wit."[5] Stack this up against the *History*'s several descriptions of decidedly unfunny New Englanders. A decade

later, an older Irving had become well established at
home as the "Dutch Herodotus," a welcome collector
(and creator) of colorful colonial annals, these all the
more welcome since dramatic history hereabouts looked
puny beside Europe's centuries of sagas.

Irving's bumptious chronicles were of the reigns of
just three Dutch governors, each broadly though dif-
ferently caricatured. From the beginning these jocose
portraits, and the half-invented milieu that framed them,
attracted a host of visual artists who shared the author's
equally broad sense of humor. While Irving tinkered
with revised editions later, getting more conservative as
he got older, the *History* still did not lose the essential
comic aspects that captured the imagination of both
readers and the special breed of book illustrators in New
World and Old.

Indeed, quite separately from these last, easel painters
were teased into their own Knickerbocker visions.
Witness, in time, the large full color painting attributed
to Britisher William Heath (1795–1840), "Peter Stuyvesant's Army entering New Amsterdam." A well-
known draftsman and engraver, Heath produced six
rollicking etchings for a British anthology *The Beauties
of Washington Irving* in 1825, a pirated collection minus
the painting's ragtag and bobtail Manna-hata militia on
parade. As a bonus to the 1850 edition already generously illustrated with "Designs by Darley," publisher Putnam added "a larger illustration on stone, from a drawing by Heath, of London, a humourous representation of
Peter Stuyvesant's Army." This is the fold-out at the
back of your volume, prepared by modern technology
inconceivable to even a Diedrich Knickerbocker.

During Irving's middle years, American literature
came of age, and art too in the Hudson River School of
Painters. The careers of James Fenimore Cooper,

Bryant, and Irving himself assisted in this development. This maturation of aesthetic sensibilities was paralleled by a vast improvement over inherited job box and composing stick methods of handset printing. The spread of stereotyping in the early 19th century was a revolution in itself. Ambitious book illustration soon became a rage, as engraving techniques (using prior artist's designs) improved apace. American skills in durable woodcuts reached a highwater mark by mid-century.[6] And here, the name of Felix Octavius Carr Darley led all the rest.

Before Darley can be brought more clearly into the picture, there is a businessman's bridge to be built between Irving and the artist. Front and center George Palmer Putnam! Putnam was, like the questing creative writers in Irving's own generation, a memorable groundbreaker. An alert and honest "Down Easter," his road to publishing success early took him from Maine to Massachusetts to New York, in a step by step involvement in the expanding world of publishing that would see him put his own name to a Manhattan-based firm in 1848.

One of his first coups was to convince Washington Irving that a multi-volumed Author's Revised Edition of his complete works would sell strongly enough to undertake this first-ever feat in American letters. Upon his return to the United States in 1846, Irving—whose last absence was spent in public service as Minister to Spain —retreated to Sunnyside, his self-styled "snuggery" on the Hudson between Tarrytown and Dobbs Ferry overlooking the Tappan Zee. But even doll-like estates run up bills and he soon had cash-flow problems. His royalties decreased as the existing editions of his works grew older. Equally disturbing was that no international copyright laws prohibited overseas literary piracy.

INTRODUCTION

As insurance, Irving dusted off his "Esquire" and played briefly at attorney in the family law office in New York City. Let George Haven Putnam, inheritor of his father's mantle, tell the rest:

> John Treat Irving the second, nephew of Washington Irving, told me more than once of the pleasurable excitement with which his uncle read this letter to his father. "There is no necessity, John," said Washington, as he kicked over the desk in front of him, "for my bothering further with the law. Here is a fool of a publisher going to give me a thousand dollars a year for doing nothing."

This 20th-century reminiscence is flawed in detail but the anecdote remains delightful enough to repeat.[7] One unassailable fact is that the resulting contract was very generous. Fifteen sturdy (but pictureless) ARE volumes came out over 1848–1851, with the dollars-and-cents commitment between these two professionals growing into a warm personal relationship.

Putnam's confidence in Irving's continuing hold on his audiences was proven profitable by sustained ARE sales. Even more profitable to the publisher, however, were the illustrated editions. Irving's contract with Putnam allowed the publisher to issue illustrated editions for which Irving would receive only his standard royalty. The balance of the profits from these higher-priced books would belong to Putnam. These illustrated editions included *The Sketch Book* (1848) and the *History of New-York* (1850). This last is the true parent of the present facsimile. These enhanced, revised texts were graced by brilliant engraving work from designs by F.O.C. Darley, already the foremost illustrator on the American scene. Putnam's golden touch in all this helps to explain why he has gone down in publishing history as "one of the most admirable of the pioneers."[8]

Felix O.C. Darley had that All-American kind of success story to tell, the self-made man who got to the top. Darley was an autodidact, who used his successes in his native Philadelphia as a springboard to a career in New York City. He arrived in time to capitalize on the renewed interest in the recently returned Irving. One key result was the commission to do six outline drawings to illustrate "Rip Van Winkle" for the American Art-Union in 1848. Another six drawings for "The Legend of Sleepy Hollow" followed in 1849. These turned out to be technical triumphs of an order unexcelled by even influential foreign masters, and were attractive in the extreme. Exhibiting clarity, sentiment, and wit, they also had an unmistakably native spirit that fitted hand-in-glove with Irving's own. Putnam's choice for an illustrator, especially for the burlesque *History of New-York,* was both logical and a happy success. This fitting combination of talents was advertised, with Darley's name prominently displayed, as "Elegantly printed in Royal Octavo. Price in cloth, $3 50 (*sic*): extra dark cloth, gilt edges, $4; dark calf, antique style, $5; morocco extra, $6."

This introduction is meant to be an open door greeting and so should not linger over biographical minutiae, though it would be interesting to learn more about Irving-*cum*-Darley than is recoverable from present sources. In the 1850's, Sunnyside itself had quite an open door policy, which brought as callers sundry accomplished visitors, and others unknown to fame. Along with these were numerous adepts with brush or pen, and even the newfangled wet plate camera. This had been a pattern in Irving's life since young manhood, when Washington Allston, Charles Robert Leslie, and Gilbert Stuart Newton were close friends. The *Alhambra* of 1832 was dedicated to his hardy companion on Spanish travels, the distinguished Scottish painter David Wilkie.

INTRODUCTION

Alas, scant references have surfaced to any publisher's conferences held in New York City, though these must have brought together for an exchange of ideas the author and illustrator. While it is a matter of conjecture, it is *likely* that more relaxed work sessions were held upriver, at Sunnyside. A drawing of Irving inscribed by Darley "from life July 1848" (*sic*) places the illustrator at Sunnyside during the planning stages of the Author's Revised Edition.

Pierre M. Irving, the author's nephew and literary executor, records in the official biography that in 1855, after speaking of favorite actors, his uncle went on about artists thus:

> Jarvis tried, but failed to embody my conception of Diedrich Knickerbocker. Leslie also. Darley hit it in the illustrated History of New York. My idea was that he should carry the air of one profoundly impressed with the truth of his own History.[9]

A 20th-century authority on Pierre's great importance in Irving's life can add, from Pierre's private journal, that on April 13, 1859, while the old man napped, a party arrived at Sunnyside that included Darley.[10] The visitors strolled in the dusk until Irving awoke and then were entertained in the parlor. This visit, ten days after the author's last birthday, must have included congratulations from admirers whose presence was welcome to the weary squire.

Today, in the little rear galley at Sunnyside, there are a number of Darley originals. These are small drawings, some wash, some pencil only, each framed and mounted. Seven derive from the *History*, including the seated Diedrich, with tricorn hat (frontis). Several drawings do not appear in Putnam's illustrated editions. And in one instance, a separate lithograph of mounted Indians in a warpath melee has on the back two trial sketches for a bareheaded Knickerbocker musing over his pages. It does not appear these were further developed for inclusion in the illustrated edition. As these items were Irving's possessions, whether asked for or given, they clearly represent "Diedrich Knickerbocker's" appreciation at being so well "Illustrated by Darley."

Sleepy Hollow Press is proud to offer this facsimile of the Irving-Putnam-Darley collaboration for modern perusal, from gold-stamped cover to cover. It is confident it will be, as once-upon-a-time the author wished for his faked but funny *History*, "thumbed and chuckled over" as its choice words and pictures deserve. Come see for yourself.

Andrew Breen Myers

INTRODUCTION

1. For a discussion of the composition and reproduction of this facsimile, see the Publisher's Note which follows.

2. William Cullen Bryant, *A Discourse on the Life...of Washington Irving. Delivered Before the New-York Historical Society at the Academy of Music in New York April* 3, 1860 (New York: G.P. Putnam, 1860), pp. 8–9.

3. Michael L. Black, "Political Satire in Knickerbocker's History" in Andrew B. Myers, ed., *The Knickerbocker Tradition: Washington Irving's New York* (Tarrytown: Sleepy Hollow Restorations, 1974), p. 66.

4. For particulars on the Albany story as well as Scott's reading of the 1812 revision sent to him by Irving's friend Henry Brevoort, see Pierre M. Irving, *The Life and Letters of Washington Irving. By His Nephew,* 4 vols. (New York: G.P. Putnam, 1862–1864), I, pp. 240, 246–247.

5. See Ralph L. Rusk, *The Life of Ralph Waldo Emerson* (New York: Charles Scribner's Sons, 1949). p. 93.

6. On the meanings of "woodcut" see Sinclair Winston, *Early American Book Illustrators and Wood Engravers, 1670–1870,* 2 vols. (Princeton: Princeton University Press, 1968), I, xxxiii, 19n, 101 ff.; II, vii, 67 ff.

7. One vitiating error is that the "father" in the quotation, J.T. Irving, I, died in 1838. As for kicking over the desk? Well, why not! For further details see George H. Putnam, *George Palmer Putnam, A Memoir* (New York: G.P. Putnam's Sons, 1912), p. 128.

8. John W. Tebell, *A History of Book Publishing in the United States,* 2 vols. (New York: R.R. Bowker Co., 1972), I, p. 299.

9. Irving, *Life and Letters,* IV, pp. 242–243. John Wesley Jarvis (1781–1839) did a well-known early portrait of Washington Irving. No surviving Knickerbocker illustrations can be located. C.R. Leslie (1794–1859) did illustrations for the *History* which have been widely reproduced.

10. On the 1859 visit, see Wayne R. Kime, *Pierre M. Irving and Washington Irving: A Collaboration in Life and Letters* (Waterloo, Ont.: Wilfrid Laurier Press, 1977), pp. 101–102, 190.

PUBLISHER'S NOTE

This facsimile edition of Diedrich Knickerbocker's *A History of New-York* represents a triumph of modern printing technology and editorial research. When George Palmer Putnam first issued the revised edition in 1850, with illustrations by F.O.C. Darley, he made use of the finest production techniques that contemporary book manufacturing had developed. By the time the 1854 impression was made available to a discerning book-buying public, the persistent wear on the existing stereoplates, brought on by intervening impressions, caused a deterioration in type integrity so severe as to make portions of the text nearly illegible. Compounding this problem was the debilitating effect of time and the elements, factors which combined to stain and spot the aging volume chosen by Sleepy Hollow Press for reproduction.

The present volume is, therefore, a carefully drawn composite of three separate editions which vary only slightly in their respective number of illustrations and dates of impression. Because of the title's scarcity and the poor condition of extant copies, strict editorial criteria were established so that the facsimile produced would be as close to the 1854 impression as possible. Each of the three volumes utilized (published in 1850,

1854, and 1860) was compared, then chosen for inclusion, on a page-by-page basis for clarity of type, completeness, and reproductive value. Since a pristine copy of *A History of New-York* could not be located, these steps were necessary before the painstakingly intricate camera work could begin.

During the selection process, a number of idiosyncrasies were detected in the 1854 impression. To determine if these were typical of the revised, illustrated *History,* the current publishers were forced to survey all known copies of the imprint, and undertake an analysis of nineteenth-century printing technology. Exhaustive research efforts have indicated that the peculiarities of the 1854 impression are typical, and lend an intrinsic and authentic value to the facsimile edition. As a result, the original impression has been left untouched, and is here reproduced in all its great beauty and glaring defects.

The reader will detect some broken typefaces throughout the text, as well as uneven baselines. These are features of the 1854 impression; no presumption of editorial oversight should be made. Equal notice will be taken of bindery guides, printed on certain pages in progressions of 8, 16, and 24. (This practice continues today, although the numbers are no longer engraved into the page plate.)

The most noticeable—and mystifying—idiosyncracy of the 1854 impression was discovered to be a number of missing illustrations. While the illustrations pages in both the 1850 and 1854 editions list sixteen Darleys and the Heath fold-out, only the 1850 imprint has that specified number. The engravings missing from the 1854 edition were tipped-in—not printed directly on the page—in the 1850 edition. It is possible that the omission in the 1854 volume was the result of excessive wear on the wood engravings or, more simply, the result of human error; either way, no definitive solution has been uncovered. For purposes of this edition, the editors have chosen to include *all* illustrative matter as listed on the 1854 illustrations page, and to print these remarkable Darleys as part of the text proper.

Two liberties have been taken by the editors in preparing this facsimile. The first involves the delightful pullout illustration of "Peter Stuyvesant's Army entering New Amsterdam," by William Heath. Without the original lithograph of this famous satirical work, reproduction of the pullout became almost a labor of love. Any number of current reproductive techniques were attempted before the printer found the correct method — preparation of a duotone negative through the application of a laser scanner. The reproduction contained at the end of this volume thus mirrors the original in subtlety of shade and tone, and only faintly shows the creases worn into the paper by the press of time.

The second liberty was also taken to ensure a full appreciation of the fine artwork represented by this volume. Both the die and original stamping of the blue, clothbound edition have been matched with great care; however, the embossing on front and back covers has been increased in size for the sake of clarity of design.

The present facsimile edition of *A History of New-York* was reproduced and printed by Aristographics, Inc., of New York City, and bound by Economy Bookbinding Corp. of Kearny, New Jersey. The cover die was prepared by Truart Engraving, also of New York. *A History of New-York* was printed on an acid-free paper manufactured especially for this edition by Mohawk Paper Mills, Inc., of Cohoes, New York. The front matter new to this edition was set in Century Oldstyle, a typeface chosen for its resemblance to the 1854 type used by G.P. Putnam.

Finally, a brief note of special acknowledgement is due to Marvin Galanty and Ellen Galanty for their expert

PUBLISHER'S NOTE

advice on the reproduction and printing of this volume.
Special thanks also go to Edward J. McLaughlin, who
designed the introductory matter and the jacket (which
is not a facsimile but an original creation for this edition);
Professor Edwin Bowden of the University of Texas at
Austin for sharing with us his knowledge of Irving editions; Robert C. Pedersen of Economy Bookbinding; and
Peter J. Malia, for his long hours of research and close
scrutiny of the editions, without which this splendid
reproduction might never have come to pass.

The Editors
Sleepy Hollow Press

KNICKERBOCKER'S HISTORY OF NEW YORK

DARLEY DEL.

J. W. ORR & ANDREW SC. N.Y.

A

HISTORY OF NEW-YORK,

FROM THE

BEGINNING OF THE WORLD TO THE END OF THE DUTCH DYNASTY;

CONTAINING, AMONG MANY SURPRISING AND CURIOUS MATTERS, THE UNUTTERABLE
PONDERINGS OF WALTER THE DOUBTER, THE DISASTROUS PROJECTS OF
WILLIAM THE TESTY, AND THE CHIVALRIC ACHIEVEMENTS OF PETER
THE HEADSTRONG—THE THREE DUTCH GOVERNORS OF NEW
AMSTERDAM: BEING THE ONLY AUTHENTIC HISTORY
OF THE TIMES THAT EVER HATH BEEN OR
EVER WILL BE PUBLISHED.

BY

Diedrich Knickerbocker.

De waarheid die in duister lag,
Die komt met klaarheid aan den dag.

WITH ILLUSTRATIONS

By FELIX O. C. DARLEY,

ENGRAVED BY EMINENT ARTISTS.

NEW-YORK:

G. P. PUTNAM & COMPANY, 10 PARK PLACE,

1854.

ILLUSTRATIONS.

CONTENTS.

BOOK I.

CONTAINING DIVERS INGENIOUS THEORIES AND PHILOSOPHIC SPECULATIONS,
CONCERNING THE CREATION AND POPULATION OF THE WORLD, AS CON-
NECTED WITH THE HISTORY OF NEW-YORK.

BOOK II.

BOOK III.

BOOK IV.

CONTAINING THE CHRONICLES OF THE REIGN OF WILLIAM THE TESTY.

BOOK V.

CONTAINING THE FIRST PART OF THE REIGN OF PETER STUYVESANT,
AND HIS TROUBLES WITH THE AMPHICTYONIC COUNCIL.

CONTENTS.

BOOK VI.

CONTAINING THE SECOND PART OF THE REIGN OF PETER THE HEADSTRONG, AND HIS GALLANT ACHIEVEMENTS ON THE DELAWARE.

BOOK VII.

THE AUTHOR'S APOLOGY.

THE following work, in which, at the outset, nothing more was contemplated than a temporary jeu d'esprit, was commenced in company with my brother, the late Peter Irving, Esq. Our idea was to parody a small hand-book which had recently appeared, entitled "A Picture of New-York." Like that, our work was to begin with an historical sketch; to be followed by notices of the customs, manners, and institutions of the city; written in a serio-comic vein, and treating local errors, follies, and abuses with good-humored satire.

To burlesque the pedantic lore displayed in certain American works, our historical sketch was to commence with the creation of the world; and we laid all kinds of works under contribution for trite citations, relevant or irrelevant, to give it the proper air of learned research. Before this crude mass of mock erudition could be digested into form, my brother departed for Europe, and I was left to prosecute the enterprise alone.

I now altered the plan of the work. Discarding all idea of a parody on the Picture of New-York, I determined that what had been originally intended as an introductory sketch, should comprise the whole work, and form a comic history of the city. I accordingly moulded the mass of citations and disquisitions into introductory chapters forming the first book; but it soon became evident to me that, like Robinson Crusoe with his boat, I had begun on too large a scale, and that, to launch my history successfully, I must reduce its proportions. I accordingly resolved to confine it to the period of the Dutch domination, which, in its rise, progress, and decline, presented that unity of subject required by classic rule. It was a period, also, at that time almost a terra incognita in history. In fact, I was surprised to find how few of my fellow-citizens were aware that New-York had ever been called New-Amsterdam, or had heard of the names of its early Dutch governors, or cared a straw about their ancient Dutch progenitors.

This, then, broke upon me as the poetic age of our city; poetic from its very obscurity; and open, like the early and obscure days of ancient Rome, to all the embellishments of heroic fiction. I hailed my native city, as fortunate above all other American cities, in having an antiquity thus extending back into the regions of doubt and fable; neither did I conceive I was committing any grievous historical sin in helping out the few facts I could collect in this remote and forgotten region with figments of my own brain, or in giving characteristic attributes to the few names connected with it which I might dig up from oblivion.

In this, doubtless, I reasoned like a young and inexperienced writer, besotted with his own fancies; and my presumptuous trespasses into this sacred, though neglected, region of history have met with deserved rebuke from men of soberer minds. It is too late, however, to recall the shaft thus rashly launched. To any one whose sense of fitness it may wound, I can only say with Hamlet,

> Let my disclaiming from a purposed evil
> Free me so far in your most generous thoughts,
> That I have shot my arrow o'er the house,
> And hurt my brother.

I will say this in further apology for my work: that if it has taken an unwarrantable liberty with our early provincial history, it has at least turned attention to that history and provoked research. It is only since this work appeared that the forgotten archives of the province have been rummaged, and the facts and personages of the olden time rescued from the dust of oblivion and elevated into whatever importance they may vitually possess.

The main object of my work, in fact, had a bearing wide from the sober aim of history; but one which, I trust, will meet with some indulgence from poetic minds. It was to embody the traditions of our city in an amusing form; to illustrate its local humors, customs, and peculiarities; to clothe home scenes and places and familiar names with those imaginative and whimsical associations so seldom met with in our new country, but which live like charms and spells about the cities of the old world, binding the heart of the native inhabitant to his home.

In this I have reason to believe I have in some measure succeeded. Before the appearance of my work the popular traditions of our city were unrecorded; the peculiar and racy customs and usages derived from our Dutch progenitors were unnoticed, or regarded with indifference, or adverted to with a sneer. Now they form a convivial currency, and are brought forward on all occasions; they link our whole community together in good humor and good fellowship; they are the rallying points of home feeling; the seasoning of our civic festivities; the staple of local tales and local pleasantries; and are so harped upon by our writers of popular fiction, that I find myself almost crowded off the legendary ground which I was the first to explore, by the host who have followed in my footsteps.

I dwell on this head because, at the first appearance of my work, its aim and drift were misapprehended by some of the descendants of the Dutch worthies; and because I understand that now and then one may still be found to regard it with a captious eye. The far greater part, however, I have reason to flatter myself, receive my good-humored picturings in the same temper with which they were executed; and when I find, after a lapse of nearly forty years, this hap-hazard production of my youth still cherished among them; when I find its very name become a "household word," and used to give the home stamp to every thing recommended for popular acceptation, such as Knickerbocker societies; Knickerbocker insurance companies; Knickerbocker steamboats; Knickerbocker omnibuses; Knickerbocker bread, and Knickerbocker ice; and when I find New-Yorkers of Dutch descent priding themselves upon being "genuine

Knickerbockers," I please myself with the persuasion that I have struck
the right chord; that my dealings with the good old Dutch times, and the
customs and usages derived from them, are in harmony with the feelings
and humors of my townsmen; that I have opened a vein of pleasant associations and quaint characteristics peculiar to my native place, and which its
inhabitants will not willingly suffer to pass away; and that, though other
histories of New-York may appear of higher claims to learned acceptation,
and may take their dignified and appropriate rank in the family library;
Knickerbocker's history will still be received with good-humored indulgence, and be thumbed and chuckled over by the family fireside.

W. I.

Sunnyside, 1848.

Notices

WHICH APPEARED IN THE NEWSPAPERS PREVIOUS TO THE PUBLICATION
OF THIS WORK.

<hr>

From the Evening Post of October 26, 1809.

DISTRESSING.

Left h.s lodgings some time since, and has not since been heard of, a small elderly gentleman, dressed in an old black coat and cocked hat, by the name of *Knickerbocker* As there are some reasons for believing he is not entirely in his right mind, and as great anxiety is entertained about him, any information concerning him left either at the Columbian Hotel, Mulberry-street, or at the office of this paper, will be thankfully received.

P. S. Printers of newspapers would be aiding the cause of humanity in giving an insertion to the above.

From the same, November 6, 1809.

To the Editor of the Evening Post:

Sir,—Having read in your paper of the 26th October last, a paragraph respecting an old gentleman by the name of *Knickerbocker*, who was missing from his lodgings; if it would be any relief to his friends, or furnish them with any clue to discover where he is, you may inform them that a person answering the description given, was seen by the passengers of the Albany stage, early in the morning, about four or five weeks since, resting himself by the side of the road, a little above King's Bridge. He had in his hand a small bundle tied in a red bandana handkerchief: he appeared to be traveling northward, and was very much fatigued and exhausted.

A TRAVELER.

From the same, November 16, 1809.

To the Editor of the Evening Post:

Sir,—You have been good enough to publish in your paper a paragraph about Mr. *Diedrich Knickerbocker*, who was missing so strangely some time since. Nothing satisfactory has been heard of the old gentleman since ; but *a very curious kind of a written book* has been found in his room, in his own handwriting. Now I wish you to notice him, if he is still alive, that if he does not return and pay off his bill for boarding and lodging, I shall have to dispose of his book to satisfy me for the same.

I am, Sir, your humble servant,

SETH HANDASIDE,
Landlord of the Independent Columbian Hotel, Mulberry-street

From the same, November 28, 1809.
LITERARY NOTICE.
INSKEEP & BRADFORD have in the press, and will shortly publish

A History of New-York,

In two volumes, duodecimo.   Price three dollars.

Containing an account of its discovery and settlement, with its internal policies, manners, customs, wars, &c. &c., under the Dutch government, furnishing many curious and interesting particulars never before published, and which are gathered from various manuscript and other authenticated sources, the whole being interspersed with philosophical speculations and moral precepts.

This work was found in the chamber of Mr. Diedrich Knickerbocker, the old gentleman whose sudden and mysterious disappearance has been noticed. It is published in order to discharge certain debts he has left behind.

From the American Citizen, December 6, 1809.
Is this day published
By INSKEEP & BRADFORD, No. 128 Broadway,
A History of New-York,
&c., &c.
(Containing same as above.)

ACCOUNT OF THE AUTHOR.

IT was some time, if I recollect right, in the early part of the autumn of 1808, that a stranger applied for lodgings at the Independent Columbian Hotel in Mulberry-street, of which I am landlord. He was a small, brisk-looking old gentleman, dressed in a rusty black coat, a pair of olive velvet breeches, and a small cocked hat. He had a few gray hairs plaited and clubbed behind, and his beard seemed to be of some eight-and-forty hours growth. The only piece of finery which he bore about him, was a bright pair of square silver shoebuckles, and all his baggage was contained in a pair of saddle-bags, which he carried under his arm. His whole appearance was something out of the common run; and my wife, who is a very shrewd body, at once set him down for some eminent country schoolmaster.

As the Independent Columbian Hotel is a very small house, I was a little puzzled at first where to put him; but my wife, who seemed taken with his looks, would needs put him in her best chamber, which is genteelly set off with the profiles of the whole family, done in black, by those two great painters, Jarvis and Wood; and commands a very pleasant view of the new grounds on the Collect, together with the rear of the Poor House and Bridewell, and a full front of the Hospital; so that it is the cheerfullest room in the whole house.

During the whole time that he stayed with us, we found him a very worthy good sort of an old gentleman, though a little queer

1*

in his ways. He would keep in his room for days together, and
if any of the children cried, or made a noise about his door, he
would bounce out in a great passion, with his hands full of papers,
and say something about " deranging his ideas ;" which made my
wife believe sometimes that he was not altogether *compos.*
Indeed, there was more than one reason to make her think so,
for his room was always covered with scraps of paper and old
mouldy books, laying about at sixes and sevens, which he would
never let any body touch ; for he said he had laid them all away
in their proper places, so that he might know where to find them ;
though for that matter, he was half his time worrying about the
house in search of some book or writing which he had carefully
put out of the way.   I shall never forget what a pother he once
made, because my wife cleaned out his room when his back was
turned, and put every thing to rights ; for he swore he would
never be able to get his papers in order again in a twelvemonth.
Upon this my wife ventured to ask him what he did with so many
books and papers ; and he told her, that he was " seeking for
immortality ;" which made her think more than ever, that the
poor old gentleman's head was a little cracked.

He was a very inquisitive body, and when not in his room
was continually poking about town, hearing all the news, and
prying into every thing that was going on : this was particularly
the case about election time, when he did nothing but bustle about
from poll to poll, attending all ward meetings and committee
rooms ; though I could never find that he took part with either
side of the question.   On the contrary, he would come home and
rail at both parties with great wrath—and plainly proved one
day, to the satisfaction of my wife and three old ladies who were
drinking tea with her, that the two parties were like two rogues,

each tugging at a skirt of the nation; and that in the end they would tear the very coat off its back, and expose its nakedness. Indeed he was an oracle among the neighbors, who would collect around him to hear him talk of an afternoon, as he smoked his pipe on the bench before the door; and I really believe he would have brought over the whole neighborhood to his own side of the question, if they could ever have found out what it was.

He was very much given to argue, or, as he called it, *philoso-phize*, about the most trifling matter; and to do him justice, I never knew any body that was a match for him, except it was a grave looking old gentleman who called now and then to see him, and often posed him in an argument. But this is nothing sur-prising, as I have since found out this stranger is the city libra-rian; who, of course, must be a man of great learning: and I have my doubts, if he had not some hand in the following history.

As our lodger had been a long time with us, and we had never received any pay, my wife began to be somewhat uneasy, and curious to find out who and what he was. She accordingly made bold to put the question to his friend, the librarian, who replied in his dry way that he was one of the *literati*, which she supposed to mean some new party in politics. I scorn to push a lodger for his pay; so I let day after day pass on without dunning the old gentleman for a farthing: but my wife, who always takes these matters on herself, and is, as I said, a shrewd kind of a woman, at last got out of patience, and hinted, that she thought it high time " some people should have a sight of some people's money." To which the old gentleman replied, in a mighty touchy manner, that she need not make herself uneasy, for that he had a treasure there, (pointing to his saddle-bags,) worth her whole house put together This was the only answer we could ever get from him; and as my wife, by some of those odd ways in which women find out every thing, learnt that he was of very great connections, being related to the Knickerbockers of Scaghtikoke, and cousin-german to the congressman of that name, she did not like to treat him uncivilly. What is more, she even offered, merely by way of making things easy, to let him live scot-free, if he would teach the children their letters; and to try her best and get her neighbors to send their children also: but the old gentleman took it in such dudgeon, and seemed so affronted at being taken for a schoolmaster, that she never dared to speak on the subject again.

About two months ago, he went out of a morning, with a bundle in his hand—and has never been heard of since. All kinds of inquiries were made after him, but in vain. I wrote to his relations at Scaghtikoke, but they sent for answer, that he had not been there since the year before last, when he had a great dispute with the congressman about politics, and left the place in a huff, and they had neither heard nor seen any thing of him from that time to this. I must own I felt very much worried about the poor old gentleman, for I thought something bad must have happened to him, that he should be missing so long, and never return to pay his bill. I therefore advertised him in the newspapers, and though my melancholy advertisement was published by several humane printers, yet I have never been able to learn any thing satisfactory about him.

My wife now said it was high time to take care of ourselves, and see if he had left any thing behind in his room, that would pay us for his board and lodging. We found nothing, however but some old books and musty writings, and his saddle-bags; which, being opened in the presence of the librarian, contained only a few articles of worn-out clothes, and a large bundle of blotted paper. On looking over this, the librarian told us, he had no doubt it was the treasure which the old gentleman had spoken about; as it proved to be a most excellent and faithful HISTORY OF NEW-YORK, which he advised us by all means to publish: assuring us that it would be so eagerly bought up by a discerning public, that he had no doubt it would be enough to pay our arrears ten times over. Upon this we got a very learned schoolmaster, who teaches our children, to prepare it for the press, which he accordingly has done; and has, moreover, added to it a number of valuable notes of his own.

This, therefore, is a true statement of my reasons for having this work printed, without waiting for the consent of the author: and I here declare, that if he ever returns, (though I much fear some unhappy accident has befallen him,) I stand ready to account with him like a true and honest man. Which is all at present,

From the public's humble servant,

SETH HANDASIDE.

Independent Columbian Hotel, New-York.

The foregoing account of the author was prefixed to the first edition of this work. Shortly after its publication a letter was received from him, by Mr. Handaside, dated at a small Dutch village on the banks of the Hudson, whither he had travelled for the purpose of inspecting certain ancient records. As this was one of those few and happy villages, into which newspapers never find their way, it is not a matter of surprise, that Mr. Knickerbocker should never have seen the numerous advertisements that were made concerning him; and that he should learn of the publication of his history by mere accident.

He expressed much concern at its premature appearance, as thereby he was prevented from making several important corrections and alterations: as well as from profiting by many curious hints which he had collected during his travels along the shores of the Tappan Sea, and his sojourn at Haverstraw and Esopus.

Finding that there was no longer any immediate necessity for his return to New-York, he extended his journey up to the residence of his relations at Scaghtikoke. On his way thither, he stopped for some days at Albany, for which city he is known to have entertained a great partiality. He found it, however, considerably altered, and was much concerned at the inroads and improvements which the Yankees were making, and the consequent decline of the good old Dutch manners. Indeed, he was informed that these intruders were making sad innovations in all parts of the state; where they had given great trouble and vexation to the regular Dutch settlers, by the introduction of turnpike gates, and country school-houses. It is said also, that Mr. Knickerbocker shook his head sorrowfully at noticing the gradual decay of the great Vander Heyden palace; but was highly indignant at finding that the ancient Dutch church, which stood in the middle of the street, had been pulled down, since his last visit.

The fame of Mr. Knickerbocker's history having reached even to Albany, he received much flattering attention from its worthy burghers, some of whom, however, pointed out two or three very great errors he had fallen into, particularly that of suspending a lump of sugar over the Albany tea-tables, which, they assured him, had been discontinued for some years past. Several families, moreover, were somewhat piqued that their ancestors had not been mentioned in his work, and showed great jealousy of their neighbors who had thus been distinguished; while the latter, it must be confessed, plumed themselves vastly thereupon; considering these recordings in the light of letters-patent of nobility, establishing their claims to ancestry—which, in this republican country, is a matter of no little solicitude and vainglory.

It is also said, that he enjoyed high favor and countenance from the governor, who once asked him to dinner, and was seen two or three times to shake hands with him, when they met in the street; which certainly was going great lengths, considering that they differed in politics. Indeed, certain of the governor's confidential friends, to whom he could venture to speak his mind freely on such matters, have assured us, that he privately entertained a considerable good will for our author—nay, he even once went so far as to declare, and that openly too, and at his own table, just after dinner, that "Knickerbocker was a very well meaning sort of an old gentleman, and no fool." From all which many have been led to suppose, that had our author been of different politics, and written for the newspapers instead of wasting his talents on histories, he might have risen to some post of honor and profit: peradventure, to be a notary public, or even a justice in the ten-pound court.

Beside the honors and civilities already mentioned, he was much caressed by the literati of Albany; particularly by Mr. John Cook, who entertained him very hospitably at his circulating library, and reading room, where they used to drink Spa water, and talk about the ancients. He found Mr. Cook a man after his own heart—of great literary research, and a curious collector of books. At parting, the latter, in testimony of friendship, made him a present of the two oldest works in his collection; which were the earliest edition of the Heidelberg Catechism, and Adrian Vander Donck's famous account of the New Netherlands: by the last of which, Mr. Knickerbocker profited greatly in this his second edition.

Having passed some time very agreeably at Albany, our author proceeded to Scaghtikoke : where, it is but justice to say, he was received with open arms, and treated with wonderful loving-kindness. He was much looked up to by the family, being the first historian of the name ; and was considered almost as great a man as his cousin the congressman—with whom, by tne by, he became perfectly reconciled, and contracted a strong friendship.

In spite, however, of the kindness of his relations, and their great attention to his comforts, the old gentleman soon became restless and discontented. His history being published, he had no longer any business to occupy his thoughts, or any scheme to excite his hopes and anticipations. This, to a busy mind like his, was a truly deplorable situation ; and, had he not been a man of inflexible morals and regular habits, there would have been great danger of his taking to politics, or drinking—both which pernicious vices we daily see men driven to, by mere spleen and idleness.

It is true, he sometimes employed himself in preparing a second edition of his history, wherein he endeavored to correct and improve many passages with which he was dissatisfied, and to rectify some mistakes that had crept into it; for he was particularly anxious that his work should be noted for its authenticity ; which, indeed, is the very life and soul of history.—But the glow of composition had departed—he had to leave many places untouched, which he would fain have altered ; and even where he did make alterations, he seemed always in doubt whether they were for the better or the worse.

After a residence of some time at Scaghtikoke, he began to feel a strong desire to return to New-York, which he ever regarded with the warmest affection ; not merely because it was his native city, but because he really considered it the very best city in the whole world.   On his return, he entered into the full enjoyment of the advantages of a literary reputation.   He was continually importuned to write advertisements, petitions, handbills, and productions of similar import ; and, although he never meddled with the public papers, yet had he the credit of writing innumerable essays, and smart things, that appeared on all subjects, and all sides of the question ; in all which he was clearly detected " by his style."

He contracted, moreover, a considerable debt at the post-office, in consequence of the numerous letters he received from authors and printers soliciting his subscription, and he was applied to by every charitable society for yearly donations, which he gave very cheerfully, considering these applications as so many compliments.   He was once invited to a great corporation dinner ; and was even twice summoned to attend as a juryman at the court of quarter sessions.   Indeed, so renowned did he become, that he could no longer pry about, as formerly, in all holes and corners of the city, according to the bent of his humor, unnoticed and uninterrupted ; but several times when he has been sauntering the streets, on his usual rambles of observation, equipped with his cane and cocked hat, the little boys at play have been known to cry, " there goes Diedrich !"—at which the old gentleman seemed not a little pleased, looking upon these salutations in the light of the praise of posterity.

In a word, if we take into consideration all these various honors and distinctions, together with an exuberant eulogium, passed on him in the Port Folio—(with which, we are told, the old gentleman was so much overpowered, that he was sick for two or three days)—it must be confessed, that few authors have ever lived to receive such illustrious rewards, or have so completely enjoyed in advance their own immortality.

After his return from Scaghtikoke, Mr. Knickerbocker took up his residence at a little rural retreat, which the Stuyvesants had granted him on the family domain, in gratitude for his honorable mention of their ancestor. It was pleasantly situated on the borders of one of the salt marshes beyond Corlear's Hook : subject, indeed, to be occasionally overflowed, and much infested, in the summer time, with musquitoes ; but otherwise very agreeable, producing abundant crops of salt grass and bulrushes.

Here, we are sorry to say, the good old gentleman fell dangerously ill of a fever, occasioned by the neighboring marshes. When he found his end approaching, he disposed of his worldly affairs, leaving the bulk of his fortune to the New-York Historical Society : his Heidelberg Catechism, and Vander Donck's work to the city library ; and his saddle-bags to Mr. Handaside. He forgave all his enemies—that is to say, all who bore any enmity towards him ; for as to himself, he declared he died in good will with all the world. And, after dictating several kind messages to his relations at Scaghtikoke, as well as to certain of our most substantial Dutch citizens, he expired in the arms of his friend the librarian.

His remains were interred, according to his own request, in St. Mark's churchyard, close by the bones of his favorite hero, Peter Stuyvesant : and it is rumored, that the Historical Society have it in mind to erect a wooden monument to his memory in the Bowling Green.

TO THE PUBLIC.

"To rescue from oblivion the memory of former incidents, and to render a just tribute of renown to the many great and wonderful transactions of our Dutch progenitors, Diedrich Knickerbocker, native of the city of New-York, produces this historical essay."* Like the great Father of History, whose words I have just quoted, I treat of times long past, over which the twilight of uncertainty had already thrown its shadows, and the night of forgetfulness was about to descend for ever. With great solicitude had I long beheld the early history of this venerable and ancient city gradually slipping from our grasp, trembling on the lips of narrative old age, and day by day dropping piecemeal into the tomb. In a little while, thought I, and those reverend Dutch burghers, who serve as the tottering monuments of good old times, will be gathered to their fathers; their children, engrossed by the empty pleasures or insignificant transactions of the present age, will neglect to treasure up the recollections of the past, and posterity will search in vain for memorials of the days of the Patriarchs. The origin of our city will be buried in eternal oblivion, and even the names and achievements of Wouter Van Twiller, William Kieft, and Peter Stuyvesant, be enveloped in doubt and fiction, like those of Romulus and Remus, of Charlemagne, king Arthur, Rinaldo, and Godfrey of Bologne.

* Beloe's Herodotus.

Determined, therefore, to avert if possible this threatened misfortune, I industriously set myself to work, to gather together all the fragments of our infant history which still existed, and like my revered prototype, Herodotus, where no written records could be found, I have endeavored to continue the chain of history by well-authenticated traditions.

In this arduous undertaking, which has been the whole business of a long and solitary life, it is incredible the number of learned authors I have consulted; and all but to little purpose. Strange as it may seem, though such multitudes of excellent works have been written about this country, there are none extant which gave any full and satisfactory account of the early history of New-York, or of its three first Dutch governors. I have, however, gained much valuable and curious matter, from an elaborate manuscript written in exceeding pure and classic low Dutch, excepting a few errors in orthography, which was found in the archives of the Stuyvesant family. Many legends, letters and other documents have I likewise gleaned, in my researches among the family chests and lumber garrets of our respectable Dutch citizens; and I have gathered a host of well-authenticated traditions from divers excellent old ladies of my acquaintance, who requested that their names might not be mentioned. Nor must I neglect to acknowledge how greatly I have been assisted by that admirable and praiseworthy institution, the NEW-YORK HISTORICAL SOCIETY, to which I here publicly return my sincere acknowledgments.

In the conduct of this inestimable work I have adopted no individual model; but on the contrary have simply contented myself with combining and concentrating the excellences of the most approved ancient historians. Like Xenophon, I have maintained the utmost impartiality, and the strictest adherence to truth throughout my history. I have enriched it after the manner of Sallust, with various characters of ancient worthies, drawn at full length and faithfully colored. I have seasoned it with profound political speculations like Thucydides, sweetened it with the graces of sentiment like Tacitus, and infused into the whole the dignity, the grandeur, and magnificence of Livy.

I am aware that I shall incur the censure of numerous very learned and judicious critics, for indulging too frequently in the bold excursive manner of my favorite Herodotus. And to be candid, I have found it impossible always to resist the allurements of those pleasing episodes which, like flowery banks and fragrant bowers, beset the dusty road of the historian, and entice him to turn aside, and refresh himself from his wayfaring. But I trust it will be found, that I have always resumed my staff, and addressed myself to my weary journey with renovated spirits, so that both my readers and myself have been benefited by the relaxation.

Indeed, though it has been my constant wish and uniform endeavor to rival Polybius himself, in observing the requisite unity of History, yet the loose and unconnected manner in which many of the facts herein recorded have come to hand, rendered such an attempt extremely difficult. This difficulty was likewise increased, by one of the grand objects contemplated in my work, which was to trace the rise of sundry customs and institutions in this best of cities, and to compare them, when in the germ of infancy, with what they are in the present old age of knowledge and improvement.

But the chief merit on which I value myself, and found my hopes for future regard, is that faithful veracity with which I

have compiled this invaluable little work; carefully winnowing
away the chaff of hypothesis, and discarding the tares of fable,
which are too apt to spring up and choke the seeds of truth and
wholesome knowledge.—Had I been anxious to captivate the
superficial throng, who skim like swallows over the surface of
literature; or had I been anxious to commend my writings to the
pampered palates of literary epicures, I might have availed myself of the obscurity that overshadows the infant years of our
city, to introduce a thousand pleasing fictions.   But I have
scrupulously discarded many a pithy tale and marvelous adventure, whereby the drowsy ear of summer indolence might be
enthralled; jealously maintaining that fidelity, gravity, and dignity,
which should ever distinguish the historian.   "For a writer of
this class," observes an elegant critic, "must sustain the character
of a wise man, writing for the instruction of posterity; one who
has studied to inform himself well, who has pondered his subject
with care, and addresses himself to our judgment, rather than to
our imagination."

Thrice happy, therefore, is this our renowned city, in having
incidents worthy of swelling the theme of history; and doubly
thrice happy is it in having such an historian as myself to relate
them.   For after all, gentle reader, cities *of themselves*, and, in
fact, empires *of themselves*, are nothing without an historian.   It
is the patient narrator who records their prosperity as they rise—
who blazons forth the splendor of their noontide meridian—who
props their feeble memorials as they totter to decay—who gathers
together their scattered fragments as they rot—and who piously,
at length, collects their ashes into the mausoleum of his work
and rears a monument that will transmit their renown to all succeeding ages.

What has been the fate of many fair cities of antiquity, whose nameless ruins encumber the plains of Europe and Asia, and awaken the fruitless inquiry of the traveler?—they have sunk into dust and silence—they have perished from remembrance for want of an historian! The philanthropist may weep over their desolation—the poet may wander among their mouldering arches and broken columns, and indulge the visionary flights of his fancy —but alas! alas! the modern historian, whose pen, like my own, is doomed to confine itself to dull matter of fact, seeks in vain among their oblivious remains, for some memorial that may tell the instructive tale of their glory and their ruin.

"Wars, conflagrations, deluges," says Aristotle, "destroy nations, and with them all their monuments, their discoveries, and their vanities.—The torch of science has more than once been extinguished and rekindled—a few individuals, who have escaped by accident, reunite the thread of generations."

The same sad misfortune which has happened to so many ancient cities, will happen again, and from the same sad cause, to nine-tenths of those which now flourish on the face of the globe. With most of them the time for recording their early history is gone by; their origin, their foundation, together with the eventful period of their youth, are for ever buried in the rubbish of years; and the same would have been the case with this fair portion of the earth, if I had not snatched it from obscurity in the very nick of time, at the moment that those matters herein recorded were about entering into the wide-spread insatiable maw of oblivion—if I had not dragged them out, as it were, by the very locks, just as the monster's adamantine fangs were closing upon them for ever! And here have I, as before observed, carefully collected, collated, and arranged them, scrip and scrap, "*punt en punt, gat en gat,*" and commenced in this little work, a history to serve as a foundation, on which other historians may hereafter raise a noble superstructure, swelling in process of time, until *Knickerbocker's New-York* may be equally voluminous with *Gibbon's Rome,* or *Hume and Smollet's England!*

And now indulge me for a moment, while I lay down my pen, skip to some little eminence at the distance of two or three hundred years ahead; and, casting back a bird's-eye glance over the waste of years that is to roll between, discover myself—little I—at this moment the progenitor, prototype, and precursor of them all, posted at the head of this host of literary worthies, with my book under my arm, and New-York on my back, pressing forward, like a gallant commander, to honor and immortality.

Such are the vainglorious imaginings that will now and then enter into the brain of the author—that irradiate, as with celestial light, his solitary chamber, cheering his weary spirits, and animating him to persevere in his labors. And I have freely given utterance to these rhapsodies whenever they have occurred; not, I trust, from an unusual spirit of egotism, but merely that the reader may for once have an idea, how an author thinks and feels while he is writing—a kind of knowledge very rare and curious, and much to be desired.

HISTORY OF NEW-YORK.

BOOK I.

CONTAINING DIVERS INGENIOUS THEORIES AND PHILOSO-
PHIC SPECULATIONS, CONCERNING THE CREATION AND
POPULATION OF THE WORLD, AS CONNECTED WITH THE
HISTORY OF NEW-YORK.

CHAPTER I.

DESCRIPTION OF THE WORLD.

ACCORDING to the best authorities, the world in which we dwell
is a huge, opaque, reflecting, inanimate mass, floating in the vast
ethereal ocean of infinite space. It has the form of an orange,
being an oblate spheroid, curiously flattened at opposite parts,
for the insertion of two imaginary poles, which are supposed to
penetrate and unite at the centre; thus forming an axis on which
the mighty orange turns with a regular diurnal revolution.

The transitions of light and darkness, whence proceed the
alternations of day and night, are produced by this diurnal revolution successively presenting the different parts of the earth to
the rays of the sun. The latter is, according to the best, that is
to say, the latest accounts, a luminous or fiery body, of a prodigious magnitude, from which this world is driven by a centrifugal
or repelling power, and to which it is drawn by a centripetal or
attractive force; otherwise called the attraction of gravitation;
the combination, or rather the counteraction of these two opposing

impulses producing a circular and annual revolution. Hence
result the different seasons of the year, viz., spring, summer,
autumn, and winter.

This I believe to be the most approved modern theory on the
subject—though there be many philosophers who have entertained
very different opinions; some, too, of them entitled to much
deference from their great antiquity and illustrious characters.
Thus it was advanced by some of the ancient sages, that the
earth was an extended plain, supported by vast pillars; and by
others, that it rested on the head of a snake, or the back of a
huge tortoise—but as they did not provide a resting place for
either the pillars or the tortoise, the whole theory fell to the
ground, for want of proper foundation.

The Brahmins assert, that the heavens rest upon the earth,
and the sun and moon swim therein like fishes in the water,
moving from east to west by day, and gliding along the edge of
the horizon to their original stations during night;[*] while, according to the Pauranicas of India, it is a vast plain, encircled by
seven oceans of milk, nectar, and other delicious liquids; that it
is studded with seven mountains, and ornamented in the centre
by a mountainous rock of burnished gold; and that a great dragon
occasionally swallows up the moon, which accounts for the phenomena of lunar eclipses.[†]

Beside these, and many other equally sage opinions, we have
the profound conjectures of ABOUL-HASSAN-ALY, son of Al Khan,
son of Aly, son of Abderrahman, son of Abdallah, son of Masoud-
el-Hadheli, who is commonly called MASOUDI, and surnamed Coth-
biddin, but who takes the humble title of Laheb-ar-rasoul, which

---

[*] Faria y Souza. Mick. lus. note b. 7.
[†] Sir W. Jones, Diss. Antiq. Ind. Zod.

means the companion of the ambassador of God. He has written
a universal history, entitled "Mouroudge-ed-dharab, or the Gold-
en Meadows, and the Mines of Precious Stones."* In this
valuable work he has related the history of the world, from the
creation down to the moment of writing; which was under the
Khaliphat of Mothi Billah, in the month Dgioumadi-el-aoual of
the 336th year of the Hegira or flight of the Prophet. He informs us that the earth is a huge bird, Mecca and Medina constituting the head, Persia and India the right wing, the land of Gog
the left wing, and Africa the tail. He informs us, moreover, that
an earth has existed before the present (which he considers as a
mere chicken of 7000 years), that it has undergone divers deluges,
and that, according to the opinion of some well-informed Brahmins of his acquaintance, it will be renovated every seventy
thousandth hazarouam; each hazarouam consisting of 12,000
years.

These are a few of the many contradictory opinions of philosophers concerning the earth, and we find that the learned have
had equal perplexity as to the nature of the sun. Some of the
ancient philosophers have affirmed that it is a vast wheel of brilliant fire;† others that it is merely a mirror or sphere of transparent crystal;‡ and a third class, at the head of whom stands
Anaxagoras, maintained that it was nothing but a huge ignited
mass of iron or stone—indeed, he declared the heavens to be merely a vault of stone—and that the stars were stones whirled up-
ward from the earth, and set on fire by the velocity of its revolu-

---

* Mss. Bibliot. Roi. Fr.

† Plutarch de placitis Philosoph. lib. ii. cap. 20.

‡ Achill. Tat. isag. cap. 19.   Ap. Petav. t. iii. p. 81.   Stob. Eclog. Phys.
lib. i. p. 56.   Plut. de Plac. Phi.

tions.* But I give little attention to the doctrines of this philosopher, the people of Athens having fully refuted them, by
banishing him from their city ; a concise mode of answering un
welcome doctrines. much resorted to in former days. Another
sect of philosophers do declare, that certain fiery particles exhale
constantly from the earth, which concentrating in a single point
of the firmament by day, constitute the sun, but being scattered
and rambling about in the dark at night, collect in various points,
and form stars. These are regularly burnt out and extinguished,
not unlike to the lamps in our street, and require a fresh supply
of exhalations for the next occasion.†

It is even recorded, that at certain remote and obscure periods,
in consequence of a great scarcity of fuel, the sun has been completely burnt out, and sometimes not rekindled for a month at a
time. A most melancholy circumstance, the very idea of which
gave vast concern to Heraclitus, that worthy weeping philosopher of antiquity. In addition to these various speculations, it
was the opinion of Herschel, that the sun is a magnificent, habitable abode ; the light it furnishes arising from certain empyreal,
luminous or phosphoric clouds, swimming in its transparent atmosphere.‡

But we will not enter farther at present into the nature of the
sun, that being an inquiry not immediately necessary to the development of this history ; neither will we embroil ourselves in

* Diogenes Laertius in Anaxag. l. ii. sec. 8. Plat. Apol. t. i. p. 26. Plut.
de Plac. Philo.   Xenoph. Mem. l iv. p. 815.

† Aristot. Meteor. l. ii. c. 2. Idem. Probl sec. 15, Stob. Ecl. Phys. l. i. p. 55
Bruck. Hist. Phil. t. i. p. 1154, &c.

‡ Philos. Trans. 1795. p. 72. Idem. 1801. p. 265. Nich. Philos. Journ. I.
p. 13.

any more of the endless disputes of philosophers touching the form of this globe, but content ourselves with the theory advanced in the beginning of this chapter, and will proceed to illustrate, by experiment, the complexity of motion therein ascribed to this our rotatory planet.

Professor Von Poddingcoft (or Puddinghead, as the name may be rendered into English,) was long celebrated in the university of Leyden, for profound gravity of deportment, and a talent at going to sleep in the midst of examinations, to the infinite relief of his hopeful students, who thereby worked their way through college with great ease and little study. In the course of one of his lectures, the learned professor, seizing a bucket of water, swung it around his head at arm's length. The impulse with which he threw the vessel from him, being a centrifugal force, the retention of his arm operating as a centripetal power, and the bucket, which was a substitute for the earth, describing a circular orbit round about the globular head and ruby visage of Professor Von Poddingcoft, which formed no bad representation of the sun. All of these particulars were duly explained to the class of gaping students around him. He apprised them, moreover, that the same principle of gravitation, which retained the water in the bucket, restrains the ocean from flying from the earth in its rapid revolutions ; and he farther informed them that should the motion of the earth be suddenly checked, it would incontinently fall into the sun, through the centripetal force of gravitation , a most ruinous event to this planet, and one which would also obscure, though it most probably would not extinguish, the solar luminary. An unlucky stripling, one of those vagrant geniuses, who seem sent into the world merely to annoy worthy men of the puddinghead order, desirous of ascertaining the correctness of the

experiment, suddenly arrested the arm of the professor, just at
the moment that the bucket was in its zenith, which immediately
deoended with astonishing precision upon the philosophic head of
the instructor of youth. A hollow sound, and a red-hot hiss, attended the contact; but the theory was in the amplest manner
illustrated, for the unfortunate bucket perished in the conflict;
but the blazing countenance of Professor Von Poddingcoft emerged
from amidst the waters, glowing fiercer than ever with unutterable indignation, whereby the students were marvelously edified,
and departed considerably wiser than before.

It is a mortifying circumstance, which greatly perplexes many
a painstaking philosopher, that nature often refuses to second his
most profound and elaborate efforts: so that after having invented
one of the most ingenious and natural theories imaginable, she
will have the perverseness to act directly in the teeth of his system,
and flatly contradict his most favorite positions. This is a manifest and unmerited grievance, since it throws the censure of the
vulgar and unlearned entirely upon the philosopher; whereas the
fault is not to be ascribed to his theory, which is unquestionably
correct, but to the waywardness of dame nature, who, with the
proverbial fickleness of her sex, is continually indulging in
coquetries and caprices, and seems really to take pleasure in vio-
lating all philosophic rules, and jilting the most learned and indefatigable of her adorers. Thus it happened with respect to the
foregoing satisfactory explanation of the motion of our planet; it
appears that the centrifugal force has long since ceased to operate,
while its antagonist remains in undiminished potency: the world,
therefore, according to the theory as it originally stood, ought in
strict propriety to tumble into the sun; philosophers were convinced
that it would do so, and awaited in anxious impatience the ful-

fillment of their prognostics. But the untoward planet pertinaciously continued her course, notwithstanding that she had reason,
philosophy, and a whole university of learned professors opposed
to her conduct. The philosophers took this in very ill part, and
it is thought they would never have pardoned the slight and af-
front which they conceived put upon them by the world, had not
a good-natured professor kindly officiated as a mediator between
the parties, and effected a reconciliation.

Finding the world would not accommodate itself to the theory,
he wisely determined to accommodate the theory to the world : he
therefore informed his brother philosophers, that the circular motion of the earth round the sun was no sooner engendered by the
conflicting impulses above described, than it became a regular
revolution, independent of the causes which gave it origin. His
learned brethren readily joined in the opinion, being heartily glad
of any explanation that would decently extricate them from their
embarrassment—and ever since that memorable era the world has
been left to take her own course, and to revolve around the sun
in such orbit as she thinks proper.

CHAPTER II.

COSMOGONY, OR CREATION OF THE WORLD; WITH A MUL-
TITUDE OF EXCELLENT THEORIES, BY WHICH THE CREA-
TION OF A WORLD IS SHOWN TO BE NO SUCH DIFFICULT
MATTER AS COMMON FOLK WOULD IMAGINE.

HAVING thus briefly introduced my reader to the world, and
given him some idea of its form and situation, he will naturally
be curious to know from whence it came, and how it was created.
And, indeed, the clearing up of these points is absolutely essential to my history, inasmuch as if this world had not been formed,
it is more than probable, that this renowned island on which is
situated the city of New-York, would never have had an existence.
The regular course of my history, therefore, requires that I should
proceed to notice the cosmogony or formation of this our globe.

And now I give my readers fair warning, that I am about to
plunge, for a chapter or two, into as complete a labyrinth as ever
historian was perplexed withal: therefore, I advise them to take
fast hold of my skirts, and keep close at my heels, venturing
neither to the right hand nor to the left, lest they get bemired in
a slough of unintelligible learning, or have their brains knocked
out by some of those hard Greek names which will be flying
about in all directions. But should any of them be too indolent

or chicken-hearted to accompany me in this perilous undertaking, they had better take a short cut round, and wait for me at the beginning of some smoother chapter.

Of the creation of the world, we have a thousand contradictory accounts; and though a very satisfactory one is furnished us by divine revelation, yet every philosopher feels himself in honor bound to furnish us with a better. As an impartial historian, I consider it my duty to notice their several theories, by which mankind have been so exceedingly edified and instructed.

Thus it was the opinion of certain ancient sages, that the earth and the whole system of the universe was the Deity himself;* a doctrine most strenuously maintained by Zenophanes and the whole tribe of Eleatics, as also by Strabo and the sect of peripatetic philosophers. Pythagoras likewise inculcated the famous numerical system of the monad, dyad, and triad, and by means of his sacred quaternary elucidated the formation of the world, the arcana of nature, and the principles both of music and morals.† Other sages adhered to the mathematical system of squares and triangles; the cube, the pyramid, and the sphere; the tetrahedron, the octahedron, the icosahedron, and the dodecahedron.‡ While others advocated the great elementary theory, which refers the construction of our globe and all that it contains, to the combinations of four material elements, air, earth, fire, and water; with the assistance of a fifth, an immaterial and vivifying principle.

Nor must I omit to mention the great atomic system taught

* Aristot. ap. Cic. lib. i. cap. 3.

† Aristot. Metaph. lib. i. c. 5. Idem. de Cœlo. l. iii. c. 1. Rousseau mem. sur Musique ancien. p. 39. Plutarch de Plac. Philos. lib. i. cap. 3.

‡ Tim. Locr. ap. Plato. t. iii. p. 90.

by old Moschus, before the siege of Troy; revived by Democritus of laughing memory; improved by Epicurus, that king of good fellows, and modernized by the fanciful Descartes. But I decline inquiring, whether the atoms, of which the earth is said to be composed, are eternal or recent; whether they are animate or inanimate; whether, agreeably to the opinion of the atheists, they were fortuitously aggregated, or, as the theists maintain, were arranged by a supreme intelligence.* Whether, in fact, the earth be an insensate clod, or whether it be animated by a soul;† which opinion was strenuously maintained by a host of philosophers, at the head of whom stands the great Plato, that temperate sage, who threw the cold water of philosophy on the form of sexual intercourse, and inculcated the doctrine of Platonic love—an exquisitely refined intercourse, but much better adapted to the ideal inhabitants of his imaginary island of Atlantis than to the sturdy race, composed of rebellious flesh and blood, which populates the little matter of fact island we inhabit.

Beside these systems, we have, moreover, the poetical theogony of old Hesiod, who generated the whole universe in the regular mode of procreation, and the plausible opinion of others, that the earth was hatched from the great egg of night, which floated in chaos, and was cracked by the horns of the celestial bull. To illustrate this last doctrine, Burnet in his theory of the earth,‡ has favored us with an accurate drawing and description, both of the form and texture of this mundane egg; which is

---

   * Aristot. Nat. Auscult. l. ii. cap. 6.   Aristoph. Metaph. lib. i. cap. 3. Cic. de Nat. Deor. lib. i. cap. 10.   Justin Mart. orat. ad gent. p. 20.

   † Mosheim in Cudw. lib. i. cap. 4.   Tim. de anim. mund. ap. Plat. lib. iii. Mem. de l'Acad. des Belles-Lettr. t. xxxii. p. 19, et al.

   ‡ Book i. ch. 5.

found to bear a marvellous resemblance to that of a goose. Such of my readers as take a proper interest in the origin of this our planet, will be pleased to learn, that the most profound sages of antiquity, among the Egyptians, Chaldeans, Persians, Greeks, and Latins, have alternately assisted at the hatching of this strange bird, and that their cacklings have been caught, and continued in different tones and inflections, from philosopher to philosopher, unto the present day.

But while briefly noticing long celebrated systems of ancient sages, let me not pass over with neglect those of other philosophers; which, though less universal and renowned, have equal claims to attention, and equal chance for correctness. Thus it is recorded by the Brahmins, in the pages of their inspired Shastah, that the angel Bistnoo, transforming himself into a great boar, plunged into the watery abyss, and brought up the earth on his tusks. Then issued from him a mighty tortoise, and a mighty snake; and Bistnoo placed the snake erect upon the back of the tortoise, and he placed the earth upon the head of the snake.*

The negro philosophers of Congo affirm that the world was made by the hands of angels, excepting their own country, which the Supreme Being constructed himself, that it might be supremely excellent. And he took great pains with the inhabitants, and made them very black, and beautiful; and when he had finished the first man, he was well pleased with him, and smoothed him over the face, and hence his nose, and the nose of all his descendants, became flat.

The Mohawk philosophers tell us, that a pregnant woman

---

* Holwell. Gent. Philosophy

fell down from heaven, and that a tortoise took her upon its back, because every place was covered with water; and that the woman, sitting upon the tortoise, paddled with her hands in the water, and raked up the earth, whence it finally happened that the earth became higher than the water.*

But I forbear to quote a number more of these ancient and outlandish philosophers, whose deplorable ignorance, in despite of all their erudition, compelled them to write in languages which but few of my readers can understand; and I shall proceed briefly to notice a few more intelligible and fashionable theories of their modern successors.

And, first, I shall mention the great Buffon, who conjectures that this globe was originally a globe of liquid fire, scintillated from the body of the sun, by the percussion of a comet, as a spark is generated by the collision of flint and steel. That at first it was surrounded by gross vapors, which, cooling and condensing in process of time, constituted, according to their densities, earth, water, and air; which gradually arranged themselves, according to their respective gravities, round the burning or vitrified mass that formed their centre.

Hutton, on the contrary, supposes that the waters at first were universally paramount; and he terrifies himself with the idea that the earth must be eventually washed away by the force of rain, rivers, and mountain torrents, until it is confounded with the ocean, or, in other words, absolutely dissolves into itself.— Sublime idea! far surpassing that of the tender-hearted damsel of antiquity, who wept herself into a fountain; or the good dame

* Johannes Megapolensis, Jun. Account of Maquaas or Mohawk Indians.

of Narbonne in France, who, for a volubility of tongue unusual
in her sex, was doomed to peel five hundred thousand and thirty-
nine ropes of onions, and actually run out at her eyes before half
the hideous task was accomplished.

Whiston, the same ingenious philosopher who rivaled Ditton
in his researches after the longitude (for which the mischief-
loving Swift discharged on their heads a most savory stanza),
has distinguished himself by a very admirable theory respecting
the earth. He conjectures that it was originally a *chaotic comet*,
which being selected for the abode of man, was removed from
its eccentric orbit, and whirled round the sun in its present
regular motion; by which change of direction, order succeeded
to confusion in the arrangement of its component parts. The
philosopher adds, that the deluge was produced by an uncourteous
salute from the watery tail of another comet; doubtless through
sheer envy of its improved condition: thus furnishing a melancholy proof that jealousy may prevail, even among the heavenly
bodies, and discord interrupt that celestial harmony of the
spheres, so melodiously sung by the poets.

But I pass over a variety of excellent theories, among which
are those of Burnet, and Woodward, and Whitehurst; regretting
extremely that my time will not suffer me to give them the notice
they deserve—and shall conclude with that of the renowned Dr.
Darwin. This learned Theban, who is as much distinguished
for rhyme as reason, and for good-natured credulity as serious
research, and who has recommended himself wonderfully to the
good graces of the ladies, by letting them into all the gallantries,
amours, debaucheries, and other topics of scandal of the court
of Flora, has fallen upon a theory worthy of his combustible
imagination. According to his opinion, the huge mass of chaos

took a sudden occasion to explode, like a barrel of gunpowder,
and in that act exploded the sun—which in its flight, by a similar
convulsion, exploded the earth, which in like guise exploded
the moon—and thus by a concatenation of explosions, the whole
solar system was produced, and set most systematically in
motion !*

By the great variety of theories here alluded to, every one
of which, if thoroughly examined, will be found surprisingly
consistent in all its parts, my unlearned readers will perhaps
be led to conclude, that the creation of a world is not so difficult
a task as they at first imagined. I have shown at least a score
of ingenious methods in which a world could be constructed;
and I have no doubt, that had any of the philosophers above
quoted the use of a good manageable comet, and the philosophical
warehouse *chaos* at his command, he would engage to manufacture a planet as good, or, if you would take his word for it,
better than this we inhabit.

And here I cannot help noticing the kindness of Providence,
in creating comets for the great relief of bewildered philosophers.
By their assistance more sudden evolutions and transitions are
effected in the system of nature than are wrought in a panto-
mimic exhibition, by the wonder-working sword of Harlequin.
Should one of our modern sages, in his theoretical flights among
the stars, ever find himself lost in the clouds, and in danger
of tumbling into the abyss of nonsense and absurdity, he has
but to seize a comet by the beard, mount astride of its tail, and
away he gallops in triumph, like an enchanter on his hyppogriff,
or a Connecticut witch on her broomstick, " to sweep the cobwebs
out of the sky."

* Drw Bot. Garden. Part I. Cant. i. l. 105.

It is an old and vulgar saying about a "beggar on horse-back," which I would not for the world have applied to these reverend philosophers: but I must confess, that some of them, when they are mounted on one of those fiery steeds, are as wild in their curvetings as was Phaeton of yore, when he aspired to manage the chariot of Phœbus. One drives his comet at full speed against the sun, and knocks the world out of him with the mighty concussion; another, more moderate, makes his comet a kind of beast of burden, carrying the sun a regular supply of food and fagots—a third, of more combustible dispo-sition, threatens to throw his comet, like a bombshell, into the world, and blow it up like a powder magazine; while a fourth, with no great delicacy to this planet, and its inhabitants, insinuates that some day or other, his comet—my modest pen blushes while I write it—shall absolutely turn tail upon our world, and deluge it with water!—Surely, as I have already observed, comets were bountifully provided by Providence for the benefit of philoso-phers, to assist them in manufacturing theories.

And now, having adduced several of the most prominent theories that occur to my recollection, I leave my judicious readers at full liberty to choose among them. They are all serious speculations of learned men—all differ essentially from each other—and all have the same title to belief. It has ever been the task of one race of philosophers to demolish the works of their predecessors, and elevate more splendid fantasies in their stead, which in their turn are demolished and replaced by the air castles of a succeeding generation. Thus it would seem that knowledge and genius, of which we make such great parade, consist but in detecting the errors and absurdities of those who have gone before, and devising new errors and absurdities, to

be detected by those who are to come after us. Theories are
the mighty soap bubbles with which the grown up children of
science amuse themselves—while the honest vulgar stand gazing
in stupid admiration, and dignify these learned vagaries with the
name of wisdom!—Surely Socrates was right in his opinion, that
philosophers are but a soberer sort of madmen, busying themselves in things totally incomprehensible, or which, if they could
be comprehended, would be found not worthy the trouble of
discovery.

For my own part, until the learned have come to an agreement among themselves, I shall content myself with the account
handed down to us by Moses; in which I do but follow the
example of our ingenious neighbors of Connecticut; who at their
first settlement proclaimed, that the colony should be governed
by the laws of God—until they had time to make better.

One thing, however, appears certain—from the unanimous
authority of the before-quoted philosophers, supported by the
evidence of our own senses, (which, though very apt to deceive
us, may be cautiously admitted as additional testimony,) it
appears, I say, and I make the assertion deliberately, without
fear of contradiction, that this globe really *was created*, and that
it is composed of *land and water*. It farther appears that it is
curiously divided and parceled out into continents and islands,
among which I boldly declare the renowned ISLAND OF NEW-
YORK will be found by any one who seeks for it in its proper
place.

CHAPTER III.

HOW THAT FAMOUS NAVIGATOR, NOAH, WAS SHAMEFULLY NICKNAMED; AND HOW HE COMMITTED AN UNPARDONABLE OVERSIGHT IN NOT HAVING FOUR SONS; WITH THE GREAT TROUBLE OF PHILOSOPHERS CAUSED THEREBY, AND THE DISCOVERY OF AMERICA.

NOAH, who is the first sea-faring man we read of, begat three sons, Shem, Ham, and Japhet. Authors, it is true, are not wanting, who affirm that the patriarch had a number of other children. Thus Berosus makes him father of the gigantic Titans, Methodius gives him a son called Jonithus, or Jonicus, and others have mentioned a son, named Thuiscon, from whom descended the Teutons or Teutonic, or in other words, the Dutch nation.

I regret exceedingly that the nature of my plan will not permit me to gratify the laudable curiosity of my readers, by investigating minutely the history of the great Noah. Indeed, such an undertaking would be attended with more trouble than many people would imagine; for the good old patriarch seems to have been a great traveler in his day, and to have passed under a different name in every country that he visited. The Chaldeans, for instance, give us his story, merely altering his

name into Xisuthrus—a trivial alteration, which, to an historian
skilled in etymologies, will appear wholly unimportant. It
appears, likewise, that he had exchanged his tarpaulin and
quadrant among the Chaldeans, for the gorgeous insignia of
royalty, and appears as a monarch in their annals. The Egyptians celebrate him under the name of Osiris; the Indians as
Menu; the Greek and Roman writers confound him with Ogyges,
and the Theban with Deucalion and Saturn. But the Chinese,
who deservedly rank among the most extensive and authentic
historians, inasmuch as they have known the world much longer
than any one else, declare that Noah was no other than Fohi;
and what gives this assertion some air of credibility is, that it
is a fact, admitted by the most enlightened literati, that Noah
traveled into China, at the time of the building of the tower
of Babel (probably to improve himself in the study of languages), and the learned Dr. Shackford gives us the additional
information, that the ark rested on a mountain on the frontiers
of China.

From this mass of rational conjectures and sage hypotheses,
many satisfactory deductions might be drawn; but I shall content
myself with the simple fact stated in the Bible, viz. that Noah
begat three sons, Shem, Ham, and Japhet. It is astonishing
on what remote and obscure contingencies the great affairs of
this world depend, and how events the most distant, and to the
common observer unconnected, are inevitably consequent the
one to the other. It remains to the philosopher to discover
these mysterious affinities, and it is the proudest triumph of
his skill, to detect and drag forth some latent chain of causation,
which at first sight appears a paradox to the inexperienced
observer. Thus many of my readers will doubtless wonder

what connection the family of Noah can possibly have with this history—and many will stare when informed, that the whole history of this quarter of the world has taken its character and course from the simple circumstance of the patriarch's having but three sons—but to explain:

Noah, we are told by sundry very credible historians, becoming sole surviving heir and proprietor of the earth, in fee simple, after the deluge, like a good father, portioned out his estate among his children. To Shem he gave Asia; to Ham, Africa; and to Japhet, Europe. Now it is a thousand times to be lamented that he had but three sons, for had there been a fourth, he would doubtless have inherited America; which, of course, would have been dragged forth from its obscurity on the occasion; and thus many a hard-working historian and philosopher would have been spared a prodigious mass of weary conjecture respecting the first discovery and population of this country. Noah, however, having provided for his three sons, looked in all probability upon our country as mere wild unsettled land, and said nothing about it; and to this unpardonable taciturnity of the patriarch may we ascribe the misfortune, that America did not come into the world as early as the other quarters of the globe.

It is true, some writers have vindicated him from this misconduct towards posterity, and asserted that he really did discover America. Thus it was the opinion of Mark Lescarbot, a French writer, possessed of that ponderosity of thought, and profoundness of reflection, so peculiar to his nation, that the immediate descendants of Noah peopled this quarter of the globe, and that the old patriarch himself, who still retained a passion for the sea-faring life, superintended the transmigration. The pious

and enlightened father, Charlevoix, a French Jesuit, remarkable
for his aversion to the marvelous, common to all great travelers,
is conclusively of the same opinion; nay, he goes still farther,
and decides upon the manner in which the discovery was effected,
which was by sea, and under the immediate direction of the
great Noah. "I have already observed," exclaims the good
father, in a tone of becoming indignation, "that it is an arbitrary
supposition that the grandchildren of Noah were not able to
penetrate into the new world, or that they never thought of it.
In effect, I can see no reason that can justify such a notion.
Who can seriously believe, that Noah and his immediate descendants knew less than we do, and that the builder and pilot of the
greatest ship that ever was, a ship which was formed to traverse
an unbounded ocean, and had so many shoals and quicksands
to guard against, should be ignorant of, or should not have
communicated to his descendants the art of sailing on the ocean?"
Therefore, they did sail on the ocean—therefore, they sailed to
America—therefore, America was discovered by Noah!

Now all this exquisite chain of reasoning, which is so
strikingly characteristic of the good father, being addressed to
the faith, rather than the understanding, is flatly opposed by
Hans de Laert, who declares it a real and most ridiculous
paradox, to suppose that Noah ever entertained the thought of
discovering America; and as Hans is a Dutch writer, I am
inclined to believe he must have been much better acquainted
with the worthy crew of the ark than his competitors, and of
course possessed of more accurate sources of information. It
is astonishing how intimate historians do daily become with the
patriarchs and other great men of antiquity. As intimacy
improves with time, and as the learned are particularly inquisi-

tive and familiar in their acquaintance with the ancients, I should
not be surprised if some future writers should gravely give us
a picture of men and manners as they existed before the flood,
far more copious and accurate than the Bible; and that, in the
course of another century, the log-book of the good Noah should
be as current among historians, as the voyages of Captain Cook,
or the renowned history of Robinson Crusoe.

I shall not occupy my time by discussing the huge mass of
additional suppositions, conjectures, and probabilities respecting
the first discovery of this country, with which unhappy historians
overload themselves, in their endeavors to satisfy the doubts of
an incredulous world. It is painful to see these laborious wights
panting, and toiling, and sweating under an enormous burden,
at the very outset of their works, which, on being opened, turns
out to be nothing but a mighty bundle of straw. As, however,
by unwearied assiduity, they seem to have established the fact,
to the satisfaction of all the world, that this country *has been
discovered*, I shall avail myself of their useful labors to be
extremely brief upon this point.

I shall not, therefore, stop to inquire, whether America was
first discovered by a wandering vessel of that celebrated Phœni-
cian fleet, which, according to Herodotus, circumnavigated Africa;
or by that Carthaginian expedition, which Pliny, the naturalist,
informs us, discovered the Canary Islands; or whether it was
settled by a temporary colony from Tyre, as hinted by Aristotle
and Seneca. I shall neither inquire whether it was first discovered by the Chinese, as Vossius with great shrewdness
advances; nor by the Norwegians in 1002, under Biorn; nor
by Behem, the German navigator, as Mr. Otto has endeavored
to prove to the savans of the learned city of Philadelphia.

Nor shall I investigate the more modern claims of the Welsh, founded on the voyage of Prince Madoc in the eleventh century, who having never returned, it has since been wisely concluded that he must have gone to America, and that for a plain reason —if he did not go there, where else could he have gone?—a question which most socratically shuts out all farther dispute.

Laying aside, therefore, all the conjectures above mentioned, with a multitude of others, equally satisfactory, I shall take for granted the vulgar opinion, that America was discovered on the 12th of October, 1492, by Christoval Colon, a Genoese, who has been clumsily nicknamed Columbus, but for what reason I cannot discern. Of the voyages and adventures of this Colon, I shall say nothing, seeing that they are already sufficiently known. Nor shall I undertake to prove that this country should have been called Colonia, after his name, that being notoriously self-evident.

Having thus happily got my readers on this side of the Atlantic, I picture them to myself, all impatience to enter upon the enjoyment of the land of promise, and in full expectation that I will immediately deliver it into their possession. But if I do, may I ever forfeit the reputation of a regular bred historian! No—no—most curious and thrice learned readers, (for thrice learned ye are if ye have read all that has gone before, and nine times learned shall ye be, if ye read that which comes after,) we have yet a world of work before us. Think you the first discoverers of this fair quarter of the globe had nothing to do but go on shore and find a country ready laid out and cultivated like a garden, wherein they might revel at their ease? No such thing—they had forests to cut down, underwood to grub up, marshes to drain, and savages to exterminate.

In like manner, I have sundry doubts to clear away, questions to resolve, and paradoxes to explain, before I permit you to range at random; but these difficulties once overcome, we shall be enabled to jog on right merrily through the rest of our history. Thus my work shall, in a manner, echo the nature of the subject, in the same manner as the sound of poetry has been found by certain shrewd critics to echo the sense—this being an improvement in history, which I claim the merit of having invented.

CHAPTER IV.

SHOWING THE GREAT DIFFICULTY PHILOSOPHERS HAVE HAD
IN PEOPLING AMERICA; AND HOW THE ABORIGINES CAME
TO BE BEGOTTEN BY ACCIDENT—TO THE GREAT RELIEF
AND SATISFACTION OF THE AUTHOR.

THE next inquiry at which we arrive in the regular course of
our history is to ascertain, if possible, how this country was
originally peopled—a point fruitful of incredible embarrassments;
for unless we prove that the Aborigines did absolutely come from
somewhere, it will be immediately asserted, in this age of skepti-
cism, that they did not come at all; and if they did not come
at all, then was this country never populated—a conclusion
perfectly agreeable to the rules of logic, but wholly irreconcilable
to every feeling of humanity, inasmuch as it must syllogistically
prove fatal to the innumerable Aborigines of this populous
region.

To avert so dire a sophism, and to rescue from logical annihi-
lation so many millions of fellow creatures, how many wings of
geese have been plundered! what oceans of ink have been
benevolently drained! and how many capacious heads of learned
historians have been addled, and for ever confounded! I pause
with reverential awe, when I contemplate the ponderous tomes,

in different languages, with which they have endeavored to solve this question, so important to the happiness of society, but so involved in clouds of impenetrable obscurity. Historian after historian has engaged in the endless circle of hypothetical argument, and after leading us a weary chase through octavos, quartos, and folios, has let us out at the end of his work just as wise as we were at the beginning. It was doubtless some philosophical wild-goose chase of the kind that made the old poet Macrobius rail in such a passion at curiosity, which he anathematizes most heartily, as "an irksome agonizing care, a superstitious industry about unprofitable things, an itching humor to see what is not to be seen, and to be doing what signifies nothing when it is done." But to proceed:

Of the claims of the children of Noah to the original population of this country I shall say nothing, as they have already been touched upon in my last chapter. The claimants next in celebrity, are the descendants of Abraham. Thus Christoval Colon (vulgarly called Columbus) when he first discovered the gold mines of Hispaniola, immediately concluded, with a shrewdness that would have done honor to a philosopher, that he had found the ancient Ophir, from whence Solomon procured the gold for embellishing the temple at Jerusalem; nay, Colon even imagined that he saw the remains of furnaces of veritable Hebraic construction, employed in refining the precious ore.

So golden a conjecture, tinctured with such fascinating extravagance, was too tempting not to be immediately snapped at by the gudgeons of learning; and accordingly, there were divers profound writers, ready to swear to its correctness, and to bring in their usual load of authorities, and wise surmises, wherewithal to prop it up. Vetablus and Robertus Stephens declared nothing

could be more clear—Arius Montanus, without the least hesita-
tion, asserts that Mexico was the true Ophir, and the Jews the
early settlers of the country.   While Possevin, Becan, and
several other sagacious writers, lug in a *supposed* prophecy of
the fourth book of Esdras, which being inserted in the mighty
hypothesis, like the keystone of an arch, gives it, in their
opinion, perpetual durability.

Scarce, however, have they completed their goodly superstructure, than in trudges a phalanx of opposite authors, with
Hans de Laet, the great Dutchman, at their head, and at one
blow tumbles the whole fabric about their ears.   Hans, in fact,
contradicts outright all the Israelitish claims to the first settlement
of this country, attributing all those equivocal symptoms, and
traces of Christianity and Judaism, which have been said to be
found in divers provinces of the new world, to the *Devil*, who
has always affected to counterfeit the worship of the true Deity.
"A remark," says the knowing old Padre d'Acosta, "made by
all good authors who have spoken of the religion of nations
newly discovered, and founded besides on the authority of the
fathers of the church."

Some writers again, among whom it is with much regret I
am compelled to mention Lopez de Gomara, and Juan de Leri,
insinuate that the Canaanites, being driven from the land of
promise by the Jews, were seized with such a panic that they
fled without looking behind them, until stopping to take breath,
they found themselves safe in America.   As they brought neither
their national language, manners, nor features with them, it is
supposed they left them behind in the hurry of their flight—
I cannot give my faith to this opinion.

I pass over the supposition of the learned Grotius, who being both an ambassador and a Dutchman to boot, is entitled to great respect; that North America was peopled by a strolling company of Norwegians, and that Peru was founded by a colony from China—Manco or Mango Capac, the first Incas, being himself a Chinese. Nor shall I more than barely mention, that father Kircher ascribes the settlement of America to the Egyptians, Rudbeck to the Scandinavians, Charron to the Gauls, Juffredus Petri to a skating party from Friesland, Milius to the Celtæ, Marinocus the Sicilian to the Romans, Le Compte to the Phœnicians, Postel to the Moors, Martyn d'Angleria to the Abyssinians, together with the sage surmise of De Laet, that England, Ireland, and the Orcades may contend for that honor.

Nor will I bestow any more attention or credit to the idea that America is the fairy region of Zipangri, described by that dreaming traveler, Marco Polo, the Venetian; or that it comprises the visionary island of Atlantis, described by Plato. Neither will I stop to investigate the heathenish assertion of Paracelsus, that each hemisphere of the globe was originally furnished with an Adam and Eve. Or the more flattering opinion of Dr. Romayne, supported by many nameless authorities, that Adam was of the Indian race—or the startling conjecture of Buffon, Helvetius, and Darwin, so highly honorable to mankind, that the whole human species is accidentally descended from a remarkable family of monkeys!

This last conjecture, I must own, came upon me very suddenly and very ungraciously. I have often beheld the clown in a pantomime, while gazing in stupid wonder at the extravagant gambols of a harlequin, all at once electrified by a sudden stroke of the wooden sword across his shoulders. Little did I think at such times, that it would ever fall to my lot to be treated with equal discourtesy, and that while I was quietly beholding these grave philosophers, emulating the eccentric transformations of the hero of pantomime, they would on a sudden turn upon me and my readers, and with one hypothetical flourish metamorphose us into beasts! I determined from that moment not to burn my fingers with any more of their theories, but content myself with detailing the different methods by which they transported the descendants of these ancient and respectable monkeys to this great field of theoretical warfare.

This was done either by migrations by land or transmigrations by water. Thus Padre Joseph D'Acosta enumerates three passages by land—first by the north of Europe, secondly by the north of Asia, and thirdly by regions southward of the Straits of Magellan. The learned Grotius marches his Norwegians by a pleasant route across frozen rivers and arms of the sea, through Iceland, Greenland, Estotiland and Naremberga: and various writers, among whom are Angleria, De Hornn, and Buffon, anxious for the accommodation of these travelers, have fastened the two continents together by a strong chain of deductions—by which means they could pass over dry-shod. But should even this fail, Pinkerton, that industrious old gentleman, who compiles books, and manufactures Geographies, has constructed a natural bridge of ice, from continent to continent, at the distance of four or five miles from Behring's Straits—for which he is entitled to the grateful thanks of all the wandering aborigines who ever did or ever will pass over it.

It is an evil much to be lamented, that none of the worthy writers above quoted could ever commence his work, without immediately declaring hostilities against every writer who had treated of the same subject. In this particular, authors may be compared to a certain sagacious bird, which in building its nest, is sure to pull to pieces the nests of all the birds in its neighborhood. This unhappy propensity tends grievously to impede the progress of sound knowledge. Theories are at best but brittle productions, and when once committed to the stream, they should take care that like the notable pots which were fellow-voyagers, they do not crack each other.

My chief surprise is, that among the many writers I have noticed, no one has attempted to prove that this country was peopled from the moon—or that the first inhabitants floated hither on islands of ice, as white bears cruise about the northern oceans —or that they were conveyed hither by balloons, as modern aeronauts pass from Dover to Calais—or by witchcraft, as Simon Magus posted among the stars—or after the manner of the renowned Scythian Abaris, who, like the New England witches or full-blooded broomsticks, made most unheard-of journeys on the back of a golden arrow, given him by the Hyperborean Apollo.

But there is still one mode left by which this country could have been peopled, which I have reserved for the last, because I consider it worth all the rest: it is—*by accident!* Speaking of the islands of Solomon, New Guinea, and New Holland, the profound father Charlevoix observes, "in fine, all these countries are peopled, and *it is possible* some have been so *by accident.* Now if it could have happened in that manner, why might it not have been at the *same time,* and by the *same means,* with *the other* parts of the globe?" This ingenious mode of deducing certain conclusions from possible premises, is an improvement in syllogistic skill, and proves the good father superior even to Archimedes, for he can turn the world without any thing to rest his lever upon. It is only surpassed by the dexterity with which the sturdy old

2*

Jesuit, in another place, cuts the gordian knot—" Nothing," says
he, " is more easy. The inhabitants of both hemispheres are certainly the descendants of the same father. The common father
of mankind received an express order from Heaven to people
the world, and *accordingly it has been peopled*. To bring this
about, it was necessary to overcome all difficulties in the way, *and
they have also been overcome!*" Pious logician! How does he
put all the herd of laborious theorists to the blush, by explaining,
in five words, what it has cost them volumes to prove they knew
nothing about!

From all the authorities here quoted, and a variety of others
which I have consulted, but which are omitted through fear of
fatiguing the unlearned reader, I can only draw the following
conclusions, which luckily, however, are sufficient for my purpose.
First, that this part of the world has actually *been peopled*,
(Q. E. D.) to support which we have living proofs in the numerous tribes of Indians that inhabit it. Secondly, that it has been
peopled in five hundred different ways, as proved by a cloud of
authors who, from the positiveness of their assertions, seem to
have been eye-witnesses to the fact. Thirdly, that the people of
this country had a *variety of fathers*, which, as it may not be
thought much to their credit by the common run of readers, the
less we say on the subject the better. The question, therefore, I
trust, is for ever at rest.

CHAPTER V.

IN WHICH THE AUTHOR PUTS A MIGHTY QUESTION TO THE ROUT, BY THE ASSISTANCE OF THE MAN IN THE MOON— WHICH NOT ONLY DELIVERS THOUSANDS OF PEOPLE FROM GREAT EMBARRASSMENT, BUT LIKEWISE CONCLUDES THIS INTRODUCTORY BOOK.

THE writer of a history may, in some respects, be likened unto an adventurous knight, who having undertaken a perilous enterprise, by way of establishing his fame, feels bound, in honor and chivalry, to turn back for no difficulty nor hardship, and never to shrink or quail, whatever enemy he may encounter. Under this impression, I resolutely draw my pen, and fall to, with might and main, at those doughty questions and subtle paradoxes, which, like fiery dragons and bloody giants, beset the entrance to my history, and would fain repulse me from the very threshold. And at this moment a gigantic question has started up, which I must needs take by the beard and utterly subdue, before I can advance another step in my historic undertaking; but I trust this will be the last adversary I shall have to contend with, and that in the next book I shall be enabled to conduct my readers in triumph into the body of my work.

The question which has thus suddenly arisen, is, What right

had the first discoverers of America to land and take possession of a country, without first gaining the consent of its inhabitants, or yielding them an adequate compensation for their territory?— a question which has withstood many fierce assaults, and has given much distress of mind to multitudes of kind-hearted folk. And indeed, until it be totally vanquished, and put to rest, the worthy people of America can by no means enjoy the soil they inhabit, with clear right and title, and quiet, unsullied consciences.

The first source of right, by which property is acquired in a country, is DISCOVERY. For as all mankind have an equal right to any thing, which has never before been appropriated, so any nation, that discovers an uninhabited country, and takes possession thereof, is considered as enjoying full property, and absolute, unquestionable empire therein.*

This proposition being admitted, it follows clearly, that the Europeans who first visited America, were the real discoverers of the same; nothing being necessary to the establishment of this fact, but simply to prove that it was totally uninhabited by man. This would at first appear to be a point of some difficulty, for it is well known, that this quarter of the world abounded with certain animals, that walked erect on two feet, had something of the human countenance, uttered certain unintelligible sounds, very much like language, in short, had a marvelous resemblance to human beings. But the zealous and enlightened fathers, who accompanied the discoverers, for the purpose of promoting the kingdom of heaven, by establishing fat monasteries and bishoprics on earth, soon cleared up this point, greatly to the satisfaction of his holiness the pope, and of all Christian voyagers and discoverers.

* Grotius. Puffendorf, b. v. c. 4. Vattel, b. i. c. 18, &c.

They plainly proved, and as there were no Indian writers arose on the other side, the fact was considered as fully admitted and established, that the two-legged race of animals before mentioned were mere cannibals, detestable monsters, and many of them giants—which last description of vagrants have, since the times of Gog, Magog, and Goliath, been considered as outlaws, and have received no quarter in either history, chivalry, or song. Indeed, even the philosophic Bacon declared the Americans to be people proscribed by the laws of nature, inasmuch as they had a barbarous custom of sacrificing men, and feeding upon man's flesh.

Nor are these all the proofs of their utter barbarism: among many other writers of discernment, Ulloa tells us "their imbecility is so visible, that one can hardly form an idea of them different from what one has of the brutes. Nothing disturbs the tranquillity of their souls, equally insensible to disasters and to prosperity. Though half naked, they are as contented as a monarch in his most splendid array. Fear makes no impression on them, and respect as little." All this is furthermore supported by the authority of M. Bouguer. "It is not easy," says he, "to describe the degree of their indifference for wealth and all its advantages. One does not well know what motives to propose to them when one would persuade them to any service. It is vain to offer them money; they answer they are not hungry." And Vanegas confirms the whole, assuring us that "ambition they have none, and are more desirous of being thought strong than valiant. The objects of ambition with us—honor, fame, reputation, riches, posts, and distinctions, are unknown among them. So that this powerful spring of action, the cause of so much *seeming* good and *real* evil in the world, has no power over them. In a word, these unhappy mortals may be compared to children, in whom the development of reason is not completed."

Now all these peculiarities, although in the unenlightened states of Greece they would have entitled their possessors to immortal honor, as having reduced to practice those rigid and abstemious maxims, the mere talking about which acquired certain old Greeks the reputation of sages and philosophers ;— yet, were they clearly proved in the present instance to betoken a most abject and brutified nature, totally beneath the human character. But the benevolent fathers, who had undertaken to turn these unhappy savages into dumb beasts, by dint of argument, advanced still stronger proofs ; for as certain divines of the sixteenth century, and among the rest Lullus, affirm—the Americans go naked, and have no beards !—" They have nothing," says Lullus, " of the reasonable animal, except the mask."—And even that mask was allowed to avail them but little, for it was soon found that they were of a hideous copper complexion—and being of a copper complexion, it was all the same as if they were negroes—and negroes are black, " and black," said the pious fathers, devoutly crossing themselves, " is the color of the Devil!" Therefore, so far from being able to own property, they had no right even to personal freedom—for liberty is too radiant a deity to inhabit such gloomy temples. All which circumstances plainly convinced the righteous followers of Cortes and Pizarro, that these miscreants had no title to the soil that they infested—that they were a perverse, illiterate, dumb, beardless, black-seed— mere wild beasts of the forests, and like them should either be subdued or exterminated.

From the foregoing arguments, therefore, and a variety of others equally conclusive, which I forbear to enumerate, it is clearly evident that this fair quarter of the globe when first visited by Europeans, was a howling wilderness, inhabited by nothing but wild beasts; and that the transatlantic visitors acquired an incontrovertible property therein, by the *right of discovery*.

This right being fully established, we now come to the next, which is the right acquired by *cultivation*. " The cultivation of the soil," we are told, " is an obligation imposed by nature on mankind. The whole world is appointed for the nourishment of its inhabitants : but it would be incapable of doing it, was it uncultivated. Every nation is then obliged by the law of nature to cultivate the ground that has fallen to its share. Those people, like the ancient Germans and modern Tartars, who, having fertile countries, disdain to cultivate the earth, and choose to live by rapine, are wanting to themselves, and *deserve to be extermi- nated as savage and pernicious beasts.*"*

Now it is notorious, that the savages knew nothing of agricul- ture, when first discovered by the Europeans, but lived a most vagabond, disorderly, unrighteous life,—rambling from place to place, and prodigally rioting upon the spontaneous luxuries of nature, without tasking her generosity to yield them any thing more ; whereas it has been most unquestionably shown, that Heaven intended the earth should be ploughed and sown, and manured, and laid out into cities, and towns, and farms, and country seats, and pleasure grounds, and public gardens, all which the Indians knew nothing about—therefore, they did not improve the talents Providence had bestowed on them— therefore, they were careless stewards—therefore, they had no right to the soil—therefore, they deserved to be exterminated.

It is true, the savages might plead that they drew all the

* Vattel, b. i. ch. 17.

benefits from the land which their simple wants required—they
found plenty of game to hunt, which, together with the roots and
uncultivated fruits of the earth, furnished a sufficient variety for
their frugal repasts;—and that as Heaven merely designed the
earth to form the abode, and satisfy the wants of man; so long
as those purposes were answered, the will of Heaven was accomplished.—But this only proves how undeserving they were of the
blessings around them—they were so much the more savages,
for not having more wants; for knowledge is in some degree an
increase of desires, and it is this superiority both in the number
and magnitude of his desires, that distinguishes the man from the
beast.   Therefore the Indians, in not having more wants, were
very unreasonable animals; and it was but just that they should
make way for the Europeans, who had a thousand wants to their
one, and, therefore, would turn the earth to more account, and by
cultivating it, more truly fulfill the will of Heaven.   Besides—
Grotius and Lauterbach, and Puffendorff, and Titius, and many
wise men beside, who have considered the matter properly, have
determined, that the property of a country cannot be acquired
by hunting, cutting wood, or drawing water in it—nothing but
precise demarcation of limits, and the intention of cultivation, can
establish the possession.   Now as the savages (probably from
never having read the authors above quoted) had never complied
with any of these necessary forms, it plainly follows that they had
no right to the soil, but that it was completely at the disposal of
the first comers, who had more knowledge, more wants, and more
elegant, that is to say, artificial desires than themselves.

   In entering upon a newly discovered, uncultivated country,
therefore, the new comers were but taking possession of what,
according to the aforesaid doctrine, was their own property—

therefore, in opposing them, the savages were invading their just rights, infringing the immutable laws of nature, and counteracting the will of Heaven—therefore, they were guilty of impiety, burglary, and trespass on the case,—therefore, they were hardened offenders against God and man—therefore, they ought to be exterminated.

But a more irresistible right than either that I have mentioned, and one which will be the most readily admitted by my reader, provided he be blessed with bowels of charity and philanthropy, is the right acquired by civilization. All the world knows the lamentable state in which these poor savages were found. Not only deficient in the comforts of life, but what is still worse, most piteously and unfortunately blind to the miseries of their situation. But no sooner did the benevolent inhabitants of Europe behold their sad condition than they immediately went to work to ameliorate and improve it. They introduced among them rum, gin, brandy, and the other comforts of life—and it is astonishing to read how soon the poor savages learned to estimate those blessings; they likewise made known to them a thousand remedies, by which the most inveterate diseases are alleviated and healed; and that they might comprehend the benefits and enjoy the comforts of these medicines, they previously introduced among them the diseases which they were calculated to cure. By these and a variety of other methods was the condition of these poor savages wonderfully improved; they acquired a thousand wants, of which they had before been ignorant; and as he has most sources of happiness who has most wants to be gratified, they were doubtlessly rendered a much happier race of beings.

But the most important branch of civilization, and which has most strenuously been extolled by the zealous and pious fathers of the Romish Church, is the introduction of the Christian faith. It was truly a sight that might well inspire horror, to behold these savages tumbling among the dark mountains of paganism, and guilty of the most horrible ignorance of religion. It is true, they neither stole nor defrauded ; they were sober, frugal, continent, and faithful to their word ; but though they acted right habitually, it was all in vain, unless they acted so from precept. The new comers, therefore, used every method to induce them to embrace and practice the true religion—except indeed that of setting them the example.

But notwithstanding all these complicated labors for their good, such was the unparalleled obstinacy of these stubborn wretches, that they ungratefully refused to acknowledge the strangers as their benefactors, and persisted in disbelieving the doctrines they endeavored to inculcate ; most insolently alleging, that from their conduct, the advocates of Christianity did not seem to believe in it themselves. Was not this too much for human patience ?—would not one suppose that the benign visitants from Europe, provoked at their incredulity, and discouraged by their stiff-necked obstinacy, would for ever have abandoned their shores, and consigned them to their original ignorance and misery ?—But no—so zealous were they to effect the temporal comfort and eternal salvation of these pagan infidels, that they even proceeded from the milder means of persuasion, to the more painful and troublesome one of persecution—let loose among them whole troops of fiery monks and furious bloodhounds—purified them by fire and sword, by stake and fagot; in consequence of which indefatigable measures the cause of Christian love and charity was so rapidly advanced, that in a few years not one-fifth of the number of unbelievers existed in South America that were found there at the time of its discovery.

What stronger right need the European settlers advance to the country than this? Have not whole nations of uninformed savages been made acquainted with a thousand imperious wants and indispensable comforts, of which they were before wholly ignorant? Have they not been literally hunted and smoked out of the dens and lurking places of ignorance and infidelity, and absolutely scourged into the right path? Have not the temporal things, the vain baubles and filthy lucre of this world, which were too apt to engage their worldly and selfish thoughts, been benevolently taken from them; and have they not, instead thereof, been taught to set their affections on things above?—And finally, to use the words of a reverend Spanish father, in a letter to his superior in Spain—" Can any one have the presumption to say that these savage Pagans have yielded any thing more than an inconsiderable recompense to their benefactors; in surrendering to them a little pitiful tract of this dirty sublunary planet in exchange for a glorious inheritance in the kingdom of heaven?"

Here then are three complete and undeniable sources of right established, any one of which was more than ample to establish a property in the newly discovered regions of America. Now, so it has happened in certain parts of this delightful quarter of the globe, that the right of discovery has been so strenuously asserted —the influence of cultivation so industriously extended, and the progress of salvation and civilization so zealously prosecuted, that, what with their attendant wars, persecutions, oppressions, diseases and other partial evils that often hang on the skirts of great benefits—the savage aborigines have, somehow or another, been utterly annihilated—and this all at once brings me to a fourth right,

which is worth all the others put together.—For the orignal claimants to the soil being all dead and buried, and no one remaining
to inherit or dispute the soil, the Spaniards, as the next immediate occupants, entered upon the possession as clearly as the
hangman succeeds to the clothes of the malefactor—and as they
have Blackstone,* and all the learned expounders of the law on
their side, they may set all actions of ejectment at defiance—and
this last right may be entitled the RIGHT BY EXTERMINATION, or
in other words, the RIGHT BY GUNPOWDER.

But lest any scruples of conscience should remain on this
head, and to settle the question of right for ever, his holiness Pope
Alexander VI. issued a bull, by which he generously granted the
newly-discovered quarter of the globe to the Spaniards and Portu-
guese ; who, thus having law and gospel on their side, and being
inflamed with great spiritual zeal, showed the Pagan savages
neither favor nor affection, but prosecuted the work of discovery,
colonization, civilization, and extermination, with ten times more
fury than ever.

Thus were the European worthies who first discovered America clearly entitled to the soil ; and not only entitled to the soil,
but likewise to the eternal thanks of these infidel savages, for
having come so far, endured so many perils by sea and land, and
taken such unwearied pains, for no other purpose but to improve
their forlorn, uncivilized, and heathenish condition—for having
made them acquainted with the comforts of life ; for having introduced among them the light of religion, and finally—for having hurried them out of the world, to enjoy its reward !

But as argument is never so well understood by us selfish mor-

* Bl. Com. b. ii. c. 1.

tals as when it comes home to ourselves, and as I am particularly anxious that this question should be put to rest for ever, I will suppose a parallel case, by way of arousing the candid attention of my readers.

Let us suppose, then, that the inhabitants of the moon, by astonishing advancement in science, and by profound insight into that lunar philosophy, the mere flickerings of which have of late years dazzled the feeble optics, and addled the shallow brains of the good people of our globe—let us suppose, I say, that the inhabitants of the moon, by these means, had arrived at such a command of their *energies*, such an enviable state of *perfectibility*, as to control the elements, and navigate the boundless regions of space. Let us suppose a roving crew of these soaring philosophers, in the course of an aerial voyage of discovery among the stars, should chance to alight upon this outlandish planet.

And here I beg my readers will not have the uncharitableness to smile, as is too frequently the fault of volatile readers, when perusing the grave speculations of philosophers. I am far from indulging in any sportive vein at present; nor is the supposition I have been making so wild as many may deem it. It has long been a very serious and anxious question with me, and many a time and oft, in the course of my overwhelming cares and contrivances for the welfare and protection of this my native planet, have I lain awake whole nights debating in my mind, whether it were most probable we should first discover and civilize the moon, or the moon discover and civilize our globe. Neither would the prodigy of sailing in the air and cruising among the stars be a whit more astonishing and incomprehensible to us, than was the European mystery of navigating floating castles, through the world of waters, to the simple natives. We have already discovered the art of coasting along the aerial shores of our planet, by means of balloons, as the savages had of venturing along their sea-coasts in canoes; and the disparity between the former, and the aerial vehicles of the philosophers from the moon, might not be greater than that between the bark canoes of the savages, and the mighty ships of their discoverers. I might here pursue an endless chain of similar speculations; but as they would be un-important to my subject, I abandon them to my reader, particu-larly if he be a philosopher, as matters well worthy of his atten-tive consideration.

To return then to my supposition—let us suppose that the aerial visitants I have mentioned, possessed of vastly superior knowledge to ourselves; that is to say, possessed of superior knowledge in the art of extermination—riding on hyppogriffs—defended with impenetrable armor—armed with concentrated sunbeams, and provided with vast engines, to hurl enormous moon-stones: in short, let us suppose them, if our vanity will permit the supposition, as superior to us in knowledge, and consequently in power, as the Europeans were to the Indians, when they first discovered them. All this is very possible; it is only our self-sufficiency that makes us think otherwise; and I warrant the poor savages, before they had any knowledge of the white men, armed in all the terrors of glittering steel and tremendous gunpowder, were as perfectly convinced that they themselves were the wisest, the most virtuous, powerful, and perfect of created beings, as are, at this present moment, the lordly inhabitants of old England, the volatile populace of France, or even the self-satisfied citizens of this most enlightened republic.

Let us suppose, moreover, that the aerial voyagers, finding

this planet to be nothing but a howling wilderness, inhabited by us, poor savages and wild beasts, shall take formal possession of it, in the name of his most gracious and philosophic excellency, the man in the moon. Finding, however, that their numbers are incompetent to hold it in complete subjection, on account of the ferocious barbarity of its inhabitants, they shall take our worthy President, the King of England, the Emperor of Hayti, the mighty Bonaparte, and the great King of Bantam, and returning to their native planet, shall carry them to court, as were the Indian chiefs led about as spectacles in the courts of Europe.

Then making such obeisance as the etiquette of the court requires, they shall address the puissant man in the moon, in, as near as I can conjecture, the following terms:

"Most serene and mighty Potentate, whose dominions extend as far as eye can reach, who rideth on the Great Bear, useth the sun as a looking-glass, and maintaineth unrivaled control over tides, madmen, and sea-crabs. We thy liege subjects have just returned from a voyage of discovery, in the course of which we have landed and taken possession of that obscure little dirty planet, which thou beholdest rolling at a distance. The five uncouth monsters, which we have brought into this august presence, were once very important chiefs among their fellow savages, who are a race of beings totally destitute of the common attributes of humanity; and differing in every thing from the inhabitants of the moon, inasmuch as they carry their heads upon their shoulders, instead of under their arms—have two eyes instead of one—are utterly destitute of tails, and of a variety of unseemly complexions, particularly of horrible whiteness—instead of pea-green.

"We have moreover found these miserable savages sunk

into a state of the utmost ignorance and depravity, every man shamelessly living with his own wife, and rearing his own children, instead of indulging in that community of wives enjoined by the law of nature, as expounded by the philosophers of the moon. In a word, they have scarcely a gleam of true philosophy among them, but are, in fact, utter heretics, ignoramuses, and barbarians. Taking compassion, therefore, on the sad condition of these sublunary wretches, we have endeavored, while we remained on their planet, to introduce among them the light of reason—and the comforts of the moon. We have treated them to mouthfuls of moonshine, and draughts of nitrous oxyd, which they swallowed with incredible voracity, particularly the females ; and we have likewise endeavored to instill into them the precepts of lunar philosophy. We have insisted upon their renouncing the contemptible shackles of religion and common sense, and adoring the profound, omnipotent, and all perfect energy, and the ecstatic, immutable, immovable perfection. But such was the unparalleled obstinacy of these wretched savages, that they persisted in cleaving to their wives, and adhering to their religion, and absolutely set at naught the sublime doctrines of the moon—nay, among other abominable heresies, they even went so far as blasphemously to declare, that this ineffable planet was made of nothing more nor less than green cheese !"

At these words, the great man in the moon (being a very profound philosopher) shall fall into a terrible passion, and possessing equal authority over things that do not belong to him, as did whilom his holiness the Pope, shall forthwith issue a formidable bull, specifying, "That, whereas a certain crew of Lunatics have lately discovered, and taken possession of a newly discovered planet called *the earth*—and that whereas it is inhabited by none but a race of two-legged animals that carry their heads on their shoulders instead of under their arms; cannot talk the lunatic language; have two eyes instead of one; are destitute of tails, and of a horrible whiteness, instead of pea-green—therefore, and for a variety of other excellent reasons, they are considered incapable of possessing any property in the planet they infest, and the right and title to it are confirmed to its original discoverers.—And furthermore, the colonists who are now about to depart to the aforesaid planet are authorized and commanded to use every means to convert these infidel savages from the darkness of Christianity, and make them thorough and absolute lunatics."

In consequence of this benevolent bull, our philosophic bene-factors go to work with hearty zeal. They seize upon our fertile territories, scourge us from our rightful possessions, relieve us from our wives, and when we are unreasonable enough to complain, they will turn upon us and say, Miserable barbarians! ungrateful wretches! have we not come thousands of miles to improve your worthless planet; have we not fed you with moon-shine; have we not intoxicated you with nitrous oxyd; does not our moon give you light every night, and have you the baseness to murmur, when we claim a pitiful return for all these benefits? But finding that we not only persist in absolute contempt of their reasoning and disbelief in their philosophy, but even go so far as daringly to defend our property, their patience shall be exhausted, and they shall resort to their superior powers of argument; hunt us with hyppogriffs, transfix us with concentrated sunbeams, demolish our cities with moon-stones; until having, by main force, converted us to the true

4

faith, they shall graciously permit us to exist in the torrid deserts of Arabia, or the frozen regions of Lapland, there to enjoy the blessings of civilization and the charms of lunar philosophy, in much the same manner as the reformed and enlightened savages of this country are kindly suffered to inhabit the inhospitable forests of the north, or the impenetrable wildernesses of South America.

Thus, I hope, I have clearly proved, and strikingly illustrated, the right of the early colonists to the possession of this country; and thus is this gigantic question completely vanquished: so having manfully surmounted all obstacles, and subdued all opposition, what remains but that I should forthwith conduct my readers into the city which we have been so long in a manner besieging? But hold; before I proceed another step, I must pause to take breath, and recover from the excessive fatigue I have undergone, in preparing to begin this most accurate of histories. And in this I do but imitate the example of a renowned Dutch tumbler of antiquity, who took a start of three miles for the purpose of jumping over a hill, but having run himself out of breath by the time he reached the foot, sat himself quietly down for a few moments to blow, and then walked over it at his leisure.

BOOK II.

TREATING OF THE FIRST SETTLEMENT OF THE PROVINCE
OF NIEUW-NEDERLANDTS.

CHAPTER I.

IN WHICH ARE CONTAINED DIVERS REASONS WHY A MAN
SHOULD NOT WRITE IN A HURRY; ALSO, OF MASTER
HENDRICK HUDSON, HIS DISCOVERY OF A STRANGE COUN-
TRY—AND HOW HE WAS MAGNIFICENTLY REWARDED BY
THE MUNIFICENCE OF THEIR HIGH MIGHTINESSES.

MY great-grandfather, by the mother's side, Hermanus Van
Clattercop, when employed to build the large stone church at
Rotterdam, which stands about three hundred yards to your left
after you turn off from the Boomkeys, and which is so conve-
niently constructed, that all the zealous Christians of Rotterdam
prefer sleeping through a sermon there to any other church in
the city—my great-grandfather, I say, when employed to build
that famous church, did in the first place send to Delft for a box
of long pipes; then having purchased a new spitting-box and
a hundred weight of the best Virginia, he sat himself down, and
did nothing for the space of three months but smoke most

laboriously. Then did he spend full three months more in trudging on foot, and voyaging in trekschuit, from Rotterdam to Amsterdam—to Delft—to Haerlem—to Leyden—to the Hague, knocking his head and breaking his pipe against every church in his road. Then did he advance gradually nearer and nearer to Rotterdam, until he came in full sight of the identical spot whereon the church was to be built. Then did he spend three months longer in walking round it and round it, contemplating it, first from one point of view, and then from another—now would he be paddled by it on the canal—now would he peep at it through a telescope from the other side of the Meuse, and now would he take a bird's-eye glance at it, from the top of one of those gigantic windmills which protect the gates of the city. The good folks of the place were on the tiptoe of expectation and impatience —notwithstanding all the turmoil of my great-grandfather, not a symptom of the church was yet to be seen; they even began to fear it would never be brought into the world, but that its great projector would lie down and die in labor of the mighty plan he had conceived. At length, having occupied twelve good months in puffing and paddling, and talking and walking—having traveled over all Holland, and even taken a peep into France and Germany—having smoked five hundred and ninety-nine pipes, and three hundred weight of the best Virginia tobacco —my great-grandfather gathered together all that knowing and industrious class of citizens who prefer attending to any body's business sooner than their own, and having pulled off his coat and five pair of breeches, he advanced sturdily up, and laid the corner-stone of the church, in the presence of the whole multitude—just at the commencement of the thirteenth month.

In a similar manner, and with the example of my worthy

ancestor full before my eyes, have I proceeded in writing this most authentic history. The honest Rotterdamers no doubt thought my great-grandfather was doing nothing at all to the purpose, while he was making such a world of prefatory bustle, about the building of his church—and many of the ingenious inhabitants of this fair city will unquestionably suppose that all the preliminary chapters, with the discovery, population, and final settlement of America, were totally irrelevant and super-fluous—and that the main business, the history of New-York, is not a jot more advanced, than if I had never taken up my pen. Never were wise people more mistaken in their conjectures; in consequence of going to work slowly and deliberately, the church came out of my grandfather's hands one of the most sumptuous, goodly, and glorious edifices in the known world—excepting that, like our magnificent capitol, at Washington, it was begun on so grand a scale that the good folks could not afford to finish more than the wing of it. So, likewise, I trust, if ever I am able to finish this work on the plan I have com-menced, (of which, in simple truth, I sometimes have my doubts,) it will be found that I have pursued the latest rules of my art, as exemplified in the writings of all the great American his-torians, and wrought a very large history out of a small subject—which, now-a-days, is considered one of the great triumphs of historic skill. To proceed, then, with the thread of my story.

In the ever memorable year of our Lord, 1609, on a Saturday morning, the five-and-twentieth day of March, old style, did that "worthy and irrecoverable discoverer, (as he has justly been called,) Master Henry Hudson," set sail from Holland in a stout vessel called the Half Moon, being employed by the Dutch East India Company, to seek a northwest passage to China.

Henry (or, as the Dutch historians call him, Hendrick)
Hudson, was a sea-faring man of renown, who had learned to
smoke tobacco under Sir Walter Raleigh, and is said to have
been the first to introduce it into Holland, which gained him much
popularity in that country, and caused him to find great favor in
the eyes of their High Mightinesses, the lords states general, and
also of the honorable West India Company. He was a short,
square, brawny old gentleman, with a double chin, a mastiff
mouth, and a broad copper nose, which was supposed in those
days to have acquired its fiery hue from the constant neighborhood of his tobacco pipe.

He wore a true Andrea Ferrara, tucked in a leathern belt,
and a commodore's cocked hat on one side of his head. He was
remarkable for always jerking up his breeches when he gave out
his orders, and his voice sounded not unlike the brattling of a
tin trumpet—owing to the number of hard northwesters which
he had swallowed in the course of his sea-faring.

Such was Hendrick Hudson, of whom we have heard so
much, and know so little: and I have been thus particular in his
description for the benefit of modern painters and statuaries, that
they may represent him as he was; and not, according to their
common custom with modern heroes, make him look like Cæsar,
or Marcus Aurelius, or the Apollo of Belvidere.

As chief mate and favorite companion, the commodore chose
master Robert Juet, of Limehouse, in England. By some his
name has been spelled *Chewit*, and ascribed to the circumstance
of his having been the first man that ever chewed tobacco; but
this I believe to be a mere flippancy; more especially as certain
of his progeny are living at this day, who write their names **Juet**.
He was an old comrade and early schoolmate of the great Hudson,

with whom he had often played truant and sailed chip boats in a neighboring pond, when they were little boys—from whence it is said the commodore first derived his bias towards a sea-faring life. Certain it is, that the old people about Limehouse declared Robert Juet to be an unlucky urchin, prone to mischief, that would one day or other come to the gallows.

He grew up as boys of that kind often grow up, a rambling, heedless varlet, tossed about in all quarters of the world—meeting with more perils and wonders than did Sindbad the Sailor, without growing a whit more wise, prudent, or ill-natured. Under every misfortune, he comforted himself with a quid of tobacco, and the truly philosophic maxim, that " it will be all the same thing a hundred years hence." He was skilled in the art of carving anchors and true lovers' knots on the bulk-heads and quarter-railings, and was considered a great wit on board ship, in consequence of his playing pranks on every body around, and now and then even making a wry face at old Hendrick, when his back was turned.

To this universal genius are we indebted for many particulars concerning this voyage; of which he wrote a history, at the request of the commodore, who had an unconquerable aversion to writing himself, from having received so many floggings about it when at school. To supply the deficiencies of master Juet's journal, which is written with true log-book brevity, I have availed myself of divers family traditions, handed down from my great-great-grandfather, who accompanied the expedition in the capacity of cabin-boy.

From all that I can learn, few incidents worthy of remark happened in the voyage; and it mortifies me exceedingly that I have

to admit so noted an expedition into my work, without making
any more of it.

Suffice it to say, the voyage was prosperous and tranquil—the
crew, being a patient people, much given to slumber and vacuity,
and but little troubled with the disease of thinking—a malady of
the mind, which is the sure breeder of discontent. Hudson had
laid in abundance of gin and sourcrout, and every man was allowed to sleep quietly at his post unless the wind blew. True it
is, some slight disaffection was shown on two or three occasions,
at certain unreasonable conduct of Commodore Hudson. Thus,
for instance, he forbore to shorten sail when the wind was light,
and the weather serene, which was considered among the most
experienced Dutch seamen, as certain *weather-breeders*, or prognostics, that the weather would change for the worse. He acted,
moreover, in direct contradiction to that ancient and sage rule of
the Dutch navigators, who always took in sail at night—put the
helm a-port, and turned in—by which precaution they had a good
night's rest—were sure of knowing where they were the next
morning, and stood but little chance of running down a continent
in the dark. He likewise prohibited the seamen from wearing
more than five jackets and six pair of breeches, under pretence
of rendering them more alert; and no man was permitted to go
aloft, and hand in sails with a pipe in his mouth, as is the invariable Dutch custom at the present day. All these grievances,
though they might ruffle for a moment the constitutional tranquillity of the honest Dutch tars, made but transient impression;
they eat hugely, drank profusely, and slept immeasurably, and
being under the especial guidance of Providence, the ship was
safely conducted to the coast of America; where, after sundry

unimportant touchings and standings off and on, she at length, on the fourth day of September, entered that majestic bay, which at this day expands its ample bosom before the city of New-York, and which had never before been visited by any European.*

It has been traditionary in our family, that when the great navigator was first blessed with a view of this enchanting island, he was observed, for the first and only time in his life, to exhibit strong symptoms of astonishment and admiration. He is said to have turned to master Juet, and uttered these remarkable words, while he pointed towards this paradise of the new world—" See ! there !"—and thereupon, as was always his way when he was uncommonly pleased, he did puff out such clouds of dense tobacco smoke, that in one minute the vessel was out of sight of land, and master Juet was fain to wait until the winds dispersed this impenetrable fog.

* True it is—and I am not ignorant of the fact, that in a certain aprocry-phal book of voyages, compiled by one Hakluyt, is to be found a letter written to Francis the First, by one Giovanne, or John Verazzani, on which some writers are inclined to found a belief that this delightful bay had been visited nearly a century previous to the voyage of the enterprising Hudson. Now this (albeit it has met with the countenance of certain very judicious and learned men) I hold in utter disbelief, and that for various good and substantial reasons: *First*, Because on strict examination it will be found, that the description given by this Verazzani applies about as well to the bay of New-York as it does to my night-cap. *Secondly*, Because that this John Verazzani, for whom I already begin to feel a most bitter enmity, is a native of Florence ; and every body knows the crafty wiles of these losel Florentines, by which they filched away the laurels from the brows of the immortal Colon, (vulgarly called Colum-bus,) and bestowed them on their officious townsman, Amerigo Vespucci ; and I make no doubt they are equally ready to rob the illustrious Hudson of the credit of discovering this beautiful island, adorned by the city of New-York,

4*

It was indeed—as my great-grandfather used to say—though in truth I never heard him, for he died, as might be expected, before I was born—" It was indeed a spot on which the eye might have reveled for ever, in ever new and never ending beauties." The island of Mannahata spread wide before them, like some sweet vision of fancy, or some fair creation of industrious magic. Its hills of smiling green swelled gently one above another, crowned with lofty trees of luxuriant growth; some pointing their tapering foliage towards the clouds, which were gloriously transparent; and others loaded with a verdant burthen of clambering vines, bowing their branches to the earth, that was covered with flowers. On the gentle declivities of the hills were scattered in gay profusion, the dog-wood, the sumach, and the wild brier, whose scarlet berries and white blossoms glowed brightly among the deep green of the surrounding foliage; and here and there a curling column of smoke rising from the little glens that opened along the shore, seemed to promise the weary voyagers a welcome at the hands of their fellow creatures. As they stood gazing with entranced attention on the scene before them, a red man, crowned with feathers, issued from one of these glens, and after contemplating in silent wonder the gallant ship,

and placing it beside their usurped discovery of South America. And, *thirdly,* I award my decision in favor of the pretensions of Hendrick Hudson, inasmuch as his expedition sailed from Holland, being truly and absolutely a Dutch enterprise—and though all the proofs in the world were introduced on the other side, I would set them at naught, as undeserving my attention. If these three reasons be not sufficient to satisfy every burgher of this ancient city—all I can say is, they are degenerate descendants from their venerable Dutch ancestors, and totally unworthy the trouble of convincing. Thus, therefore, the title of Hendrick Hudson to his renowned discovery is fully vindicated.

as she sat like a stately swan swimming on a silver lake, sounded the warhoop, and bounded into the woods like a wild deer, to the utter astonishment of the phlegmatic Dutchmen, who had never heard such a noise, or witnessed such a caper in their whole lives.

Of the transactions of our adventurers with the savages, and how the latter smoked copper pipes, and ate dried currants; how they brought great store of tobacco and oysters; how they shot one of the ship's crew, and how he was buried, I shall say nothing; being that I consider them unimportant to my history. After tarrying a few days in the bay, in order to refresh themselves after their sea-faring, our voyagers weighed anchor, to explore a mighty river which emptied into the bay. This river, it is said, was known among the savages by the name of the *Shatemuck;* though we are assured in an excellent little history published in 1674, by John Josselyn, Gent., that it was called the *Mohegan,** and master Richard Bloome, who wrote some time afterwards, asserts the same—so that I very much incline in favor of the opinion of these two honest gentlemen. Be this as it may, up this river did the adventurous Hendrick proceed, little doubting but it would turn out to be the much looked for passage to China!

The journal goes on to make mention of divers interviews between the crew and the natives, in the voyage up the river; but as they would be impertinent to my history, I shall pass over them in silence, except the following dry joke, played off by the old commodore and his school-fellow, Robert Juet, which does

---

* This river is likewise laid down in Ogilvy's map as Manhattan—Noordt Montaigne and Mauritius river.

such vast credit to their experimental philosophy, that I cannot
refrain from inserting it. " Our master and his mate determined
to try some of the chiefe men of the countrey, whether they had
any treacherie in them. So they tooke them downe into the cabin,
and gave them so much wine and aqua vitæ, that they were all
merrie ; and one of them had his wife with him, which sate so
modestly, as any of our countrey women would do in a strange
place. In the end, one of them was drunke, which had been
aborde of our ship all the time that we had been there, and that
was strange to them, for they could not tell how to take it."*

Having satisfied himself by this ingenious experiment, that
the natives were an honest, social race of jolly roysters, who had
no objection to a drinking bout, and were very merry in their
cups, the old commodore chuckled hugely to himself, and thrusting a double quid of tobacco in his cheek, directed master Juet
to have it carefully recorded, for the satisfaction of all the natural philosophers of the university of Leyden—which done, he
proceeded on his voyage, with great self-complacency. After
sailing, however, above an hundred miles up the river, he found
the watery world around him began to grow more shallow and
confined, the current more rapid, and perfectly fresh—phenomena not uncommon in the ascent of rivers, but which puzzled the
honest Dutchmen prodigiously. A consultation was therefore
called, and having deliberated full six hours, they were brought
to a determination, by the ship's running aground—whereupon
they unanimously concluded, that there was but little chance of
getting to China in this direction. A boat, however, was dispatched to explore higher up the river, which, on its return, con-

* Juet's Journ. Purch. Pil.

firmed the opinion—upon this the ship was warped off and put about, with great difficulty, being like most of her sex, exceedingly hard to govern; and the adventurous Hudson, according to the account of my great-great-grandfather, returned down the river —with a prodigious flea in his ear!

Being satisfied that there was little likelihood of getting to China, unless, like the blind man, he returned from whence he sat out, and took a fresh start, he forthwith recrossed the sea to Holland, where he was received with great welcome by the honorable East India Company, who were very much rejoiced to see him come back safe—with their ship; and at a large and respectable meeting of the first merchants and burgomasters of Amsterdam, it was unanimously determined, that as a munificent reward for the eminent services he had performed, and the important discovery he had made, the great river Mohegan should be called after his name!—and it continues to be called Hudson river unto this very day.

CHAPTER II.

THE delectable accounts given by the great Hudson, and master Juet, of the country they had discovered, excited not a little talk and speculation among the good people of Holland. Letters patent were granted by government to an association of merchants, called the West India Company, for the exclusive trade on Hudson river, on which they erected a trading-house called Fort Aurania, or Orange, from whence did spring the great city of Albany. But I forbear to dwell on the various commercial and colonizing enterprises which took place; among which was that of Mynheer Adrian Block, who discovered and gave a name to Block Island, since famous for its cheese—and shall barely confine myself to that which gave birth to this renowned city.

It was some three or four years after the return of the immortal Hendrick, that a crew of honest, Low Dutch colonists set sail from the city of Amsterdam, for the shores of America. It is an irreparable loss to history, and a great proof of the

darkness of the age, and the lamentable neglect of the noble art
of book-making, since so industriously cultivated by knowing sea-
captains, and learned supercargoes, that an expedition so interesting and important in its results, should be passed over in utter
silence. To my great-great-grandfather am I again indebted for
the few facts I am enabled to give concerning it—he having once
more embarked for this country, with a full determination, as he
said, of ending his days here—and of begetting a race of Knickerbockers, that should rise to be great men in the land.

The ship in which these illustrious adventurers set sail was
called the *Goede Vrouw,* or good woman, in compliment to the
wife of the President of the West India Company, who was allowed by every body (except her husband) to be a sweet-tem-
pered lady—when not in liquor. It was in truth a most gallant
vessel, of the most approved Dutch construction, and made by the
ablest ship-carpenters of Amsterdam, who, it is well known, always model their ships after the fair forms of their countrywomen.
Accordingly, it had one hundred feet in the beam, one hundred
feet in the keel, and one hundred feet from the bottom of the
stern-post to the tafferel. Like the beauteous model, who was declared to be the greatest belle in Amsterdam, it was full in the
bows, with a pair of enormous cat-heads, a copper bottom, and
withal a most prodigious poop!

The architect, who was somewhat of a religious man, far from
decorating the ship with pagan idols, such as Jupiter, Neptune, or
Hercules, (which heathenish abominations, I have no doubt occasion the misfortunes and shipwreck of many a noble vessel,) he,
I say, on the contrary, did laudably erect for a head, a goodly
image of St. Nicholas, equipped with a low, broad-brimmed hat,
a huge pair of Flemish trunk hose, and a pipe that reached to the

end of the bowsprit. Thus gallantly furnished, the stanch ship floated sideways, like a majestic goose, out of the harbor of the great city of Amsterdam, and all the bells, that were not otherwise engaged, rang a triple bobmajor on the joyful occasion.

My great-great-grandfather remarks, that the voyage was uncommonly prosperous, for, being under the especial care of the ever-revered St. Nicholas, the Goede Vrouw seemed to be endowed with qualities unknown to common vessels. Thus she made as much leeway as headway, could get along very nearly as fast with the wind ahead, as when it was a-poop—and was particularly great in a calm; in consequence of which singular advantages, she made out to accomplish her voyage in a very few months, and came to anchor at the mouth of the Hudson, a little to the east of Gibbet Island.

Here lifting up their eyes, they beheld, on what is at present called the Jersey shore, a small Indian village, pleasantly embowered in a grove of spreading elms, and the natives all collected on the beach, gazing in stupid admiration at the Goede Vrouw. A boat was immediately dispatched to enter into a treaty with them, and approaching the shore, hailed them through a trumpet, in the most friendly terms; but so horribly confounded were these poor savages at the tremendous and uncouth sound of the Low Dutch language, that they one and all took to their heels, and scampered over the Bergen hills; nor did they stop until they had buried themselves, head and ears, in the marshes on the other side, where they all miserably perished to a man—and their bones being collected and decently covered by the Tammany Society of that day, formed that singular mound called RATTLE-SNAKE HILL, which rises out of the centre of the salt marshes, a little to the east of the Newark Causeway.

Animated by this unlooked-for victory, our valiant heroes sprang ashore in triumph, took possession of the soil as conquerors, in the name of their High Mightinesses the Lords States General; and marching fearlessly forward, carried the village of COMMUNIPAW by storm, notwithstanding that it was vigorously defended by some half a score of old squaws and pappooses. On looking about them they were so transported with the excellencies of the place, that they had very little doubt the blessed St. Nicholas had guided them thither, as the very spot whereon to settle their colony. The softness of the soil was wonderfully adapted to the driving of piles; the swamps and marshes around them afforded ample opportunities for the constructing of dykes and dams; the shallowness of the shore was peculiarly favorable to the building of docks—in a word, this spot abounded with all the requisites for the foundation of a great Dutch city. On making a faithful report, therefore, to the crew of the Goede Vrouw, they one and all determined that this was the destined end of their voyage. Accordingly they descended from the Goede Vrouw, men, women, and children, in goodly groups, as did the animals of yore from the ark, and formed themselves into a thriving settlement, which they called by the Indian name COMMUNIPAW.

As all the world is doubtless perfectly acquainted with Communipaw, it may seem somewhat superfluous to treat of it in the present work; but my readers will please to recollect, that notwithstanding it is my chief desire to satisfy the present age, yet I write likewise for posterity, and have to consult the understanding and curiosity of some half a score of centuries yet to come; by which time, perhaps, were it not for this invaluable history, the great Communipaw, like Babylon, Carthage, Nineveh, and other great cities, might be perfectly extinct—sunk and forgotten in its

own mud—its inhabitants turned into oysters,* and even its situation a fertile subject of learned controversy and hard-headed in-
vestigation among indefatigable historians.   Let me then piously
rescue from oblivion the humble relics of a place, which was the
egg from whence was hatched the mighty city of New-York !

Communipaw is at present but a small village, pleasantly
situated, among rural scenery, on that beauteous part of the
Jersey shore which was known in ancient legends by the name
of Pavonia,† and commands a grand prospect of the superb bay
of New-York.   It is within but half an hour's sail of the latter
place, provided you have a fair wind, and may be distinctly seen
from the city.   Nay, it is a well known fact, which I can testify
from my own experience, that on a clear still summer evening,
you may hear, from the battery of New-York, the obstreperous
peals of broad-mouthed laughter of the Dutch negroes at Communipaw, who, like most other negroes, are famous for their
risible powers.   This is peculiarly the case on Sunday evenings,
when, it is remarked by an ingenious and observant philosopher,
who has made great discoveries in the neighborhood of this city,
that they always laugh loudest—which he attributes to the circumstance of their having their holiday clothes on.

These negroes, in fact, like the monks in the dark ages,
engross all the knowledge of the place, and being infinitely more
adventurous and more knowing than their masters, carry on all
the foreign trade ; making frequent voyages to town in canoes
loaded with oysters, buttermilk, and cabbages.   They are great
astrologers, predicting the different changes of weather almost as

* Men by inaction degenerate into oysters.—*Kaimes.*

† Pavonia, in the ancient maps, is given to a tract of country extending
from about Hoboken to Amboy.

accurately as an almanac—they are moreover exquisite per-
formers on three-stringed fiddles : in whistling they almost boast
the far-famed powers of Orpheus's lyre, for not a horse or an ox
in the place, when at the plough or before the wagon, will budge
a foot until he hears the well known whistle of his black driver
and companion.—And from their amazing skill at casting up
accounts upon their fingers, they are regarded with as much
veneration as were the disciples of Pythagoras of yore, when
initiated into the sacred quaternary of numbers.

As to the honest burghers of Communipaw, like wise men
and sound philosophers, they never look beyond their pipes, nor
trouble their heads about any affairs out of their immediate
neighborhood; so that they live in profound and enviable ignorance of all the troubles, anxieties, and revolutions of this
distracted planet. I am even told that many among them do
verily believe that Holland, of which they have heard so much
from tradition, is situated somewhere on Long Island—that
Spiking-devil and *the Narrows* are the two ends of the world—
that the country is still under the dominion of their High
Mightinesses, and that the city of New-York still goes by the
name of Nieuw Amsterdam. They meet every Saturday afternoon, at the only tavern in the place, which bears as a sign, a
square-headed likeness of the Prince of Orange, where they
smoke a silent pipe, by way of promoting social conviviality, and
invariably drink a mug of cider to the success of Admiral
Van Tromp, who they imagine is still sweeping the British
channel, with a broom at his mast-head.

Communipaw, in short, is one of the numerous little villages
in the vicinity of this most beautiful of cities, which are so many
strong-holds and fastnesses, whither the primitive manners of our

Dutch forefathers have retreated, and where they are cherished with devout and scrupulous strictness. The dress of the original settlers is handed down inviolate, from father to son—the identical broad-brimmed hat, broad-skirted coat, and broad-bottomed breeches, continue from generation to generation; and several gigantic knee-buckles of massy silver, are still in wear, that made gallant display in the days of the patriarchs of Communipaw. The language likewise continues unadulterated by barbarous innovations; and so critically correct is the village schoolmaster in his dialect, that his reading of a Low Dutch psalm has much the same effect on the nerves as the filing of a handsaw.

CHAPTER III.

IN WHICH IS SET FORTH THE TRUE ART OF MAKING A BARGAIN
—TOGETHER WITH THE MIRACULOUS ESCAPE OF A GREAT
METROPOLIS IN A FOG—AND THE BIOGRAPHY OF CERTAIN
HEROES OF COMMUNIPAW.

HAVING, in the trifling digression which concluded the last
chapter, discharged the filial duty which the city of New-York
owed to Communipaw, as being the mother settlement; and having given a faithful picture of it as it stands at present, I return
with a soothing sentiment of self-approbation, to dwell upon its
early history. The crew of the Goede Vrouw being soon rein-
forced by fresh importations from Holland, the settlement went.
jollily on, increasing in magnitude and prosperity. The neighboring Indians in a short time became accustomed to the uncouth
sound of the Dutch language, and an intercourse gradually took
place between them and the new comers. The Indians were
much given to long talks, and the Dutch to long silence—in this
particular, therefore, they accommodated each other completely.
The chiefs would make long speeches about the big bull, the Wabash, and the Great Spirit, to which the others would listen very
attentively, smoke their pipes, and grunt *yah, myn-her*—whereat

the poor savages were wondrously delighted.   They instructed
the new settlers in the best art of curing and smoking tobacco,
while the latter, in return, made them drunk with true Hollands—
and then taught them the art of making bargains.

A brisk trade for furs was soon opened: the Dutch traders
were scrupulously honest in their dealings, and purchased by
weight, establishing it as an invariable table of avoirdupois, that
the hand of a Dutchman weighed one pound, and his foot two
pounds.   It is true, the simple Indians were often puzzled by the
great disproportion between bulk and weight, for let them place a
bundle of furs, never so large, in one scale, and a Dutchman put
his hand or foot in the other, the bundle was sure to kick the
beam—never was a package of furs known to weigh more than
two pounds in the market of Communipaw!

This is a singular fact—but I have it direct from my great-
great-grandfather, who had risen to considerable importance in
the colony, being promoted to the office of weigh-master, on
account of the uncommon heaviness of his foot.

The Dutch possessions in this part of the globe began now to
assume a very thriving appearance, and were comprehended
under the general title of Nieuw Nederlandts, on account, as the
sage Vander Donck observes, of their great resemblance to the
Dutch Netherlands—which indeed was truly remarkable, excepting that the former were rugged and mountainous, and the latter
level and marshy.   About this time the tranquillity of the Dutch
colonists was doomed to suffer a temporary interruption.   In
1614, Captain Sir Samuel Argal, sailing under a commission
from Dale, governor of Virginia, visited the Dutch settlements on
Hudson River, and demanded their submission to the English
crown and Virginian dominion.   To this arrogant demand, as

they were in no condition to resist it, they submitted for the time, like discreet and reasonable men.

It does not appear that the valiant Argal molested the settlement of Communipaw; on the contrary, I am told that when his vessel first hove in sight, the worthy burghers were seized with such a panic, that they fell to smoking their pipes with astonishing vehemence; insomuch that they quickly raised a cloud, which, combining with the surrounding woods and marshes, completely enveloped and concealed their beloved village, and overhung the fair regions of Pavonia—so that the terrible Captain Argal passed on, totally unsuspicious that a sturdy little Dutch settlement lay snugly couched in the mud, under cover of all this pestilent vapor. In commemoration of this fortunate escape, the worthy inhabitants have continued to smoke, almost without intermission, unto this very day; which is said to be the cause of the remarkable fog which often hangs over Communipaw of a clear afternoon.

Upon the departure of the enemy, our worthy ancestors took full six months to recover their wind and get over the consternation into which they had been thrown. They then called a council of safety to smoke over the state of the province. At this council presided one Oloffe Van Kortlandt, a personage who was held in great reverence among the sages of Communipaw for the variety and darkness of his knowledge. He had originally been one of a set of peripatetic philosophers who passed much of their time sunning themselves on the side of the great canal of Amsterdam in Holland; enjoying, like Diogenes, a free and unincumbered estate in sunshine. His name Kortlandt (Shortland or Lackland) was supposed, like that of the illustrious Jean Sansterre, to indicate that he had *no land*; but he insisted, on the contrary, that he had great landed estates somewhere in Terra

Incognita; and he had come out to the new world to look after them. He was the first great land speculator that we read of in these parts.

Like all land speculators, he was much given to dreaming. Never did any thing extraordinary happen at Communipaw but he declared that he had previously dreamt it; being one of those infallible prophets who predict events after they have come to pass. This supernatural gift was as highly valued among the burghers of Pavonia as among the enlightened nations of antiquity. The wise Ulysses was more indebted to his sleeping than his waking moments for his most subtle achievements, and seldom undertook any great exploit without first soundly sleeping upon it; and the same may be said of Oloffe Van Kortlandt, who was thence aptly denominated Oloffe the Dreamer.

As yet his dreams and speculations had turned to little personal profit; and he was as much a lack-land as ever. Still he carried a high head in the community; if his sugar-loaf hat was rather the worse for wear, he set it off with a taller cock's-tail; if his shirt was none of the cleanest, he puffed it out the more at the bosom; and if the tail of it peeped out of a hole in his breeches, it at least proved that it really had a tail and was not mere ruffle.

The worthy Van Kortlandt, in the council in question, urged the policy of emerging from the swamps of Communipaw and seeking some more eligible site for the seat of empire. Such, he said, was the advice of the good St. Nicholas, who had appeared to him in a dream the night before; and whom he had known by his broad hat, his long pipe, and the resemblance which he bore to the figure on the bow of the Goede Vrouw.

Many have thought this dream was a mere invention of Oloffe

Van Kortlandt; who, it is said, had ever regarded Communipaw
with an evil eye because he had arrived there after all the land
had been shared out, and who was anxious to change the seat of
empire to some new place, where he might be present at the
distribution of "town lots." But we must not give heed to such
insinuations, which are too apt to be advanced against those worthy gentlemen engaged in laying out towns, and in other land
speculations. For my own part, I am disposed to place the same
implicit faith in the vision of Oloffe the Dreamer that was manifested by the honest burghers of Communipaw, who one and all
agreed that an expedition should be forthwith fitted out to go on
a voyage of discovery in quest of a new seat of empire.

This perilous enterprise was to be conducted by Oloffe himself; who chose as lieutenants or coadjutors Mynheers Abraham
Hardenbroeck, Jacobus Van Zandt, and Winant Ten Broeck—
three indubitably great men, but of whose history, although I
have made diligent inquiry, I can learn but little previous to
their leaving Holland. Nor need this occasion much surprise;
for adventurers, like prophets, though they make great noise
abroad, have seldom much celebrity in their own countries; but
this much is certain, that the overflowings and offscourings of a
country are invariably composed of the richest parts of the soil.
And here I cannot help remarking how convenient it would be
to many of our great men and great families of doubtful origin,
could they have the privilege of the heroes of yore, who, whenever their origin was involved in obscurity, modestly announced
themselves descended from a god—and who never visited a foreign country but what they told some cock and bull stories about
their being kings and princes at home. This venal trespass on
the truth, though it has been occasionally played off by some

pseudo marquis, baronet, and other illustrious foreigner, in out land of good-natured credulity, has been completely discountenanced in this skeptical, matter of fact age—and I even question whether any tender virgin, who was accidentally and unaccountably enriched with a bantling, would save her character at parlor firesides and evening tea-parties by ascribing the phenomenon to a swan, a shower of gold, or a river god.

Had I the benefit of mythology and classic fable above alluded to, I should have furnished the first of the trio with a pedigree equal to that of the proudest hero of antiquity. His name, Van Zandt, that is to say, *from the sand*, or in common parlance, from the dirt, gave reason to suppose that like Triptolemus, Themes, the Cyclops and the Titans, he had sprung from Dame Terra, or the earth! This supposition is strongly corroborated by his size, for it is well known that all the progeny of mother earth were of a gigantic stature; and Van Zandt, we are told, was a tall, raw-boned man, above six feet high—with an astonishingly hard head. Nor is this origin of the illustrious Van Zandt a whit more improbable or repugnant to belief than what is related and universally admitted of certain of our greatest, or rather richest men; who, we are told with the utmost gravity, did originally spring from a dunghill!

Of the second of the trio, but faint accounts have reached to this time, which mention that he was a sturdy, obstinate, worrying, bustling little man; and, from being usually equipped in an old pair of buckskins, was familiarly dubbed Harden Broeck; that is to say, Hard in the Breech; or, as it was generally rendered, Tough Breeches.

Ten Broeck completed this junto of adventurers. It is a singular but ludicrous fact, which, were I not scrupulous in recording the whole truth, I should almost be tempted to pass over in silence as incompatible with the gravity and dignity of history; that this worthy gentleman should likewise have been nicknamed from what in modern times is considered the most ignoble part of the dress. But in truth the small clothes seems to have been a very dignified garment in the eyes of our venerated ancestors, in all probability from its covering that part of the body which has been pronounced "the seat of honor."

The name of Ten Broeck, or as it was sometimes spelled Tin Broeck, has been indifferently translated into Ten Breeches and Tin Breeches. Certain elegant and ingenious writers on the subject declare in favor of *Tin*, or rather *Thin* Breeches; whence they infer that the original bearer of it was a poor but merry rogue, whose galligaskins were none of the soundest, and who, peradventure, may have been the author of that truly philosophical stanza:

> "Then why should we quarrel for riches,
>   Or any such glittering toys;
> A light heart and *thin pair of breeches*
>   Will go thorough the world, my brave boys!"

The more accurate commentators, however, declare in favor of the other reading, and affirm that the worthy in question, was a burly, bulbous man, who, in sheer ostentation of his venerable progenitors, was the first to introduce into the settlement the ancient Dutch fashion of ten pair of breeches.

Such was the trio of coadjutors chosen by Oloffe the Dreamer, to accompany him in this voyage into unknown realms; as to the names of his crews they have not been handed down by history.

Having, as I before observed, passed much of his life in the open air, among the peripatetic philosophers of Amsterdam, Oloffe had become familiar with the aspect of the heavens, and could as accurately determine when a storm was brewing or a squall rising, as a dutiful husband can foresee, from the brow of his spouse, when a tempest is gathering about his ears. Having pitched upon a time for his voyage, when the skies appeared propitious he exhorted all his crews to take a good night's rest; wind up their family affairs and make their wills; precautions taken by our forefathers even in after times when they became more adventurous, and voyaged to Haverstraw, or Kaatskill, or Groodt Esopus, or any other far country, beyond the great waters of the Tappaan Zee.

CHAPTER IV.

HOW THE HEROES OF COMMUNIPAW VOYAGED TO HELL-GATE, AND HOW THEY WERE RECEIVED THERE.

AND now the rosy blush of morn began to mantle in the east, and soon the rising sun, emerging from amidst golden and purple clouds, shed his blithsome rays on the tin weathercocks of Communipaw. It was that delicious season of the year, when nature, breaking from the chilling thraldom of old winter, like a blooming damsel from the tyranny of a sordid old father, threw herself, blushing with ten thousand charms, into the arms of youthful spring. Every tufted copse and blooming grove resounded with the notes of hymeneal love. The very insects, as they sipped the dew that gemmed the tender grass of the meadows, joined in the joyous epithalamium—the virgin bud timidly put forth its blushes, "the voice of the turtle was heard in the land," and the heart of man dissolved away in tenderness. Oh! sweet Theocritus! had I thine oaten reed, wherewith thou erst did charm the gay Sicilian plains—Or Oh! gentle Bion! thy pastoral pipe, wherein the happy swains of the Lesbian isle so much delighted, then might I attempt to sing, in soft Bucolic or negligent Idyllium, the rural beauties of the scene—but having nothing, save this jaded goose quill, wherewith to wing my flight, I must fain resign all poetic disportings of the fancy, and pursue my narrative in humble prose; comforting myself with the hope, that though it may not steal so sweetly upon the imagination of my reader, yet it may commend itself, with virgin modesty, to his better judgment, clothed in the chaste and simple garb of truth.

No sooner did the first rays of cheerful Phœbus dart into the windows of Communipaw, than the little settlement was all in motion. Forth issued from his castle the sage Van Kortlandt, and seizing a conch shell, blew a far resounding blast, that soon summoned all his lusty followers. Then did they trudge resolutely down to the water side, escorted by a multitude of relatives and friends, who all went down, as the common phrase expresses it, "to see them off." And this shows the antiquity of those long family processions, often seen in our city, composed of all ages, sizes, and sexes, laden with bundles and bandboxes, escorting some bevy of country cousins, about to depart for home in a market-boat.

The good Oloffe bestowed his forces in a squadron of three canoes, and hoisted his flag on board a little round Dutch boat, shaped not unlike a tub, which had formerly been the jolly-boat of the Goede Vrouw. And now, all being embarked, they bade farewell to the gazing throng upon the beach, who continued shouting after them, even when out of hearing, wishing them a happy voyage, advising them to take good care of themselves, not to get drowned—with an abundance other of those sage and invaluable cautions, generally given by landsmen to such as go down to the sea in ships, and adventure upon the deep waters. In the meanwhile the voyagers cheerily urged their course across the crystal bosom of the bay, and soon left behind them the green shores of ancient Pavonia.

And first they touched at two small islands which lie nearly opposite Communipaw, and which are said to have been brought into existence about the time of the great irruption of the Hudson, when it broke through the Highlands and made its way to the ocean.* For in this tremendous uproar of the waters, we are told that many huge fragments of rock and land were rent from the mountains and swept down by this runaway river, for sixty or seventy miles; where some of them ran aground on the shoals just opposite Communipaw, and formed the identical islands in question, while others drifted out to sea, and were never heard of more! A sufficient proof of the fact is, that the rock which forms the bases of these islands is exactly similar to that of the Highlands, and moreover one of our philosophers, who has diligently compared the agreement of their respective surfaces, has even gone so far as to assure me, in confidence, that Gibbet Island was originally nothing more nor less than a wart on Anthony's nose.†

Leaving these wonderful little isles, they next coasted by Governor's Island, since terrible from its frowning fortress and grinning batteries. They would by no means, however, land

---

* It is a matter long since established by certain of our philosophers, that is to say, having been often advanced, and never contradicted, it has grown to be pretty nigh equal to a settled fact, that the Hudson was originally a lake dammed up by the mountains of the Highlands. In process of time, however, becoming very mighty and obstreperous, and the mountains waxing pursy, dropsical, and weak in the back, by reason of their extreme old age, it suddenly rose upon them, and after a violent struggle effected its escape. This is said to have come to pass in very remote time, probably before that rivers had lost the art of running up hill. The foregoing is a theory in which I do not pretend to be skilled, notwithstanding that I do fully give it my belief.

† A promontory in the Highlands.

upon this island, since they doubted much it might be the abode of demons and spirits, which in those days did greatly abound throughout this savage and pagan country.

Just at this time a shoal of jolly porpoises came rolling and tumbling by, turning up their sleek sides to the sun, and spouting up the briny element in sparkling showers. No sooner did the sage Oloffe mark this than he was greatly rejoiced. " This," exclaimed he, " if I mistake not, augurs well—the porpoise is a fat, well-conditioned fish—a burgomaster among fishes—his looks betoken ease, plenty, and prosperity—I greatly admire this round fat fish, and doubt not but this is a happy omen of the success of our undertaking." So saying, he directed his squadron to steer in the track of these alderman fishes.

Turning, therefore, directly to the left, they swept up the strait vulgarly called the East River. And here the rapid tide which courses through this strait, seizing on the gallant tub in which Commodore Van Kortlandt had embarked, hurried it forward with a velocity unparalleled in a Dutch boat, navigated by Dutchmen; insomuch that the good commodore, who had all his life long been accustomed only to the drowsy navigation of canals, was more than ever convinced that they were in the hands of some supernatural power, and that the jolly porpoises were towing them to some fair haven that was to fulfill all their wishes and expectations.

Thus born away by the resistless current, they doubled that boisterous point of land since called Corlear's Hook,* and leaving to the right the rich winding cove of the Wallabout, they drifted into a magnificent expanse of water, surrounded by

* Properly spelt *hoeck*, (i. e. a point of land.)

pleasant shores, whose verdure was exceedingly refreshing to the eye. While the voyagers were looking around them, on what they conceived to be a serene and sunny lake, they beheld at a distance a crew of painted savages, busily employed in fishing, who seemed more like the genii of this romantic region— their slender canoe lightly balanced like a feather on the undulating surface of the bay.

At sight of these the hearts of the heroes of Communipaw were not a little troubled. But, as good fortune would have it, at the bow of the commodore's boat was stationed a very valiant man, named Hendrick Kip, (which being interpreted, means *chicken*, a name given him in token of his courage.) No sooner did he behold these varlet heathens than he trembled with excessive valor, and although a good half mile distant, he seized a musketoon that lay at hand, and turning away his head, fired it most intrepidly in the face of the blessed sun. The blundering weapon recoiled and gave the valiant Kip an ignominious kick, which laid him prostrate with uplifted heels in the bottom of the boat. But such was the effect of this tremendous fire, that the wild men of the woods, struck with consternation, seized hastily upon their paddles, and shot away into one of the deep inlets of the Long Island shore.

This signal victory gave new spirits to the voyagers, and in honor of the achievement they gave the name of the valiant Kip to the surrounding bay, and it has continued to be called KIP'S BAY from that time to the present. The heart of the good Van Kortlandt—who, having no land of his own, was a great admirer of other people's—expanded to the full size of a pepper-corn at the sumptuous prospect of rich unsettled country around him, and falling into a delicious revery, he straightway

5*

began to riot in the possession of vast meadows of salt marsh and interminable patches of cabbages. From this delectable vision he was all at once awakened by the sudden turning of the tide, which would soon have hurried him from this land of promise, had not the discreet navigator given signal to steer for shore; where they accordingly landed hard by the rocky heights of Bellevue—that happy retreat, where our jolly aldermen eat for the good of the city, and fatten the turtle that are sacrificed on civic solemnities.

Here, seated on the green-sward, by the side of a small stream that ran sparkling among the grass, they refreshed themselves after the toils of the seas, by feasting lustily on the ample stores which they had provided for this perilous voyage. Thus having well fortified their deliberative powers, they fell into an earnest consultation, what was farther to be done. This was the first council dinner ever eaten at Bellevue by Christian burghers, and here, as tradition relates, did originate the great family feud between the Hardenbroecks and the Tenbroecks, which afterwards had a singular influence on the building of the city. The sturdy Hardenbroeck, whose eyes had been wondrously delighted with the salt marshes which spread their reeking bosoms along the coast, at the bottom of Kip's Bay, counseled by all means to return thither, and found the intended city. This was strenuously opposed by the unbending Ten Broeck, and many testy arguments passed between them. The particulars of this controversy have not reached us, which is ever to be lamented; this much is certain, that the sage Oloffe put an end to the dispute, by determining to explore still farther in the route which the mysterious porpoises had so clearly pointed out—whereupon the sturdy Tough Breeches abandoned the expedition, took possession of a neighboring hill, and in a fit of great wrath peopled all that tract of country, which has continued to be inhabited by the Hardenbroecks unto this very day.

By this time the jolly Phœbus, like some wanton urchin sporting on the side of a green hill, began to roll down the declivity of the heavens; and now, the tide having once more turned in their favor, the Pavonians again committed themselves to its discretion, and coasting along the western shores, were borne towards the straits of Blackwell's Island.

And here the capricious wanderings of the current occasioned not a little marvel and perplexity to these illustrious mariners. Now would they be caught by the wanton eddies, and, sweeping round a jutting point, would wind deep into some romantic little cove, that indented the fair island of Manna-hatta; now were they hurried narrowly by the very bases of impending rocks, mantled with the flaunting grape-vine, and crowned with groves which threw a broad shade on the waves beneath; and anon they were borne away into the mid-channel and wafted along with a rapidity that very much discomposed the sage Van Kortlandt, who as he saw the land swiftly receding on either side, began exceedingly to doubt that terra firma was giving them the slip.

Wherever the voyagers turned their eyes, a new creation seemed to bloom around. No signs of human thrift appeared to check the delicious wildness of nature, who here reveled in all her luxuriant variety. Those hills, now bristled, like the fretful porcupine, with rows of poplars, (vain upstart plants! minions of wealth and fashion!) were then adorned with the vigorous natives of the soil; the lordly oak, the generous chestnut, the graceful elm—while here and there the tulip-tree reared its majestic head, the giant of the forest. Where now are seen the gay retreats of luxury—villas half buried in twilight bowers, whence the amorous flute oft breathes the sighings of some city swain— there the fish-hawk built his solitary nest, on some dry tree that overlooked his watery domain. The timid deer fed undisturbed along those shores now hallowed by the lover's moonlight walk, and printed by the slender foot of beauty; and a savage solitude extended over those happy regions, where now are reared the stately towers of the Joneses, the Schermerhornes, and the Rhine-landers.

Thus gliding in silent wonder through these new and unknown scenes, the gallant squadron of Pavonia swept by the foot of a promontory, which strutted forth boldly into the waves, and seemed to frown upon them as they brawled against its base. This is the bluff well known to modern mariners by the name of Gracie's point, from the fair castle which, like an elephant, it carries upon its back. And here broke upon their view a wild and varied prospect, where land and water were beauteously intermingled, as though they had combined to heighten and set off each other's charms. To their right lay the sedgy point of Blackwell's Island, drest in the fresh garniture of living green—beyond it stretched the pleasant coast of Sundswick, and the small harbor well known by the name of Hallet's Cove—a place infamous in latter days, by reason of its being the haunt of pirates who infest these seas, robbing orchards and watermelon patches, and insulting gentlemen navigators, when voyaging in their pleasure boats. To the left a deep bay, or rather creek, gracefully receded between shores fringed with forests, and forming a kind of vista, through which were beheld the silvan regions of Haerlem, Morrissania, and East Chester. Here the eye reposed with delight on a richly wooded country, diversified by tufted knolls, shadowy intervals, and waving lines of upland, swelling above each other; while over the whole, the purple mists of spring diffused a hue of soft voluptuousness.

Just before them the grand course of the stream, making a sudden bend, wound among embowered promontories and shores of emerald verdure, that seemed to melt into the wave. A character of gentleness and mild fertility prevailed around. The sun had just descended, and the thin haze of twilight, like a transparent veil drawn over the bosom of virgin beauty, heightened the charms which it half concealed.

Ah! witching scenes of foul delusion Ah! hapless voyagers, gazing with simple wonder on these Circean shores! Such, alas! are they, poor easy souls, who listen to the seductions of a wicked world—treacherous are its smiles! fatal its caresses. He who yields to its enticements launches upon a whelming tide, and trusts his feeble bark among the dimpling eddies of a whirlpool! And thus it fared with the worthies of Pavonia, who, little mistrusting the guileful scene before them, drifted quietly on, until they were aroused by an uncommon tossing and agitation of their vessels. For now the late dimpling current began to brawl around them, and the waves to boil and foam with horrific fury. Awakened as if from a dream, the astonished Oloffe bawled aloud to put about, but his words were lost amid the roaring of the waters. And now ensued a scene of direful consternation. At one time they were borne with dreadful velocity among tumultuous breakers; at another, hurried down boisterous rapids. Now they were nearly dashed upon the Hen and Chickens; (infamous rocks!—more voracious than Scylla and her whelps;) and anon they seemed sinking into yawning gulfs, that threatened to entomb them beneath the waves. All the elements

combined to produce a hideous confusion. The waters raged—
the winds howled—and as they were hurried along, several of
the astonished mariners beheld the rocks and trees of the neighboring shores driving through the air!

At length the mighty tub of Commodore Van Kortlandt was
drawn into the vortex of that tremendous whirlpool called the
Pot, where it was whirled about in giddy mazes, until the senses
of the good commander and his crew were overpowered by the
horror of the scene, and the strangeness of the revolution.

How the gallant squadron of Pavonia was snatched from the
jaws of this modern Charybdis, has never been truly made known,
for so many survived to tell the tale, and, what is still more wonderful, told it in so many different ways, that there has ever prevailed a great variety of opinions on the subject.

As to the commodore and his crew, when they came to their
senses they found themselves stranded on the Long Island shore.
The worthy commodore, indeed, used to relate many and wonderful stories of his adventures in this time of peril; how that he
saw spectres flying in the air, and heard the yelling of hobgoblins,
and put his hand into the pot when they were whirled round, and
found the water scalding hot, and beheld several uncouth looking
beings seated on rocks and skimming it with huge ladles—but particularly he declared with great exultation, that he saw the losel
porpoises, which had betrayed them into this peril, some broiling
on the Gridiron and others hissing on the Frying-pan!

These, however, were considered by many as mere phanta-
sies of the commodore, while he lay in a trance; especially as
he was known to be given to dreaming; and the truth of them
has never been clearly ascertained. It is certain, however,
that to the accounts of Oloffe and his followers may be traced the

various traditions handed down of this marvelous strait—as how the devil has been seen there, sitting astride of the Hog's Back and playing on the fiddle—how he broils fish there before a storm; and many other stories, in which we must be cautious of putting too much faith.   In consequence of all these terrific circumstances, the Pavonian commander gave this pass the name of *Helle-gat,* or as it has been interpreted, *Hell-Gate;** which it continues to bear at the present day.

* This is a narrow strait in the Sound, at the distance of six miles above New-York. It is dangerous to shipping, unless under the care of skillful pilots, by reason of numerous rocks, shelves, and whirlpools. These have received sundry appellations, such as the Gridiron, Frying-pan, Hog's Back, Pot, &c., and are very violent and turbulent at certain times of tide. Certain mealy-mouthed men, of squeamish consciences, who are loth to give the Devil his due, have softened the above characteristic name into *Hurl*-gate, forsooth! Let those take care how they venture into the Gate, or they may be hurled into the Pot before they are aware of it. The name of this strait, as given by our author, is supported by the map in Vander Donck's history, published in 1656—by Ogilvie's History of America, 1671—as also by a journal still extant, written in the 16th century, and to be found in Hazard's State Papers And an old MS. written in French, speaking of various alterations in names about this city, observes, " De *Helle-gat* trou d'Enfer, ils ont fait *Hell-gate,* Porte d'Enfer."

CHAPTER V.

THE darkness of night had closed upon this disastrous day, and
a doleful night was it to the shipwrecked Pavonians, whose ears
were incessantly assailed with the raging of the elements, and the
howling of the hobgoblins that infested this perfidious strait.   But
when the morning dawned, the horrors of the preceding evening
had passed away, rapids, breakers, and whirlpools had disappeared,
the stream again ran smooth and dimpling, and having changed
its tide, rolled gently back, towards the quarter where lay their
much-regretted home.

The wo-begone heroes of Communipaw eyed each other with
rueful countenances ; their squadron had been totally dispersed by
the late disaster.   Some were cast upon the western shore, where,
headed by one Ruleff Hopper, they took possession of all the
country lying about the six mile stone ; which is held by the Hoppers at this present writing.

The Waldrons were driven by stress of weather to a distant
coast, where, having with them a jug of genuine Hollands, they
were enabled to conciliate the savages, setting up a kind of

tavern; whence, it is said, did spring the fair town of Haerlem, in which their descendants have ever since continued to be
reputable publicans. As to the Suydams, they were thrown
upon the Long Island coast, and may still be found in those
parts. But the most singular luck attended the great Ten
Broeck, who, falling overboard, was miraculously preserved from
sinking by the multitude of his nether garments. Thus buoyed
up, he floated on the waves like a merman, or like an angler's
dobber, until he landed safely on a rock, where he was found the
next morning busily drying his many breeches in the sunshine.

I forbear to treat of the long consultation of Oloffe with his
remaining followers, in which they determined that it would
never do to found a city in so diabolical a neighborhood. Suffice
it in simple brevity to say that they once more committed themselves, with fear and trembling, to the briny element, and steered
their course back again through the scenes of their yesterday's
voyage, determined no longer to roam in search of distant sites,
but to settle themselves down in the marshy regions of Pavonia.

Scarce, however, had they gained a distant view of Communipaw when they were encountered by an obstinate eddy which
opposed their homeward voyage. Weary and dispirited as they
were, they yet tugged a feeble oar against the stream; until, as
if to settle the strife, half a score of potent billows rolled the tub
of Commodore Van Kortlandt high and dry on the long point of
an island which divided the bosom of the bay.

Some pretend that these billows were sent by old Neptune to
strand the expedition on a spot whereon was to be founded his
strong-hold in this western world: others more pious, attribute
every thing to the guardianship of the good St. Nicholas; and
after events will be found to corroborate this opinion. Oloffe

Van Kortlandt was a devout trencherman. Every repast was a kind of religious rite with him; and his first thought on finding him once more on dry ground, was how he should contrive to celebrate his wonderful escape from Hell-gate and all its horrors by a solemn banquet. The stores which had been provided for the voyage by the good housewives of Communi-paw were nearly exhausted, but, in casting his eyes about, the commodore beheld that the shore abounded with oysters. A great store of these was instantly collected; a fire was made at the foot of a tree; all hands fell to roasting and broiling and stewing and frying, and a sumptuous repast was soon set forth. This is thought to be the origin of those civic feasts with which, to the present day, all our public affairs are celebrated, and in which the oyster is ever sure to play an important part.

On the present occasion the worthy Van Kortlandt was observed to be particularly zealous in his devotions to the trencher; for having the cares of the expedition especially committed to his care, he deemed it incumbent on him to eat profoundly for the public good. In proportion as he filled himself to the very brim with the dainty viands before him, did the heart of this excellent burgher rise up towards his throat, until he seemed crammed and almost choked with good eating and good nature. And at such times it is, when a man's heart is in his throat, that he may more truly be said to speak from it, and his speeches abound with kindness and good fellowship. Thus having swallowed the last possible morsel, and washed it down with a fervent potation, Oloffe felt his heart yearning, and his whole frame in a manner dilating with unbounded benevolence. Every thing around him seemed excellent and delightful; and laying his hands on each side of his capacious periphery, and rolling his half closed eyes around on the beautiful diversity of land and water before him, he exclaimed, in a fat half smothered voice, " What a charming prospect !" The words died away in his throat—he seemed to ponder on the fair scene for a moment —his eyelids heavily closed over their orbs—his head drooped upon his bosom—he slowly sank upon the green turf, and a deep sleep stole gradually over him.

And the sage Oloffe dreamed a dream—and lo, the good St. Nicholas came riding over the tops of the trees, in that self-same wagon wherein he brings his yearly presents to children, and he descended hard by where the heroes of Communipaw had made their late repast. And he lit his pipe by the fire, and sat himself down and smoked; and as he smoked the smoke from his pipe ascended into the air and spread like a cloud overhead. And Oloffe bethought him, and he hastened and climbed up to the top of one of the tallest trees, and saw that the smoke spread over a great extent of country—and as he considered it more attentively, he fancied that the great volume of smoke assumed a variety of marvelous forms, where in dim obscurity he saw shadowed out palaces and domes and lofty spires, all of which lasted but a moment, and then faded away, until the whole rolled off, and nothing but the green woods were left. And when St. Nicholas had smoked his pipe, he twisted it in his hat-band, and laying his finger beside his nose, gave the astonished Van Kortlandt a very significant look, then mounting his wagon, he returned over the tree-tops and disappeared.

And Van Kortlandt awoke from his sleep greatly instructed, and he aroused his companions, and related to them his dream, and interpreted it, that it was the will of St. Nicholas that they should settle down and build the city here. And that the smoke of the pipe was a type how vast would be the extent of the city; inasmuch as the volumes of its smoke would spread over a wide extent of country. And they all with one voice assented to this interpretation excepting Mynheer Ten Broeck, who declared the meaning to be that it would be a city wherein a little fire would occasion a great smoke, or in other words, a very vaporing little city—both which interpretations have strangely come to pass!

The great object of their perilous expedition, therefore, being thus happily accomplished, the voyagers returned merrily to Communipaw, where they were received with great rejoicings. And here calling a general meeting of all the wise men and the dignitaries of Pavonia, they related the whole history of their voyage, and of the dream of Oloffe Van Kortlandt. And the people lifted up their voices and blessed the good St. Nicholas, and from that time forth the sage Van Kortlandt was held in more honor than ever, for his great talent at dreaming, and was pronounced a most useful citizen and a right good man—when he was asleep.

CHAPTER VI.

CONTAINING AN ATTEMPT AT ETYMOLOGY—AND OF THE FOUND-
ING OF THE GREAT CITY OF NEW-AMSTERDAM.

THE original name of the island whereon the squadron of Communipaw was thus propitiously thrown, is a matter of some
dispute, and has already undergone considerable vitiation—a
melancholy proof of the instability of all sublunary things, and
the vanity of all our hopes of lasting fame; for who can expect
his name will live to posterity, when even the names of mighty
islands are thus soon lost in contradiction and uncertainty!

The name most current at the present day, and which is likewise countenanced by the great historian Vander Donck, is
MANHATTAN; which is said to have originated in a custom
among the squaws, in the early settlement, of wearing men's
hats, as is still done among many tribes. "Hence," as we are
told by an old governor who was somewhat of a wag, and
flourished almost a century since, and had paid a visit to the wits
of Philadelphia, "hence arose the appellation of man-hat-on,
first given to the Indians, and afterwards to the island"—a stupid
joke!—but well enough for a governor.

Among the more venerable sources of information on this subject, is that valuable history of the American possessions. written by Master Richard Blome, in 1687, wherein it is called Manhadaes and Manahanent; nor must I forget the excellent little book, full of precious matter, of that authentic historian, John Josselyn, Gent., who expressly calls it Manadaes.

Another etymology still more ancient, and sanctioned by the countenance of our ever to be lamented Dutch ancestors, is that found in certain letters still exant;* which passed between the early governors and their neighboring powers, wherein it is called indifferently Monhattoes—Munhatos, and Manhattoes, which are evidently unimportant variations of the same name; for our wise forefathers set little store by those niceties either in orthography or orthoepy, which form the sole study and ambition of many learned men and women of this hypercritical age. This last name is said to be derived from the great Indian spirit Manetho; who was supposed to make this island his favorite abode, on account of its uncommon delights. For the Indian traditions affirm that the bay was once a translucid lake, filled with silver and golden fish, in the midst of which lay this beautiful island, covered with every variety of fruits and flowers; but that the sudden irruption of the Hudson laid waste these blissful scenes, and Manetho took his flight beyond the great waters of Ontario.

These, however, are very fabulous legends, to which very cautious credence must be given; and though I am willing to admit the last quoted orthography of the name as very fit for prose, yet is there another which I peculiarly delight in, as at once poetical, melodious, and significant—and which we have on the authority of Master Juet; who, in his account of the voyage of the great Hudson, calls this MANNA-HATA—that is to say, the island

---

* Vide Hazard's Col. Stat. Pap.

of manna—or, in other words, a land flowing with milk and honey.

Still my deference to the learned obliges me to notice the opinion of the worthy Dominie Heckwelder, which ascribes the name to a great drunken bout held on the island by the Dutch discoverers, whereat they made certain of the natives most extatically drunk for the first time in their lives; who, being delighted with their jovial entertainment gave the place the name of Mannahattanink; that is to say, The Island of Jolly Topers: a name which it continues to merit to the present day.*

* MSS. of the Rev. John Heckwelder, in the archives of the New-York Historical Society.

CHAPTER VII.

IT having been solemnly resolved that the seat of empire should
be removed from the green shores of Pavonia to the pleasant
island of Manna-hata, every body was anxious to embark under
the standard of Oloffe the Dreamer, and to be among the first
sharers of the promised land. A day was appointed for the
grand migration, and on that day little Communipaw was in a
buzz and a bustle like a hive in swarming time. Houses were
turned inside out and stripped of the venerable furniture which
had come from Holland; all the community, great and small,
black and white, man, woman, and child, was in commotion, forming lines from the houses to the water side, like lines of ants from
an ant-hill; every body laden with some article of household
furniture; while busy housewives plied backwards and forwards
along the lines, helping every thing forward by the nimbleness of
their tongues.

By degrees a fleet of boats and canoes were piled up with
all kinds of household articles: ponderous tables; chests of
drawers resplendent with brass ornaments; quaint corner cup-

boards; beds and bedsteads; with any quantity of pots, kettles, frying-pans, and Dutch ovens. In each boat embarked a whole family, from the robustious burgher down to the cats and dogs and little negroes. In this way they set off across the mouth of the Hudson, under the guidance of Oloffe the Dreamer, who hoisted his standard on the leading boat.

This memorable migration took place on the first of May, and was long cited in tradition as the *grand moving*. The anniversary of it was piously observed among the "sons of the pilgrims of Communipaw," by turning their houses topsy-turvy and carrying all the furniture through the streets, in emblem of the swarming of the parent hive; and this is the real origin of the universal agitation and "moving" by which this most restless of cities is literally turned out of doors on every May day.

As the little squadron from Communipaw drew near to the shores of Manna-hata, a sachem, at the head of a band of warriors, appeared to oppose their landing. Some of the most zealous of the pilgrims were for chastising this insolence with powder and ball, according to the approved mode of discoverers; but the sage Oloffe gave them the significant sign of St. Nicholas, laying his finger beside his nose and winking hard with one eye; whereupon his followers perceived that there was something sagacious in the wind. He now addressed the Indians in the blandest terms; and made such tempting display of beads, hawks'-bells, and red blankets, that he was soon permitted to land, and a great land speculation ensued. And here let me give the true story of the original purchase of the site of this renowned city, about which so much has been said and written. Some affirm that the first cost was but sixty guilders. The learned Dominie Heck-

6

welder records a tradition* that the Dutch discoverers bargained for only so much land as the hide of a bullock would cover; but that they cut the hide in strips no thicker than a child's finger, so as to take in a large portion of land, and to take in the Indians into the bargain. This, however, is an old fable which the worthy Dominie may have borrowed from antiquity. The true version is, that Oloffe Van Kortlandt bargained for just so much land as a man could cover with his nether garments. The terms being concluded, he produced his friend Mynheer Tenbroeck, as the man whose breeches were to be used in measurement. The simple savages, whose ideas of a man's nether garments had never expanded beyond the dimensions of a breech clout, stared with astonishment and dismay as they beheld this bulbous-bottomed burgher peeled like an onion, and breeches after breeches spread forth over the land until they covered the actual site of this venerable city.

This is the true history of the adroit bargain by which the island of Manhattan was bought for sixty guilders; and in corroboration of it I will add, that Mynheer Ten Breeches, for his services on this memorable occasion, was elevated to the office of land measurer; which he ever afterwards exercised in the colony.

* MSS. of the Rev. John Heckwelder; New-York Historical Society.

DARLEY DEL

CHAPTER VIII.

OF THE FOUNDING AND NAMING OF THE NEW CITY; OF THE
CITY ARMS; AND OF THE DIREFUL FEUD BETWEEN TEN
BREECHES AND TOUGH BREECHES.

THE land being thus fairly purchased of the Indians, a circumstance very unusual in the history of colonization, and strongly illustrative of the honesty of our Dutch progenitors, a stockade fort and trading house were forthwith erected on an eminence in front of the place where the good St. Nicholas had appeared in a vision to Oloffe the Dreamer; and which, as has already been observed, was the identical place at present known as the Bowling Green.

Around this fort a progeny of little Dutch-built houses, with tiled roofs and weathercocks, soon sprang up, nestling themselves under its walls for protection, as a brood of half-fledged chickens nestle under the wings of the mother hen. The whole was surrounded by an inclosure of strong palisadoes, to guard against any sudden irruption of the savages. Outside of these extended the corn-fields and cabbage-gardens of the community; with here and there an attempt at a tobacco plantation; all covering those tracts of country at present called Broadway, Wall-street, William-street and Pearl-street.

I must not omit to mention that in portioning out the land, a goodly "bowerie" or farm was allotted to the sage Oloffe in consideration of the service he had rendered to the public by his talent at dreaming; and the site of his "bowerie" is known by the name of Kortlandt (or Courtlandt) street to the present day.

And now the infant settlement having advanced in age and stature, it was thought high time it should receive an honest Christian name. Hitherto it had gone by the original Indian name Manna-hata, or as some will have it, "The Manhattoes;" but this was now decried as savage and heathenish, and as tending to keep up the memory of the pagan brood that originally possessed it. Many were the consultations held upon the subject, without coming to a conclusion, for though every body condemned the old name, nobody could invent a new one. At length, when the council was almost in despair, a burgher, remarkable for the size and squareness of his head, proposed that they should call it New-Amsterdam. The proposition took every body by surprise; it was so striking, so apposite, so ingenious. The name was adopted by acclamation, and New-Amsterdam the metropolis was thenceforth called. Still, however, the early authors of the province continued to call it by the general appellation of "The Manhattoes," and the poets fondly clung to the euphonious name of Manna-hata; but those are a kind of folk whose tastes and notions should go for nothing in matters of this kind.

Having thus provided the embryo city with a name, the next was to give it an armorial bearing or device, as some cities have a rampant lion, others a soaring eagle; emblematical, no doubt, of the valiant and high-flying qualities of the inhabitants : so after mature deliberation a sleek beaver was emblazoned on the city

standard as indicative of the amphibious origin, and patient, persevering habits of the New-Amsterdammers.

The thriving state of the settlement and the rapid increase of
houses soon made it necessary to arrange some plan upon which
the city should be built; but at the very first consultation held on
the subject, a violent discussion arose; and I mention it with much
sorrowing as being the first altercation on record in the councils
of New-Amsterdam. It was, in fact, a breaking forth of the
grudge and heart-burning that had existed between those two
eminent burghers, Mynheers Tenbroeck and Hardenbroeck, ever
since their unhappy dispute on the coast of Bellevue. The
great Hardenbroeck had waxed very wealthy and powerful, from
his domains, which embraced the whole chain of Apulean mountains that stretched along the gulf of Kip's Bay, and from part
of which his descendants have been expelled in latter ages by the
powerful clans of the Joneses and the Schermerhorns.

An ingenious plan for the city was offered by Mynheer Hardenbroeck, who proposed that it should be cut up and intersected by
canals, after the manner of the most admired cities in Holland.
To this Mynheer Tenbroeck was diametrically opposed, suggest-
ing in place thereof, that they should run out docks and wharves,
by means of piles driven into the bottom of the river, on which
the town should be built. "By these means," said he, triumphantly, "shall we rescue a considerable space of territory from
these immense rivers, and build a city that shall rival Amsterdam, Venice, or any amphibious city in Europe." To this proposition, Hardenbroeck (or Tough Breeches) replied, with a look
of as much scorn as he could possibly assume. He cast the utmost censure upon the plan of his antagonist, as being preposterous, and against the very order of things, as he would leave to

every true Hollander. " For what," said he, " is a town without canals ?—it is like a body without veins and arteries, and must perish for want of a free circulation of the vital fluid."—Ten Breeches, on the contrary, retorted with a sarcasm upon his antago- nist, who was somewhat of an arid, dry-boned habit; he remarked, that as to the circulation of the blood being necessary to existence, Mynheer Tough Breeches was a living contradiction to his own assertion; for every body knew there had not a drop of blood circulated through his wind-dried carcase for good ten years, and yet there was not a greater busy-body in the whole colony. Personalities have seldom much effect in making converts in argu- ment—nor have I ever seen a man convinced of error by being convicted of deformity. At least such was not the case at pre- sent. If Ten Breeches was very happy in sarcasm, Tough Breeches, who was a sturdy little man, and never gave up the last word, rejoined with increasing spirit—Ten Breeches had the advantage of the greatest volubility, but Tough Breeches had that invaluable coat of mail in argument called obstinacy—Ten Breeches had, therefore, the most mettle, but Tough Breeches the best bottom—so that though Ten Breeches made a dreadful clattering about his ears, and battered and belabored him with hard words and sound arguments, yet Tough Breeches hung on most resolutely to the last. They parted, therefore, as is usual in all arguments where both parties are in the right, without coming to any conclusion—but they hated each other most heartily for ever after, and a similar breach with that between the houses of Capulet and Montague, did ensue between the families of Ten Breeches and Tough Breeches.

I would not fatigue my reader with these dull matters of fact, but that my duty as a faithful historian, requires that I should be particular—and in truth, as I am now treating of the critical period, when our city, like a young twig, first received the twists and turns which have since contributed to give it its present picturesque irregularity, I cannot be too minute in detailing their first causes.

After the unhappy altercation I have just mentioned, I do not find that any thing farther was said on the subject worthy of being recorded. The council, consisting of the largest and oldest heads in the community, met regularly once a week, to ponder on this momentous subject; but, either they were deterred by the war of words they had witnessed, or they were naturally averse to the exercise of the tongue, and the consequent exercise of the brains —certain it is, the most profound silence was maintained—the question as usual lay on the table—the members quietly smoked their pipes, making but few laws, without ever enforcing any, and in the meantime the affairs of the settlement went on—as it pleased God.

As most of the council were but little skilled in the mystery of combining pot-hooks and hangers, they determined most judiciously not to puzzle either themselves or posterity with voluminous records. The secretary, however, kept the minutes of the council with tolerable precision, in a large vellum folio, fastened with massy brass clasps; the journal of each meeting consisted but of two lines, stating in Dutch, that "the council sat this day, and smoked twelve pipes, on the affairs of the colony."—By which it appears that the first settlers did not regulate their time by hours, but pipes, in the same manner as they measure distances in Holland at this very time; an admirably exact measurement, as a pipe in the mouth of a true-born Dutchman is never liable to those accidents and irregularities that are continually putting our clocks out of order.

In this manner did the profound council of NEW-AMSTERDAM smoke, and doze, and ponder, from week to week, month to month, and year to year, in what manner they should construct their infant settlement—meanwhile, the town took care of itself, and like a sturdy brat which is suffered to run about wild, unshackled by clouts and bandages, and other abominations by which your notable nurses and sage old women cripple and disfigure the children of men, increased so rapidly in strength and magnitude, that before the honest burgomasters had determined upon a plan, it was too late to put it in execution—whereupon they wisely abandoned the subject altogether.

CHAPTER IX.

HOW THE CITY OF NEW-AMSTERDAM WAXED GREAT UNDER THE PROTECTION OF ST. NICHOLAS AND THE ABSENCE OF LAWS AND STATUTES. HOW OLOFFE THE DREAMER BEGAN TO DREAM OF AN EXTENSION OF EMPIRE, AND OF THE EFFECT OF HIS DREAMS.

THERE is something exceedingly delusive in thus looking back, through the long vista of departed years, and catching a glimpse of the fairy realms of antiquity. Like a landscape melting into distance, they receive a thousand charms from their very obscurity, and the fancy delights to fill up their outlines with graces and excellences of its own creation. Thus loom on my imagination those happier days of our city, when as yet New-Amsterdam was a mere pastoral town, shrouded in groves of sycamores and willows, and surrounded by trackless forests and wide-spreading waters, that seemed to shut out all the cares and vanities of a wicked world.

In those days did this embryo city present the rare and noble spectacle of a community governed without laws; and thus being left to its own course, and the fostering care of Providence, increased as rapidly as though it had been burthened with a dozen panniers full of those sage laws usually heaped on the backs of young cities—in order to make them grow. And in this particular I greatly admire the wisdom and sound knowledge of human nature, displayed by the sage Oloffe the Dreamer and his fellow legislators. For my part, I have not so bad an opinion of mankind as many of my brother philosophers. I do not think poor human nature so sorry a piece of workmanship as they would make it out to be; and as far as I have observed, I am fully satisfied that man, if left to himself, would about as readily go right as wrong. It is only this eternally sounding in his ears that it is his duty to go right, which makes him go the very reverse. The noble independence of his nature revolts at this intolerable tyranny of law, and the perpetual interference of officious morality, which are ever besetting his path with finger-posts and directions to " keep to the right, as the law directs ;" and like a spirited urchin, he turns directly contrary, and gallops through mud and mire, over hedges and ditches, merely to show that he is a lad of spirit, and out of his leading-strings. And these opinions are amply substantiated by what I have above said of our worthy ancestors ; who never being be-preached and be-lectured, and guided and governed by statutes and laws and by-laws, as are their more enlightened descendants, did one and all demean themselves honestly and peaceably, out of pure ignorance, or in other words—because they knew no better.

Nor must I omit to record one of the earliest measures of this infant settlement, inasmuch as it shows the piety of our forefathers, and that, like good Christians, they were always ready to serve God, after they had first served themselves. Thus, having quietly settled themselves down, and provided for their own comfort, they bethought themselves of testifying their gratitude to the great and good St. Nicholas, for his protecting care, in guiding them to this delectable abode. To this end they built a fair and goodly chapel within the fort, which they consecrated to his name; whereupon he immediately took the town of New-Amsterdam under his peculiar patronage, and he has ever since been, and I devoutly hope will ever be, the tutelar saint of this excellent city.

At this early period was instituted that pious ceremony, still religiously observed in all our ancient families of the right breed, of hanging up a stocking in the chimney on St. Nicholas eve: which stocking is always found in the morning miraculously filled; for the good St. Nicholas has ever been a great giver of gifts, particularly to children.

I am moreover told that there is a little legendary book, somewhere extant, written in Low Dutch, which says, that the image of this renowned saint, which whilom graced the bowsprit of the Goede Vrouw, was elevated in front of this chapel, in the centre of what, in modern days, is called the Bowling Green—on the very spot, in fact, where he appeared in vision to Oloffe the Dreamer. And the legend further treats of divers miracles wrought by the mighty pipe, which the saint held in his mouth; a whiff of which was a sovereign cure for an indigestion— an invaluable relic in this colony of brave trenchermen. As, however, in spite of the most diligent search, I cannot lay my hands upon this little book, I must confess that I entertain considerable doubt on the subject.

Thus benignly fostered by the good St. Nicholas, the infant city thrived apace. Hordes of painted savages, it is true, still lurked about the unsettled parts of the island. The hunter still pitched his bower of skins and bark beside the rills that ran through the cool and shady glens, while here and there might be seen on some sunny knoll, a group of Indian wigwams, whose smoke arose above the neighboring trees, and floated in the transparent atmosphere. A mutual good-will, however, existed between these wandering beings and the burghers of New-Amsterdam. Our benevolent forefathers endeavored as much as possible to ameliorate their situation, by giving them gin, rum, and glass beads, in exchange for their peltries; for it seems the kind-hearted Dutchmen had conceived a great friendship for their savage neighbors, on account of their being pleasant men to trade with, and little skilled in the art of making a bargain.

Now and then a crew of these half human sons of the forest would make their appearance in the streets of New-Amsterdam, fantastically painted and decorated with beads and flaunting feathers, sauntering about with an air of listless indifference—sometimes in the market-place, instructing the little Dutch boys in the use of the bow and arrow—at other times, inflamed with liquor, swaggering and whooping and yelling about the town like so many fiends, to the great dismay of all the good wives, who would hurry their children into the house, fasten the doors, and throw water upon the enemy from the garret windows. It is worthy of mention here, that our forefathers were very particular in holding up these wild men as excellent domestic examples—and for reasons that may be gathered from the history of master Ogilby, who tells us, that "for the least offence the bridegroom soundly beats his wife and turns her out of doors, and marries another, insomuch that some of them have every year a new wife." Whether this awful example had any influence or not, history does not mention; but it is certain that our grandmothers were miracles of fidelity and obedience.

True it is, that the good understanding between our ancestors and their savage neighbors was liable to occasional interruptions,

Darley. Del.   CHILD. Sc.

and I have heard my grandmother, who was a very wise old woman, and well versed in the history of these parts, tell a long story of a winter's evening, about a battle between the New-Amsterdammers and the Indians, which was known by the name of the *Peach War*, and which took place near a peach orchard, in a dark glen, which for a long while went by the name of Murderer's Valley.

The legend of this sylvan war was long current among the nurses, old wives, and other ancient chroniclers of the place ; but time and improvement have almost obliterated both the tradition and the scene of battle ; for what was once the blood-stained valley is now in the centre of this populous city, and known by the name of *Dey-street*.

I know not whether it was to this "Peach war," and the acquisitions of Indian land which may have grown out of it, that we may ascribe the first seeds of the spirit of "annexation" which now began to manifest themselves. Hitherto the ambition of the worthy burghers had been confined to the lovely island of Manna-hata ; and Spiten Devil on the Hudson, and Hell-gate on the Sound, were to them the pillars of Hercules, the *ne plus ultra* of human enterprise. Shortly after the Peach war, however, a restless spirit was observed among the New-Amsterdammers, who began to cast wistful looks upon the wild lands of their Indian neighbors ; for somehow or other wild Indian land always looks greener in the eyes of settlers than the land they occupy. It is hinted that Oloffe the Dreamer encouraged these notions : having, as has been shown, the inherent spirit of a land speculator, which had been wonderfully quickened and expanded since he had become a land holder. Many of the common people, who had never before owned a foot of land, now began to be

discontented with the town lots which had fallen to their shares;
others who had snug farms and tobacco plantations, found they
had not sufficient elbow-room, and began to question the rights of
the Indians to the vast regions they pretended to hold,—while
the good Oloffe indulged in magnificent dreams of foreign conquest and great patroonships in the wilderness.

The result of these dreams were certain exploring expeditions
sent forth in various directions to " sow the seeds of empire," as
it was said.   The earliest of these were conducted by Hans
Reinier Oothout, an old navigator famous for the sharpness of
his vision, who could see land when it was quite out of sight to
ordinary mortals, and who had a spy-glass covered with a bit
of tarpauling, with which he could spy up the crookedest river,
quite to its head waters.   He was accompanied by Mynheer
Ten Breeches, as land measurer, in case of any dispute with the
Indians.

What was the consequence of these exploring expeditions?
In a little while we find a frontier post or trading-house called
Fort Nassau, established far to the south on Delaware River;
another called Fort Goed Hoep (or Good Hope), on the Varsche
or Fresh, or Connecticut River; and another called Fort Aurania
(now Albany) away up the Hudson River; while the boundaries
of the province kept extending on every side, nobody knew
whither, far into the regions of Terra Incognita.

Of the boundary feuds and troubles which the ambitious little
province brought upon itself by these indefinite expansions of
its territory, we shall treat at large in the after pages of this
eventful history; sufficient for the present is it to say that the
swelling importance of the New-Netherlands awakened the attention of the mother country, who finding it likely to yield much

revenue and no trouble, began to take that interest in its welfare which knowing people evince for rich relations.

But as this opens a new era in the fortunes of New-Amsterdam, I will here put an end to this second book of my history, and will treat of the maternal policy of the mother country in my next.

BOOK III.

IN WHICH IS RECORDED THE GOLDEN REIGN OF WOUTER
VAN TWILLER.

CHAPTER I.

OF THE RENOWNED WOUTER VAN TWILLER, HIS UNPARAL-
LELED VIRTUES—AS LIKEWISE HIS UNUTTERABLE WISDOM
IN THE LAW CASE OF WANDLE SCOONHOVEN AND BARENT
BLEECKER—AND THE GREAT ADMIRATION OF THE PUBLIC
THEREAT.

GRIEVOUS and very much to be commiserated is the task of the
feeling historian, who writes the history of his native land. If
it fall to his lot to be the recorder of calamity or crime, the
mournful page is watered with his tears—nor can he recall the
most prosperous and blissful era, without a melancholy sigh at
the reflection, that it has passed away for ever! I know not
whether it be owing to an immoderate love for the simplicity of
former times, or to that certain tenderness of heart incident to all
sentimental historians; but I candidly confess that I cannot look
back on the happier days of our city, which I now describe
without great dejection of spirits. With faltering hand do I
withdraw the curtain of oblivion, that veils the modest merit of

our venerable ancestors, and as their figures rise to my mental vision, humble myself before their mighty shades.

Such are my feelings when I revisit the family mansion of the Knickerbockers, and spend a lonely hour in the chamber where hang the portraits of my forefathers, shrouded in dust, like the forms they represent. With pious reverence do I gaze on the countenances of those renowned burghers, who have preceded me in the steady march of existence—whose sober and temperate blood now meanders through my veins, flowing slower and slower in its feeble conduits, until its current shall soon be stopped for ever!

These, I say to myself, are but frail memorials of the mighty men who flourished in the days of the patriarchs; but who, alas, have long since mouldered in that tomb, towards which my steps are insensibly and irresistibly hastening! As I pace the darkened chamber and lose myself in melancholy musings, the shadowy images around me almost seem to steal once more into existence—their countenances to assume the animation of life—their eyes to pursue me in every movement! Carried away by the delusions of fancy, I almost imagine myself surrounded by the shades of the departed, and holding sweet converse with the worthies of antiquity! Ah, hapless Diedrich! born in a degenerate age, abandoned to the buffetings of fortune—a stranger and a weary pilgrim in thy native land—blest with no weeping wife, nor family of helpless children; but doomed to wander neglected through those crowded streets, and elbowed by foreign upstarts from those fair abodes where once thine ancestors held sovereign empire!

Let me not, however, lose the historian in the man, nor suffer the doting recollections of age to overcome me, while dwelling with fond garrulity on the virtuous days of the patriarchs—on those sweet days of simplicity and ease, which never more will dawn on the lovely island of Manna-hata.

These melancholy reflections have been forced from me by the growing wealth and importance of New-Amsterdam, which, I plainly perceive, are to involve it in all kinds of perils and disasters. Already, as I observed at the close of my last book, they had awakened the attention of the mother country. The usual mark of protection shown by mother countries to wealthy colonies was forthwith manifested; a governor being sent out to rule over the province and squeeze out of it as much revenue as possible. The arrival of a governor of course put an end to the protectorate of Oloffe the Dreamer. He appears, however, to have dreamt to some purpose during his sway, as we find him afterwards living as a patroon on a great landed estate on the banks of the Hudson; having virtually forfeited all right to his ancient appellation of Kortlandt or Lackland.

It was in the year of our Lord 1629 that Mynheer Wouter Van Twiller was appointed governor of the province of Nieuw-Nederlandts, under the commission and control of their High Mightinesses the Lords States General of the United Netherlands, and the privileged West India Company.

This renowned old gentleman arrived at New-Amsterdam in the merry month of June, the sweetest month in all the year; when dan Apollo seems to dance up the transparent firmament— when the robin, the thrush, and a thousand other wanton song-sters make the woods to resound with amorous ditties, and the luxurious little boblincon revels among the clover blossoms of the meadows—all which happy coincidence persuaded the old dames of New-Amsterdam, who were skilled in the art of foretelling

events, that this was to be a happy and prosperous administration.

The renowned Wouter (or Walter) Van Twiller, was descended from a long line of Dutch burgomasters, who had
successively dozed away their lives, and grown fat upon the
bench of magistracy in Rotterdam; and who had comported
themselves with such singular wisdom and propriety, that they
were never either heard or talked of—which, next to being
universally applauded, should be the object of ambition of all
magistrates and rulers. There are two opposite ways by which
some men make a figure in the world; one by talking faster than
they think; and the other by holding their tongues and not thinking at all. By the first many a smatterer acquires the reputation
of a man of quick parts; by the other many a dunderpate, like
the owl, the stupidest of birds, comes to be considered the very
type of wisdom. This, by the way, is a casual remark, which I
would not for the universe have it thought I apply to Governor
Van Twiller. It is true he was a man shut up within himself,
like an oyster, and rarely spoke except in monosyllables; but
then it was allowed he seldom said a foolish thing. So invincible
was his gravity that he was never known to laugh or even to
smile through the whole course of a long and prosperous life.
Nay if a joke were uttered in his presence, that set light-minded
hearers in a roar, it was observed to throw him into a state of
perplexity. Sometimes he would deign to inquire into the
matter, and when, after much explanation, the joke was made as
plain as a pike-staff; he would continue to smoke his pipe in
silence, and at length, knocking out the ashes would exclaim,
"Well! I see nothing in all that to laugh about."

With all his reflective habits, he never made up his mind on a

subject. His adherents accounted for this by the astonishing magnitude of his ideas. He conceived every subject on so grand a scale that he had not room in his head to turn it over and examine both sides of it. Certain it is that if any matter were propounded to him on which ordinary mortals would rashly determine at first glance, he would put on a vague, mysterious look; shake his capacious head; smoke some time in profound silence, and at length observe that "he had his doubts about the matter," which gained him the reputation of a man slow of belief, and not easily imposed upon. What is more, it gained him a lasting name: for to this habit of the mind has been attributed his surname of Twiller; which is said to be a corruption of the original Twijfler, or, in plain English, *Doubter*.

The person of this illustrious old gentleman was formed and proportioned, as though it had been moulded by the hands of some cunning Dutch statuary, as a model of majesty and lordly grandeur. He was exactly five feet six inches in height, and six feet five inches in circumference. His head was a perfect sphere, and of such stupendous dimensions, that dame Nature with all her sex's ingenuity, would have been puzzled to construct a neck capable of supporting it; wherefore she wisely declined the attempt, and settled it firmly on the top of his back-bone, just between the shoulders. His body was oblong and particularly capacious at bottom; which was wisely ordered by Providence, seeing that he was a man of sedentary habits, and very averse to the idle labor of walking. His legs were short, but sturdy in proportion to the weight they had to sustain; so that when erect he had not a little the appearance of a beer barrel on skids. His face, that infallible index of the mind, presented a vast expanse, unfurrowed by any of those lines and angles which disfigure the human countenance with what is termed expression. Two small gray eyes twinkled feebly in the midst, like two stars of lesser magnitude in a hazy firmament; and his full-fed cheeks, which seemed to have taken toll of every thing that went into his mouth, were curiously mottled and streaked with dusky red, like a spitzenberg apple.

His habits were as regular as his person. He daily took his four stated meals, appropriating exactly an hour to each; he smoked and doubted eight hours, and he slept the remaining twelve of the four-and-twenty. Such was the renowned Wouter Van Twiller—a true philosopher, for his mind was either elevated above, or tranquilly settled below, the cares and perplexities of this world. He had lived in it for years, without feeling the least curiosity to know whether the sun revolved round it, or it round the sun; and he had watched, for at least half a century, the smoke curling from his pipe to the ceiling, without once troubling his head with any of those numerous theories, by which a philosopher would have perplexed his brain, in accounting for its rising above the surrounding atmosphere.

In his council he presided with great state and solemnity. He sat in a huge chair of solid oak, hewn in the celebrated forest of the Hague, fabricated by an experienced timmerman of Amsterdam, and curiously carved about the arms and feet, into exact imitations of gigantic eagle's claws. Instead of a sceptre he swayed a long Turkish pipe, wrought with jasmin and amber, which had been presented to a stadtholder of Holland, at the conclusion of a treaty with one of the petty Barbary powers. In this stately chair would he sit, and this magnificent pipe would he smoke, shaking his right knee with a constant motion, and fixing his eye for hours together upon a little print of Amsterdam, which hung in a black frame against the opposite wall of the council chamber. Nay, it has even been said, that when any deliberation of extraordinary length and intricacy was on the carpet, the renowned Wouter would shut his eyes for full two hours at a time, that he might not be disturbed by external objects—and at such times the internal commotion of his mind was evinced by certain regular guttural sounds, which his admirers declared were merely the noise of conflict, made by his contending doubts and opinions.

It is with infinite difficulty I have been enabled to collect these biographical anecdotes of the great man under consideration. The facts respecting him were so scattered and vague, and divers of them so questionable in point of authenticity, that I have had to give up the search after many, and decline the admission of still more, which would have tended to heighten the coloring of his portrait.

I have been the more anxious to delineate fully the person and habits of Wouter Van Twiller, from the consideration that he was not only the first, but also the best governor that ever presided over this ancient and respectable province ; and so tranquil and benevolent was his reign, that I do not find throughout the whole of it, a single instance of any offender being brought to punishment—a most indubitable sign of a merciful governor, and a case unparalleled, excepting in the reign of the illustrious King Log, from whom, it is hinted, the renowned Van Twiller was a lineal descendant.

The very outset of the career of this excellent magistrate was distinguished by an example of legal acumen, that gave flattering presage of a wise and equitable administration. The morning after he had been installed in office, and at the moment that he was making his breakfast from a prodigious earthen dish, filled with milk and Indian pudding, he was interrupted by the appearance of Wandle Schoonhoven, a very important old burgher of New-Amsterdam, who complained bitterly of one Barent Bleecker, inasmuch as he refused to come to a settlement of accounts, seeing that there was a heavy balance in favor of the said Wandle. Governor Van Twiller, as I have already observed, was a man of few words; he was likewise a mortal enemy to multiplying writings—or being disturbed at his breakfast. Having listened attentively to the statement of Wandle Schoonhoven, giving an occasional grunt, as he shoveled a spoonful of Indian pudding into his mouth—either as a sign that he relished the dish, or comprehended the story—he called unto him his constable, and pulling out of his breeches pocket a huge jack-knife, dispatched it after the defendant as a summons, accompanied by his tobacco-box as a warrant.

This summary process was as effectual in those simple days as was the seal ring of the great Haroun Alraschid among the true believers. The two parties being confronted before him, each produced a book of accounts, written in a language and character that would have puzzled any but a High Dutch commentator, or a learned decipherer of Egyptian obelisks. The sage Wouter took them one after the other, and having poised them in his hands, and attentively counted over the number of leaves, fell straightway into a very great doubt, and smoked for half an hour without saying a word; at length, laying his finger beside his nose, and shutting his eyes for a moment, with the air of a man who has just caught a subtle idea by the tail, he slowly took his pipe from his mouth, puffed forth a column of tobacco smoke, and with marvellous gravity and solemnity pronounced —that having carefully counted over the leaves and weighed the books, it was found, that one was just as thick and as heavy as the other—therefore it was the final opinion of the court that the accounts were equally balanced—therefore Wandle should give Barent a receipt, and Barent should give Wandle a receipt—and the constable should pay the costs.

This decision being straightway made known, diffused general joy throughout New-Amsterdam, for the people immediately perceived, that they had a very wise and equitable magistrate to rule over them. But its happiest effect was, that not another lawsuit took place throughout the whole of his administration—and the office of constable fell into such decay, that there was not one of those losel scouts known in the province for many years. I am the more particular in dwelling on this transaction, not only because I deem it one of the most sage and righteous judgments on record, and well worthy the attention of modern magistrates; but because it was a miraculous event in the history of the renowned Wouter—being the only time he was ever known to come to a decision in the whole course of his life.

CHAPTER II.

IN treating of the early governors of the province, I must caution my readers against confounding them, in point of dignity and power, with those worthy gentlemen, who are whimsically denominated governors in this enlightened republic—a set of unhappy victims of popularity, who are in fact the most dependent hen-pecked beings in the community: doomed to bear the secret goadings and corrections of their own party, and the sneers and revilings of the whole world beside. Set up, like geese at Christmas holidays, to be pelted and shot at by every whipster and vagabond in the land. On the contrary, the Dutch governors enjoyed that uncontrolled authority, vested in all commanders of distant colonies or territories. They were in a manner absolute despots in their little domains, lording it, if so disposed, over both law and gospel, and accountable to none but the mother country; which it is well known is astonishingly deaf to all complaints against its governors, provided they discharge the main duty of their station—squeezing out a good revenue. This hint will be of importance, to prevent my readers from being seized with doubt and incredulity, whenever, in the course of this authentic history, they encounter the uncommon circumstance of a governor acting with independence, and in opposition to the opinions of the multitude.

To assist the doubtful Wouter in the arduous business of legislation, a board of magistrates was appointed, which presided immediately over the police. This potent body consisted of a schout or bailiff, with powers between those of the present mayor and sheriff—five burgermeesters, who were equivalent to aldermen, and five schepens, who officiated as scrubs, subdevils, or bottle-holders to the burgermeesters, in the same manner as do assistant aldermen to their principals at the present day; it being their duty to fill the pipes of the lordly burgermeesters—hunt the markets for delicacies for corporation dinners, and to discharge such other little offices of kindness as were occasionally required. It was, moreover, tacitly understood, though not specifically enjoined, that they should consider themselves as butts for the blunt wits of the burgermeesters, and should laugh most heartily at all their jokes; but this last was a duty as rarely called in action in those days as it is at present, and was shortly remitted, in consequence of the tragical death of a fat little schepen—who actually died of suffocation in an unsuccessful effort to force a laugh at one of burgermeester Van Zandt's best jokes.

In return for these humble services, they were permitted to say *yes* and *no* at the council-board, and to have that enviable privilege, the run of the public kitchen—being graciously permitted to eat, and drink, and smoke, at all those snug junketings and public gormandizings, for which the ancient magistrates were

equally famous with their modern successors. The post of schepen, therefore, like that of assistant alderman, was eagerly coveted
by all your burghers of a certain description, who have a huge
relish for good feeding, and an humble ambition to be great men
in a small way—who thirst after a little brief authority, that shall
render them the terror of the alms-house and the bridewell—
that shall enable them to lord it over obsequious poverty, vagrant
vice, outcast prostitution, and hunger-driven dishonesty—that
shall give to their beck a hound-like pack of catchpolls and
bumbailiffs—tenfold greater rogues than the culprits they hunt
down !—My readers will excuse this sudden warmth, which I
confess is unbecoming of a grave historian—but I have a mortal
antipathy to catchpolls, bumbailiffs, and little great men.

The ancient magistrates of this city corresponded with those
of the present time no less in form, magnitude, and intellect, than
in prerogative and privilege. The burgomasters, like our aldermen, were generally chosen by weight—and not only the weight
of the body, but likewise the weight of the head. It is a maxim
practically observed in all honest, plain-thinking, regular cities,
that an alderman should be fat—and the wisdom of this can be
proved to a certainty. That the body is in some measure an
image of the mind, or rather that the mind is moulded to the
body, like melted lead to the clay in which it is cast, has been
insisted on by many philosophers, who have made human nature
their peculiar study—for as a learned gentleman of our own city
observes, " there is a constant relation between the moral character of all intelligent creatures, and their physical constitution—
between their habits and the structure of their bodies." Thus
we see that a lean, spare, diminutive body is generally accompanied by a petulant, restless, meddling mind—either the mind

wears down the body, by its continual motion; or else the body, not affording the mind sufficient house-room, keeps it continually in a state of fretfulness, tossing and worrying about from the uneasiness of its situation.   Whereas your round, sleek, fat, unwieldy periphery is ever attended by a mind like itself, tranquil, torpid, and at ease; and we may always observe, that your well fed, robustious burghers are in general very tenacious of their ease and comfort; being great enemies to noise, discord, and disturbance—and surely none are more likely to study the public tranquillity than those who are so careful of their own. Who ever hears of fat men heading a riot, or herding together in turbulent mobs?—no—no—it is your lean, hungry men who are continually worrying society, and setting the whole community by the ears.

The divine Plato, whose doctrines are not sufficiently attended to by philosophers of the present age, allows to every man three souls—one immortal and rational, seated in the brain, that it may overlook and regulate the body—a second consisting of the surly and irascible passions which, like belligerent powers, lie encamped around the heart—a third mortal and sensual, destitute of reason, gross and brutal in its propensities, and enchained in the belly, that it may not disturb the divine soul by its ravenous howlings. Now, according to this excellent theory, what can be more clear, than that your fat alderman is most likely to have the most regular and well-conditioned mind.   His head is like a huge spherical chamber, containing a prodigious mass of soft brains, whereon the rational soul lies softly and snugly couched, as on a feather bed; and the eyes, which are the windows of the bed-chamber, are usually half closed, that its slumberings may not be disturbed by external objects.   A mind thus comfortably lodged, and protected

from disturbance, is manifestly most likely to perform its func-
tions with regularity and ease. By dint of good feeding moreover, the mortal and malignant soul, which is confined in the
belly, and which, by its raging and roaring, puts the irritable soul
in the neighborhood of the heart in an intolerable passion, and
thus renders men crusty and quarrelsome when hungry, is completely pacified, silenced, and put to rest—whereupon a host of
honest, good-fellow qualities and kind-hearted affections, which
had lain perdue, slyly peeping out of the loop-holes of the heart,
finding this cerberus asleep, do pluck up their spirits, turn out one
and all in their holiday suits, and gambol up and down the dia-
phragm—disposing their possessor to laughter, good humor, and
a thousand friendly offices towards his fellow mortals.

As a board of magistrates, formed on this principle, think but
very little, they are the less likely to differ and wrangle about
favorite opinions—and as they generally transact business upon
a hearty dinner, they are naturally disposed to be lenient and
indulgent in the administration of their duties. Charlemagne
was conscious of this, and therefore ordered in his cartularies,
that no judge should hold a court of justice, except in the morning, on an empty stomach.—A pitiful rule, which I can never
forgive, and which I warrant bore hard upon all the poor culprits
in the kingdom. The more enlightened and humane generation
of the present day have taken an opposite course, and have so
managed, that the aldermen are the best fed men in the community; feasting lustily on the fat things of the land, and gorging so
heartily on oysters and turtles, that in process of time they
acquire the activity of the one, and the form, the waddle, and the
green fat of the other. The consequence is, as I have just said,
these luxurious feastings do produce such a dulcet equanimity

and repose of the soul, rational and irrational, that their transactions are proverbial for unvarying monotony—and the profound laws which they enact in their dozing moments, amid the labors of digestion, are quietly suffered to remain as dead letters, and never enforced, when awake. In a word, your fair, round-bellied burgomaster, like a full-fed mastiff, dozes quietly at the house-door, always at home, and always at hand to watch over its safety—but as to electing a lean, meddling candidate to the office, as has now and then been done, I would as lief put a greyhound to watch the house, or a race-horse to draw an ox wagon.

The burgomasters then, as I have already mentioned, were wisely chosen by weight, and the schepens, or assistant aldermen, were appointed to attend upon them, and help them eat; but the latter, in the course of time, when they had been fed and fattened into sufficient bulk of body and drowsiness of brain, became very eligible candidates for the burgomasters' chairs, having fairly eaten themselves into office, as a mouse eats his way into a comfortable lodgment in a goodly, blue-nosed, skimmed milk, New-England cheese.

Nothing could equal the profound deliberations that took place between the renowned Wouter, and these his worthy compeers, unless it be the sage divans of some of our modern corporations. They would sit for hours smoking and dozing over public affairs, without speaking a word to interrupt that perfect stillness, so necessary to deep reflection. Under the sober sway of Wouter Van Twiller and these his worthy coadjutors, the infant settlement waxed vigorous apace, gradually emerging from the swamps and forests, and exhibiting that mingled appearance of town and country, customary in new cities, and which at this day may be witnessed in the city of Washington; that immense metropolis, which makes so glorious an appearance on paper.

It was a pleasing sight in those times, to behold the honest burgher, like a patriarch of yore, seated on the bench at the door of his whitewashed house, under the shade of some gigantic sycamore or overhanging willow. Here would he smoke his pipe of a sultry afternoon, enjoying the soft southern breeze, and listening with silent gratulation to the clucking of his hens, the cackling of his geese, and the sonorous grunting of his swine; that combination of farm-yard melody, which may truly be said to have a silver sound, inasmuch as it conveys a certain assurance of profitable marketing.

The modern spectator, who wanders through the streets of this populous city, can scarcely form an idea of the different appearance they presented in the primitive days of the Doubter. The busy hum of multitudes, the shouts of revelry, the rumbling equipages of fashion, the rattling of accursed carts, and all the spirit-grieving sounds of brawling commerce, were unknown in the settlement of New-Amsterdam. The grass grew quietly in the highways—the bleating sheep and frolicksome calves sported about the verdant ridge, where now the Broadway loungers take their morning stroll—the cunning fox or ravenous wolf skulked in the woods, where now are to be seen the dens of Gomez and his righteous fraternity of money-brokers—and flocks of vociferous geese cackled about the fields, where now the great Tammany wigwam and the patriotic tavern of Martling echo with the wranglings of the mob.

In these good times did a true and enviable equality of rank and property prevail, equally removed from the arrogance of wealth, and the servility and heart-burnings of repining poverty —and what in my mind is still more conducive to tranquillity and harmony among friends, a happy equality of intellect was likewise to be seen. The minds of the good burghers of New-Amsterdam seemed all to have been cast in one mould, and to be those honest, blunt minds, which, like certain manufactures, are made by the gross, and considered as exceedingly good for common use.

Thus it happens that your true dull minds are generally preferred for public employ, and especially promoted to city honors; your keen intellects, like razors, being considered too sharp for common service. I know that it is common to rail at the unequal distribution of riches, as the great source of jealousies, broils, and heart-breakings; whereas, for my part, I verily believe it is the sad inequality of intellect that prevails, that embroils communities more than any thing else; and I have remarked that your knowing people, who are so much wiser than any body else, are eternally keeping society in a ferment. Happily for New-Amsterdam, nothing of the kind was known within its walls—the very words of learning, education, taste, and talents were unheard of —a bright genius was an animal unknown, and a blue stocking lady would have been regarded with as much wonder as a horned frog or a fiery dragon. No man in fact seemed to know more than his neighbor, nor any man to know more than an honest man ought to know, who has nobody's business to mind but his own; the parson and the council clerk were the only men that could read in the community, and the sage Van Twiller always signed his name with a cross.

Thrice happy and ever to be envied little Burgh! existing in all the security of harmless insignificance—unnoticed and unenvied by the world, without ambition, without vainglory, without

7*

riches, without learning, and all their train of carking cares—and as of yore, in the better days of man, the deities were wont to visit him on earth and bless his rural habitations, so we are told, in the sylvan days of New-Amsterdam, the good St. Nicholas would often make his appearance in his beloved city, of a holiday afternoon, riding jollily among the tree-tops, or over the roofs of the houses, now and then drawing forth magnificent presents from his breeches pockets, and dropping them down the chimneys of his favorites. Whereas in these degenerate days of iron and brass he never shows us the light of his countenance, nor ever visits us, save one night in the year; when he rattles down the chimneys of the descendants of the patriarchs, confining his presents merely to the children, in token of the degeneracy of the parents.

Such are the comfortable and thriving effects of a fat government. The province of the New-Netherlands, destitute of wealth, possessed a sweet tranquillity that wealth could never purchase. There were neither public commotions, nor private quarrels; neither parties, nor sects, nor schisms; neither persecutions, nor trials, nor punishments; nor were there counsellors, attorneys, catchpolls, or hangmen. Every man attended to what little business he was lucky enough to have, or neglected it if he pleased, without asking the opinion of his neighbor. In those days nobody meddled with concerns above his comprehension; nor thrust his nose into other people's affairs; nor neglected to correct his own conduct, and reform his own character, in his zeal to pull to pieces the characters of others—but in a word, every respectable citizen eat when he was not hungry, drank when he was not thirsty, and went regularly to bed when the sun set and the fowls went to roost, whether he were sleepy or not; all which tended so remarkably to the population of the settlement, that I am told every dutiful wife throughout New-Amsterdam made a point of enriching her husband with at least one child a year, and very often a brace—this superabundance of good things clearly constituting the true luxury of life, according to the favorite Dutch maxim, that "more than enough constitutes a feast." Every thing, therefore, went on exactly as it should do, and in the usual words employed by historians to express the welfare of a country, "the profoundest *tranquillity* and *repose* reigned throughout the province."

CHAPTER III.

MANIFOLD are the tastes and dispositions of the enlightened lite-rati, who turn over the pages of history. Some there be whose hearts are brimful of the yeast of courage, and whose bosoms do work, and swell, and foam, with untried valor, like a barrel of new cider, or a train-band captain, fresh from under the hands of his tailor. This doughty class of readers can be satisfied with nothing but bloody battles, and horrible encounters; they must be continually storming forts, sacking cities, springing mines, marching up to the muzzles of cannon, charging bayonet through every page, and reveling in gunpowder and carnage. Others, who are of a less martial, but equally ardent imagination, and who, withal, are a little given to the marvelous, will dwell with wondrous satisfaction on descriptions of prodigies, unheard-of events, hair-breadth escapes, hardy adventures, and all those as-tonishing narrations, which just amble along the boundary line of possibility. A third class, who, not to speak slightly of them, are of a lighter turn, and skim over the records of past times, as they do over the edifying pages of a novel, merely for relaxation and innocent amusement, do singularly delight in treasons, executions, Sabine rapes, Tarquin outrages, conflagrations, murders, and all the other catalogue of hideous crimes, which like cayenne in cookery, do give a pungency and flavor to the dull detail of history—while a fourth class, of more philosophic habits, do diligently pore over the musty chronicles of time, to investigate the operations of the human kind, and watch the gradual changes in men and manners, effected by the progress of knowledge, the vicissitudes of events, or the influence of situation.

If the three first classes find but little wherewithal to solace themselves in the tranquil reign of Wouter Van Twiller, I entreat them to exert their patience for a while, and bear with the tedious picture of happiness, prosperity, and peace, which my duty as a faithful historian obliges me to draw; and I promise them that as soon as I can possibly alight upon any thing horrible, uncommon, or impossible, it shall go hard but I will make it afford them entertainment. This being premised, I turn with great complacency to the fourth class of my readers, who are men, or, if possible, women after my own heart; grave, philosophical, and investigating; fond of analyzing characters, of taking a start from first causes, and so hunting a nation down, through all the mazes of innovation and improvement. Such will naturally be anxious to witness the first development of the newly hatched colony, and the primitive manners and customs prevalent among its inhabitants, during the halcyon reign of Van Twiller or the Doubter.

I will not grieve their patience, however, by describing minutely the increase and improvement of New-Amsterdam. Their own imaginations will doubtless present to them the good burghers, like so many painstaking and persevering beavers, slowly and surely pursuing their labors—they will behold the prosperous transformation from the rude log hut to the stately Dutch mansion, with brick front, glazed windows, and tiled roof; from the tangled thicket to the luxuriant cabbage garden; and from the skulking Indian to the ponderous burgomaster. In a word, they will picture to themselves the steady, silent, and undeviating march of prosperity, incident to a city destitute of pride or ambition, cherished by a fat government, and whose citizens do nothing in a hurry.

The sage council, as has been mentioned in a preceding chapter, not being able to determine upon any plan for the building of their city—the cows, in a laudable fit of patriotism, took it under their peculiar charge, and as they went to and from pasture, established paths through the bushes, on each side of which the good folks built their houses; which is one cause of the rambling and picturesque turns and labyrinths, which distinguish certain streets of New-York at this very day.

The houses of the higher class were generally constructed of wood, excepting the gable end, which was of small black and yellow Dutch bricks, and always faced on the street, as our ancestors, like their descendants, were very much given to outward show, and were noted for putting the best leg foremost. The house was always furnished with abundance of large doors and small windows on every floor, the date of its erection was curiously designated by iron figures on the front, and on the top of the roof was perched a fierce little weathercock, to let the family into the important secret, which way the wind blew. These, like the weathercocks on the tops of our steeples, pointed so many different ways, that every man could have a wind to his mind ;—the most stanch and loyal citizens, however, always went according to the weathercock on the top of the governor's house, which was certainly the most correct, as he had a trusty servant employed every morning to climb up and set it to the right quarter.

In those good days of simplicity and sunshine, a passion for cleanliness was the leading principle in domestic economy, and the universal test of an able housewife—a character which formed the utmost ambition of our unenlightened grandmothers. The front door was never opened except on marriages, funerals, new year's days, the festival of St. Nicholas, or some such great occasion. It was ornamented with a gorgeous brass knocker, curiously wrought, sometimes in the device of a dog, and sometimes of a lion's head, and was daily burnished with such religious zeal, that it was ofttimes worn out by the very precautions taken for its preservation. The whole house was constantly in a state of inundation, under the discipline of mops and brooms and scrubbing brushes; and the good housewives of those days were a kind of amphibious animal, delighting exceedingly to be dabbling in water—insomuch that an historian of the day gravely tells us, that many of his townswomen grew to have webbed fingers like unto a duck; and some of them, he had little doubt, could the matter be examined into, would be found to have the tails of mermaids—but this I look upon to be a mere sport of fancy, or what is a worse, a wilful misrepresentation.

The grand parlor was the sanctum sanctorum, where the passion for cleaning was indulged without control. In this sacred apartment no one was permitted to enter, excepting the mistress and her confidential maid, who visited it once a week, for the purpose of giving it a thorough cleaning, and putting things to

rights—always taking the precaution of leaving their shoes at
the door, and entering devoutly on their stocking feet. After
scrubbing the floor, sprinkling it with fine white sand, which was
curiously stroked into angles, and curves, and rhomboids with a
broom—after washing the windows, rubbing and polishing the
furniture, and putting a new bunch of evergreens in the fire-
place—the window shutters were again closed to keep out the
flies, and the room carefully locked up until the revolution of
time brought round the weekly cleaning day.

As to the family, they always entered in at the gate, and most
generally lived in the kitchen.   To have seen a numerous household assembled round the fire, one would have imagined that he
was transported back to those happy days of primeval simplicity,
which float before our imaginations like golden visions.   The
fireplaces were of a truly patriarchal magnitude, where the
whole family, old and young, master and servant, black and
white, nay, even the very cat and dog, enjoyed a community of
privilege, and had each a right to a corner.   Here the old
burgher would sit in perfect silence, puffing his pipe, looking in
the fire with half shut eyes, and thinking of nothing for hours
together; the goede vrouw on the opposite side would employ
herself diligently in spinning yarn, or knitting stockings.   The
young folks would crowd around the hearth, listening with breathless attention to some old crone of a negro, who was the oracle
of the family, and who, perched like a raven in a corner of the
chimney, would croak forth for a long winter afternoon a string
of incredible stories about New England witches—grisly ghosts,
horses without heads—and hair-breadth escapes and bloody encounters among the Indians.

In those happy days a well regulated family always rose with the dawn, dined at eleven, and went to bed at sunset. Dinner was invariably a private meal, and the fat old burghers showed incontestable signs of disapprobation and uneasiness at being surprised by a visit from a neighbor on such occasions. But though our worthy ancestors were thus singularly averse to giving dinners, yet they kept up the social bands of intimacy by occasional banquetings, called tea-parties.

These fashionable parties were generally confined to the higher classes, or noblesse, that is to say, such as kept their own cows, and drove their own wagons. The company commonly assembled at three o'clock, and went away about six, unless it was in winter time, when the fashionable hours were a little earlier, that the ladies might get home before dark. The tea-table was crowned with a huge earthen dish, well stored with slices of fat pork, fried brown, cut up into morsels, and swimming in gravy. The company being seated round the genial board, and each furnished with a fork, evinced their dexterity in launching at the fattest pieces in this mighty dish—in much the same manner as sailors harpoon porpoises at sea, or our Indians spear salmon in the lakes. Sometimes the table was graced with immense apple pies, or saucers full of preserved peaches and pears; but it was always sure to boast an enormous dish of balls of sweetened dough, fried in hog's fat, and called doughnuts, or olykoeks—a delicious kind of cake, at present scarce known in this city, except in genuine Dutch families.

The tea was served out of a majestic delft tea-pot, ornamented with paintings of fat little Dutch shepherds and shepherdesses tending pigs—with boats sailing in the air, and houses built in the clouds, and sundry other ingenious Dutch fantasies. The beaux distinguished themselves by their adroitness in replenishing this pot from a huge copper tea-kettle, which would have made the pigmy macaronies of these degenerate days sweat merely to look at it. To sweeten the beverage, a lump of sugar was laid beside each cup—and the company alternately nibbled and sipped with great decorum, until an improvement was introduced by a shrewd and economic old lady, which was to suspend a large lump directly over the tea-table, by a string from the ceiling, so that it could be swung from mouth to mouth—an ingenious expedient, which is still kept up by some families in Albany; but which prevails without exception in Communipaw, Bergen, Flatbush, and all our uncontaminated Dutch villages.

At these primitive tea-parties the utmost propriety and dignity of deportment prevailed. No flirting nor coqueting—no gambling of old ladies nor hoyden chattering and romping of young ones—no self-satisfied struttings of wealthy gentlemen, with their brains in their pockets—nor amusing conceits, and monkey divertisements, of smart young gentlemen, with no brains at all. On the contrary, the young ladies seated themselves demurely in their rush-bottomed chairs, and knit their own woolen stockings; nor ever opened their lips excepting to say *yah Mynheer*, or *yah ya Vrouw*, to any question that was asked them; behaving, in all things, like decent, well-educated damsels. As to the gentlemen, each of them tranquilly smoked his pipe, and seemed lost in contemplation of the blue and white tiles with which the fireplaces were decorated; wherein sundry passages of Scripture were piously portrayed—Tobit and his dog figured to great advantage; Haman swung conspicuously on his gibbet, and Jonah appeared most manfully bouncing out of the whale, like Harlequin through a barrel of fire.

The parties broke up without noise and without confusion.

They were carried home by their own carriages, that is to say, by the vehicles nature had provided them, excepting such of the wealthy as could afford to keep a wagon. The gentlemen gallantly attended their fair ones to their respective abodes, and took leave of them with a hearty smack at the door: which, as it was an established piece of etiquette, done in perfect simplicity and honesty of heart, occasioned no scandal at that time, nor should it at the present—if our great-grandfathers approved of the custom, it would argue a great want of reverence in their descendants to say a word against it.

CHAPTER IV

CONTAINING FURTHER PARTICULARS OF THE GOLDEN AGE, AND
WHAT CONSTITUTED A FINE LADY AND GENTLEMAN IN THE
DAYS OF WALTER THE DOUBTER.

IN this dulcet period of my history, when the beauteous island of
Manna-hata presented a scene, the very counterpart of those
glowing pictures drawn of the golden reign of Saturn, there was,
as I have before observed, a happy ignorance, an honest simplicity
prevalent among its inhabitants, which, were I even able to de-
pict, would be but little understood by the degenerate age for
which I am doomed to write. Even the female sex, those arch
innovators upon the tranquillity, the honesty, and gray-beard customs of society, seemed for a while to conduct themselves with
incredible sobriety and comeliness.

Their hair, untortured by the abominations of art, was scrupulously pomatumed back from their foreheads with a candle, and
covered with a little cap of quilted calico, which fitted exactly to
their heads. Their petticoats of linsey-woolsey were striped with
a variety of gorgeous dyes—though I must confess these gallant
garments were rather short, scarce reaching below the knee; but
then they made up in the number, which generally equaled that
of the gentlemen's small clothes; and what is still more praise-

worthy, they were all of their own manufacture—of which circumstance, as may well be supposed, they were not a little vain.

These were the honest days, in which every woman staid at home, read the Bible, and wore pockets—ay, and that too of a goodly size, fashioned with patchwork into many curious devices, and ostentatiously worn on the outside. These, in fact, were convenient receptacles, where all good housewives carefully stored away such things as they wished to have at hand; by which means they often came to be incredibly crammed—and I remember there was a story current when I was a boy, that the lady of Wouter Van Twiller once had occasion to empty her right pocket in search of a wooden ladle, when the contents filled a couple of corn baskets, and the utensil was discovered lying among some rubbish in one corner—but we must not give too much faith to all these stories; the anecdotes of those remote periods being very subject to exaggeration.

Besides these notable pockets, they likewise wore scissors and pincushions suspended from their girdles by red ribands, or among the more opulent and showy classes, by brass, and even silver chains—indubitable tokens of thrifty housewives and industrious spinsters. I cannot say much in vindication of the shortness of the petticoats; it doubtless was introduced for the purpose of giving the stockings a chance to be seen, which were generally of blue worsted with magnificent red clocks—or perhaps to display a well-turned ankle, and a neat, though serviceable foot, set off by a high-heeled leathern shoe, with a large and splendid silver buckle. Thus we find that the gentle sex in all ages have shown the same disposition to infringe a little upon the laws of decorum, in order to betray a lurking beauty, or gratify an innocent love of finery.

From the sketch here given, it will be seen that our good grandmothers differed considerably in their ideas of a fine figure from their scantily dressed descendants of the present day. A fine lady, in those times, waddled under more clothes, even on a fair summer's day, than would have clad the whole bevy of a modern ball-room. Nor were they the less admired by the gentlemen in consequence thereof. On the contrary, the greatness of a lover's passion seemed to increase in proportion to the magnitude of its object—and a voluminous damsel, arrayed in a dozen of petticoats, was declared by a Low Dutch sonneteer of the province to be radiant as a sunflower, and luxuriant as a full-blown cabbage. Certain it is, that in those days the heart of a lover could not contain more than one lady at a time ; whereas the heart of a modern gallant has often room enough to accommodate half a dozen. The reason of which I conclude to be, that either the hearts of the gentlemen have grown larger, or the persons of the ladies smaller —this, however, is a question for physiologists to determine.

But there was a secret charm in these petticoats, which, no doubt, entered into the consideration of the prudent gallants. The wardrobe of a lady was in those days her only fortune; and she who had a good stock of petticoats and stockings, was as absolutely an heiress as is a Kamschatka damsel with a store of bear skins, or a Lapland belle with a plenty of reindeer. The ladies, therefore, were very anxious to display these powerful attractions to the greatest advantage ; and the best rooms in the house, instead of being adorned with caricatures of dame Nature, in watercolors and needle-work, were always hung round with abundance of homespun garments, the manufacture and the property of the females—a piece of laudable ostentation that still prevails among the heiresses of our Dutch villages.

The gentlemen, in fact, who figured in the circles of the gay world in these ancient times, corresponded, in most particulars, with the beauteous damsels whose smiles they were ambitious to deserve. True it is, their merits would make but a very inconsiderable impression upon the heart of a modern fair; they neither drove their curricles nor sported their tandems, for as yet those gaudy vehicles were not even dreamt of—neither did they distinguish themselves by their brilliancy at the table, and their consequent rencontres with watchmen, for our forefathers were of too pacific a disposition to need those guardians of the night, every soul throughout the town being sound asleep before nine o'clock. Neither did they establish their claims to gentility at the expense of their tailors—for as yet those offenders against the pockets of society, and the tranquillity of all aspiring young gentlemen, were unknown in New-Amsterdam; every good housewife made the clothes of her husband and family, and even the goede vrouw of Van Twiller himself thought it no disparagement to cut out her husband's linsey-woolsey galligaskins.

Not but what there were some two or three youngsters who manifested the first dawning of what is called fire and spirit; who held all labor in contempt; skulked about docks and market places; loitered in the sunshine; squandered what little money they could procure at hustle-cap and chuck-farthing; swore, boxed, fought cocks, and raced their neighbor's horses—in short, who promised to be the wonder, the talk, and abomination of the town, had not their stylish career been unfortunately cut short by an affair of honor with a whipping-post.

Far other, however, was the truly fashionable gentleman of those days—his dress, which served for both morning and evening, street and drawing-room, was a linsey-woolsey coat, made,

perhaps, by the fair hands of the mistress of his affections, and
gallantly bedecked with abundance of large brass buttons—half
a score of breeches heightened the proportions of his figure—his
shoes were decorated by enormous copper buckles—a low-crowned
broad-brimmed hat overshadowed his burly visage, and his hair
dangled down his back in a prodigious queue of eelskin.

Thus equipped, he would manfully sally forth with pipe in
mouth to besiege some fair damsel's obdurate heart—not such a
pipe, good reader, as that which Acis did sweetly tune in praise
of his Galatea, but one of true Delft manufacture, and furnished
with a charge of fragrant tobacco.   With this would he resolutely set himself down before the fortress, and rarely failed, in
the process of time, to smoke the fair enemy into a surrender,
upon honorable terms.

Such was the happy reign of Wouter Van Twilier, celebrated
in many a long forgotten song as the real golden age, the rest
being nothing but counterfeit copper-washed coin.   In that delightful period, a sweet and holy calm reigned over the whole
province.   The burgomaster smoked his pipe in peace—the substantial solace of his domestic cares, after her daily toils were
done, sat soberly at the door, with her arms crossed over her
apron of snowy white, without being insulted by ribald street-
walkers or vagabond boys—those unlucky urchins, who do so
infest our streets, displaying under the roses of youth the thorns
and briers of iniquity.   Then it was that the lover with ten
breeches, and the damsel with petticoats of half a score, indulged
in all the innocent endearments of virtuous love without fear and
without reproach ; for what had that virtue to fear, which was
defended by a shield of good linsey-woolseys, equal at least to the
seven bull-hides of the invincible Ajax ?

Ah blissful, and never to be forgotten age! when every thing was better than it has ever been since, or ever will be again— when Buttermilk Channel was quite dry at low water—when the shad in the Hudson were all salmon, and when the moon shone with a pure and resplendent whiteness, instead of that melancholy yellow light which is the consequence of her sickening at the abominations she every night witnesses in this degenerate city!

Happy would it have been for New-Amsterdam could it always have existed in this state of blissful ignorance and lowly simplicity, but alas! the days of childhood are too sweet to last! Cities, like men, grow out of them in time, and are doomed alike to grow into the bustle, the cares, and miseries of the world. Let no man congratulate himself, when he beholds the child of his bosom or the city of his birth increasing in magnitude and importance—let the history of his own life teach him the dangers of the one, and this excellent little history of Manna-hata convince him of the calamities of the other.

CHAPTER V.

IT has already been mentioned that, in the early times of Oloffe
the Dreamer, a frontier post, or trading-house, called Fort Aurania, had been established on the upper waters of the Hudson, precisely on the site of the present venerable city of Albany; which
was at that time considered at the very end of the habitable world.
It was, indeed, a remote possession with which, for a long time,
New-Amsterdam held but little intercourse. Now and then the
"Company's Yacht," as it was called, was sent to the Fort with
supplies, and to bring away the peltries which had been purchased
of the Indians. It was like an expedition to the Indias, or the
North Pole, and always made great talk in the settlement. Sometimes an adventurous burgher would accompany the expedition,
to the great uneasiness of his friends; but, on his return, had so
many stories to tell of storms and tempests on the Tappaan Zee,
of hobgoblins in the Highlands and at the Devils Dans Kam-
mer, and of all the other wonders and perils with which the river

abounded in those early days, that he deterred the less **adven-**turous inhabitants from following his example.

Matters were in this state, when, one day, as **Walter the** Doubter and his burgermeesters were smoking and pondering **over** the affairs of the province, they were roused by the report **of a** cannon. Sallying forth, they beheld a strange vessel at anchor in the bay. It was unquestionably of Dutch build; broad bot-tomed and high pooped, and bore the flag of their High Mighti-nesses at the mast-head.

After a while a boat put off for land, and a stranger stepped on shore, a lofty, lordly kind of man, tall and dry, with a meagre face, furnished with huge moustaches. He was clad in Flemish doublet and hose, and an insufferably tall hat, with a cocktail feather. Such was the patroon Killian Van Rensellaer, who had come out from Holland to found a colony or patroonship on a great tract of wild land, granted to him by their High Mighti-nesses the Lords States General, in the upper regions of the Hudson.

Killian Van Rensellaer was a nine days' wonder in New-Amsterdam ; for he carried a high head, looked down upon the portly, short-legged burgomasters, and owned no allegiance to the governor himself; boasting that he held his patroonship directly from the Lords States General.

He tarried but a short time in New-Amsterdam ; merely to beat up recruits for his colony. Few, however, ventured to enlist for those remote and savage regions ; and when they embarked, their friends took leave of them as if they should never see them more ; and stood gazing with tearful eye as the stout, round-sterned little vessel ploughed and splashed its way up the Hudson, with great noise and little progress, taking nearly a day to get out of sight of the city.

And now, from time to time, floated down tidings to the Manhattoes of the growing importance of this new colony. Every account represented Killian Van Rensellaer as rising in importance and becoming a mighty patroon in the land. He had received more recruits from Holland. His patroonship of Rensellaerwick lay immediately below Fort Aurania, and extended for several miles on each side of the Hudson, beside embracing the mountainous region of the Helderberg. Over all this he claimed to hold separate jurisdiction independent of the colonial authorities at New-Amsterdam.

All these assumptions of authority were duly reported to Governor Van Twiller and his council, by dispatches from Fort Aurania; at each new report the governor and his counsellors looked at each other, raised their eyebrows, gave an extra puff or two of smoke, and then relapsed into their usual tranquillity.

At length tidings came that the patroon of Rensellaerwick had extended his usurpations along the river, beyond the limits granted him by their High Mightinesses; and that he had even seized upon a rocky island in the Hudson, commonly known by the name of Bearn or Bear's Island; where he was erecting a fortress to be called by the lordly name of Rensellaerstein.

Wouter Van Twiller was roused by this intelligence. After consulting with his burgomasters, he dispatched a letter to the patroon of Rensellaerwick, demanding by what right he had seized upon this island, which lay beyond the bounds of his patroonship. The answer of Killian Van Rensellaer was in his own lordly style, "*By wapen recht !*" that is to say, by the right

of arms, or, in common parlance, by club-law. This answer
plunged the worthy Wouter in one of the deepest doubts he had
in the whole course of his administration ; in the meantime, while
Wouter doubted, the lordly Killian went on to finish his fortress
of Rensellaerstein, about which I foresee I shall have something
to record in a future chapter of this most eventful history.

CHAPTER VI.

IN the year of our Lord one thousand eight hundred and four, on a fine afternoon in the glowing month of September, I took my customary walk upon the battery, which is at once the pride and bulwark of this ancient and impregnable city of New-York. The ground on which I trod was hallowed by recollections of the past, and as I slowly wandered through the long alley of poplars, which, like so many birch brooms standing on end, diffused a melancholy and lugubrious shade, my imagination drew a contrast between the surrounding scenery, and what it was in the classic days of our forefathers. Where the government house by name, but the custom house by occupation, proudly reared its brick walls and wooden pillars, there whilom stood the low, but substantial, red-tiled mansion of the renowned Wouter Van Twiller. Around it the mighty bulwarks of Fort Amsterdam frowned defiance to every absent foe; but, like many a whiskered warrior and gallant militia captain, confined their martial deeds to frowns alone. The mud breastworks had long been leveled with the earth, and their site converted into the green lawns and leafy alleys of the battery; where the gay apprentice sported his Sunday coat, and the laborious mechanic, relieved from the dirt and drudgery of the week, poured his weekly tale of love into the half averted ear of the sentimental chambermaid. The capacious bay still presented the same expansive sheet of water, studded with islands, sprinkled with fishing boats, and bounded by shores of picturesque beauty. But the dark forests which once clothed those shores had been violated by the savage hand of cultivation, and their tangled mazes, and impenetrable thickets, had degenerated into teeming orchards and waving fields of grain. Even Governor's Island, once a smiling garden, appertaining to the sovereigns of the province, was now covered with fortifications, inclosing a tremendous block-house—so that this once peaceful island resembled a fierce little warrior in a big cocked hat, breathing gunpowder and defiance to the world!

For some time did I indulge in a pensive train of thought; contrasting, in sober sadness, the present day with the hallowed years behind the mountains; lamenting the melancholy progress of improvement, and praising the zeal with which our worthy burghers endeavor to preserve the wrecks of venerable customs, prejudices, and errors, from the overwhelming tide of modern innovation—when by degrees my ideas took a different turn, and I insensibly awakened to an enjoyment of the beauties around me.

It was one of those rich autumnal days which heaven particularly bestows upon the beauteous island of Manna-hata and its vicinity—not a floating cloud obscured the azure firmament— the sun, rolling in glorious splendor through his ethereal course, seemed to expand his honest Dutch countenance into an unusual expression of benevolence, as he smiled his evening salutation upon a city which he delights to visit with his most bounteous beams—the very winds seemed to hold in their breaths in mute attention, lest they should ruffle the tranquillity of the hour—and the waveless bosom of the bay presented a polished mirror, in which nature beheld herself and smiled. The standard of our city, reserved like a choice handkerchief, for days of gala, hung motionless on the flag-staff, which forms the handle of a gigantic churn ; and even the tremulous leaves of the poplar and the aspen ceased to vibrate to the breath of heaven. Every thing seemed to acquiesce in the profound repose of nature. The formidable eighteen-pounders slept in the embrazures of the wooden batteries, seemingly gathering fresh strength to fight the battles of their country on the next fourth of July—the solitary drum on Governor's Island forgot to call the garrison to their *shovels*—the evening gun had not yet sounded its signal for all the regular well-meaning poultry throughout the country to go to roost ; and the fleet of canoes at anchor between Cibbet Island and Communipaw, slumbered on their rakes, and suffered the innocent oysters to lie for a while unmolested in the soft mud of their native banks !—My own feelings sympathized with the contagious tranquillity, and I should infallibly have dozed upon one of those fragments of benches, which our benevolent magistrates have provided for the benefit of convalescent loungers, had not the extraordinary inconvenience of the couch set all repose at defiance.

In the midst of this slumber of the soul, my attention was attracted to a black speck, peering above the western horizon, just in the rear of Bergen steeple—gradually it augments and overhangs the would-be cities of Jersey, Harsimus, and Hoboken, which, like three jockies, are starting on the course of existence, and jostling each other at the commencement of the race. Now it skirts the long shore of ancient Pavonia, spreading its wide shadows from the high settlements of Weehawk quite to the lazaretto and quarantine, erected by the sagacity of our police, for the embarrassment of commerce—now it climbs the serene vault of heaven, cloud rolling over cloud, shrouding the orb of day, darkening the vast expanse, and bearing thunder and hail and tempest in its bosom. The earth seems agitated at the confusion of the heavens—the late waveless mirror is lashed into furious waves that roll in hollow murmurs to the shore—the oyster boats that erst sported in the placid vicinity of Gibbet Island, now hurry affrighted to the land—the poplar writhes and twists and whistles in the blast—torrents of drenching rain and sounding hail deluge the battery walks—the gates are thronged by apprentices, servant maids, and little Frenchmen, with pocket handkerchiefs over their hats, scampering from the storm—the late beauteous prospect presents one scene of anarchy and wild uproar, as though old Chaos had resumed his reign, and was hurling back into one vast turmoil the conflicting elements of nature.

Whether I fled from the fury of the storm, or remained boldly at my post, as our gallant train-band captains, who march their soldiers through the rain without flinching, are points which I leave to the conjecture of the reader. It is possible he may be a little perplexed also to know the reason why I introduced this tremendous tempest to disturb the serenity of my work. On this latter point I will gratuitously instruct his ignorance. The panorama view of the battery was given merely to gratify the reader with a correct description of that celebrated place, and the parts adjacent—secondly, the storm was played off partly to give a little bustle and life to this tranquil part of my work, and to keep

8*

my drowsy readers from falling asleep—and partly to serve as an overture to the tempestuous times which are about to assail the pacific province of Nieuw-Nederlandts—and which overhang the slumbrous administration of the renowned Wouter Van Twiller. It is thus the experienced playwright puts all the fiddles, the French-horns, the kettle-drums, and trumpets of his orchestra in requisition, to usher in one of those horrible and brimstone up-roars called Melodrames—and it is thus he discharges his thunder, his lightning, his rosin, and saltpetre, preparatory to the rising of a ghost, or the murdering of a hero.—We will now proceed with our history.

Whatever may be advanced by philosophers to the contrary, I am of opinion that, as to nations, the old maxim, that "honesty is the best policy," is a sheer and ruinous mistake. It might have answered well enough in the honest times when it was made ; but in these degenerate days, if a nation pretends to rely merely upon the justice of its dealings, it will fare something like the honest man who fell among thieves, and found his honesty a poor protection against bad company. Such, at least, was the case with the guileless government of the New-Netherlands ; which, like a worthy unsuspicious old burgher, quietly settled itself down in the city of New-Amsterdam, as into a snug elbow chair—and fell into a comfortable nap—while, in the meantime, its cunning neighbors stepped in and picked its pockets. In a word, we may ascribe the commencement of all the woes of this great province, and its magnificent metropolis, to the tranquil security, or, to speak more accurately, to the unfortunate honesty of its govern-ment. But as I dislike to begin an important part of my history towards the end of a chapter ; and as my readers, like myself, must doubtless be exceedingly fatigued with the long walk we have taken, and the tempest we have sustained—I hold it meet we shut up the book, smoke a pipe, and having thus refreshed our spirits, take a fair start in a new chapter.

CHAPTER VII.

THAT my readers may the more fully comprehend the extent of
the calamity, at this very moment impending over the honest,
unsuspecting province of Nieuw-Nederlandts, and its dubious
governor, it is necessary that I should give some account of a
horde of strange barbarians, bordering upon the eastern frontier.

Now so it came to pass, that many years previous to the time
of which we are treating, the sage cabinet of England had adopted
a certain national creed, a kind of public walk of faith, or rather
a religious turnpike, in which every loyal subject was directed to
travel to Zion—taking care to pay the *toll-gatherers* by the way.

Albeit a certain shrewd race of men, being very much given
to indulge their own opinions on all manner of subjects (a propensity exceedingly offensive to your free governments of Europe),
did most presumptuously dare to think for themselves in matters
of religion, exercising what they considered a natural and unex-
tinguishable right—the liberty of conscience.

As, however, they possessed that ingenuous habit of mind

which always thinks aloud; which rides cock-a-hoop on the tongue, and is for ever galloping into other people's ears, it naturally followed that their liberty of conscience likewise implied *liberty of speech*, which being freely indulged, soon put the country in a hubbub, and aroused the pious indignation of the vigilant fathers of the church.

The usual methods were adopted to reclaim them, which in those days were considered efficacious in bringing back stray sheep to the fold; that is to say, they were coaxed, they were admonished, they were menaced, they were buffeted—line upon line, precept upon precept, lash upon lash, here a little and there a great deal, were exhausted without mercy, and without success; until the worthy pastors of the church, wearied out by their unparalleled stubbornness, were driven in the excess of their tender mercy, to adopt the Scripture text, and literally to "heap live embers on their heads."

Nothing, however, could subdue that independence of the tongue which has ever distinguished this singular race, so that, rather than subject that heroic member to further tyranny, they one and all embarked for the wilderness of America, to enjoy, unmolested, the inestimable right of talking. And, in fact, no sooner did they land upon the shore of this free-spoken country, than they all lifted up their voices, and made such a clamor of tongues, that we are told they frightened every bird and beast out of the neighborhood, and struck such mute terror into certain fish, that they have been called *dumb-fish* ever since.

This may appear marvelous, but it is nevertheless true, in proof of which I would observe, that the dumb-fish has ever since become an object of superstitious reverence, and forms the Saturday's dinner of every true Yankee.

The simple aborigines of the land for a while contemplated these strange folk in utter astonishment, but discovering that they wielded harmless, though noisy weapons, and were a lively, ingenious, good-humored race of men, they became very friendly and sociable, and gave them the name of *Yanokies,* which in the Mais-Tchusaeg (or Massachusett) language signifies *silent men*—a waggish appellation, since shortened into the familiar epithet of YANKEES, which they retain unto the present day.

True it is, and my fidelity as a historian will not allow me to pass over the fact, that having served a regular apprenticeship in the school of persecution, these ingenious people soon showed that they had become masters of the art. The great majority were of one particular mode of thinking in matters of religion ; but to their great surprise and indignation, they found that divers papists, quakers and anabaptists were springing up among them, and all claiming to use the liberty of speech. This was at once pronounced a daring abuse of the liberty of conscience ; which they now insisted was nothing more than the liberty to think as one pleased in matters of religion—provided one thought right; for otherwise it would be giving a latitude to damnable heresies. Now as they, the majority, were convinced that they alone thought right, it consequently followed, that whoever thought different from them thought wrong—and whoever thought wrong, and obstinately persisted in not being convinced and converted, was a flagrant violator of the inestimable liberty of conscience, and a corrupt and infectious member of the body politic, and deserved to be lopped off and cast into the fire. The consequence of all which was a fiery persecution of divers sects, and especially of quakers.

Now I'll warrant there are hosts of my readers, ready at once to lift up their hands and eyes, with that virtuous indignation with which we contemplate the faults and errors of our neighbors, and, to exclaim at the preposterous idea of convincing the mind by tormenting the body, and establishing the doctrine of charity and forbearance by intolerant persecution. But in simple truth, what are we doing at this very day, and in this very enlightened nation, but acting upon the very same principle in our political controversies? Have we not within but a few years released ourselves from the shackles of a government which cruelly denied us the privilege of governing ourselves, and using in full latitude that invaluable member, the tongue? and are we not at this very moment striving our best to tyrannize over the opinions, tie up the tongues, and ruin the fortunes of one another? What are our great political societies, but mere political inquisitions—our pothouse committees but little tribunals of denunciation—our newspapers but mere whipping-posts and pillories, where unfortunate individuals are pelted with rotten eggs—and our council of appointment, but a grand *auto da fe*, where culprits are annually sacrificed for their political heresies?

Where then is the difference in principle between our measures and those you are so ready to condemn among the people I am treating of? There is none; the difference is merely circumstantial.—Thus we *denounce*, instead of banishing—we *libel*, instead of scourging—we *turn out of office*, instead of hanging—and where they burnt an offender in proper person, we either tar and feather or *burn him in effigy*—this political persecution being, somehow or other, the grand palladium of our liberties, and an incontrovertible proof that this is *a free country!*

But notwithstanding the fervent zeal with which this holy war was prosecuted against the whole race of unbelievers, we do not find that the population of this new colony was in anywise hindered thereby ; on the contrary, they multiplied to a degree which would be incredible to any man unacquainted with the marvelous fecundity of this growing country.

This amazing increase may, indeed, be partly ascribed to a singular custom prevalent among them, commonly known by the name of *bundling,*—a superstitious rite observed by the young people of both sexes, with which they usually terminated their festivities ; and which was kept up with religious strictness by the more bigoted part of the community. This ceremony was likewise, in those primitive times, considered as an indispensable preliminary to matrimony ; their courtships commencing where ours usually finish—by which means they acquired that intimate acquaintance with each others' good qualities before marriage, which has been pronounced by philosophers the sure basis of a happy union. Thus early did this cunning and ingenious people display a shrewdness of making a bargain, which has ever since distingnished them—and a strict adherence to the good old vulgar maxim about "buying a pig in a poke."

To this sagacious custom, therefore, do I chiefly attribute the unparalleled increase of the Yanokie or Yankee race ; for it is a certain fact, well authenticated by court records and parish registers, that wherever the practice of bundling prevailed, there was an amazing number of sturdy brats annually born unto the State, without the license of the law, or the benefit of clergy. Neither did the irregularity of their birth operate in the least to their disparagement. On the contrary, they grew up a long-sided, raw-boned, hardy race of whoreson whalers, wood-cutters, fishermen, and pedlers, and strapping corn-fed wenches ; who by their united efforts tended marvelously towards peopling those notable tracts of country called Nantucket, Piscataway, and Cape Cod.

CHAPTER VIII.

HOW THESE SINGULAR BARBARIANS TURNED OUT TO BE NO-
TORIOUS SQUATTERS—HOW THEY BUILT AIR CASTLES, AND
ATTEMPTED TO INITIATE THE NEDERLANDERS INTO THE
MYSTERY OF BUNDLING.

IN the last chapter I have given a faithful and unprejudiced
account of the origin of that singular race of people, inhabiting
the country eastward of the Nieuw-Nederlandts; but I have yet
to mention certain peculiar habits which rendered them exceedingly annoying to our ever honored Dutch ancestors.

The most prominent of these was a certain rambling propensity, with which, like the sons of Ishmael, they seem to have been
gifted by heaven, and which continually goads them on, to shift
their residence from place to place, so that a Yankee farmer is
in a constant state of migration; *tarrying* occasionally here and
there; clearing lands for other people to enjoy, building houses
for others to inhabit, and in a manner may be considered the
wandering Arab of America.

His first thought, on coming to the years of manhood, is to
settle himself in the world—which means nothing more nor less
than to begin his rambles. To this end he takes unto himself for
a wife some buxom country heiress, passing rich in red ribands,
glass beads, and mock tortoise-shell combs, with a white gown

and morocco shoes for Sunday, and deeply skilled in the mystery of making apple sweatmeats, long sauce, and pumpkin pie.

Having thus provided himself, like a pedler with a heavy knapsack, wherewith to regale his shoulders through the journey of life, he literally sets out on the peregrination. His whole family, household furniture, and farming utensils, are hoisted into a covered cart; his own and his wife's wardrobe packed up in a firkin—which done, he shoulders his axe, takes staff in hand, whistles "yankee doodle," and trudges off to the woods, as confident of the protection of Providence, and relying as cheerfully upon his own resources, as did ever a patriarch of yore, when he journeyed into a strange country of the Gentiles. Having buried himself in the wilderness, he builds himself a log hut, clears away a cornfield and potato patch, and Providence smiling upon his labors, is soon surrounded by a snug farm and some half a score of flaxen-headed urchins, who, by their size, seem to have sprung all at once out of the earth, like a crop of toadstools.

But it is not the nature of this most indefatigable of speculators to rest contented with any state of sublunary enjoyment—*improvement* is his darling passion, and having thus improved his lands, the next care is to provide a mansion worthy the residence of a landholder. A huge palace of pine boards immediately springs up in the midst of the wilderness, large enough for a parish church, and furnished with windows of all dimensions, but so rickety and flimsy withal, that every blast gives it a fit of the ague.

By the time the outside of this mighty air castle is completed, either the funds or the zeal of our adventurer are exhausted, so that he barely manages to half finish one room within, where the whole family burrow together—while the rest of the house is

devoted to the curing of pumpkins, or storing of carrots and potatoes, and is decorated with fanciful festoons of dried apples and
peaches.   The outside remaining unpainted, grows venerably
black with time; the family wardrobe is laid under contribution
for old hats, petticoats, and breeches, to stuff into the broken windows, while the four winds of heaven keep up a whistling and
howling about this aerial palace, and play as many unruly gambols as they did of yore in the cave of old Æolus.

The humble log hut, which whilom nestled this *improving*
family snugly within its narrow but comfortable walls, stands hard
by, in ignominious contrast, degraded into a cow-house or pig-
sty; and the whole scene reminds one forcibly of a fable, which
I am surprised has never been recorded, of an aspiring snail, who
abandoned his humble habitation, which he had long filled with
great respectability, to crawl into the empty shell of a lobster—
where he would no doubt have resided with great style and splendor, the envy and the hate of all the painstaking snails in the
neighborhood, had he not perished with cold, in one corner of his
stupendous mansion.

Being thus completely settled, and, to use his own words, " to
rights," one would imagine that he would begin to enjoy the comforts of his situation, to read newspapers, talk politics, neglect his
own business, and attend to the affairs of the nation, like a useful
and patriotic citizen; but now it is that his wayward disposition
begins again to operate.   He soon grows tired of a spot where
there is no longer any room for improvement—sells his farm, air
castle, petticoat windows and all, reloads his cart, shoulders his
axe, puts himself at the head of his family, and wanders away in
search of new lands—again to fell trees—again to clear cornfields
—again to build a shingle palace, and again to sell off and wander.

Such were the people of Connecticut, who bordered upon the eastern frontier of New-Netherlands, and my readers may easily imagine what uncomfortable neighbors this light-hearted but restless tribe must have been to our tranquil progenitors. If they cannot, I would ask them, if they have ever known one of our regular, well-organized Dutch families, whom it hath pleased heaven to afflict with the neighborhood of a French boarding-house? The honest old burgher cannot take his afternoon s pipe on the bench before his door, but he is persecuted with the scraping of fiddles, the chattering of women, and the squalling of children—he cannot sleep at night for the horrible melodies of some amateur, who chooses to serenade the moon, and display his terrible proficiency in *execution*, on the clarionet, hautboy, or some other soft-toned instrument—nor can he leave the street door open, but his house is defiled by the unsavory visits of a troop of pup dogs, who even sometimes carry their loathsome ravages into the sanctum sanctorum, the parlor!

If my readers have ever witnessed the sufferings of such a family, so situated, they may form some idea how our worthy ancestors were distressed by their mercurial neighbors of Connecticut.

Gangs of these marauders, we are told, penetrated into the New-Netherland settlements, and threw whole villages into consternation by their unparalleled volubility, and their intolerable inquisitiveness—two evil habits hitherto unknown in those parts, or only known to be abhorred; for our ancestors were noted as being men of truly Spartan taciturnity, and who neither knew nor cared aught about any body's concerns but their own. Many enormities were committed on the highways, where several unoffending burghers were brought to a stand, and tortured with questions and guesses, which outrages occasioned as much vexation and heart-burning as does the modern right of search on the high seas.

Great jealousy did they likewise stir up, by their intermeddling and successes among the divine sex; for being a race of brisk, likely, pleasant-tongued varlets, they soon seduced the light affections of the simple damsels from their ponderous Dutch gallants. Among other hideous customs, they attempted to introduce among them that of *bundling*, which the Dutch lasses of the Nederlandts, with that eager passion for novelty and foreign fashions natural to their sex, seemed very well inclined to follow, but that their mothers, being more experienced in the world, and better acquainted with men and things, strenuously discountenanced all such outlandish innovations.

But what chiefly operated to embroil our ancestors with these strange folk, was an unwarrantable liberty which they occasionally took of entering in hordes into the territories of the New-Netherlands, and settling themselves down, without leave or license, to *improve* the land, in the manner I have before noticed. This unceremonious mode of taking possession of *new land* was technically termed *squatting*, and hence is derived the appellation of *squatters*; a name odious in the ears of all great landholders, and which is given to those enterprising worthies who seize upon land first, and take their chance to make good their title to it afterwards.

All these grievances, and many others which were constantly accumulating, tended to form that dark and portentous cloud, which, as I observed in a former chapter, was slowly gathering over the tranquil province of New-Netherlands. The pacific cabinet of Van Twiller, however, as will be perceived in the sequel, bore them all with a magnanimity that redounds to their immortal credit—becoming by passive endurance inured to this increasing mass of wrongs; like that mighty man of old, who by dint of carrying about a calf from the time it was born, continued to carry it without difficulty when it had grown to be an ox.

CHAPTER IX.

HOW THE FORT GOED HOOP WAS FEARFULLY BELEAGUERED—
HOW THE RENOWNED WOUTER FELL INTO A PROFOUND
DOUBT, AND HOW HE FINALLY EVAPORATED.

BY this time my readers must fully perceive what an arduous
task I have undertaken—exploring a little kind of Herculaneum
of history, which had lain nearly for ages buried under the rubbish of years, and almost totally forgotten—raking up the limbs
and fragments of disjointed facts, and endeavoring to put them
scrupulously together, so as to restore them to their original form
and connection—now lugging forth the character of an almost
forgotten hero, like a mutilated statue—now deciphering a half
defaced inscription, and now lighting upon a mouldering manuscript, which, after painful study, scarce repays the trouble of
perusal.

In such case how much has the reader to depend upon the
honor and probity of his author, lest, like a cunning antiquarian,
he either impose upon him some spurious fabrication of his own,
for a precious relic from antiquity—or else dress up the dismem-
bered fragment with such false trappings, that it is scarcely possible to distinguish the truth from the fiction with which it is en
veloped. This is a grievance which I have more than once had

to lament, in the course of my wearisome researches among the works of my fellow historians, who have strangely disguised and distorted the facts respecting this country; and particularly respecting the great province of New-Netherlands; as will be perceived by any who will take the trouble to compare their romantic effusions, tricked out in the meretricious gauds of fable, with this authentic history.

I have had more vexations of the kind to encounter, in those parts of my history which treat of the transactions on the eastern border, than in any other, in consequence of the troops of historians who have infested those quarters, and have shown the honest people of Nieuw-Nederlandts no mercy in their works. Among the rest, Mr. Benjamin Trumbull arrogantly declares, that "the Dutch were always mere intruders."—Now to this I shall make no other reply, than to proceed in the steady narration of my history, which will contain not only proofs that the Dutch had clear title and possession in the fair valleys of the Connecticut, and that they were wrongfully dispossessed thereof—but likewise, that they have been scandalously maltreated ever since, by the misrepresentations of the crafty historians of New-England. And in this I shall be guided by a spirit of truth and impartiality, and a regard to immortal fame—for I would not wittingly dishonor my work by a single falsehood, misrepresentation, or prejudice, though it should gain our forefathers the whole country of New-England.

I have already noticed in a former chapter of my history, that the territories of the Nieuw-Nederlandts extended on the east, quite to the Varshe or fresh, or Connecticut river. Here, at an early period, had been established a frontier post on the bank of the river, and called Fort Goed Hoop, not far from the site of the present fair city of Hartford. It was placed under the command of Jacobus Van Curlet, or Curlis, as some historians will have it; a doughty soldier, of that stomachful class famous for eating all they kill. He was long in the body and short in the limb, as though a tall man's body had been mounted on a little man's legs. He made up for this turnspit construction by striding to such an extent, that you would have sworn he had on the seven-leagued boots of Jack the Giant-killer; and so high did he tread on parade, that his soldiers were sometimes alarmed lest he should trample himself under foot.

But notwithstanding the erection of this fort and the appointment of this ugly little man of war as commander, the Yankees continued the interlopings hinted at in my last chapter, and at length had the audacity to *squat* themselves down within the jurisdiction of Fort Goed Hoop.

The long-bodied Van Curlet protested with great spirit against these unwarrantable encroachments, couching his protest in Low Dutch, by way of inspiring more terror, and forthwith dispatched a copy of the protest to the governor at New-Amsterdam, together with a long and bitter account of the aggressions of the enemy. This done, he ordered his men, one and all, to be of good cheer—shut the gate of the fort, smoked three pipes, went to bed, and awaited the result with a resolute and intrepid tranquillity, that greatly animated his adherents, and no doubt struck sore dismay and affright into the hearts of the enemy.

Now it came to pass, that about this time, the renowned Wouter Van Twiller, full of years and honors, and council dinners, had reached that period of life and faculty which, according to the great Gulliver, entitles a man to admission into the ancient order of Struldbruggs. He employed his time in smoking his

9

Turkish pipe, amid an assemblage of sages, equally enlightened, and nearly as venerable as himself, and who, for their silence, their gravity, their wisdom, and their cautious averseness to coming to any conclusion in business, are only to be equaled by certain profound corporations which I have known in my time. Upon reading the protest of the gallant Jacobus Van Curlet, therefore, his excellency fell straightway into one of the deepest doubts that ever he was known to encounter; his capacious head gradually drooped on his chest, he closed his eyes, and inclined his ear to one side, as if listening with great attention to the discussion that was going on in his belly; and which all who knew him declared to be the huge court-house or council-chamber of his thoughts; forming to his head what the house of representatives does to the senate. An inarticulate sound, very much resembling a snore, occasionally escaped him—but the nature of this internal cogitation was never known, as he never opened his lips on the subject to man, woman, or child. In the meantime. the protest of Van Curlet laid quietly on the table, where it served to light the pipes of the venerable sages assembled in council; and in the great smoke which they raised, the gallant Jacobus, his protest, and his mighty fort Goed Hoop, were soon as completely beclouded and forgotten, as is a question of emergency swallowed up in the speeches and resolutions of a modern session of Congress.

There are certain emergencies when your profound legislators and sage deliberative councils are mightily in the way of a nation; and when an ounce of hair-brained decision is worth a pound of sage doubt and cautious discussion. Such, at least, was the case at present; for while the renowned Wouter Van Twiller was daily battling with his doubts, and his resolution growing weaker and weaker in the contest, the enemy pushed farther and farther into his territories, and assumed a most formidable appearance in the neighborhood of fort Goed Hoop. Here they founded the mighty town of *Pyquag*, or, as it has since been called, *Weathersfield*, a place which, if we may credit the assertions of that worthy historian, John Josselyn, Gent., "hath been infamous by reason of the witches therein."—And so daring did these men of Pyquag become, that they extended those plantations of onions, for which their town is illustrious, under the very noses of the garrison of fort Goed Hoop—insomuch that the honest Dutchmen could not look toward that quarter without tears in their eyes.

This crying injustice was regarded with proper indignation by the gallant Jacobus Van Curlet.—He absolutely trembled with the violence of his choler and the exacerbations of his valor; which were the more turbulent in their workings, from the length of the body in which they were agitated. He forthwith proceeded to strengthen his redoubts, heighten his breastworks, deepen his fosse, and fortify his position with a double row of abbatis; after which he dispatched a fresh courier with accounts of his perilous situation.

The courier chosen to bear the dispatches was a fat oily little man, as being less liable to be worn out, or to lose leather on the journey: and to insure his speed, he was mounted on the fleetest wagon horse in the garrison, remarkable for length of limb, largeness of bone, and hardness of trot; and so tall, that the little messenger was obliged to climb on his back by means of his tail and crupper. Such extraordinary speed did he make, that he arrived at fort Amsterdam in a little less than a month, though the distance was full two hundred pipes, or about one hundred and twenty miles.

With an appearance of great hurry and business, and smoking
a short traveling-pipe, he proceeded on a long swing trot
through the muddy lanes of the metropolis, demolishing whole
batches of dirt pies, which the little Dutch children were making
in the road; and for which kind of pastry the children of this city
have ever been famous.   On arriving at the governor's house, he
climbed down from his steed; roused the gray-headed door-
keeper, old Skaats, who, like his lineal descendant and faithful re-
presentative, the venerable crier of our court, was nodding at his
post—rattled at the door of the council chamber, and startled the
members as they were dozing over a plan for establishing a public market.

At that very moment a gentle grunt, or rather a deep-drawn
snore, was heard from the chair of the governor ; a whiff of smoke
was at the same instant observed to escape from his lips, and a
light cloud to ascend from the bowl of his pipe.   The council, of
course, supposed him engaged in deep sleep for the good of the community, and, according to custom in all such cases established, every
man bawled out silence, when, of a sudden, the door flew open,
and the little courier straddled into the apartment, cased to the
middle in a pair of Hessian boots, which he had got into for the
sake of expedition.   In his right hand he held forth the ominous
dispatches, and with his left he grasped firmly the waistband of
his galligaskins, which had unfortunately given way, in the exertion of descending from his horse.   He stumped resolutely up to
the governor, and with more hurry than perspicuity, delivered his
message.   But fortunately his ill tidings came too late to ruffle
the tranquillity of this most tranquil of rulers.   His venerable
excellency had just breathed and smoked his last—his lungs and
his pipe having been exhausted together. and his peaceful soul

having escaped in the last whiff that curled from his tobacco pipe.
In a word, the renowned Walter the Doubter, who had so often
slumbered with his contemporaries, now slept with his fathers, and
Wilhelmus Kieft governed in his stead.

BOOK IV.

CONTAINING THE CHRONICLES OF THE REIGN OF WILLIAM
THE TESTY.

CHAPTER I.

SHOWING THE NATURE OF HISTORY IN GENERAL; CONTAINING
FARTHERMORE THE UNIVERSAL ACQUIREMENTS OF WILLIAM
THE TESTY, AND HOW A MAN MAY LEARN SO MUCH AS TO
RENDER HIMSELF GOOD FOR NOTHING.

WHEN the lofty Thucydides is about to enter upon his description
of the plague that desolated Athens, one of his modern commentators assures the reader, that the history is now going to be exceeding solemn, serious, and pathetic; and hints, with that air of
chuckling gratulation with which a good dame draws forth a choice
morsel from a cupboard to regale a favorite, that this plague will
give his history a most agreeable variety.

In like manner did my heart leap within me, when I came
to the dolorous dilemma of Fort Good Hope, which I at once
perceived to be the forerunner of a series of great events and en-
tertaining disasters. Such are the true subjects for the historic
pen. For what is history, in fact, but a kind of Newgate calen-

dar, a register of the crimes and miseries that man has inflicted
on his fellow man? It is a huge libel on human nature, to which
we industriously add page after page, volume after volume,
as if we were building up a monument to the honor, rather than
the infamy of our species. If we turn over the pages of these
chronicles that man has written of himself, what are the characters dignified by the appellation of great, and held up to the admiration of posterity? Tyrants, robbers, conquerors, renowned only
for the magnitude of their misdeeds, and the stupendous wrongs
and miseries they have inflicted on mankind—warriors, who have
hired themselves to the trade of blood, not from motives of virtuous
patriotism, or to protect the injured and defenceless, but merely to
gain the vaunted glory of being adroit and successful in massa-
cring their fellow-beings! What are the great events that constitute a glorious era?—The fall of empires—the desolation of
happy countries—splendid cities smoking in their ruins—the
proudest works of art tumbled in the dust—the shrieks and groans
of whole nations ascending unto heaven!

It is thus the historian may be said to thrive on the miseries
of mankind, like birds of prey which hover over the field of battle,
to fatten on the mighty dead. It was observed by a great projector of inland lock navigation, that rivers, lakes, and oceans,
were only formed to feed canals.—In like manner I am tempted
to believe, that plots, conspiracies, wars, victories, and massacres,
are ordained by Providence only as food for the historian.

It is a source of great delight to the philosopher, in studying
the wonderful economy of nature, to trace the mutual dependencies of things, how they are created reciprocally for each other,
and how the most noxious and apparently unnecessary animal
has its uses. Thus those swarms of flies, which are so often

execrated as useless vermin, are created for the sustenance of spiders—and spiders, on the other hand, are evidently made to devour flies. So those heroes who have been such scourges to the world, were bounteously provided as themes for the poet and historian, while the poet and the historian were destined to record the achievements of heroes!

These, and many similar reflections, naturally arose in my mind, as I took up my pen to commence the reign of William Kieft: for now the stream of our history, which hitherto has rolled in a tranquil current, is about to depart for ever from its peaceful haunts, and brawl through many a turbulent and rugged scene.

As some sleek ox, sunk in the rich repose of a clover-field, dozing and chewing the cud, will bear repeated blows before it raises itself; so the province of Nieuw Nederlandts, having waxed fat under the drowsy reign of the Doubter, needed cuffs and kicks to rouse it into action. The reader will now witness the manner in which a peaceful community advances towards a state of war; which is apt to be like the approach of a horse to a drum, with much prancing and little progress, and too often with the wrong end foremost.

Wilhelmus Kieft, who, in 1634, ascended the gubernatorial chair (to borrow a favorite though clumsy appellation of modern phraseologists), was of a lofty descent, his father being inspector of wind-mills in the ancient town of Saardam; and our hero, we are told, when a boy, made very curious investigations into the nature and operation of these machines, which was one reason why he afterwards came to be so ingenious a governor. His name, according to the most authentic etymologists, was a corruption of Kyver; that is to say, a *wrangler* or *scolder*; and ex-

9*

pressed the characteristic of his family, which, for nearly two
centuries, had kept the windy town of Saardam in hot water, and
produced more tartars and brimstones than any ten families in the
place; and so truly did he inherit this family peculiarity, that he
had not been a year in the government of the province, before he
was universally denominated William the Testy. His appearance answered to his name. He was a brisk, wiry, waspish little
old gentleman; such a one as may now and then be seen stumping about our city in a broad-skirted coat with huge buttons, a
cocked hat stuck on the back of his head, and a cane as high as
his chin. His face was broad, but his features were sharp; his
cheeks were scorched into a dusky red, by two fiery little gray
eyes; his nose turned up, and the corners of his mouth turned
down, pretty much like the muzzle of an irritable pug-dog.

I have heard it observed by a profound adept in human physi-
ology, that if a woman waxes fat with the progress of years, her
tenure of life is somewhat precarious, but if haply she withers as
she grows old, she lives for ever. Such promised to be the case
with William the Testy, who grew tough in proportion as he
dried. He had withered, in fact, not through the process of years,
but through the tropical fervor of his soul, which burnt like a
vehement rush-light in his bosom; inciting him to incessant
broils and bickerings. Ancient traditions speak much of his
learning, and of the gallant inroads he had made into the dead
languages in which he had made captive a host of Greek nouns
and Latin verbs; and brought off rich booty in ancient saws and
apothegms; which he was wont to parade in his public harangues,
as a triumphant general of yore, his *spolia opima*. Of meta-
physics he knew enough to confound all hearers and himself into
the bargain. In logic, he knew the whole family of syllogisms

and dilemmas, and was so proud of his skill that he never suffered even a self-evident fact to pass unargued. It was observed, however, that he seldom got into an argument without getting into a perplexity, and then into a passion with his adversary for not being convinced gratis.

He had, moreover, skirmished smartly on the frontiers of several of the sciences, was fond of experimental philosophy, and prided himself upon inventions of all kinds. His abode, which he had fixed at a Bowerie or country-seat at a short distance from the city, just at what is now called Dutch-street, soon abounded with proofs of his ingenuity: patent smoke-jacks that required a horse to work them; Dutch ovens that roasted meat without fire; carts that went before the horses; weather-cocks that turned against the wind; and other wrong-headed contrivances that astonished and confounded all beholders. The house, too, was beset with paralytic cats and dogs, the subjects of his experimental philosophy; and the yelling and yelping of the latter unhappy victims of science, while aiding in the pursuit of knowledge, soon gained for the place the name of " Dog's Misery," by which it continues to be known even at the present day.

It is in knowledge as in swimming; he who flounders and splashes on the surface, makes more noise, and attracts more attention, than the pearl-diver who quietly dives in quest of treasures to the bottom. The vast acquirements of the new governor were the theme of marvel among the simple burghers of New-Amsterdam; he figured about the place as learned a man as a Bonze at Pekin, who has mastered one half of the Chinese alphabet: and was unanimously pronounced a " universal genius !"

I have known in my time many a genius of this stamp; but, to speak my mind freely, I never knew one who, for the ordinary purposes of life, was worth his weight in straw. In this respect, a little sound judgment and plain common sense is worth all the sparkling genius that ever wrote poetry or invented theories. Let us see how the universal acquirements of William the Testy aided him in the affairs of government.

CHAPTER II.

No sooner had this bustling little potentate been blown by a
whiff of fortune into the seat of government than he called his
council together to make them a speech on the state of affairs.

Caius Gracchus, it is said, when he harangued the Roman
populace, modulated his tone by an oratorical flute or pitch-pipe;
Wilhelmus Kieft, not having such an instrument at hand, availed
himself of that musical organ or trump which nature has implanted
in the midst of a man's face; in other words, he preluded his
address by a sonorous blast of the nose; a preliminary flourish
much in vogue among public orators.

He then commenced by expressing his humble sense of his utter unworthiness of the high post to which he had been appointed;
which made some of the simple burghers wonder why he undertook it, not knowing that it is a point of etiquette with a public
orator never to enter upon office without declaring himself unworthy to cross the threshold. He then proceeded in a manner
highly classic and erudite to speak of government generally, and
of the governments of ancient Greece in particular; together

14

with the wars of Rome and Carthage; and the rise and fall of
sundry outlandish empires which the worthy burghers had never
read nor heard of. Having thus, after the manner of your
learned orators, treated of things in general, he came by a natural, roundabout transition, o the matter in hand, namely, the
daring aggressions of the Yankees.

As my readers are well aware of the advantage a potentate
has of handling his enemies as he pleases in his speeches and
bulletins, where he has the talk all on his own side, they may rest
assured that William the Testy did not let such an opportunity
escape of giving the Yankees what is called "a taste of his quality." In speaking of their inroads into the territories of their
High Mightinesses, he compared them to the Gauls who desolated Rome; the Goths and Vandals who overran the fairest
plains of Europe; but when he came to speak of the unparalleled
audacity with which they of Weathersfield had advanced their
patches up to the very walls of Fort Goed Hoop, and threatened
to smother the garrison in onions, tears of rage started into his
eyes, as though he nosed the very offence in question.

Having thus wrought up his tale to a climax, he assumed a
most belligerent look, and assured the council that he had devised
an instrument, potent in its effects, and which he trusted would
soon drive the Yankees from the land. So saying, he thrust his
hand into one of the deep pockets of his broad-skirted coat and
drew forth, not an infernal machine, but an instrument in writing,
which he laid with great emphasis upon the table.

The burghers gazed at it for a time in silent awe, as a wary
housewife does at a gun, fearful it may go off half-cocked. The
document in question had a sinister look, it is true; it was crabbed in text, and from a broad red ribbon dangled the great seal

BOBBETT & EDMONDS. Sc.

of the province, about the size of a buckwheat pancake. Still, after all, it was but an instrument in writing. Herein, however, existed the wonder of the invention. The document in question was a PROCLAMATION, ordering the Yankees to depart instantly from the territories of their High Mightinesses under pain of suffering all the forfeitures and punishments in such case made and provided. It was on the moral effect of this formidable instrument that Wilhelmus Kieft calculated; pledging his valor as a governor that, once fulminated against the Yankees, it would, in less than two months, drive every mother's son of them across the borders.

The council broke up in perfect wonder, and nothing was talked of for some time among the old men and women of New-Amsterdam but the vast genius of the governor, and his new and cheap mode of fighting by proclamation.

As to Wilhelmus Kieft, having dispatched his proclamation to the frontiers, he put on his cocked hat and corduroy small-clothes, and mounting a tall raw-boned charger, trotted out to his rural retreat of Dog's Misery. Here, like the good Numa, he reposed from the toils of state, taking lessons in government, not from the nymph Egeria, but from the honored wife of his bosom; who was one of that class of females sent upon the earth a little after the flood, as a punishment for the sins of mankind, and commonly known by the appellation of *knowing women*. In fact, my duty as an historian obliges me to make known a circumstance which was a great secret at the time, and consequently was not a subject of scandal at more than half the tea-tables in New-Amsterdam, but which, like many other great secrets, has leaked out in the lapse of years—and this was, that Wilhelmus the Testy, though one of the most potent little men that ever

breathed, yet submitted at home to a species of government, neither laid down in Aristotle nor Plato; in short, it partook of the
nature of a pure, unmixed tyranny, and is familiarly denominated
petticoat government.—An absolute sway, which, although exceedingly common in these modern days, was very rare among
the ancients, if we may judge from the rout made about the
domestic economy of honest Socrates; which is the only ancient
case on record.

The great Kieft, however, warded off all the sneers and
sarcasms of his particular friends, who are ever ready to joke
with a man on sore points of the kind, by alleging that it was a
government of his own election, to which he submitted through
choice; adding at the same time a profound maxim which he had
found in an ancient author, hat "he who would aspire to *govern*
should first learn to *obey.*"

CHAPTER III.

NEVER was a more comprehensive, a more expeditious, or, what is still better, a more economical measure devised, than this of defeating the Yankees by proclamation—an expedient, likewise, so gentle and humane, there were ten chances to one in favor of its succeeding,—but then there was one chance to ten that it would not succeed—as the ill-natured fates would have it, that single chance carried the day! The proclamation was perfect in all its parts, well constructed, well written, well sealed, and well published—all that was wanting to insure its effect was, that the Yankees should stand in awe of it; but, provoking to relate, they treated it with the most absolute contempt, applied it to an unseemly purpose, and thus did the first warlike proclamation come to a shameful end—a fate which I am credibly informed has befallen but too many of its successors.

So far from abandoning the country, those varlets continued their encroachments, squatting along the green banks of the Varsche river, and founding Hartford, Stamford, New Haven, and

other border towns. I have already shown how the onion patches
of Pyquag were an eyesore to Jacobus Van Curlet and his garrison; but now these moss-troopers increased in their atrocities,
kidnapping hogs, impounding horses, and sometimes grievously
rib-roasting their owners. Our worthy forefathers could scarcely
stir abroad without danger of being outjockied in horseflesh, or
taken in in bargaining; while, in their absence, some daring
Yankee pedler would penetrate to their household, and nearly
ruin the good housewives with tin-ware and wooden bowls.*

    I am well aware of the perils which environ me in this part
of my history. While raking, with curious hand but pious heart,
among the mouldering remains of former days, anxious to draw
therefrom the honey of wisdom, I may fare somewhat like that

    * The following cases in point appear in Hazard's Collection of State
Papers.

    " In the meantime, they of Hartford have not onely usurped and taken in
the lands of Connecticott, although unrighteously and against the lawes of nations but have hindered our nation in sowing theire own purchased broken np
lands, but have also sowed them with corne in the night, which the Nederlanders had broken up and intended to sowe : and have beaten the servants of
the high and mighty the honored companie, which were laboring upon theire
master's lands, from theire lands, with sticks and plow staves in hostile manner
laming, and among the rest, struck Ever Duckings [Evert Duyckink] a hole in
his head, with a stick, so that the bloode ran downe very strongly downe upon
his body."

    " Those of Hartford sold a hogg, that belonged to the honored companie,
under pretence that it had eaten of theire grounde grass, when they had not
any foot of inheritance. They proffered the hogg for 5s. if the commissioners
would have given 5s. for damage ; which the commissioners denied, because
noe man's own hogg (as men used to say) can trespass upon his owne master's
grounde."

valiant worthy, Samson, who, in meddling with the carcass of a
dead lion, drew a swarm of bees about his ears. Thus, while
narrating the many misdeeds of the Yanokie or Yankee race, it
is ten chances to one but I offend the morbid sensibilities of certain of their unreasonable descendants, who may fly out and raise
such a buzzing about this unlucky head of mine, that I shall need
the tough hide of an Achilles, or an Orlando Furioso, to protect
me from their stings.

Should such be the case, I should deeply and sincerely lament
—not my misfortune in giving offence—but the wrong-headed
perverseness of an ill-natured generation, in taking offence at any
thing I say. That their ancestors did use my ancestors ill is
true, and I am very sorry for it. I would, with all my heart, the
fact were otherwise; but as I am recording the sacred events of
history, I'd not bate one nail's breadth of the honest truth, though
I were sure the whole edition of my work would be bought up
and burnt by the common hangman of Connecticut. And in
sooth, now that these testy gentlemen have drawn me out, I will
make bold to go farther, and observe that this is one of the grand
purposes for which we impartial historians are sent into the world
—to redress wrongs and render justice on the heads of the guilty.
So that, though a powerful nation may wrong its neighbors with
temporary impunity, yet sooner or later an historian springs up,
who wreaks ample chastisement on it in return.

Thus these moss-troopers of the east little thought, I'll warrant it, while they were harassing the inoffensive province of
Nieuw-Nederlands, and driving its unhappy governor to his wit's
end, that an historian would ever arise, and give them their
own, with interest. Since, then, I am but performing my bounden
duty as an historian, in avenging the wrongs of our revered an-

cestors, I shall make no further apology, and, indeed, when it is
considered that I have all these ancient borderers of the east in
my power, and at the mercy of my pen, I trust that it will be
admitted I conduct myself with great humanity and moderation.

It was long before William the Testy could be persuaded that
his much vaunted war measure was ineffectual; on the contrary,
he flew in a passion whenever it was doubted, swearing that
though slow in operating, yet when it once began to work, it would
soon purge the land of these invaders. When convinced, at
length, of the truth, like a shrewd physician he attributed the
failure to the quantity, not the quality of the medicine, and resolved to double the dose. He fulminated, therefore, a second
proclamation more vehement than the first, forbidding all intercourse with these Yankee intruders; ordering the Dutch burghers
on the frontiers to buy none of their pacing horses, measly pork,
apple sweetmeats, Weathersfield onions, or wooden bowls, and to
furnish them with no supplies of gin, gingerbread, or sourkrout.

Another interval elapsed, during which the last proclamation
was as little regarded as the first, and the nonintercourse was
especially set at naught by the young folks of both sexes, if we
may judge by the active bundling which took place along the
borders.

At length one day the inhabitants of New-Amsterdam were
aroused by a furious barking of dogs, great and small, and beheld,
to their surprise, the whole garrison of Fort Good Hope straggling into town all tattered and wayworn, with Jacobus Van Curlet
at their head, bringing the melancholy intelligence of the capture
of Fort Good Hope by the Yankees.

The fate of this important fortress is an impressive warning
to all military commanders. It was neither carried by storm nor

famine ; nor was it undermined ; nor bombarded ; nor set on fire by red-hot shot ; but was taken by a stratagem no less singular than effectual, and which can never fail of success, whenever an opportunity occurs of putting it in practice.

It seems that the Yankees had received intelligence that the garrison of Jacobus Van Curlet had been reduced nearly one-eighth by the death of two of his most corpulent soldiers, who had overeaten themselves on fat salmon caught in the Varsche river. A secret expedition was immediately set on foot to surprise the fortress. The crafty enemy knowing the habits of the garrison to sleep soundly after they had eaten their dinners and smoked their pipes, stole upon them at the noontide of a sultry summer's day, and surprised them in the midst of their slumbers.

In an instant the flag of their High Mightinesses was lowered, and the Yankee standard elevated in its stead, being a dried codfish, by way of a spread eagle. A strong garrison was appointed, of long-sided, hard-fisted Yankees, with Weathersfield onions for cockades and feathers. As to Jacobus Van Curlet and his men, they were seized by the nape of the neck, conducted to the gate, and one by one dismissed with a kick in the crupper, as Charles XIIth dismissed the heavy-bottomed Russians at the battle of Narva ; Jacobus Van Curlet receiving two kicks in consideration of his official dignity.

CHAPTER IV.

CONTAINING THE FEARFUL WRATH OF WILLIAM THE TESTY, AND THE ALARM OF NEW-AMSTERDAM—HOW THE GOVERNOR DID STRONGLY FORTIFY THE CITY—OF THE RISE OF ANTHONY THE TRUMPETER, AND THE WINDY ADDITION TO THE ARMORIAL BEARINGS OF NEW-AMSTERDAM.

LANGUAGE cannot express the awful ire of William the Testy on hearing of the catastrophe at Fort Goed Hoop. For three good hours his rage was too great for words, or rather the words were too great for him, (being a very small man,) and he was nearly choked by the misshapen, nine-cornered Dutch oaths and epithets which crowded at once into his gullet. At length his words found vent, and for three days he kept up a constant discharge, anathematizing the Yankees, man, woman, and child, for a set of dieven, schobbejacken, deugenieten, twistzoekeren, blaes-kaken, loosen-schalken, kakken-bedden, and a thousand other names, of which, unfortunately for posterity, history does not make mention. Finally, he swore that he would have nothing more to do with such a squatting, bundling, guessing, questioning, swapping, pumpkin-eating, molasses-daubing, shingle-splitting, cider-watering, horse-jockeying, notion-peddling crew—that they might stay at fort Goed Hoop and rot, before he would dirty his hands by attempting to drive them away; in proof of which he ordered the new-raised troops to be marched forthwith into winter quarters, although it was not as yet quite midsummer. Great despondency now fell upon the city of New-Amsterdam. It was feared that the conquerors of fort Goed Hoop, flushed with victory and apple-brandy, might march on to the capital, take it by storm, and annex the whole province to Connecticut. The name of Yankee became as terrible among the Nieuw-Nederlanders as was that of Gaul among the ancient Romans; insomuch that the good wives of the Manhattoes used it as a bugbear wherewith to frighten their unruly children.

Every body clamored around the governor, imploring him to put the city in a complete posture of defence, and he listened to their clamors. Nobody could accuse William the Testy of being idle in time of danger, or at any other time. He was never idle, but then he was often busy to very little purpose. When a young-ling he had been impressed with the words of Solomon, " Go to the ant, thou sluggard, observe her ways and be wise," in con-formity to which he had ever been of a restless, ant-like turn; hurrying hither and thither, nobody knew why or wherefore, busying himself about small matters with an air of great impor-tance and anxiety, and toiling at a grain of mustard-seed in the full conviction that he was moving a mountain. In the present instance, he called in all his inventive powers to his aid, and was continually pondering over plans, making diagrams, and wor-rying about with a troop of workmen and projectors at his heels. At length, after a world of consultation and contrivance, his plans of defence ended in rearing a great flag-staff in the centre of the fort, and perching a wind-mill on each bastion.

These warlike preparations in some measure allayed the public alarm, especially after an additional means of securing the safety of the city had been suggested by the governor's lady. It has already been hinted in this most authentic history, that in the domestic establishment of William the Testy "the gray mare was the better horse;" in other words, that his wife "ruled the roast," and, in governing the governor, governed the province, which might thus be said to be under petticoat government.

Now it came to pass, that about this time there lived in the Manhattoes a jolly, robustious trumpeter, named Antony Van Corlear, famous for his long wind; and who, as the story goes, could twang so potently upon his instrument, that the effect upon all within hearing was like that ascribed to the Scotch bagpipe when it sings right lustily i' the nose.

This sounder of brass was moreover a lusty bachelor, with a pleasant, burly visage, a long nose, and huge whiskers. He had his little *bowerie*, or retreat in the country, where he led a roystering life, giving dances to the wives and daughters of the burghers of the Manhattoes, insomuch that he became a prodigious favorite with all the women, young and old. He is said to have been the first to collect that famous toll levied on the fair sex at Kissing Bridge, on the highway to Hellgate.*

To this sturdy bachelor the eyes of all the women were turned in this time of darkness and peril, as the very man to second and carry out the plans of defence of the governor. A kind of petticoat council was forthwith held at the government house, at which the governor's lady presided; and this lady, as has been hinted,

---

* The bridge here mentioned by Mr. Knickerbocker still exists; but it is said that the toll is seldom collected now-a-days excepting on sleighing parties, by the descendants of the patriarchs, who still preserve the traditions of the city.

being all potent with the governor, the result of these councils was the elevation of Antony the Trumpeter to the post of commandant of wind-mills and champion of New-Amsterdam.

The city being thus fortified and garrisoned, it would have done one's heart good to see the governor snapping his fingers and fidgeting with delight, as the trumpeter strutted up and down the ramparts twanging defiance to the whole Yankee race, as does a modern editor to all the principalities and powers on the other side of the Atlantic. In the hands of Antony Van Corlear this windy instrument appeared to him as potent as the horn of the paladin Astolpho, or even the more classic horn of Alecto; nay, he had almost the temerity to compare it with the rams' horns celebrated in holy writ, at the very sound of which the walls of Jericho fell down.

Be all this as it may, the apprehensions of hostilities from the east gradually died away. The Yankees made no further invasion; nay, they declared they had only taken possession of fort Goed Hoop as being erected within their territories. So far from manifesting hostility, they continued to throng to New-Amsterdam with the most innocent countenances imaginable, filling the market with their notions, being as ready to trade with the Nederlanders as ever—and not a whit more prone to get to the windward of them in a bargain.

The old wives of the Manhattoes who took tea witL the governor's lady attributed all this affected moderation to the awe inspired by the military preparations of the governor, and the windy prowess of Antony the Trumpeter.

There were not wanting illiberal minds, however, who sneered at the governor for thinking to defend his city as he governed it, by mere wind; but William Kieft was not to be

10

jeered out of his wind-mills—he had seen them perched upon the ramparts of his native city of Saardam, and was persuaded they were connected with the great science of defence; nay, so much piqued was he by having them made a matter of ridicule, that he introduced them into the arms of the city, where they remain to this day, quartered with the ancient beaver of the Manhattoes, an emblem and memento of his policy.

I must not omit to mention that certain wise old burghers of the Manhattoes, skillful in expounding signs and mysteries, after events have come to pass, consider this early intrusion of the wind-mill into the escutcheon of our city, which before had been wholly occupied by the beaver, as portentous of its after fortune, when the quiet Dutchman would be elbowed aside by the enterprising Yankee, and patient industry overtopped by windy speculation.

CHAPTER V.

AMONG the wrecks and fragments of exalted wisdom which have
floated down the stream of time from venerable antiquity, and
been picked up by those humble, but industrious wights who ply
along the shores of literature, we find a shrewd ordinance of Charondas the Locrian legislator. Anxious to preserve the judicial
code of the State from the additions and amendments of country
members and seekers of popularity, he ordained that, whoever proposed a new law should do it with a halter about his neck;
whereby, in case his proposition were rejected, they just hung him
up—and there the matter ended.

The effect was, that for more than two hundred years there
was but one trifling alteration in the judicial code ; and legal matters were so clear and simple that the whole race of lawyers
starved to death for want of employment. The Locrians, too,
being freed from all incitement to litigation, lived very lovingly
together, and were so happy a people that they make scarce any
figure in history ; it being only your litigious, quarrelsome, rantipole nations who make much noise in the world.

I have been reminded of these historical facts in coming to
treat of the internal policy of William the Testy. Well would

it have been for him had he in the course of his universal acquirements stumbled upon the precaution of the good Charondas ;
or had he looked nearer home at the protectorate of Oloffe the
Dreamer, when the community was governed without laws. Such
legislation, however, was not suited to the busy, meddling mind of
William the Testy.   On the contrary, he conceived that the true
wisdom of legislation consisted in the multiplicity of laws.   He
accordingly had great punishments for great crimes, and little punishments for little offences.   By degrees the whole surface of society was cut up by ditches and fences, and quickset hedges of the
law, and even the sequestered paths of private life so beset by
petty rules and ordinances, too numerous to be remembered, that
one could scarce walk at large without the risk of letting off a
spring-gun or falling into a man-trap.

In a little while the blessings of innumerable laws became ap-
parent—a class of men arose to expound and confound them.
Petty courts were instituted to take cognizance of petty offences,
pettifoggers began to abound ; and the community was soon set
together by the ears.

Let me not be thought as intending any thing derogatory to
the profession of the law, or to the distinguished members of that
illustrious order.   Well am I aware that we have in this ancient
city innumerable worthy gentlemen, the knights-errants of modern
days, who go about redressing wrongs and defending the defenceless, not for the love of filthy lucre, nor the selfish cravings of
renown, but merely for the pleasure of doing good.   Sooner would
I throw this trusty pen into the flames, and cork up my ink-bottle
for ever, than infringe even for a nail's breadth upon the dignity
of these truly benevolent champions of the distressed.   On the
contrary I allude merely to those caitiff scouts who, in these latter

days of evil, infest the skirts of the profession, as did the recreant
Cornish knights of yore, the honorable order of chivalry; who,
under its auspices, commit flagrant wrongs; who thrive by quib-
bles, by quirks and chicanery, and like vermin increase the corruption in which they are engendered.

Nothing so soon awakens the malevolent passions as the facility
of gratification. The courts of law would never be so crowded
with petty, vexatious and disgraceful suits, were it not for the
herds of pettifoggers. These tamper with the passions of the
poorer and more ignorant classes; who, as if poverty were not a
sufficient misery in itself, are ever ready to imbitter it by litigation.
These, like quacks in medicine, excite the malady to profit by the
cure, and retard the cure to augment the fees. As the quack exhausts the constitution, the pettifogger exhausts the purse; and as
he who has once been under the hands of a quack, is for ever
after prone to dabble in drugs, and poison himself with infallible
prescriptions; so the client of the pettifogger is ever after prone
to embroil himself with his neighbors, and impoverish himself
with successful lawsuits.—My readers will excuse this digression
into which I have been unwarily betrayed; but I could not avoid
giving a cool and unprejudiced account of an abomination too
prevalent in this excellent city, and with the effects of which I
am ruefully acquainted: having been nearly ruined by a lawsuit which was decided against me; and my ruin having been
completed by another, which was decided in my favor.

To return to our theme. There was nothing in the whole
range of moral offences against which the jurisprudence of Wil
liam the Testy was more strenuously directed, than the crying
sin of poverty. He pronounced it the root of all evil, and determined to cut it up root and branch, and extirpate it from the

land. He had been struck, in the course of his travels in the old countries of Europe, with the wisdom of those notices posted up in country towns, that "any vagrant found begging there would be put in the stocks," and he had observed, that no beggars were to be seen in these neighborhoods; having doubtless thrown off their rags and their poverty and become rich under the terror of the law. He determined to improve upon this hint. In a little while a new machine of his own invention, was erected hard by Dog's Misery. This was nothing more nor less than a gibbet, of a very strange, uncouth, and unmatchable construction, far more efficacious, as he boasted, than the stocks, for the punishment of poverty. It was for altitude not a whit inferior to that of Haman, so renowned in Bible history; but the marvel of the contrivance was, that the culprit, instead of being suspended by the neck according to venerable custom, was hoisted by the waistband, and kept dangling and sprawling between heaven and earth for an hour or two at a time—to the infinite entertainment and edification of the respectable citizens who usually attend exhibitions of the kind.

It is incredible how the little governor chuckled at beholding caitiff vagrants and sturdy beggars thus swinging by the crupper, and cutting antic gambols in the air. He had a thousand pleasantries, and mirthful conceits to utter upon these occasions. He called them his dandle-lions—his wild-fowl—his high-fliers—his spread-eagles—his goshawks—his scare-crows—and finally, his *gallows-birds ;* which ingenious appellation, though originally confined to worthies who had taken the air in this strange manner, has since grown to be a cant-name given to all candidates for legal elevation. This punishment, moreover, if we may credit the assertions of certain grave etymologists, gave the first hint for a kind of harnessing, or strapping, by which our forefathers braced up their multifarious breeches, and which has of late years been revived, and continues to be worn at the present day.

Such was the punishment of all petty delinquents, vagrants and beggars and others detected in being guilty of poverty in a small way ; as to those who had offended on a great scale, who had been guilty of flagrant misfortunes and enormous backslidings of the purse, and who stood convicted of large debts, which they were unable to pay, William Kieft had them straightway inclosed within the stone walls of a prison, there to remain until they should reform and grow rich. This notable expedient, however, does not appear to have been more efficacious under William the Testy than in more modern days : it being found that the longer a poor devil was kept in prison the poorer he grew.

CHAPTER VI.

PROJECTS OF WILLIAM THE TESTY FOR INCREASING THE CUR-
RENCY—HE IS OUTWITTED BY THE YANKEES—THE GREAT
OYSTER WAR.

NEXT to his projects for the suppression of poverty, may be
classed those of William the Testy, for increasing the wealth of
New-Amsterdam. Solomon, of whose character for wisdom the
little governor was somewhat emulous, had made gold and silver
as plenty as the stones in the streets of Jerusalem. William Kieft
could not pretend to vie with him as to the precious metals, but
he determined, as an equivalent, to flood the streets of New-Amsterdam with Indian money. This was nothing more nor less
than strings of beads wrought out of clams, periwinkles, and
other shell-fish, and called seawant or wampum. These had
formed a native currency among the simple savages ; who were
content to take them of the Dutchmen in exchange for peltries.
In an unlucky moment, William the Testy, seeing this money of
easy production, conceived the project of making it the current
coin of the province. It is true it had an intrinsic value among
the Indians, who used it to ornament their robes and moccasons,
but among the honest burghers it had no more intrinsic value than
those rags which form the paper currency of modern days. This

consideration, however, had no weight with William Kieft. He began by paying all the servants of the company, and all the debts of government, in strings of wampum. He sent emissaries to sweep the shores of Long Island, which was the Ophir of this modern Solomon, and abounded in shell-fish. These were transported in loads to New-Amsterdam, coined into Indian money, and launched into circulation.

And now, for a time, affairs went on swimmingly; money became as plentiful as in the modern days of paper currency, and, to use the popular phrase, "a wonderful impulse was given to public prosperity." Yankee traders poured into the province, buying every thing they could lay their hands on, and paying the worthy Dutchmen their own price—in Indian money. If the latter, however, attempted to pay the Yankees in the same coin for their tinware and wooden bowls, the case was altered; nothing would do but Dutch guilders and such like "metallic currency." What was worse, the Yankees introduced an inferior kind of wampum made of oyster-shells, with which they deluged the province, carrying off in exchange all the silver and gold, the Dutch herrings, and Dutch cheeses: thus early did the knowing men of the east manifest their skill in bargaining the New-Amsterdammers out of the oyster, and leaving them the shell.*

It was a long time before William the Testy was made sen-

---

* In a manuscript record of the province, dated 1659, Library of the New-York Historical Society, is the following mention of Indian money.

Seawant alias wampum. Beads manufactured from the *Quahang* or *wilk;* a shell-fish formerly abounding on our coasts, but lately of more rare occurrence, of two colors, black and white ; the former twice the value of the latter. Six beads of the white and three of the black for an English penny. The seawant depreciates from time to time. The New England people make use of it as a

sible how completely his grand project of finance was turned
against him by his eastern neighbors ; nor would he probably have
ever found it out, had not tidings been brought him that the Yankees had made a descent upon Long Island, and had established
a kind of mint at Oyster Bay, where they were coining up all the
oyster banks.

Now this was making a vital attack upon the province in a
double sense, financial and gastronomical. Ever since the council
dinner of Oloffe the Dreamer at the founding of New-Amsterdam, at which banquet the oyster figured so conspicuously, this
divine shell-fish has been held in a kind of superstitious reverence
at the Manhattoes ; as witness the temples erected to its cult in
every street and lane and alley.   In fact it is the standard luxury
of the place, as is the terrapin at Philadelphia, the soft crab at
Baltimore, or the canvas-back at Washington.

The seizure of Oyster Bay, therefore, was an outrage not
merely on the pockets, but the larders of the New-Amsterdammers ; the whole community was aroused, and an oyster crusade
was immediately set on foot against the Yankees.   Every stout
trencherman hastened to the standard ; nay, some of the most corpulent Burgomasters and Schepens joined the expedition as a
corps de reserve, only to be called into action when the sacking
commenced.

means of barter, not only to carry away the best cargoes which we send thither,
but to accumulate a large quantity of beavers and other furs ; by which the
company is defrauded of her revenues, and the merchants disappointed in
making returns with that speed with which they might wish to meet their engagements : while their commissioners and the inhabitants remain overstocked
with seawant—a sort of currency of no value except with the New-Netherland
savages, &c.

The conduct of the expedition was intrusted to a valiant Dutchman, who for size and weight might have matched with Colbrand the Danish champion, slain by Guy of Warwick. He was famous throughout the province for strength of arm and skill at quarter-staff, and hence was named Stoffel Brinkerhoff; or rather, Brinkerhoofd; that is to stay, Stoffel the head-breaker.

This sturdy commander, who was a man of few words but vigorous deeds, led his troops resolutely on through Nineveh, and Babylon, and Jericho, and Patch-hog, and other Long Island towns, without encountering any difficulty of note; though it is said that some of the burgomasters gave out at Hard-scramble Hill and Hungry Hollow; and that others lost heart and turned back at Puss-panick. With the rest he made good his march until he arrived in the neighborhood of Oyster Bay.

Here he was encountered by a host of Yankee warriors headed by Preserved Fish, and Habakkuk Nutter, and Return Strong, and Zerubbabel Fisk, and Determined Cock! at the sound of whose names Stoffel Brinkerhoff verily believed the whole parliament of Praise-God Barebones had been let loose upon him. He soon found, however, that they were merely the "selectmen" of the settlement, armed with no weapon but the tongue, and disposed only to meet him on the field of argument. Stoffel had but one mode of arguing; that was, with the cudgel; but he used it with such effect that he routed his antagonists, broke up the settlement, and would have driven the inhabitants into the sea if they had not managed to escape across the Sound to the mainland by the Devil's stepping-stones, which remain to this day monuments of this great Dutch victory over the Yankees.

Stoffel Brinkerhoff made great spoil of oysters and clams,

coined and uncoined, and then set out on his return to the Manhattoes. A grand triumph, after the manner of the ancients,
was prepared for him by William the Testy.   He entered New-
Amsterdam as a conqueror, mounted on a Narraganset pacer.
Five dried codfish on poles, standards taken from the enemy,
were borne before him, and an immense store of oysters and
clams, Weathersfield onions, and Yankee "notions" formed the
spolia opima; while several coiners of oyster-shells were led captive to grace the hero's triumph.

The procession was accompanied by a full band of boys and
negroes performing on the popular instruments of rattle-bones
and clam-shells, while Antony Van Corlear sounded his trumpet
from the ramparts.

A great banquet was served up in the stadthouse from the
clams and oysters taken from the enemy; while the governor
sent the shells privately to the mint and had them coined into
Indian money, with which he paid his troops.

It is moreover said that the governor, calling to mind the
practice among the ancients to honor their victorious general with
public statues, passed a magnanimous decree, by which every
tavern-keeper was permitted to paint the head of Stoffel Brinkerhoff upon his sign !

CHAPTER VII.

GROWING DISCONTENTS OF NEW-AMSTERDAM UNDER THE GOVERNMENT OF WILLIAM THE TESTY.

IT has been remarked by the observant writer of the Stuyvesant manuscript, that under the administration of William Kieft the disposition of the inhabitants of New-Amsterdam experienced an essential change, so that they became very meddlesome and factious. The unfortunate propensity of the little governor to experiment and innovation, and the frequent exacerbations of his temper, kept his council in a continual worry; and the council being to the people at large what yeast or leaven is to a batch, they threw the whole community in a ferment; and the people at large being to the city what the mind is to the body, the unhappy commotions they underwent operated most disastrously upon New-Amsterdam—insomuch that, in certain of their paroxysms of consternation and perplexity, they begat several of the most crooked, distorted, and abominable streets, lanes, and alleys, with which this metropolis is disfigured.

The fact was, that about this time the community, like Balaam's ass, began to grow more enlightened than its rider, and to show a disposition for what is called "self-government." This restive propensity was first evinced in certain popular meetings, in which the burghers of New-Amsterdam met to talk and smoke over the complicated affairs of the province, gradually obfuscating themselves with politics and tobacco-smoke. Hither resorted those idlers and squires of low degree who hang loose on society and are blown about by every wind of doctrine. Cobblers abandoned their stalls to give lessons on political economy; blacksmiths suffered their fires to go out while they stirred up the fires of faction; and even tailors, though said to be the ninth parts of humanity, neglected their own measures to criticise the measures of government.

Strange! that the science of government, which seems to be so generally understood, should invariably be denied to the only one called upon to exercise it. Not one of the politicians in question, but, take his word for it, could have administered affairs ten times better than William the Testy.

Under the instructions of these political oracles the good people of New-Amsterdam soon became exceedingly enlightened; and as a matter of course, exceedingly discontented. They gradually found out the fearful error in which they had indulged, of thinking themselves the happiest people in creation; and were convinced that, all circumstances to the contrary notwithstanding, they were a very unhappy, deluded, and consequently ruined people!

We are naturally prone to discontent, and avaricious after imaginary causes of lamentation. Like lubberly monks we belabor our own shoulders, and take a vast satisfaction in the music of our own groans. Nor is this said by way of paradox; daily experience shows the truth of these observations. It is almost impossible to elevate the spirits of a man groaning under ideal calamities; but nothing is easier than to render him wretched, though on the pinnacle of felicity; as it would be an Herculean task to hoist a man to the top of a steeple, though the merest child could topple him off thence.

I must not omit to mention that these popular meetings were generally held at some noted tavern; these public edifices possessing what in modern times are thought the true fountains of political inspiration. The ancient Germans deliberated upon a matter when drunk, and reconsidered it when sober. Mob politicians in modern times dislike to have two minds upon a subject; so they both deliberate and act when drunk; by this means a world of delay is spared; and as it is universally allowed that a man when drunk sees double, it follows conclusively that he sees twice as well as his sober neighbors.

CHAPTER VIII.

WILHELMUS KIEFT, as has already been observed, was a great legislator on a small scale, and had a microscopic eye in public affairs. He had been greatly annoyed by the factious meetings of the good people of New-Amsterdam, but, observing that on these occasions the pipe was ever in their mouth, he began to think that the pipe was at the bottom of the affair, and that there was some mysterious affinity between politics and tobacco smoke. Determined to strike at the root of the evil, he began, forthwith, to rail at tobacco, as a noxious, nauseous weed; filthy in all its uses; and as to smoking he denounced it as a heavy tax upon the public pocket; a vast consumer of time, a great encourager of idleness, and a deadly bane to the prosperity and morals of the people. Finally he issued an edict, prohibiting the smoking of tobacco throughout the New-Netherlands. Ill fated Kieft! Had he lived in the present age and attempted to check the unbounded license of the press, he could not have struck more sorely upon the sensibilities of the million. The pipe, in fact, was the great organ of reflection and deliberation of the New-Netherlander. It was his constant companion and solace—was he gay, he smoked; was he sad, he smoked; his pipe was never out of his mouth; it was a part of his physiognomy; without it his best friends would not know him. Take away his pipe? You might as well take away his nose!

The immediate effect of the edict of William the Testy was a popular commotion. A vast multitude armed with pipes and tobacco-boxes, and an immense supply of ammunition, sat themselves down before the governor's house, and fell to smoking with tremendous violence. The testy William issued forth like a wrathful spider, demanding the reason of this lawless fumigation. The sturdy rioters replied by lolling back in their seats, and puffing away with redoubled fury; raising such a murky cloud that the governor was fain to take refuge in the interior of his castle.

A long negotiation ensued through the medium of Antony the Trumpeter. The governor was at first wrathful and unyielding, but was gradually smoked into terms. He concluded by permitting the smoking of tobacco, but he abolished the fair long pipes used in the days of Wouter Van Twiller, denoting ease, tranquillity, and sobriety of deportment; these he condemned as incompatible with the dispatch of business, in place whereof he substituted little captious short pipes, two inches in length, which, he observed, could be stuck in one corner of the mouth, or twisted in the hat-band; and would never be in the way. Thus ended this alarming insurrection, which was long known by the name of The Pipe Plot, and which, it has been somewhat quaintly observed, did end. like most plots and seditions, in mere smoke.

But mark, oh, reader! the deplorable evils which did afterwards result. The smoke of these villanous little pipes, continually ascending in a cloud about the nose, penetrated into and befogged the cerebellum; dried up all the kindly moisture of the brain, and rendered the people who used them as vaporish and testy as the governor himself. Nay, what is worse, from being goodly, burly, sleek-conditioned men, they became, like our Dutch yeomanry who smoke short pipes, a lantern-jawed, smoke-dried, leathern-hided race.

Nor was this all. From this fatal schism in tobacco pipes we may date the rise of parties in the Nieuw-Nederlands. The rich and self-important burghers who had made their fortunes, and could afford to be lazy, adhered to the ancient fashion, and formed a kind of aristocracy known as the *Long Pipes ;* while the lower order, adopting the reform of William Kieft as more convenient in their handicraft employments, were branded with the plebeian name of *Short Pipes.*

A third party sprang up, headed by the descendants of Robert Chewit, the companion of the great Hudson. These discarded pipes altogether and took to chewing tobacco ; hence they were called *Quids ;* an appellation since given to those political mongrels, which sometimes spring up between two great parties, as a mule is produced between a horse and an ass.

And here I would note the great benefit of party distinctions in saving the people at large the trouble of thinking. Hesiod divides mankind into three classes, those who think for themselves, those who think as others think, and those who do not think at all. The second class comprises the great mass of society ; for most people require a set creed and a file-leader. Hence the origin of party : which means a large body of people, some few of whom think, and all the rest talk. The former take the lead and discipline the latter ; prescribing what they must say ; what they must approve ; what they must hoot at ; whom they must support; but, above all, whom they must hate ; for no one can be a right good partisan, who is not a thorough-going hater.

The enlightened inhabitants of the Manhattoes, therefore, being divided into parties, were enabled to hate each other with great accuracy. And now the great business of politics went bravely on, the long pipes and short pipes assembling in separate beer-houses, and smoking at each other with implacable vehemence, to the great support of the state and profit of the tavern-keepers. Some, indeed, went so far as to bespatter their adversaries with those odoriferous little words which smell so strong in the Dutch language; believing, like true politicians, that they served their party, and glorified themselves in proportion as they bewrayed their neighbors. But, however they might differ among themselves, all parties agreed in abusing the governor; seeing that he was not a governor of their choice, but appointed by others to rule over them.

Unhappy William Kieft! exclaims the sage writer of the Stuyvesant manuscript, doomed to contend with enemies too knowing to be entrapped, and to reign over a people too wise to be governed. All his foreign expeditions were baffled and set at naught by the all-pervading Yankees; all his home measures were canvassed and condemned by "numerous and respectable meetings" of pot-house politicians.

In the multitude of counselors, we are told, there is safety; but the multitude of counselors was a continual source of perplexity to William Kieft. With a temperament as hot as an old radish, and a mind subject to perpetual whirlwinds and tornadoes, he never failed to get into a passion with every one who undertook to advise him. I have observed, however, that your passionate little men, like small boats with large sails, are easily upset or blown out of their course; so was it with William the Testy, who was prone to be carried away by the last piece of

advice blown into his ear.   The consequence was, that, though a
projector of the first class, yet, by continually changing his projects, he gave none a fair trial ; and by endeavoring to do every
thing, he in sober truth did nothing.

In the meantime, the sovereign people having got into the
saddle, showed themselves, as usual, unmerciful riders ; spurring
on the little governor with harangues and petitions, and thwarting
him with memorials and reproaches, in much the same way as
holyday apprentices manage an unlucky devil of a hack-horse—
so that Wilhelmus Kieft was kept at a worry or a gallop throughout the whole of his administration.

CHAPTER IX.

IF we could but get a peep at the tally of dame Fortune, where
like a vigilant landlady she chalks up the debtor and creditor
accounts of thoughtless mortals, we should find that every good is
checked off by an evil; and that however we may apparently
revel scotfree for a season, the time will come when we must
ruefully pay off the reckoning. Fortune in fact is a pestilent
shrew, and withal an inexorable creditor; and though for a time
she may be all smiles and curtsies and indulge us in long credits,
yet sooner or later she brings up her arrears with a vengeance,
and washes out her scores with our tears. "Since," says good
old Boetius, "no man can retain her at his pleasure, what are
her favors but sure prognostications of approaching trouble and
calamity?"

This is the fundamental maxim of that sage school of philosophers the croakers, who esteem it true wisdom to doubt and
despond when other men rejoice; well knowing that happiness is
at best but transient; that the higher one is elevated on the see-

saw balance of fortune, the lower must be his subsequent depression; that he who is on the uppermost round of a ladder has most to suffer from a fall, while he who is at the bottom runs very little risk of breaking his neck by tumbling to the top.

Philosophical readers of this stamp must have doubtless indulged in dismal forebodings all through the tranquil reign of Walter the Doubter, and considered it what Dutch seamen call a weather-breeder. They will not be surprised, therefore, that the foul weather which gathered during his days, should now be rattling from all quarters on the head of William the Testy.

The origin of some of these troubles may be traced quite back to the discoveries and annexations of Hans Reinier Oothout the explorer and Wynant Ten Breeches the land measurer, made in the twilight days of Oloffe the Dreamer; by which the territories of the Nieuw Nederlands were carried far to the south, to Delaware river and parts beyond. The consequence was, many disputes and brawls with the Indians, which now and then reached the drowsy ears of Walter the Doubter and his council, like the muttering of distant thunder from behind the mountains, without, however, disturbing their repose. It was not till the time of William the Testy that the thunderbolt reached the Manhattoes. While the little governor was diligently protecting his eastern boundaries from the Yankees, word was brought him of the irruption of a vagrant colony of Swedes in the south, who had landed on the banks of the Delaware and displayed the banner of that redoubtable virago Queen Christina, and taken possession of the country in her name. These had been guided in their expedition by one Peter Minuits or Minnewits, a renegade Dutchman, formerly in the service of their High Mightinesses; but who now declared himself governor of all the surrounding country, to which was given the name of the province of NEW SWEDEN.

It is an old saying that " a little pot is soon hot," which was the case with William the Testy. Being a little man he was soon in a passion, and once in a passion he socn boiled over. Summoning his council on the receipt of this news, he belabored the Swedes in the longest speech that had been heard in the colony since the wordy warfare of Ten Breeches and Tough Breeches. Having thus taken off the fire-edge of his valor, he resorted to his favorite measure of proclamation, and dispatched a document of the kind, ordering the renegade Minnewits and his gang of Swedish vagabonds to leave the country immediately, under pain of the vengeance of their High Mightinesses the Lords States General, and of the potentates of the Manhattoes.

This strong measure was not a whit more effectual than its predecessors, which had been thundered against the Yankees ; and William Kieft was preparing to follow it up with something still more formidable, when he received intelligence of other invaders on his southern frontier ; who had taken possession of the banks of the Schuylkill, and built a fort there. They were represented as a gigantic, gunpowder race of men, exceedingly expert at boxing, biting, gouging, and other branches of the rough and tumble mode of warfare, which they had learned from their prototypes and cousins-german, the Virginians, to whom they have ever borne considerable resemblance. Like them, too, they were great roysters, much given to revel on hoe-cake and bacon, mintjulep and apple-toddy ; whence their newly-formed colony had already acquired the name of Merryland ; which, with a slight modification, it retains to the present day.

In fact the Merrylanders and their cousins, the Virginians,

were represented to William Kieft as offsets from the same original stock as his bitter enemies the Yanokie, or Yankee tribes of
the east; having both come over to this country for the liberty of
conscience; or, in other words, to live as they pleased: the Yankees taking to praying and money-making, and converting quakers;
and the Southerners to horse-racing and cock-fighting, and breeding negroes.

Against these new invaders Wilhelmus Kieft immediately dispatched a naval armament of two sloops and thirty men, under
Jan Jansen Alpendam, who was armed to the very teeth with one
of the little governor's most powerful speeches, written in vigorous
Low Dutch.

Admiral Alpendam arrived without accident in the Schuylkill,
and came upon the enemy just as they were engaged in a great
" barbecue," a kind of festivity or carouse much practised in
Merryland. Opening upon them with the speech of William the
Testy, he denounced them as a pack of lazy, canting, julep-tip-
pling, cock-fighting, horse-racing, slave-driving, tavern-haunting,
Sabbath-breaking, mulatto-breeding upstarts; and concluded by
ordering them to evacuate the country immediately: to which
they laconically replied in plain English, " they'd see him d——d
first !"

Now this was a reply on which neither Jan Jansen Alpendam
nor Wilhelmus Kieft had made any calculation. Finding himself,
therefore, totally unprepared to answer so terrible a rebuff with
suitable hostility, the admiral concluded his wisest course would
be to return home and report progress. He accordingly steered
his course back to New-Amsterdam, where he arrived safe,
having accomplished this hazardous enterprise at small expense
of treasure, and no loss of life. His saving policy gained him

the universal appellation of the Saviour of his Country ; and his services were suitably rewarded by a shingle monument, erected by subscription on the top of Flattenbarrack-hill, where it immortalized his name for three whole years, when it fell to pieces and was burnt for firewood.

CHAPTER X.

ABOUT this time the testy little governor of the New-Netherlands
appears to have had his hands full, and with one annoyance and
the other to have been kept continually on the bounce. He was
on the very point of following up the expedition of Jan Jansen
Alpendam by some belligerent measures against the marauders
of Merryland, when his attention was suddenly called away by
belligerent troubles springing up in another quarter, the seeds of
which had been sown in the tranquil days of Walter the Doubter

The reader will recollect the deep doubt into which that most
pacific governor was thrown on Killian Van Rensellaer's taking
possession of Bearn Island by *wapen recht*. While the governor
doubted and did nothing, the lordly Killian went on to complete
his sturdy little castellum of Rensellaerstein, and to garrison it
with a number of his tenants from the Helderberg, a mountain
region famous for the hardest heads and hardest fists in the province. Nicholas Koorn, a faithful squire of the patroon, accustomed to strut at his heels, wear his cast-off clothes, and imitate
his lofty bearing, was established in this post as wacht-meester.

His duty it was to keep an eye on the river and oblige every vessel that passed, unless on the service of their High Mightinesses, to strike its flag, lower its peak, and pay toll to the lord of Rensellaerstein.

This assumption of sovereign authority within the territories of the Lords States General, however it might have been tolerated by Walter the Doubter, had been sharply contested by William the Testy on coming into office, and many written remonstrances had been addressed by him to Killian Van Rensellaer, to which the latter never deigned a reply. Thus by degrees a sore place, or in Hibernian parlance a *raw*, had been established in the irritable soul of the little governor, insomuch that he winced at the very name of Rensellaerstein.

Now it came to pass, that on a fine sunny day the Company's yacht the Half-Moon, having been on one of its stated visits to Fort Aurania, was quietly tiding it down the Hudson; the commander, Govert Lockerman, a veteran Dutch skipper of few words but great bottom, was seated on the high poop, quietly smoking his pipe, under the shadow of the proud flag of Orange, when, on arriving abreast of Bearn Island, he was saluted by a stentorian voice from the shore, " Lower thy flag, and be d——d to thee !"

Govert Lockerman, without taking his pipe out of his mouth, turned up his eye from under his broad-brimmed hat to see who hailed him thus discourteously. There, on the ramparts of the fort, stood Nicholas Koorn, armed to the teeth, flourishing a brass-hilted sword, while a steeple-crowned hat and cock's tail-feather, formerly worn by Killian Van Rensellaer himself, gave an inexpressible loftiness to his demeanor.

Govert Lockerman eyed the warrior from top to toe, but was

not to be dismayed. Taking the pipe slowly out of his mouth,
" To whom should I lower my flag ?" demanded he. " To the
high and mighty Killian Van Renssellaer, the lord of Rensellaerstein !" was the reply.

" I lower it to none but the Prince of Orange and my masters
the Lords States General." So saying, he resumed his pipe and
smoked with an air of dogged determination.

Bang ! went a gun from the fortress ; the ball cut both sail
and rigging. Govert Lockerman said nothing, but smoked the
more doggedly.

Bang ! went another gun ; the shot whistling close astern.

" Fire, and be d—d," cried Govert Lockerman, cramming a
new charge of tobacco into his pipe, and smoking with still
increasing vehemence.

Bang ! went a third gun. The shot passed over his head,
tearing a hole in the " princely flag of Orange."

This was the hardest trial of all for the pride and patience of
Govert Lockerman ; he maintained a stubborn though swelling
silence, but his smothered rage might be perceived by the short
vehement puffs of smoke emitted from his pipe, by which he
might be tracked for miles, as he slowly floated out of shot and
out of sight of Bearn Island. In fact he never gave vent to his
passion until he got fairly among the highlands of the Hudson ;
when he let fly whole volleys of Dutch oaths, which are said to
linger to this very day among the echoes of the Dunderberg, and to
give particular effect to the thunder-storms in that neighborhood.

It was the sudden apparition of Govert Lockerman at Dog's
Misery, bearing in his hand the tattered flag of Orange, that arrested the attention of William the Testy, just as he was devising
a new expedition against the marauders of Merryland. I will

not pretend to describe the passion of the little man when he heard of the outrage of Rensellaerstein. Suffice it to say, in the first transports of his fury, he turned Dog's Misery topsy-turvy ; kicked every cur out of doors, and threw the cats out of the window ; after which, his spleen being in some measure relieved, he went into a council of war with Govert Lockerman, the skipper, assisted by Antony Van Corlear, the trumpeter.

CHAPTER XI.

OF THE DIPLOMATIC MISSION OF ANTONY THE TRUMPETER
TO THE FORTRESS OF RENSELLAERSTEIN—AND HOW HE
WAS PUZZLED BY A CABALISTIC REPLY.

THE eyes of all New-Amsterdam were now turned to see what
would be the end of this direful feud between William the Testy
and the patroon of Rensellaerwick; and some observing the
consultations of the governor with the skipper and the trumpeter, predicted warlike measures by sea and land. The wrath of
William Kieft however, though quick to rise, was quick to
evaporate. He was a perfect brush-heap in a blaze, snapping
and crackling for a time and then ending in smoke. Like many
other valiant potentates, his first thoughts were all for war, his
sober second thoughts for diplomacy.

Accordingly, Govert Lockerman was once more dispatched
up the river in the Company's yacht, the Goed Hoop, bearing
Antony the Trumpeter as ambassador, to treat with the belligerent powers of Rensellaerstein   In the fullness of time the yacht
arrived before Bearn Island, and Antony the Trumpeter, mounting
the poop, sounded a parley to the fortress. In a little while the
steeple-crowned hat of Nicholas Koorn, the wacht-meester, rose
above the battlements, followed by his iron visage, and ultimately

his whole person, armed, as before, to the very teeth: while one by one a whole row of Helderbergers reared their round burly heads above the wall, and beside each pumpkin-head peered the end of a rusty musket. Nothing daunted by this formidable array, Antony Van Corlear drew forth and read with audible voice a missive from William the Testy, protesting against the usurpation of Bearn Island, and ordering the garrison to quit the premises, bag and baggage, on pain of the vengeance of the potentate of the Manhattoes.

In reply the wacht-meester applied the thumb of his right hand to the end of his nose, and the thumb of the left hand to the little finger of the right, and spreading each hand like a fan made an aerial flourish with his fingers. Antony Van Corlear was sorely perplexed to understand this sign, which seemed to him something mysterious and masonic. Not liking to betray his ignorance, he again read with a loud voice the missive of William the Testy, and again Nicholas Koorn applied the thumb of his right hand to the end of his nose, and the thumb of his left hand to the little finger of the right and repeated this kind of nasal weather-cock. Antony Van Corlear now persuaded himself that this was some short-hand sign or symbol, current in diplomacy; which though unintelligible to a new diplomat, like himself, would speak volumes to the experienced intellect of Willliam the Testy; considering his embassy therefore at an end, he sounded his trumpet with great complacency and set sail on his return down the river, every now and then practising this mysterious sign of the wacht-meester, to keep it accurately in mind.

Arrived at New Amsterdam he made a faithful report of his embassy to the governor, accompanied by a manual exhibition of the response of Nicholas Koorn. The governor was equally

perplexed with his ambassador. He was deeply versed in the
mysteries of freemasonry; but they threw no light on the matter. He knew every variety of wind-mill and weather-cock, but
was not a whit the wiser as to the aerial sign in question. He
had even dabbled in Egyptian hieroglyphics and the mystic sym-
bols of the obelisks, but none furnished a key to the reply of
Nicholas Koorn. He called a meeting of his council. Antony
Van Corlear stood forth in the midst, and putting the thumb of
his right hand to his nose and the thumb of his left hand to the
finger of the right, he gave a faithful fac-simile of the portentous
sign. Having a nose of unusual dimensions it was as if the
reply had been put in capitals, but all in vain; the worthy burgomasters were equally perplexed with the governor. Each
one put his thumb to the end of his nose, spread his fingers
like a fan, imitated the motion of Antony Van Corlear, and
then smoked on in dubious silence. Several times was Antony
obliged to stand forth like a fugleman and repeat the sign, and
each time a circle of nasal weather-cocks might be seen in the
council chamber.

Perplexed in the extreme, William the Testy sent for all the
soothsayers, and fortunetellers and wise men of the Manhattoes,
but none could interpret the mysterious reply of Nicholas
Koorn. The council broke up in sore perplexity. The matter
got abroad, Antony Van Corlear was stopped at every corner to
repeat the signal to a knot of anxious newsmongers, each of
whom departed with his thumb to his nose and his fingers in the
air, to carry the story home to his family. For several days all
business was neglected in New-Amsterdam; nothing was talked
of but the diplomatic mission of Antony the Trumpeter, nothing
was to be seen but knots of politicians with their thumbs to their

noses. In the meantime the fierce feud between William the Testy and Killian Van Rensellaer, which at first had menaced deadly warfare, gradually cooled off, like many other war questions, in the prolonged delays of diplomacy.

Still to this early affair of Rensellaerstein may be traced the remote origin of those windy wars in modern days which rage in the bowels of the Helderberg, and have well nigh shaken the great patroonship of the Van Rensellaers to its foundation; for we are told that the bully boys of the Helderberg, who served under Nicholas Koorn the wacht-meester, carried back to their mountains the hieroglyphic sign which had so sorely puzzled Antony Van Corlear and the sages of the Manhattoes; so that to the present day the thumb to the nose and the fingers in the air is apt to be the reply of the Helderbergers whenever called upon for any long arrears of rent.

11*

CHAPTER XII.

CONTAINING THE RISE OF THE GREAT AMPHICTYONIC COUNCIL.
OF THE PILGRIMS, WITH THE DECLINE AND FINAL EXTINC-
TION OF WILLIAM THE TESTY.

IT was asserted by the wise men of ancient times, who had a
nearer opportunity of ascertaining the fact, that at the gate of
Jupiter's palace lay two huge tuns, one filled with blessings,
the other with misfortunes; and it would verily seem as if the
latter had been completely overturned and left to deluge the
unlucky province of Nieuw-Nederlands: for about this time, while
harassed and annoyed from the south and the north, incessant forays
were made by the border chivalry of Connecticut upon the pig-
styes and hen-roosts of the Nederlanders. Every day or two
some broad-bottomed express-rider, covered with mud and mire,
would come floundering into the gate of New-Amsterdam, freighted
with some new tale of aggression from the frontier; whereupon
Antony Van Corlear, seizing his trumpet, the only substitute for
a newspaper in those primitive days, would sound the tidings
from the ramparts with such doleful notes and disastrous cadence,
as to throw half the old women in the city into hysterics; all
which tended greatly to increase his popularity; there being
nothing for which the public are more grateful than being frequently treated to a panic; a secret well known to modern editors.

But, oh ye powers! into what a paroxysm of passion did each new outrage of the Yankees throw the choleric little governor! Letter after letter, protest after protest, bad Latin, worse English, and hideous Low Dutch, were incessantly fulminated upon them, and the four-and-twenty letters of the alphabet, which formed his standing army, were worn out by constant campaigning. All, however, was ineffectual; even the recent victory at Oyster Bay, which had shed such a gleam of sunshine between the clouds of his foul weather reign, was soon followed by a more fearful gathering up of those clouds, and indications of more portentous tempest; for the Yankee tribe on the banks of the Connecticut, finding on this memorable occasion their incompetency to cope in fair fight with the sturdy chivalry of the Manhattoes, had called to their aid all the ten tribes of their brethren, who inhabit the east country, which from them has derived the name of Yankee land. This call was promptly responded to. The consequence was a great confederacy of the tribes of Massachusetts, Connecticut, New-Plymouth and New-Haven, under the title of the " United Colonies of New-England ;" the pretended object of which was mutual defence against the savages ; but the real object the subjugation of the Nieuw-Nederlands.

For, to let the reader into one of the great secrets of history, the Nieuw-Nederlands had long been regarded by the whole Yankee race as the modern land of promise, and themselves as the chosen and peculiar people destined, one day or other, by hook or by crook, to get possession of it. In truth they are a wonderful and all-prevalent people ; of that class who only require an inch to gain an ell, or a halter to gain a horse. From the time they first gained a foothold on Plymouth Rock, they began to migrate, progressing and progressing from place to place, and land to land, making a little here and a little there, and controverting the old proverb, that a rolling stone gathers no moss. Hence they have facetiously received the nickname of THE PILGRIMS : that is to say, a people who are always seeking a better country than their own.

The tidings of this great Yankee league struck William Kieft with dismay, and for once in his life he forgot to bounce on receiving a disagreeable piece of intelligence. In fact, on turning over in his mind all that he had read at the Hague about leagues and combinations, he found that this was a counterpart of the Amphictyonic league, by which the states of Greece attained such power and supremacy ; and the very idea made his heart quake for the safety of his empire at the Manhattoes.

The affairs of the confederacy were managed by an annual council of delegates held at Boston, which Kieft denominated the Delphos of this truly classic league. The very first meeting gave evidence of hostility to the Nieuw-Nederlanders, who were charged in their dealings with the Indians, with carrying on a traffic in "guns, powther and shott—a trade damnable and injurious to the colonists." It is true the Connecticut traders were fain to dabble a little in this damnable traffic ; but then they always dealt in what were termed Yankee guns ; ingeniously calculated to burst in the pagan hands which used them.

The rise of this potent confederacy was a death-blow to the glory of William the Testy, for from that day forward he never held up his head, but appeared quite crest-fallen. It is true, as the grand council augmented in power, and the league rolling onward, gathered about the red hills of New-Haven, threatening to overwhelm the Nieuw-Nederlands, he continued occasionally to fulminate proclamations and protests, as a shrewd sea-captain fires his guns into a water-spout; but alas! they had no more effect than so many blank cartridges.

Thus end the authenticated chronicles of the reign of William the Testy; for henceforth, in the troubles, perplexities, and confusion of the times, he seems to have been totally overlooked, and to have slipped for ever through the fingers of scrupulous history. It is a matter of deep concern that such obscurity should hang over his latter days; for he was in truth a mighty and great little man, and worthy of being utterly renowned, seeing that he was the first potentate that introduced into this land the art of fighting by proclamation, and defending a country by trumpeters and wind-mills.

It is true, that certain of the early provincial poets, of whom there were great numbers in the Nieuw-Nederlands, taking advantage of his mysterious exit, have fabled that, like Romulus, he was translated to the skies, and forms a very fiery little star, somewhere on the left claw of the crab; while others, equally fanciful, declare that he had experienced a fate similar to that of the good king Arthur; who, we are assured by ancient bards, was carried away to the delicious abodes of fairy land, where he still exists, in pristine worth and vigor, and will one day or another return to restore the gallantry, the honor, and the immaculate probity, which prevailed in the glorious days of the Round Table.*

* The old Welsh bards believed that king Arthur was not dead, but carried awaie by the fairies into some pleasant place, where he sholde remaine for a time, and then returne againe and reigne in as great authority as ever.—Hollinshed.

The Britons suppose that he shall come yet and conquere all Britaigne, for certes, this is the prophicye of Merlyn—He say'd that his deth shall be doubt-

All these, however, are but pleasing fantasies, the cobweb visions of those dreaming varlets, the poets, to which I would not have my judicious reader attach any credibility. Neither am I disposed to credit an ancient and rather apocryphal historian, who asserts that the ingenious Wilhelmus was annihilated by the blowing down of one of his wind-mills; nor a writer of later times, who affirms that he fell a victim to an experiment in natural history, having the misfortune to break his neck from a garret window of the stadthouse in attempting to catch swallows by sprinkling salt upon their tails. Still less do I put my faith in the tradition that he perished at sea in conveying home to Holland a treasure of golden ore, discovered somewhere among the haunted regions of the Catskill mountains.*

eous; and said soth, for men thereof yet have doubte and shullen for ever more—for men wyt not whether that he lyveth or is dede.—DE LEEW. CHRON.

* Diedrich Knickerbocker, in his scrupulous search after truth, is sometimes too fastidious in regard to facts which border a little on the marvelous. The story of the golden ore rests on something better than mere tradition. The venerable Adrian Van der Donck, Doctor of Laws, in his description of the New Netherlands, asserts it from his own observation as an eye-witness. He was present, he says, in 1645 at a treaty between Governor Kieft and the Mo-hawk Indians, in which one of the latter, in painting himself for the ceremony, used a pigment the weight and shining appearance of which excited the curi-osity of the governor and Mynheer Van der Donck. They obtained a lump and gave it to be proved by a skillful doctor of medicine, Johannes de la Montagne, one of the councilors of the New Netherlands. It was put into a crucible, and yielded two pieces of gold worth about three guilders. All this, continues Adrian Van der Donck, was kept secret. As soon as peace was made with the Mohawks, an officer and a few men were sent to the mountain (in the region of the Kaatskill) under the guidance of an Indian, to search for the precious mineral. They brought back a bucket full of ore; which being submitted to the crucible, proved as productive as the first. William Kieft now thought the discovery certain. He sent a confidential person, Arent Corsen,

The most probable account declares, that what with the constant troubles on his frontiers—the incessant schemings and projects going on in his own pericranium—the memorials, petitions, remonstrances, and sage pieces of advice of respectable meetings of the sovereign people, and the refractory disposition of his councilors, who were sure to differ from him on every point, and uniformly to be in the wrong—his mind was kept in a furnace heat, until he became as completely burnt out as a Dutch family pipe which has passed through three generations of hard smokers. In this manner did he undergo a kind of animal combustion, consuming away like a farthing rush-light—so that when grim death finally snuffed him out, there was scarce left enough of him to bury!

with a bag full of the mineral, to New-Haven, to take passage in an English ship for England, thence to proceed to Holland. The vessel sailed at Christmas, but never reached her port. All on board perished.

In the year 1647, Wilhelmus Kieft himself embarked on board the Princess, taking with him specimens of the supposed mineral. The ship was never heard of more!

Some have supposed that the mineral in question was not gold, but pyrites; but we have the assertion of Adrian Van der Donck, an eye-witness, and the experiment of Johannes de la Montagne, a learned doctor of medicine, on the golden side of the question. Cornelius Van Tienhooven, also, at that time secretary of the New-Netherlands, declared in Holland that he had tested several specimens of the mineral, which proved satisfactory.*

It would appear, however, that these golden treasures of the Kaatskill always brought ill luck; as is evidenced in the fate of Arent Corsen and Wilhelmus Kieft, and the wreck of the ships in which they attempted to convey the treasure across the ocean. The golden mines have never since been explored, but remain among the mysteries of the Kaatskill mountains, and under the protection of the goblins which haunt them.

* See Van der Donck's Description of the New-Netherlands. Collect. New-York Hist Society, Vol. I. p. 161.

BOOK V.

CONTAINING THE FIRST PART OF THE REIGN OF PETER
STUYVESANT, AND HIS TROUBLES WITH THE AMPHIC-
TYONIC COUNCIL.

CHAPTER I.

IN WHICH THE DEATH OF A GREAT MAN IS SHOWN TO BE NO
VERY INCONSOLABLE MATTER OF SORROW—AND HOW PE-
TER STUYVESANT ACQUIRED A GREAT NAME FROM THE UN-
COMMON STRENGTH OF HIS HEAD.

To a profound philosopher like myself, who am apt to see clear
through a subject, where the penetration of ordinary people extends but half way, there is no fact more simple and manifest than
that the death of a great man is a matter of very little importance.
Much as we may think of ourselves, and much as we may excite
the empty plaudits of the million, it is certain that the greatest
among us do actually fill but an exceeding small space in the
world; and it is equally certain, that even that small space is
quickly supplied when we leave it vacant. "Of what consequence is it," said Pliny, "that individuals appear, or make their
exit? the world is a theatre whose scenes and actors are continu-

ally changing." Never did philosopher speak more correctly, and I only wonder that so wise a remark could have existed so many ages, and mankind not have laid it more to heart. Sage follows on in the footsteps of sage ; one hero just steps out of his triumphal car, to make way for the hero who comes after him ; and of the proudest monarch it is merely said that, " he slept with his fathers, and his successor reigned in his stead."

The world, to tell the private truth, cares but little for their loss, and if left to itself would soon forget to grieve, and though a nation has often been figuratively drowned in tears on the death of a great man, yet it is ten to one if an individual tear has been shed on the occasion, excepting from the forlorn pen of some hungry author. It is the historian, the biographer, and the poet, who have the whole burden of grief to sustain ; who—kind souls ! —like undertakers in England, act the part of chief mourners— who inflate a nation with sighs it never heaved, and deluge it with tears it never dreamt of shedding. Thus, while the patriotic author is weeping and howling, in prose, in blank verse, and in rhyme, and collecting the drops of public sorrow into his volume, as into a lachrymal vase, it is more than probable his fellow-citi- zens are eating and drinking, fiddling and dancing, as utterly ignorant of the bitter lamentations made in their name, as are those men of straw, John Doe and Richard Roe, of the plaintiffs for whom they are generously pleased to become sureties.

The most glorious hero that ever desolated nations might have mouldered into oblivion among the rubbish of his own monument, did not some historian take him into favor, and benevolently transmit his name to posterity—and much as the valiant William Kieft worried, and bustled, and turmoiled, while he had the desti- nies of a whole colony in his hand, I question seriously whether he will not be obliged to this authentic history for all his future celebrity.

His exit occasioned no convulsion in the city of New-Amsterdam nor its vicinity : the earth trembled not, neither did any stars shoot from their spheres—the heavens were nct shrouded in black, as poets would fain persuade us they have been, on the death of a hero—the rocks (hard-hearted varlets !) melted not into tears, nor did the trees hang their heads in silent sorrow ; and as to the sun, he lay a-bed the next night just as long, and showed as jolly a face when he rose, as he ever did on the same day of the month in any year, either before or since. The good people of New-Amsterdam, one and all, declared that he had been a very busy, active, bustling little governor ; that he was "the father of his country"—that he was "the noblest work of God"—that "he was a man, take him for all in all, they ne'er should look upon his like again"—together with sundry other civil and affectionate speeches regularly said on the death of all great men ; after which they smoked their pipes, thought no more about him, and Peter Stuyvesant succeeded to his station.

Peter Stuyvesant was the last, and, like the renowned Wouter Van Twiller, the best of our ancient Dutch governors. Wouter having surpassed all who preceded him, and Pieter or Piet, as he was sociably called by the old Dutch burghers, who were ever prone to familiarize names, having never been equalled by any successor. He was in fact the very man fitted by nature to retrieve the desperate fortunes of her beloved province, had not the fates, those most potent and unrelenting of all ancient spinsters, destined them to inextricable confusion.

To say merely that he was a hero would be doing him

great injustice—he was in truth a combination of heroes—for he was of a sturdy, rawboned make like Ajax Telamon, with a pair of round shoulders that Hercules would have given his hide for (meaning his lion's hide,) when he undertook to ease old Atlas of his load.   He was, moreover, as Plutarch describes Coriolanus, not only terrible for the force of his arm, but likewise of his voice, which sounded as though it came out of a barrel ; and, like the self-same warrior, he possessed a sovereign contempt for the sovereign people, and an iron aspect, which was enough of itself to make the very bowels of his adversaries quake with terror and dismay.   All this martial excellency of appearance was inexpressibly heightened by an accidental advantage, with which I am surprised that neither Homer nor Virgil have graced any of their heroes.   This was nothing less than a wooden leg, which was the only prize he had gained in bravely fighting the battles of his country, but of which he was so proud, that he was often heard to declare he valued it more than all his other limbs put together ; indeed so highly did he esteem it, that he had it gallantly enchased and relieved with silver devices, which caused it to be related in divers histories and legends that he wore a silver leg.*

Like that choleric warrior Achilles, he was somewhat subject to extempore bursts of passion, which were rather unpleasant to his favorites and attendants, whose perceptions he was apt to quicken, after the manner of his illustrious imitator, Peter the Great, by anointing their shoulders with his walking-staff.

Though I cannot find that he had read Plato, or Aristotle, or Hobbes, or Bacon, or Algernon Sydney, or Tom Paine, yet

---

* See the histories of Masters Josselyn and Blome.

did he sometimes manifest a shrewdness and sagacity in his measures, that one would hardly expect from a man who did not know Greek, and had never studied the ancients. True it is, and I confess it with sorrow, that he had an unreasonable aversion to experiments, and was fond of governing his province after the simplest manner—but then he contrived to keep it in better order than did the erudite Kieft, though he had all the philosophers, ancient and modern, to assist and perplex him. I must likewise own that he made but very few laws, but then again he took care that those few were rigidly and impartially enforced—and I do not know but justice on the whole was as well administered as if there had been volumes of sage acts and statutes yearly made, and daily neglected and forgotten.

He was, in fact, the very reverse of his predecessors, being neither tranquil and inert, like Walter the Doubter, nor restless and fidgeting, like William the Testy; but a man, or rather a governor, of such uncommon activity and decision of mind, that he never sought nor accepted the advice of others; depending bravely upon his single head as would a hero of yore upon his single arm, to carry him through all difficulties and dangers. To tell the simple truth he wanted nothing more to complete him as a statesman than to think always right, for no one can say but that he always acted as he thought. He was never a man to flinch when he found himself in a scrape; but to dash forward through thick and thin, trusting, by hook or by crook, to make all things straight in the end. In a word, he possessed in an eminent degree that great quality in a statesman, called perseverance by the polite, but nicknamed obstinacy by the vulgar. A wonderful salve for official blunders; since he who perseveres in error without flinching, gets the credit of boldness and consistency, while he who wavers in seeking to do what is right gets stigmatized as a trimmer. This much is certain; and it is a maxim well worthy the attention of all legislators great and small, who stand shaking in the wind, irresolute which way to steer, that a ruler who follows his own will pleases himself, while he who seeks to satisfy the wishes and whims of others runs great risk of pleasing nobody. There is nothing too like putting down one's foot resolutely, when in doubt; and letting things take their course. The clock that stands still points right twice in the four and twenty hours: while others may keep going continually and be continually going wrong.

Nor did this magnanimous quality escape the discernment of the good people of Nieuw-Nederlands; on the contrary, so much were they struck with the independent will and vigorous resolution displayed on all occasions by their new governor, that they universally called him Hard-Koppig Piet; or Peter the Head-strong—a great compliment to the strength of his understanding.

If, from all that I have said, thou dost not gather, worthy reader, that Peter Stuyvesant was a tough, sturdy, valiant, weather-beaten, mettlesome, obstinate, leathern-sided, lion-hearted, generous-spirited old governor, either I have written to but little purpose, or thou art very dull at drawing conclusions.

This most excellent governor commenced his administration on the 29th of May, 1647; a remarkably stormy day, distinguished in all the almanacs of the time which have come down to us by the name of *Windy Friday*. As he was very jealous of his personal and official dignity, he was inaugurated into office with great ceremony; the goodly oaken chair of the renowned Wouter Van Twiller being carefully preserved for such occasions, in like manner as the chair and stone were reverentially preserved at Schone, in Scotland, for the coronation of the Caledonian monarchs.

I must not omit to mention, that the tempestuous state of the elements, together with its being that unlucky day of the week termed "hanging day," did not fail to excite much grave speculation and divers very reasonable apprehensions among the more ancient and enlightened inhabitants; and several of the sager sex, who were reputed to be not a little skilled in the mysteries of astrology and fortunetelling, did declare outright that they were omens of a disastrous administration—an event that came to be lamentably verified, and which proves, beyond dispute, the wisdom of attending to those preternatural intimations furnished by dreams and visions, the flying of birds, falling of stones, and cackling of geese, on which the sages and rulers of ancient times placed such reliance—or to those shootings of stars, eclipses of the moon, howlings of dogs, and flarings of candles, carefully noted and interpreted by the oracular sybils of our day; who, in my humble opinion, are the legitimate inheritors and preservers of the ancient science of divination. This much is certain, that Governor Stuyvesant succeeded to the chair of state at a turbulent period; when foes thronged and threatened from without; when anarchy and stiff-necked opposition reigned rampant within; when the authority of their High Mightinesses the Lords States-General, though supported by economy, and defended by speeches, protests and proclamations, yet tottered to its very centre; and when the great city of New-Amsterdam, though fortified by flag-staffs, trumpeters, and wind-mills, seemed, like some fair lady of easy virtue, to lie open to attack, and ready to yield to the first invader.

CHAPTER II.

THE very first movements of the great Peter, on taking the reins
of government, displayed his magnanimity, though they occasioned not a little marvel and uneasiness among the people of the
Manhattoes. Finding himself constantly interrupted by the opposition, and annoyed by the advice of his privy council, the
members of which had acquired the unreasonable habit of thinking and speaking for themselves during the preceding reign, he
determined at once to put a stop to such grievous abominations.
Scarcely, therefore, had he entered upon his authority, than he
turned out of office all the meddlesome spirits of the factious cabinet of William the Testy ; in place of whom he chose unto
himself counselors from those fat, somniferous, respectable
burghers who had flourished and slumbered under the easy reign
of Walter the Doubter. All these he caused to be furnished
with abundance of fair long pipes, and to be regaled with frequent corporation dinners, admonishing them to smoke, and eat,
and sleep, for the good of the nation, while he took the burden of

government upon his own shoulders—an arrangement to which they all gave hearty acquiescence.

Nor did he stop here, but made a hideous rout among the inventions and expedients of his learned predecessor—rooting up his patent gallows, where caitiff vagabonds were suspended by the waistband—demolishing his flag-staffs and wind-mills, which, like mighty giants, guarded the ramparts of New-Amsterdam— pitching to the duyvel whole batteries of quaker guns—and, in a word, turning topsy-turvy the whole philosophic, economic, and wind-mill system of the immortal sage of Saardam.

The honest folk of New-Amsterdam began to quake now for the fate of their matchless champion, Antony the Trumpeter, who had acquired prodigious favor in the eyes of the women, by means of his whiskers and his trumpet. Him did Peter the Headstrong cause to be brought into his presence, and eyeing him for a moment from head to foot, with a countenance that would have appalled any thing else than a sounder of brass— " Pr'ythee, who and what art thou?" said he. " Sire," replied the other, in no wise dismayed, " for my name, it is Anthony Van Corlear—for my parentage, I am the son of my mother—for my profession, I am champion and garrison of this great city of New-Amsterdam." " I doubt me much," said Peter Stuyvesant, " that thou art some scurvy costard-monger knave :—how didst thou acquire this paramount honor and dignity ?" " Marry, sir," replied the other, " like many a great man before me, simply *by sounding my own trumpet.*" " Ay, is it so ?" quoth the governor; " why then let us have a relish of thy art." Whereupon the good Antony put his instrument to his lips, and sounded a charge with such a tremendous outset, such a delectable quaver, and such a triumphant cadence, that it was enough to make one's heart leap

12

out of one's mouth only to be within a mile of it.   Like as a war-worn charger, grazing in peaceful plains, starts at a strain of martial music, pricks up his ears, and snorts, and paws, and kindles at the noise, so did the heroic Peter joy to hear the clangor of the trumpet; for of him might truly be said, what was recorded of the renowned St. George of England, " there was nothing in all the world that more rejoiced his heart than to hear the pleasant sound of war, and see the soldiers brandish forth their steeled weapons."   Casting his eye more kindly, therefore, upon the sturdy Van Corlear, and finding him to be a jovial varlet, shrewd in his discourse, yet of great discretion and immeasurable wind, he straightway conceived a vast kindness for him, and discharging him from the troublesome duty of garrisoning, defending, and alarming the city, ever after retained him about his person, as his chief favorite, confidential envoy, and trusty squire. Instead of disturbing the city with disastrous notes, he was in structed to play so as to delight the governor while at his repasts, as did the minstrels of yore in the days of glorious chivalry—and on all public occasions to rejoice the ears of the people with warlike melody—thereby keeping alive a noble and martial spirit.

But the measure of the valiant Peter which produced the greatest agitation in the community, was his laying his hand upon the currency.   He had old-fashioned notions in favor of gold and silver, which he considered the true standards of wealth and mediums of commerce, and one of his first edicts was, that all duties to government should be paid in those precious metals, and that seawant, or wampum, should no longer be a legal tender.

Here was a blow at public prosperity !   All those who speculated on the rise and fall of this fluctuating currency, found their calling at an end: those, too, who had hoarded Indian money by barrels full, found their capital shrunk in amount; but, above all, the Yankee traders, who were accustomed to flood the market with newly-coined oyster-shells, and to abstract Dutch merchandise in exchange, were loud-mouthed in decrying this " tampering with the currency." It was clipping the wings of commerce; it was checking the development of public prosperity; trade would be at an end; goods would moulder on the shelves; grain would rot in the granaries; grass would grow in the market-place. In a word, no one who has not heard the outcries and howlings of a modern Tarshish, at any check upon " paper money," can have any idea of the clamor against Peter the Headstrong, for checking the circulation of oyster-shells.

In fact, trade did shrink into narrower channels; but then the stream was deep as it was broad; the honest Dutchmen sold less goods; but then they got the worth of them, either in silver and gold, or in codfish, tin-ware, apple-brandy, Weathersfield onions, wooden bowls, and other articles of Yankee barter. The ingenious people of the east, however, indemnified themselves in another way for having to abandon the coinage of oyster-shells, for about this time we are told that wooden nutmegs made their first appearance in New-Amsterdam, to the great annoyance of the Dutch housewives.

NOTE.

From a manuscript record of the province; Lib. N. Y. Hist. Society.— We have been unable to render your inhabitants wiser and prevent their being further imposed upon than to declare absolutely and peremptorily that henceforward seawant shall be bullion—not longer admissible in trade, without any value, as it is indeed. So that every one may be upon his guard to barter no longer away his wares and merchandises for these bubbles—at least not to accept them at a higher rate or in a larger quantity than as they may want them in their trade with the savages.

In this way your English [Yankee] neighbors shall no longer be enabled to draw the best wares and merchandises from our country for nothing—the beavers and furs not excepted. This has indeed long since been insufferable, although it ought chiefly to be imputed to the imprudent penuriousness of our own merchants and inhabitants, who, it is to be hoped, shall through the abolition of this seawant become wiser and more prudent.

27th January, 1662.

Seawant falls into disrepute—duties to be paid in silver coin.

CHAPTER III.

Now it came to pass, that while Peter Stuyvesant was busy regulating the internal affairs of his domain, the great Yankee league, which had caused such tribulation to William the Testy, continued to increase in extent and power. The grand Amphictyonic council of the league was held at Boston, where it spun a web, which threatened to link within it all the mighty principalities and powers of the east. The object proposed by this formidable combination was mutual protection and defence against their savage neighbors; but all the world knows the real aim was to form a grand crusade against the Nieuw-Nederlands and to get possession of the city of the Manhattoes—as devout an object of enterprise and ambition to the Yankees as was ever the capture of Jerusalem to ancient crusaders.

In the very year following the inauguration of Governor Stuyvesant, a grand deputation departed from the city of Providence (famous for its dusty streets and beauteous women) in behalf of the plantation of Rhode Island, praying to be admitted into the league.

The following minute of this deputation appears in the ancient records of the council.*

" Mr. Will. Cottington and Captain Partridg of Rhoode Island presented this insewing request to the commissioners in wrighting—

" Our request and motion is in behalfe of Rhoode Iland, that wee the Ilanders of Roode-Iland may be rescauied into combination with all the united colonyes of New England in a firme and perpetual league of friendship and amity of ofence and defence, mutuall advice and succor upon all just occasions for our mutuall safety and wellfaire, etc.

" WILL COTTINGTON,

" ALICXSANDER PARTRIDG."

There was certainly something in the very physiognomy of this document that might well inspire apprehension. The name of Alexander, however misspelt, has been warlike in every age, and though its fierceness is in some measure softened by being coupled with the gentle cognomen of Partridge, still, like the color of scarlet, it bears an exceeding great resemblance to the sound of a trumpet. From the style of the letter, moreover, and the soldierlike ignorance of orthography displayed by the noble captain Alicxsander Partridg in spelling his own name, we may picture to ourselves this mighty man of Rhodes, strong in arms, potent in the field, and as great a scholar as though he had been educated among that learned people of Thrace, who, Aristotle assures us, could not count beyond the number four.

The result of this great Yankee league was augmented auda-

* Haz. Col. Stat. Pap.

city on the part of the moss-troopers of Connecticut—pushing their encroachments farther and farther into the territories of their High Mightinesses, so that even the inhabitants of New-Amsterdam began to draw short breath and to find themselves exceedingly cramped for elbow-room.

Peter Stuyvesant was not a man to submit quietly to such intrusions; his first impulse was to march at once to the frontier and kick these squatting Yankees out of the country; but, be-thinking himself in time that he was now a governor and legis-lator, the policy of the statesman for once cooled the fire of the old soldier, and he determined to try his hand at negotiation. A correspondence accordingly ensued between him and the grand council of the league, and it was agreed that commissioners from either side should meet at Hartford, to settle boundaries, adjust grievances, and establish a " perpetual and happy peace."

The commissioners on the part of the Manhattoes were chosen, according to immemorial usage of that venerable metropolis, from among the " wisest and weightiest" men of the community; that is to say, men with the oldest heads and heaviest pockets. Among these sages the veteran navigator, Hans Reinier Oothout, who had made such extensive discoveries during the time of Oloffe the Dreamer, was looked up to as an oracle in all matters of the kind; and he was ready to produce the very spy-glass with which he first spied the mouth of the Connecticut River from his mast-head, and all the world knows that the discovery of the mouth of a river gives prior right to all the lands drained by its waters.

It was with feelings of pride and exultation that the good people of the Manhattoes saw two of the richest and most pon-derous burghers departing on this embassy; men whose word on 'change was oracular, and in whose presence no poor man ventured

to appear without taking off his hat : when it was seen, too, that
the veteran Reinier Oothout accompanied them with his spy-glass
under his arm, all the old men and old women predicted that men
of such weight, with such evidence, would leave the Yankees no
alternative but to pack up their tin kettles and wooden wares ;
put wife and children in a cart, and abandon all the lands of their
High Mightinesses, on which they had squatted.

In truth, the commissioners sent to Hartford by the league,
seemed in nowise calculated to compete with men of such capacity.
They were two lean Yankee lawyers, litigious-looking varlets, and
evidently men of no substance, since they had no rotundity in the
belt, and there was no jingling of money in their pockets ; it is
true they had longer heads than the Dutchmen ; but if the heads
of the latter were flat at top, they were broad at bottom, and what
was wanting in height of forehead, was made up by a double
chin.

The negotiation turned as usual upon the good old corner-
stone of original discovery ; according to the principle that he
who first sees a new country, has an unquestionable right to it.
This being admitted, the veteran Oothout, at a concerted signal,
stepped forth in the assembly with the identical tarpauling spy-
glass in his hand, with which he had discovered the mouth of the
Connecticut, while the worthy Dutch commissioners lolled back in
their chairs, secretly chuckling at the idea of having for once got
the weather-gage of the Yankees ; but what was their dismay
when the latter produced a Nantucket whaler with a spy-glass,
twice as long, with which he discovered the whole coast, quite
down to the Manhattoes ; and so crooked that he had spied with
it up the whole course of the Connecticut River.   This principle
pushed home, therefore, the Yankees had a right to the whole

country bordering on the Sound; nay, the city of New-Amsterdam was a mere Dutch squatting-place on their territories.

I forbear to dwell upon the confusion of the worthy Dutch commissioners at finding their main pillar of proof thus knocked from under them; neither will I pretend to describe the consternation of the wise men at the Manhattoes when they learnt how their commissioner had been out-trumped by the Yankees, and how the latter pretended to claim to the very gates of New-Amsterdam.

Long was the negotiation protracted, and long was the public mind kept in a state of anxiety. There are two modes of settling boundary questions when the claims of the opposite parties are irreconcilable. One is by an appeal to arms, in which case the weakest party is apt to lose its right, and get a broken head into the bargain; the other mode is by compromise, or mutual conces sion; that is to say, one party cedes half of its claims, and the other party half of its rights; he who grasps most gets most, and the whole is pronounced an equitable division, "perfectly honorable to both parties."

The latter mode was adopted in the present instance. The Yankees gave up claims to vast tracts of the Nieuw-Nederlands which they had never seen, and all right to the island of Manna-hata and the city of New-Amsterdam, to which they had no right at all; while the Dutch, in return, agreed that the Yankees should retain possession of the frontier places where they had squatted, and of both sides of the Connecticut river.

When the news of this treaty arrived at New-Amsterdam, the whole city was in an uproar of exultation. The old women rejoiced that there was to be no war, the old men that their cabbage-gardens were safe from invasion; while the political sages

pronounced the treaty a great triumph over the Yankees, considering how much they had claimed, and how little they had been
" fobbed off with."

And now my worthy reader is, doubtless, like the great and
good Peter, congratulating himself with the idea, that his feelings
will no longer be harassed by afflicting details of stolen horses,
broken heads, impounded hogs, and all the other catalogue of
heart-rending cruelties that disgraced these border wars.   But if
he should indulge in such expectations, it is a proof that he is
but little versed in the paradoxical ways of cabinets; to convince
him of which, I solicit his serious attention to my next chapter,
wherein I will show that Peter Stuyvesant has already committed
a great error in politics; and by effecting a peace, has materially
hazarded the tranquillity of the province.

CHAPTER IV.

CONTAINING DIVERS SPECULATIONS ON WAR AND NEGOTIA-
TIONS—SHOWING THAT A TREATY OF PEACE IS A GREAT
NATIONAL EVIL.

IT was the opinion of that poetical philosopher, Lucretius, that war was the original state of man, whom he described as being primitively a savage beast of prey, engaged in a constant state of hostility with his own species, and that this ferocious spirit was tamed and ameliorated by society. The same opinion has been advocated by Hobbes,* nor have there been wanting many other philosophers to admit and defend it.

For my part, though prodigiously fond of these valuable speculations, so complimentary to human nature, yet, in this instance, I am inclined to take the proposition by halves, believing with Horace,† that though war may have been originally the favorite amusement and industrious employment of our progenitors, yet, like many other excellent habits, so far from being

---

* Hobbes's Leviathan.   Part i. ch. 13.

† Quum prorepserunt primis animalia terris,
　Mutuum ac turpe pecus, glandem atque cubilia propter,
　Unguibus et pugnis, dein fustibus, atque ita porro
　Pugnabant armis, quæ post fabricaverat usus.

HOR. Sat. L. i. S. 3.

ameliorated, it has been cultivated and confirmed by refinement and civilization, and increases in exact proportion as we approach towards that state of perfection, which is the *ne plus ultra* of modern philosophy.

The first conflict between man and man was the mere exertion of physical force, unaided by auxiliary weapons—his arm was his buckler, his fist was his mace, and a broken head the catastrophe of his encounters. The battle of unassisted strength was succeeded by the more rugged one of stones and clubs, and war assumed a sanguinary aspect. As man advanced in refinement, as his faculties expanded, and as his sensibilities became more exquisite, he grew rapidly more ingenious and experienced in the art of murdering his fellow-beings. He invented a thousand devices to defend and to assault—the helmet, the cuirass, and the buckler, the sword, the dart, and the javelin, prepared him to elude the wound as well as to launch the blow. Still urging on, in the career of philanthropic invention, he enlarges and heightens his powers of defence and injury:—The Aries, the Scorpio, the Balista, and the Catapulta, give a horror and sublimity to war, and magnify its glory, by increasing its desolation. Still insatiable, though armed with machinery that seemed to reach the limits of destructive invention, and to yield a power of injury commensurate even with the desires of revenge—still deeper researches must be made in the diabolical arcana. With furious zeal he dives into the bowels of the earth; he toils midst poisonous minerals and deadly salts—the sublime discovery of gunpowder blazes upon the world—and finally the dreadful art of fighting by proclamation seems to endow the demon of war with ubiquity and omnipotence!

This, indeed, is grand!—this, indeed, marks the powers of

mind, and bespeaks that divine endowment of reason, which distinguishes us from the animals, our inferiors. The unenlightened brutes content themselves with the native force which Providence has assigned them.—The angry bull butts with his horns, as did his progenitors before him—the lion, the leopard, and the tiger seek only with their talons and their fangs to gratify their sanguinary fury ; and even the subtle serpent darts the same venom, and uses the same wiles, as did his sire before the flood. Man alone, blessed with the inventive mind, goes on from discovery to discovery—enlarges and multiplies his powers of destruction ; arrogates the tremendous weapons of Deity itself, and tasks creation to assist him in murdering his brother worm !

In proportion as the art of war has increased in improvement has the art of preserving peace advanced in equal ratio ; and as we have discovered, in this age of wonders and inventions, that proclamation is the most formidable engine in war, so have we discovered the no less ingenious mode of maintaining peace by perpetual negotiations.

A treaty, or, to speak more correctly, a negotiation, therefore, according to the acceptation of experienced statesmen, learned in these matters, is no longer an attempt to accommodate differences, to ascertain rights, and to establish an equitable exchange of kind offices ; but a contest of skill between two powers, which shall overreach and take in the other. It is a cunning endeavor to obtain by peaceful manœuvre, and the chicanery of cabinets, those advantages which a nation would otherwise have wrested by force of arms ; in the same manner as a conscientious highwayman reforms and becomes a quiet and praiseworthy citizen, contenting himself with cheating his neighbor out of that property he would formerly have seized with open violence.

In fact, the only time when two nations can be said to be in a state of perfect amity is when a negotiation is open, and a treaty pending. Then, when there are no stipulations entered into, no bonds to restrain the will, no specific limits to awaken the captious jealousy of right implanted in our nature ; when each party has some advantage to hope and expect from the other, then it is that the two nations are wonderfully gracious and friendly; their ministers professing the highest mutual regard, exchanging billets-doux, making fine speeches, and indulging in all those little diplomatic flirtations, coquetries, and fondlings, that do so marvelously tickle the good humor of the respective nations. Thus it may paradoxically be said, that there is never so good an understanding between two nations as when there is a little mis-understanding—and that so long as they are on no terms at all, they are on the best terms in the world!

I do not by any means pretend to claim the merit of having made the above discovery. It has, in fact, long been secretly acted upon by certain enlightened cabinets, and is, together with divers other notable theories, privately copied out of the common-place book of an illustrious gentleman, who has been member of congress, and enjoyed the unlimited confidence of heads of departments. To this principle may be ascribed the wonderful ingenuity shown of late years in protracting and interrupting negotiations.—Hence the cunning measure of appointing as ambassador some political pettifogger skilled in delays, so-phisms, and misapprehensions, and dexterous in the art of baffling argument—or some blundering statesman, whose errors and misconstructions may be a plea for refusing to ratify his engagements. And hence, too, that most notable expedient, so popular with our government, of sending out a brace of ambassadors; between whom, having each an individual will to consult, character to establish, and interest to promote, you may as well look for unanimity and concord as between two lovers with one mistress, two dogs with one bone, or two naked rogues with one pair of breeches. This disagreement, therefore, is continually breeding delays and impediments, in consequence of which the negotiation goes on swimmingly—inasmuch as there is no prospect of its ever coming to a close. Nothing is lost by these delays and obstacles but time ; and in a negotiation, according to the theory I have exposed, all time lost is in reality so much time gained :—with what delightful paradoxes does modern political economy abound!

Now all that I have here advanced is so notoriously true, that I almost blush to take up the time of my readers with treating of matters which must many a time have stared them in the face. But the proposition to which I would most earnestly call their attention is this, that though a negotiation be the most harmonizing of all national transactions, yet a treaty of peace is a great political evil, and one of the most fruitful sources of war.

I have rarely seen an instance of any special contract between individuals that did not produce jealousies, bickerings, and often downright ruptures between them ; nor did I ever know of a treaty between two nations that did not occasion continual misunderstandings. How many worthy country neighbors have I known, who, after living in peace and good fellowship for years, have been thrown into a state of distrust, caviling, and animosity, by some ill-starred agreement about fences, runs of water and stray cattle ! And how many well-meaning nations, who would otherwise have remained in the most amicable disposition towards each other, have been brought to swords' points about the

infringement or misconstruction of some treaty, which in an evil
hour they had concluded, by way of making their amity more
sure!

Treaties at best are but complied with so long as interest requires their fulfillment; consequently they are virtually binding
on the weaker party only, or, in plain truth, they are not binding
at all.   No nation will wantonly go to war with another if it has
nothing to gain thereby, and therefore needs no treaty to restrain
it from violence; and if it have any thing to gain, I much question, from what I have witnessed of the righteous conduct of nations, whether any treaty could be made so strong that it could
not thrust the sword through—nay, I would hold ten to one, the
treaty itself would be the very source to which resort would be
had to find a pretext for hostilities.

Thus, therefore, I conclude—that though it is the best of all
policies for a nation to keep up a constant negotiation with its
neighbors, yet it is the summit of folly for it ever to be beguiled
into a treaty; for then comes on non-fulfillment and infraction,
then remonstrance, then altercation, then retaliation, then recrimi-
nation, and finally open war.   In a word, negotiation is like
courtship, a time of sweet words, gallant speeches, soft looks, and
endearing caresses—but the marriage ceremony is the signal for
hostilities.

If my painstaking reader be not somewhat perplexed by the
ratiocination of the foregoing passage, he will perceive, at a
glance, that the Great Peter, in concluding a treaty with his
eastern neighbors, was guilty of lamentable error in policy.   In
fact, to this unlucky agreement may be traced a world of bickerings and heart-burnings between the parties, about fancied or
pretended infringements of treaty stipulations; in all which the

Yankees were prone to indemnify themselves by a " dig into the sides" of the New-Netherlands. But, in sooth, these border feuds, albeit they gave great annoyance to the good burghers of Manna-hata, were so pitiful in their nature, that a grave historian like myself, who grudges the time spent in any thing less than the revolutions of states and fall of empires, would deem them un-worthy of being inscribed on his page. The reader is, therefore, to take it for granted, though I scorn to waste, in the detail, that time which my furrowed brow and trembling hand inform me is invaluable, that all the while the Great Peter was occupied in those tremendous and bloody contests which I shall shortly re-hearse, there was a continued series of little, dirty, sniveling scourings, broils, and maraudings, kept up on the eastern frontiers by the moss-troopers of Connecticut. But, like that mirror of chivalry, the sage and valorous Don Quixote, I leave these petty contests for some future Sancho Panza of a historian, while I reserve my prowess and my pen for achievements of higher dignity; for at this moment I hear a direful and portentous note issuing from the bosom of the great council of the league, and resounding throughout the regions of the east, menacing the fame and fortunes of Peter Stuyvesant. I call, therefore, upon the reader to leave behind him all the paltry brawls of the Connecti-cut borders, and to press forward with me to the relief of our favorite hero, who, I foresee, will be wofully beset by the implaca-ble Yankees in the next chapter.

CHAPTER V.

THAT the reader may be aware of the peril at this moment
menacing Peter Stuyvesant and his capital, I must remind him
of the old charge advanced in the council of the league in the
time of William the Testy, that the Nederlanders were carrying
on a trade "damnable and injurious to the colonists," in furnishing
the savages with "guns, powther, and shott." This, as I then suggested, was a crafty device of the Yankee confederacy to have a
snug cause of war *in petto*, in case any favorable opportunity
should present of attempting the conquest of the New-Neder-
lands: the great object of Yankee ambition.

Accordingly we now find, when every other ground of com-
plaint had apparently been removed by treaty, this nefarious
charge revived with tenfold virulence, and hurled like a thunderbolt at the very head of Peter Stuyvesant; happily his head, like
that of the great bull of the Wabash, was proof against such
missiles.

To be explicit, we are told that, in the year 1651, the great confederacy of the east accused the immaculate Peter, the soul of honor and heart of steel, of secretly endeavoring, by gifts and promises, to instigate the Narroheganset, Mohaque, and Pequot Indians, to surprise and massacre the Yankee settlements. " For," as the grand council observed, " the Indians round about for divers hundred miles cercute seeme to have drunk deepe of an intoxicating cupp, att or from the Manhattoes against the English, whoe have sought their good, both in bodily and spirituall respects."

This charge they pretended to support by the evidence of divers Indians, who were probably moved by that spirit of truth which is said to reside in the bottle, and who swore to the fact as sturdily as though they had been so many Christian troopers.

Though descended from a family which suffered much injury from the losel Yankees of those times, my great-grandfather having had a yoke of oxen and his best pacer stolen, and having received a pair of black eyes and a bloody nose in one of these border wars; and my grandfather, when a very little boy tending pigs, having been kidnapped and severely flogged by a long-sided Connecticut schoolmaster—yet I should have passed over all these wrongs with forgiveness and oblivion—I could even have suffered them to have broken Everet Ducking's head; to have kicked the doughty Jacobus Van Curlet and his ragged regiment out of doors; to have carried every hog into captivity, and depopulated every henroost on the face of the earth with perfect impunity— but this wanton attack upon one of the most gallant and irreproachable heroes of modern times, is too much even for me to digest; and has overset, with a single puff, the patience of the historian, and the forbearance of the Dutchman.

Oh reader, it was false! I swear to thee, it was false!—If

thou hast any respect to my word—if the undeviating character for veracity, which I have endeavored to maintain throughout this work, has its due weight with thee, thou wilt not give thy faith to this tale of slander; for I pledge my honor and my immortal fame to thee, that the gallant Peter Stuyvesant was not only innocent of this foul conspiracy, but would have suffered his right arm or even his wooden leg to consume with slow and everlasting flames, rather than attempt to destroy his enemies in any other way than open, generous warfare—beshrew those caitiff scouts, that conspired to sully his honest name by such an imputation!

Peter Stuyvesant, though haply he may never have heard of a knight-errant, had as true a heart of chivalry as ever beat at the round table of King Arthur. In the honest bosom of this heroic Dutchman dwelt the seven noble virtues of knighthood, flourishing among his hardy qualities like wild flowers among rocks. He was, in truth, a hero of chivalry struck off by nature at a single heat, and though little care may have been taken to refine her workmanship, he stood forth a miracle of her skill. In all his dealings he was headstrong perhaps, but open and above board; if there was any thing in the whole world he most loathed and despised it was cunning and secret wile; "straight forward" was his motto, and he would at any time rather run his hard head against a stone wall than attempt to get round it.

Such was Peter Stuyvesant, and if my admiration of him has on this occasion transported my style beyond the sober gravity which becomes the philosophic recorder of historic events, I must plead as an apology, that though a little gray-headed Dutchman, arrived almost at the down-hill of life, I still retain a lingering spark of that fire which kindles in the eye of youth when contemplating the virtues of ancient worthies. Blessed, thrice and nine times blessed be the good St. Nicholas, if I have indeed escaped that apathy which chills the sympathies of age and paralyzes every glow of enthusiasm.

The first measure of Peter Stuyvesant, on hearing of this slanderous charge, would have been worthy of a man who had studied for years in the chivalrous library of Don Quixote. Drawing his sword and laying it across the table, to put him in proper tune, he took pen in hand and indited a proud and lofty letter to the council of the league, reproaching them with giving ear to the slanders of heathen savages against a Christian, a soldier, and a cavalier; declaring that whoever charged him with the plot in question, lied in his throat; to prove which he offered to meet the president of the council or any of his compeers; or their champion, Captain Alicxsander Partridg, that mighty man of Rhodes, in single combat; wherein he trusted to vindicate his honor by the prowess of his arm.

This missive was intrusted to his trumpeter and squire, Antony Van Corlear, that man of emergencies, with orders to travel night and day, sparing neither whip nor spur, seeing that he carried the vindication of his patron's fame in his saddle-bags.

The loyal Antony accomplished his mission with great speed and considerable loss of leather. He delivered his missive with becoming ceremony, accompanying it with a flourish of defiance on his trumpet to the whole council, ending with a significant and nasal twang full in the face of Captain Partridg, who nearly jumped out of his skin in an ecstasy of astonishment.

The grand council was composed of men too cool and practical to be put readily in a heat, or to indulge in knight-errantry; and above all to run a tilt with such a fiery hero as Peter the Headstrong. They knew the advantage, however, to have always a snug, justifiable cause of war in reserve with a neighbor, who had territories worth invading; so they devised a reply to Peter Stuyvesant, calculated to keep up the "raw" which they had established.

On receiving this answer, Antony Van Corlear remounted the Flanders mare which he always rode, and trotted merrily back to the Manhattoes, solacing himself by the way according to his wont—twanging his trumpet like a very devil, so that the sweet valleys and banks of the Connecticut resounded with the warlike melody—bringing all the folks to the windows as he passed through Hartford and Pyquag, and Middletown, and all the other border towns, ogling and winking at the women, and making aerial wind-mills from the end of his nose at their husbands —and stopping occasionally in the villages to eat pumpkin-pies, dance at country frolics, and bundle with the Yankee lasses— whom he rejoiced exceedingly with his soul-stirring instrument.

CHAPTER VI.

HOW PETER STUYVESANT DEMANDED A COURT OF HONOR—AND OF THE COURT OF HONOR AWARDED TO HIM.

THE reply of the grand council to Peter Stuyvesant was couched in the coolest and most diplomatic language. They assured him that "his confident denials of the barbarous plot alleged against him would weigh little against the testimony of divers sober and respectable Indians;" that "his guilt was proved to their perfect satisfaction," so that they must still require and seek due *satisfaction and security;* ending with—" so we rest, sir—Yours in ways of righteousness.'

I forbear to say how the lion-hearted Peter roared and ramped at finding himself more and more entangled in the meshes thus artfully drawn round him by the knowing Yankees. Impatient, however, of suffering so gross an aspersion to rest upon his honest name, he sent a second messenger to the council, reiterating his denial of the treachery imputed to him, and offering to submit his conduct to the scrutiny of a court of honor. His offer was readily accepted; and now he looked forward with confidence to an august tribunal to be assembled at the Manhattoes, formed of high-minded cavaliers, peradventure governors and commanders of the confederate plantations, where the matter might be investigated by his peers, in a manner befitting his rank and dignity.

While he was awaiting the arrival of such high functionaries, behold, one sunshiny afternoon there rode into the great gate of the Manhattoes two lean, hungry-looking Yankees, mounted on Narraganset pacers, with saddle-bags under their bottoms, and green satchels under their arms, who looked marvelously like two pettifogging attorneys beating the hoof from one county court to another in quest of lawsuits: and, in sooth, though they may have passed under different names at the time, I have reason to suspect they were the identical varlets who had negotiated the worthy Dutch commissioners out of the Connecticut river.

It was a rule with these indefatigable missionaries never to let the grass grow under their feet. Scarce had they, therefore, alighted at the inn and deposited their saddle-bags, than they made their way to the residence of the governor. They found him, according to custom, smoking his afternoon pipe on the "stoop," or bench at the porch of his house, and announced themselves, at once, as commissioners sent by the grand council of the east to investigate the truth of certain charges advanced against him.

The good Peter took his pipe from his mouth, and gazed at them for a moment in mute astonishment. By way of expediting business, they were proceeding on the spot to put some preliminary questions; asking him, peradventure, whether he pleaded guilty or not guilty, considering him something in the light of culprit at the bar; when they were brought to a pause by seeing him lay down his pipe and begin to fumble with his walking-staff. For a moment, those present would not have given half a crown for both the crowns of the commissioners; but Peter Stuyvesant repressed his mighty wrath and stayed his hand; he scanned the varlets from head to foot, satchels and all, with a look of ineffable scorn; then strode into the house, slammed the door after him, and commanded that they should never again be admitted to his presence.

The knowing commissioners winked to each other, and made a certificate on the spot that the governor had refused to answer their interrogatories or to submit to their examination. They then proceeded to rummage about the city for two or three days, in quest of what they called evidence, perplexing Indians and old women with their cross-questioning until they had stuffed their satchels and saddle-bags with all kinds of apocryphal tales, rumors and calumnies: with these they mounted their Narraganset pacers and traveled back to the grand council; neither did the proud-hearted Peter trouble himself to hinder their researches nor impede their departure; he was too mindful of their sacred character as envoys; but I warrant me had they played the same tricks with William the Testy, he would have had them tucked up by the waistband and treated to an aerial gambol on his patent gallows.

13

CHAPTER VII.

HOW "DRUM ECCLESIASTIC" WAS BEATEN THROUGHOUT CON-
NECTICUT FOR A CRUSADE AGAINST THE NEW-NETHER-
LANDS, AND HOW PETER STUYVESANT TOOK MEASURES TO
FORTIFY HIS CAPITAL.

THE grand council of the East held a solemn meeting on the
return of their envoys. As no advocate appeared in behalf of
Peter Stuyvesant every thing went against him. His haughty
refusal to submit to the questioning of the commissioners was
construed into a consciousness of guilt. The contents of the
satchels and saddle-bags were poured forth before the council
and appeared a mountain of evidence. A pale bilious orator
took the floor, and declaimed for hours and in belligerent terms.
He was one of those furious zealots who blow the bellows of
faction until the whole furnace of politics is red-hot with sparks
and cinders. What was it to him if he should set the house on
fire, so that he might boil his pot by the blaze? He was from
the borders of Connecticut; his constituents lived by marauding
their Dutch neighbors, and were the greatest poachers in Christendom, excepting the Scotch border nobles. His eloquence had
its effect, and it was determined to set on foot an expedition
against the Nieuw-Nederlands.

It was necessary, however, to prepare the public mind for this measure. Accordingly the arguments of the orator were echoed from the pulpit for several succeeding Sundays, and a crusade was preached up against Peter Stuyvesant and his devoted city.

This is the first we hear of the "drum ecclesiastic" beating up for recruits in worldly warfare in our country. It has since been called into frequent use. A cunning politician often lurks under the clerical robe; things spiritual and things temporal are strangely jumbled together, like drugs on an apothecary's shelf; and instead of a peaceful sermon, the simple seeker after right-eousness has often a political pamphlet thrust down his throat, labeled with a pious text from Scripture.

And now nothing was talked of but an expedition against the Manhattoes. It pleased the populace, who had a vehement pre-judice against the Dutch, considering them a vastly inferior race, who had sought the new world for the lucre of gain, not the liberty of conscience; who were mere heretics and infidels, inas-much as they refused to believe in witches and sea-serpents, and had faith in the virtues of horse-shoes nailed to the door; ate pork without molasses; held pumpkins in contempt, and were in perpetual breach of the eleventh commandment of all true Yan-kees, "Thou shalt have codfish dinners on Saturdays."

No sooner did Peter Stuyvesant get wind of the storm that was brewing in the east than he set to work to prepare for it. He was not one of those economical rulers, who postpone the expense of fortifying until the enemy is at the door. There is nothing, he would say, that keeps off enemies and crows more than the smell of gunpowder. He proceeded, therefore, with all diligence, to put the province and its metropolis in a posture of defence.

Among the remnants which remained from the days of William the Testy, were the militia laws; by which the inhabitants were obliged to turn out twice a year, with such military equipments as it pleased God; and were put under the command of tailors and man-milliners, who, though on ordinary occasions they might have been the meekest, most pippin-hearted little men in the world, were very devils at parades, when they had cocked hats on their heads and swords by their sides. Under the instructions of these periodical warriors, the peaceful burghers of the Manhattoes were schooled in iron war, and became so hardy in the process of time, that they could march through sun and rain, from one end of the town to the other, without flinching; and so intrepid and adroit, that they could face to the right, wheel to the left, and fire without winking or blinking.

Peter Stuyvesant, like all old soldiers who have seen service and smelt gunpowder, had no great respect for militia troops; however, he determined to give them a trial, and accordingly called for a general muster, inspection, and review. But, oh Mars and Bellona! what a turning out was here! Here came old Roelant Cuckaburt, with a short blunderbuss on his shoulder, and a long horseman's sword trailing by his side; and Barent Dirkson, with something that looked like a copper kettle turned upside down on his head, and a couple of old horse-pistols in his belt; and Dirk Volkertson, with a long duck fowling-piece without any ramrod; and a host more, armed higgledy-piggledy—with swords, hatchets, snickersnees, crowbars, broomsticks, and what not; the officers distinguished from the rest by having their slouched hats cocked up with pins, and surmounted with cock-tail feathers.

The sturdy Peter eyed this non-descript host with some such

rueful aspect as a man would eye the devil, and determined to give his featherbed soldiers a seasoning. He accordingly put them through their manual exercise over and over again ; trudged them backwards and forwards about the streets of New-Amsterdam until their short legs ached and their fat sides sweated again, and finally encamped them in the evening on the summit of a hill without the city, to give them a taste of camp life, intending the next day to renew the toils and perils of the field. But so it came to pass that in the night there fell a great and heavy rain, and melted away the army, so that in the morning when Gaffer Phoebus shed his first beams upon the camp scarce a warrior remained excepting Peter Stuyvesant and his trumpeter Van Corlear.

This awful desolation of a whole army would have appalled a commander of less nerve; but it served to confirm Peter's want of confidence in the militia system, which he thenceforward used to call, in joke—for he sometimes indulged in a joke—William the Testy's broken reed. He now took into his service a goodly number of burly, broad-shouldered, broad-bottomed Dutchmen ; whom he paid in good silver and gold, and of whom he boasted that whether they could stand fire or not, they were at least water-proof.

He fortified the city, too, with pickets and pallisadoes, extending across the island from river to river; and above all, cast up mud batteries or redoubts on the point of the island, where it divided the beautiful bosom of the bay.

These latter redoubts, in process of time, came to be pleasantly overrun by a carpet of grass and clover, and overshadowed by wide-spreading elms and sycamores; among the branches of which the birds would build their nests and rejoice the ear with

their melodious notes.   Under these trees, too, the old burghers
would smoke their afternoon pipe; contemplating the golden sun
as he sank in the west, an emblem of the tranquil end toward
which they were declining.   Here, too, would the young men and
maidens of the town take their evening stroll, watching the silver
moonbeams as they trembled along the calm bosom of the bay, or
lit up the sail of some gliding bark; and peradventure inter-
changing the soft vows of honest affection; for to evening strolls
in this favored spot were traced most of the marriages in New-
Amsterdam.

Such was the origin of that renowned promenade, THE BAT-
TERY, which though ostensibly devoted to the stern purposes of
war, has ever been consecrated to the sweet delights of peace.
The scene of many a gambol in happy childhood—of many a
tender assignation in riper years—of many a soothing walk in
declining age—the healthful resort of the feeble invalid—the
Sunday refreshment of the dusty tradesman—in fine, the ornament and delight of New-York, and the pride of the lovely island
of Manna-hata.

CHAPTER VIII.

HAVING thus provided for the temporary security of New-Amsterdam, and guarded it against any sudden surprise, the gallant Peter took a hearty pinch of snuff, and snapping his fingers, set the great council of Amphictyons and their champion, the redoubtable Alicxsander Partridg, at defiance. In the meantime the moss-troopers of Connecticut; the warriors of New-Haven and Hartford, and Pyquag, otherwise called Weathersfield, famous for its onions and its witches—and of all the other border towns were in a prodigious turmoil; furbishing up their rusty weapons, shouting aloud for war, and anticipating easy conquests, and glorious rummaging of the fat little Dutch villages.

In the midst of these warlike preparations, however, they received the chilling news that the colony of Massachusetts refused to back them in this righteous war. It seems that the gallant conduct of Peter Stuyvesant, the generous warmth of his vindication and the chivalrous spirit of his defiance, though lost upon the grand council of the league, had carried conviction to the general court of Massachusetts, which nobly refused to believe him guilty of the villanous plot laid at his door.*

The defection of so important a colony paralyzed the councils of the league, some such dissension arose among its members as prevailed of yore in the camp of the brawling warriors of Greece, and in the end the crusade against the Manhattoes was abandoned.

It is said that the moss-troopers of Connecticut were sorely disappointed; but well for them that their belligerent cravings were not gratified: for by my faith, whatever might have been the ultimate result of a conflict with all the powers of the east, in the interim the stomachful heroes of Pyquag would have been choked with their own onions, and all the border towns of Connecticut would have had such a scouring from the lion-hearted Peter and his robustious myrmidons, that I warrant me they would not have had the stomach to squat on the land or invade the henroost of a Nederlander for a century to come.

But it was not merely the refusal of Massachusetts to join in their unholy crusade that confounded the councils of the league; for about this time broke out in the New England provinces the awful plague of witchcraft, which spread like pestilence through the land. Such a howling abomination could not be suffered to remain long unnoticed; it soon excited the fiery indignation of those guardians of the commonwealth, who whilom had evinced such active benevolence in the conversion of Quakers and Anabaptists. The grand council of the league publicly set their faces against the crime, and bloody laws were enacted against all " solem conversing or compacting with the divil by the way of conju

* Hazard's State Papers.

racion or the like."*   Strict search too was made after witches,
who were easily detected by devil's pinches; by being able to
weep but three tears, and those out of the left eye; and by having a most suspicious predilection for black cats and broomsticks ! What is particularly worthy of admiration is, that this
terrible art, which has baffled the studies and researches of philosophers, astrologers, theurgists, and other sages, was chiefly
confined to the most ignorant, decrepit, and ugly old women in
the community, with scarce more brains than the broomsticks
they rode upon.

When once an alarm is sounded, the public, who dearly love
to be in a panic, are always ready to keep it up. Raise but the
cry of yellow fever, and immediately every headache, indigestion,
and overflowing of the bile is pronounced the terrible epidemic;
cry out mad dog, and every unlucky cur in the street is in jeopardy: so in the present instance, whoever was troubled with
colic or lumbago was sure to be bewitched—and woe to any
unlucky old woman living in the neighborhood.

It is incredible the number of offences that were detected,
"for every one of which," says the reverend Cotton Mather, in
that excellent work, the History of New England, "we have
such a sufficient evidence, that no reasonable man in this whole
country ever did question them; *and it will be unreasonable to
do it in any other.*"†

Indeed, that authentic and judicious historian, John Josselyn,
Gent., furnishes us with unquestionable facts on this subject.
"There are none," observes he, "that beg in this country, but
there be witches too many—bottle-bellied witches and others,

* New Plymouth record.

† Mather's Hist. New Eng. B. 6. ch. 7.

13*

that produce many strange apparitions, if you will believe report of a shallop at sea manned with women—and of a ship and great red horse standing by the main-mast; the ship being in a small cove to the eastward vanished of a sudden," etc.

The number of delinquents, however, and their magical devices, were not more remarkable than their diabolical obstinacy. Though exhorted in the most solemn, persuasive, and affectionate manner, to confess themselves guilty, and be burnt for the good of religion, and the entertainment of the public; yet did they most pertinaciously persist in asserting their innocence. Such incredible obstinacy was in itself deserving of immediate punishment, and was sufficient proof, if proof were necessary, that they were in league with the devil, who is perverseness itself. But their judges were just and merciful, and were determined to punish none that were not convicted on the best of testimony; not that they needed any evidence to satisfy their own minds, for, like true and experienced judges, their minds were perfectly made up, and they were thoroughly satisfied of the guilt of the prisoners before they proceeded to try them: but still something was necessary to convince the community at large—to quiet those prying quidnuncs who should come after them—in short, the world must be satisfied. Oh the world—the world!—all the world knows the world of trouble the world is eternally occasioning!—The worthy judges, therefore, were driven to the necessity of sifting, detecting, and making evident as noon-day, matters which were at the commencement all clearly understood and firmly decided upon in their own pericraniums—so that it may truly be said, that the witches were burnt to gratify the populace of the day—but were tried for the satisfaction of the whole world that should come after them!

Finding therefore, that neither exhortation, sound reason, nor friendly entreaty had any avail on these hardened offenders, they resorted to the more urgent arguments of torture; and having thus absolutely wrung the truth from their stubborn lips, they condemned them to undergo the roasting due unto the heinous crimes they had confessed. Some even carried their perverseness so far as to expire under the torture, protesting their innocence to the last; but these were looked upon as thoroughly and absolutely possessed by the devil, and the pious bystanders only lamented that they had not lived a little longer, to have perished in the flames.

In the city of Ephesus, we are told that the plague was expelled by stoning a ragged old beggar to death, whom Apollonius pointed out as being the evil spirit that caused it, and who actually showed himself to be a demon, by changing into a shagged dog. In like manner, and by measures equally sagacious, a salutary check was given to this growing evil. The witches were all burnt, banished, or panic-struck, and in a little while there was not an ugly old woman to be found throughout New England—which is doubtless one reason why all the young women there are so handsome. Those honest folk who had suffered from their incantations gradually recovered, excepting such as had been afflicted with twitches and aches, which, however, assumed the less alarming aspects of rheumatisms, sciatics, and lumbagos— and the good people of New England, abandoning the study of the occult sciences, turned their attention to the more profitable hocus pocus of trade, and soon became expert in the legerdemain art of turning a penny. Still, however, a tinge of the old leaven is discernible, even unto this day, in their characters—witches occasionally start up among them in different disguises, as

physicians, civilians, and divines. The people at large show a
keenness, a cleverness, and a profundity of wisdom, that savors
strongly of witchcraft—and it has been remarked, that whenever
any stones fall from the moon, the greater part of them is sure to
tumble into New England!

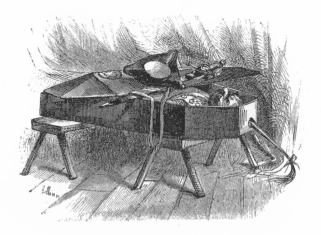

CHAPTER IX.

WHICH RECORDS THE RISE AND RENOWN OF A MILITARY COM-
MANDER, SHOWING THAT A MAN, LIKE A BLADDER, MAY
BE PUFFED UP TO GREATNESS BY MERE WIND; TOGETHER
WITH THE CATASTROPHE OF A VETERAN AND HIS QUEUE.

WHEN treating of these tempestuous times the unknown writer of the Stuyvesant manuscript breaks out into an apostrophe in praise of the good St. Nicholas, to whose protecting care he ascribes the disssensions which broke out in the council of the league, and the direful witchcraft which filled all Yankee land as with Egyptian darkness.

A portentous gloom, says he, hung lowering over the fair valleys of the East: the pleasant banks of the Connecticut no longer echoed to the sounds of rustic gayety; grisly phantoms glided about each wild brook and silent glen; fearful apparitions were seen in the air; strange voices were heard in solitary places, and the border towns were so occupied in detecting and punishing losel witches, that, for a time, all talk of war was suspended, and New-Amsterdam and its inhabitants seemed to be totally forgotten.

I must not conceal the fact that at one time there was some danger of this plague of witchcraft extending into the New

Netherlands; and certain witches mounted on broomsticks are said to have been seen whisking in the air over some of the Dutch villages near the borders; but the worthy Nederlanders took the precaution to nail horseshoes to their doors, which it is well known are effectual barriers against all diabolical vermin of the kind. Many of those horseshoes may be seen at this very day on ancient mansions and barns remaining from the days of the patriarchs; nay, the custom is still kept up among some of our legitimate Dutch yeomanry, who inherit from their fore-fathers a desire to keep witches and Yankees out of the country.

And now the great Peter, having no immediate hostility to apprehend from the east, turned his face, with characteristic vigilance to his southern frontiers. The attentive reader will recollect that certain freebooting Swedes had become very troublesome in this quarter in the latter part of the reign of William the Testy, setting at naught the proclamations of that veritable potentate, and putting his admiral, the intrepid Jan Jansen Alpendam, to a perfect nonplus. To check the incursions of these Swedes, Peter Stuyvesant now ordered a force to that frontier, giving the command of it to General Jacobus Van Pof-fenburgh, an officer who had risen to great importance during the reign of Wilhelmus Kieft. He had, if histories speak true, been second in command to the doughty Van Curlet, when he and his warriors were inhumanly kicked out of Fort Goed Hoop by the Yankees. In that memorable affair Van Poffenburgh is said to have received more kicks in a certain honorable part, than any of his comrades, in consequence of which, on the resignation of Van Curlet, he had been promoted to his place, being considered a hero who had seen service, and suffered in his country's cause.

It is tropically observed by honest old Socrates, that heaven infuses into some men at their birth a portion of intellectual gold; into others of intellectual silver; while others are intellectually furnished with iron and brass. Of the last class was General Van Poffenburgh, and it would seem as if dame Nature, who will sometimes be partial, had given him brass enough for a dozen ordinary braziers. All this he had contrived to pass off upon William the Testy for genuine gold, and the little governor would sit for hours and listen to his gunpowder stories of exploits, which left those of Tirante the White, Don Belianis of Greece, or St. George and the Dragon quite in the background. Having been promoted by William Kieft to the command of his whole disposable forces, he gave importance to his station by the grandiloquence of his bulletins, always styling himself Commander-in-chief of the Armies of the New-Netherlands; though in sober truth, these armies were nothing more than a handful of hen-stealing, bottle-bruising ragamuffins.

In person he was not very tall, but exceedingly round; neither did his bulk proceed from his being fat, but windy; being blown up by a prodigious conviction of his own importance, until he resembled one of those bags of wind given by Eolus, in an incredible fit of generosity, to that vagabond warrior, Ulysses. His windy endowments had long excited the admiration of Antony Van Corlear, who is said to have hinted more than once to William the Testy that in making Van Poffenburgh a general he had spoiled an admirable trumpeter.

As it is the practice in ancient story to give the reader a description of the arms and equipments of every noted warrior, I will bestow a word upon the dress of this redoubtable commander. It comported with his character, being so crossed and slashed, and embroidered with lace and tinsel, that he seemed to have as much

brass without, as nature had stored away within.   He was swathed
too, in a crimson sash, of the size and texture of a fishing-net,
doubtless to keep his swelling heart from bursting through his
ribs.   His face glowed with furnace heat from between a huge
pair of well-powdered whiskers; and his valorous soul seemed
ready to bounce out of a pair of large, glassy, blinking eyes, projecting like those of a lobster.

I swear to thee, worthy reader, if history and tradition belie
not this warrior, I would give all the money in my pocket to have
seen him accoutred cap-a-pie—booted to the middle—sashed to
the chin—collared to the ears—whiskered to the teeth—crowned
with an overshadowing cocked hat, and girded with a leathern
belt ten inches broad, from which trailed a falchion, of a length
that I dare not mention.   Thus equipped, he strutted about, as
bitter-looking a man of war as the far-famed More, of More-hall,
when he sallied forth to slay the Dragon of Wantley.   For what
says the ballad?

> " Had you but seen him in this dress,
>   How fierce he looked and how big,
>   You would have thought him for to be
>   Some Egyptian porcupig.
>   He frighted all—cats, dogs and all,
>   Each cow, each horse, and each hog;
>   For fear they did flee, for they took him to be
>   Some strange outlandish hedge-hog."*

I must confess this general, with all his outward valor and
ventosity, was not exactly an officer to Peter Stuyvesant's taste,
but he stood foremost in the army list of William the Testy, and

* Ballad of Dragon of Wantley.

it is probable the good Peter, who was conscientious in his dealings with all men, and had his military notions of precedence,
thought it but fair to give him a chance of proving his right to
his dignities.

To this copper captain, therefore, was confided the command
of the troops destined to protect the southern frontier; and scarce
had he departed for his station than bulletins began to arrive from
him, describing his undaunted march through savage deserts, over
insurmountable mountains, across impassable rivers, and through
impenetrable forests, conquering vast tracts of uninhabited country, and encountering more perils than did Xenophon in his far-
famed retreat with his ten thousand Grecians.

Peter Stuyvesant read all these grandiloquent dispatches with
a dubious screwing of the mouth and shaking of the head; but
Antony Van Corlear repeated these contents in the streets and
market-places with an appropriate flourish upon his trumpet, and
the windy victories of the general resounded through the streets
of New-Amsterdam.

On arriving at the southern frontier, Van Poffenburgh proceeded to erect a fortress, or strong-hold, on the South or Delaware river. At first he bethought him to call it Fort Stuyvesant,
in honor of the governor, a lowly kind of homage prevalent in
our country among speculators, military commanders, and office-
seekers of all kinds, by which our maps come to be studded with
the names of political patrons and temporary great men; in the
present instance, Van Poffenburgh carried his homage to the
most lowly degree, giving his fortress the name of Fort Casimir,
in honor, it is said, of a favorite pair of brimstone trunk breeches
of his excellency.

As this fort will be found to give rise to important events, it

may be worth while to notice that it was afterwards called Nieuw-
Amstel, and was the germ of the present flourishing town of
New-Castle, or, more properly speaking, No Castle, there being
nothing of the kind on the premises.

His fortress being finished, it would have done any man's
heart good to behold the swelling dignity with which the general
would stride in and out a dozen times a day, surveying it in front
and in rear; on this side and on that; how he would strut backwards and forwards, in full regimentals, on the top of the ramparts; like a vainglorious cock-pigeon, swelling and vaporing on
the top of a dove-cote.

There is a kind of valorous spleen which, like wind, is apt to
grow unruly in the stomachs of newly-made soldiers, compelling
them to box-lobby brawls and broken-headed quarrels, unless
there can be found some more harmless way to give it vent. It
is recorded in the delectable romance of Pierce Forest, that a
young knight, being dubbed by King Alexander, did incontinently
gallop into an adjacent forest and belabor the trees with such
might and main, that he not merely eased off the sudden effer-
vescence of his valor, but convinced the whole court that he
was the most potent and courageous cavalier on the face of the
earth. In like manner the commander of Fort Casimir, when he
found his martial spirit waxing too hot within him, would sally
forth into the fields and lay about him most lustily with his sabre;
decapitating cabbages by platoons; hewing down lofty sunflowers,
which he termed gigantic Swedes, and if, perchance, he espied a
colony of big-bellied pumpkins quietly basking in the sun, "ah!
caitiff Yankees!" would he roar, "have I caught ye at last?"
So saying, with one sweep of his sword, he would cleave the unhappy vegetables from their chins to their waistbands; by which

DARLEY.

warlike havoc, his choler being in some sort allayed, he would return into the fortress with the full conviction that he was a very miracle of military prowess.

He was a disciplinarian, too, of the first order. Woe to any unlucky soldier who did not hold up his head and turn out his toes when on parade ; or, who did not salute the general in proper style as he passed. Having one day, in his Bible researches, encountered the history of Absalom and his melancholy end, the general bethought him that, in a country abounding with forests, his soldiers were in constant risk of a like catastrophe ; he there-fore, in an evil hour, issued orders for cropping the hair of both officers and men throughout the garrison.

Now so it happened, that among his officers was a sturdy veteran named Keldermeester ; who had cherished, through a long life, a mop of hair not a little resembling the shag of a New-foundland dog, terminating in a queue like the handle of a fry-ing-pan, and queued so tightly to his head that his eyes and mouth generally stood ajar, and his eyebrows were drawn up to the top of his forehead. It may naturally be supposed that the possessor of so goodly an appendage would resist with abhorrence an order condemning it to the shears. On hearing the general orders, he discharged a tempest of veteran, soldier-like oaths, and dunder and blixums—swore he would break any man's head who attempted to meddle with his tail—queued it stiffer than ever, and whisked it about the garrison as fiercely as the tail of a crocodile.

The eelskin queue of old Keldermeester became instantly an affair of the utmost importance. The commander-in-chief was too enlightened an officer not to perceive that the discipline of the garrison, the subordination and good order of the armies of the Nieuw-Nederlands, the consequent safety of the whole province,

and ultimately the dignity and prosperity of their High Mightinesses the Lords States General, imperiously demanded the dock-
ing of that stubborn queue. He decreed, therefore, that old
Keldermeester should be publicly shorn of his glories in presence
of the whole garrison—the old man as resolutely stood on the
defensive—whereupon he was arrested and tried by a court-mar-
tial for mutiny, desertion, and all the other list of offences noticed
in the articles of war, ending with a " videlicet, in wearing an
eelskin queue, three feet long, contrary to orders." Then came
on arraignments, and trials, and pleadings ; and the whole garrison was in a ferment about this unfortunate queue. As it is well
known that the commander of a frontier post has the power of
acting pretty much after his own will, there is little doubt but that
the veteran would have been hanged or shot at least, had he not
luckily fallen ill of a fever, through mere chagrin and mortifica-
tion—and deserted from all earthly command, with his beloved
locks unviolated. His obstinacy remained unshaken to the very
last moment, when he directed that he should be carried to his
grave with his eelskin queue sticking out of a hole in his coffin.

This magnanimous affair obtained the general great credit as
a disciplinarian ; but it is hinted that he was ever afterwards subject to bad dreams and fearful visitations in the night ; when the
grizzly spectrum of old Keldermeester would stand sentinel by his
bedside, erect as a pump, his enormous queue strutting out like
the handle.

BOOK VI.

CONTAINING THE SECOND PART OF THE REIGN OF PETER
THE HEADSTRONG, AND HIS GALLANT ACHIEVEMENTS
ON THE DELAWARE.

CHAPTER I.

IN WHICH IS EXHIBITED A WARLIKE PORTRAIT OF THE GREAT
PETER—OF THE WINDY CONTEST OF GENERAL VAN POF-
FENBURGH AND GENERAL PRINTZ, AND OF THE MOSQUITO
WAR ON THE DELAWARE.

HITHERTO, most venerable and courteous reader, have I shown
thee the administration of the valorous Stuyvesant, under the
mild moonshine of peace, or rather the grim tranquillity of awful
expectation; but now the war drum rumbles from afar, the brazen
trumpet brays its thrilling note, and the rude clash of hostile
arms speaks fearful prophecies of coming troubles. The gallant warrior starts from soft repose; from golden visions, and
voluptuous ease; where in the dulcet, "piping time of peace,"
he sought sweet solace after all his toils. No more in beauty's
siren lap reclined, he weaves fair garlands for his lady's brows;
no more entwines with flowers his shining sword, nor through

the livelong lazy summer's day chants forth his love-sick soul in madrigals.   To manhood roused, he spurns the amorous flute; doffs from his brawny back the robe of peace, and clothes his pampered limbs in panoply of steel.   O'er his dark brow, where late the myrtle waved, where wanton roses breathed enervate love, he rears the beaming casque and nodding plume; grasps the bright shield, and shakes the ponderous lance; or mounts with eager pride his fiery steed, and burns for deeds of glorious chivalry!

But soft, worthy reader! I would not have you imagine that any *preux chevalier*, thus hideously begirt with iron, existed in the city of New-Amsterdam.   This is but a lofty and gigantic mode, in which we heroic writers always talk of war, thereby to give it a noble and imposing aspect; equipping our warriors with bucklers, helms, and lances, and such like outlandish and obsolete weapons, the like of which perchance they had never seen or heard of; in the same manner that a cunning statuary arrays a modern general or an admiral in the accoutrements of a Cæsar or an Alexander.   The simple truth then of all this oratorical flourish is this—that the valiant Peter Stuyvesant all of a sudden found it necessary to scour his rusty blade, which too long had rusted in its scabbard, and prepare himself to undergo those hardy toils of war, in which his mighty soul so much delighted.

Methinks I at this moment behold him in my imagination— or rather, I behold his goodly portrait, which still hangs up in the family mansion of the Stuyvesants—arrayed in all the terrors of a true Dutch general.   His regimental coat of German blue, gorgeously decorated with a goodly show of large brass buttons, reaching from his waistband to his chin: the voluminous skirts turned up at the corners and separating gallantly behind, so as to display the seat of a sumptuous pair of brimstone-colored trunk-breeches—a graceful style still prevalent among the warriors of our day, and which is in conformity to the custom of ancient heroes, who scorned to defend themselves in rear. His face rendered exceeding terrible and warlike by a pair of black mustachios; his hair strutting out on each side in stiffly pomatumed ear-locks, and descending in a rat-tail queue below his waist; a shining stock of black leather supporting his chin, and a little but fierce cocked hat, stuck with a gallant and fiery air over his left eye. Such was the chivalric port of Peter the Headstrong; and when he made a sudden halt, planted himself firmly on his solid supporter, with his wooden leg inlaid with silver a little in advance, in order to strengthen his position, his right hand grasping a gold-headed cane, his left resting upon the pummel of his sword, his head dressing spiritedly to the right, with a most appalling and hard-favored frown upon his brow—he presented altogether one of the most commanding, bitter-looking and soldier-like figures that ever strutted upon canvas.—Proceed we now to inquire the cause of this warlike preparation.

In the preceding chapter we have spoken of the founding of Fort Casimir, and of the merciless warfare waged by its commander upon cabbages, sunflowers and pumpkins, for want of better occasion to flesh his sword. Now it came to pass that higher up the Delaware, at his strong-hold of Tinnekonk, resided one Jan Printz, who styled himself Governor of New-Sweden. If history belie not this redoubtable Swede, he was a rival worthy of the windy and inflated commander of Fort Casimir, for master David Pieterzen de Vrie, in his excellent book of voyages, describes him as "weighing upwards of four hundred pounds," a huge feeder and bowser in proportion, taking three potations pottle-deep at every meal. He had a garrison after his own heart at Tinnekonk, guzzling, deep-drinking swashbucklers, who made the wild woods ring with their carousals.

No sooner did this robustious commander hear of the erection of Fort Casimir, than he sent a message to Van Poffenburgh, warning him off the land, as being within the bounds of his juris-diction.

To this General Van Poffenburgh replied that the land be-longed to their High Mightinesses, having been regularly pur-chased of the natives, as discoverers from the Manhattoes, as witness the breeches of their land measurer Ten Broeck.

To this the governor rejoined that the land had previously been sold by the Indians to the Swedes, and consequently was under the petticoat government of her Swedish majesty, Christina; and woe be to any mortal that wore a breeches who should dare to meddle even with the hem of her sacred garment.

I forbear to dilate upon the war of words which was kept up for some time by these windy commanders; Van Poffenburgh, however, had served under William the Testy, and was a veteran in this kind of warfare. Governor Printz, finding he was not to be dislodged by these long shots, now determined upon coming to closer quarters. Accordingly he descended the river in great force and fume, and erected a rival fortress just one Swedish mile below Fort Casimir, to which he gave the name of Helsen-burg.

And now commenced a tremendous rivalry between these two doughty commanders; striving to outstrut and outswell each other like a couple of belligerent turkeycocks. There was a con-test who should run up the tallest flag-staff and display the broad-est flag; all day long there was a furious rolling of drums and twanging of trumpets in either fortress, and, whichever had the wind in its favor, would keep up a continual firing of cannon, to taunt its antagonist with the smell of gunpowder.

On all these points of windy warfare the antagonists were well matched; but so it happened that the Swedish fortress being lower down the river, all the Dutch vessels bound to Fort Casimir with supplies, had to pass it. Governor Printz at once took advantage of this circumstance, and compelled them to lower their flags as they passed under the guns of his battery.

This was a deadly wound to the Dutch pride of General Van Poffenburgh, and sorely would he swell when from the ramparts of Fort Casimir he beheld the flag of their High Mightinesses struck to the rival fortress. To heighten his vexation, Governor Printz, who, as has been shown, was a huge trencherman, took the liberty of having the first rummage of every Dutch merchant-ship, and securing to himself and his guzzling garrison all the little round Dutch cheeses, all the Dutch herrings, the gingerbread, the sweetmeats, the curious stone jugs of gin, and all the other Dutch luxuries, on their way for the solace of Fort Casimir. It is possible he may have paid to the Dutch skippers the full value of their commodities, but what consolation was this to Jacobus Van Poffenburgh and his garrison, who thus found their favorite supplies cut off, and diverted into the larders of the hostile camp? For some time this war of the cupboard was carried on to the great festivity and jollification of the Swedes, while the warriors of Fort Casimir found their hearts, or rather their stomachs, daily failing them. At length the summer heats and summer showers set in, and now, lo and behold, a great miracle was wrought for the relief of the Nederlands, not a little resembling one of the plagues of Egypt; for it came to pass that a great cloud

14

of musquetoes arose out of the marshy borders of the river and settled upon the fortress of Helsenburg, being, doubtless, attracted by the scent of the fresh blood of these Swedish gormandizers. Nay, it is said that the body of Jan Printz alone, which was as big and as full of blood as that of a prize ox, was sufficient to attract the musquetoes from every part of the country. For some time the garrison endeavored to hold out, but it was all in vain; the musquetoes penetrated into every chink and crevice, and gave them no rest day nor night; and as to Governor Jan Printz, he moved about as in a cloud, with musqueto music in his ears, and musqueto stings to the very end of his nose. Finally the garrison was fairly driven out of the fortress, and obliged to retreat to Tinnekonk; nay, it is said that the musquetoes followed Jan Printz even thither, and absolutely drove him out of the country; certain it is, he embarked for Sweden shortly afterwards, and Jan Claudius Risingh was sent to govern New-Sweden in his stead.

Such was the famous musqueto war on the Delaware, of which General Van Poffenburgh would fain have been the hero; but the devout people of the Nieuw-Nederlands always ascribed the discomfiture of the Swedes to the miraculous intervention of St. Nicholas. As to the fortress of Helsenburg, it fell to ruin, but the story of its strange destruction was perpetuated by the Swedish name of Myggen-borg, that is to say, Musqueto Castle.*

* Acrelius' History N. Sweden. For some notice of this miraculous discomfiture of the Swedes, see N. Y. Hist. Col., new series, vol. 1, p. 412.

CHAPTER II.

JAN CLAUDIUS RISINGH, who succeeded to the command of New-Sweden, looms largely in ancient records as a gigantic Swede, who, had he not been rather knock-kneed and splay-footed, might have served for the model of a Samson or a Hercules. He was no less rapacious than mighty, and, withal, as crafty as he was rapacious, so that there is very little doubt that, had he lived some four or five centuries since, he would have figured as one of those wicked giants, who took a cruel pleasure in pocketing beautiful princesses and distressed damsels, when gadding about the world, and locking them up in enchanted castles, without a toilet, a change of linen, or any other convenience.—In consequence of which enormities they fell under the high displeasure of chivalry, and all true, loyal, and gallant knights were instructed to attack and slay outright any miscreant they might happen to find above six feet high; which is doubtless one reason why the race of large men is nearly extinct, and the generations of latter ages are so exceedingly small.

Governor Risingh, notwithstanding his giantly condition, was, as I have hinted, a man of craft. He was not a man to ruffle the vanity of General Van Poffenburgh, or to rub his self-conceit against the grain.   On the contrary, as he sailed up the Delaware, he paused before Fort Casimir, displayed his flag, and fired a royal salute before dropping anchor.   The salute would doubttess have been returned, had not the guns been dismounted ; as it was, a veteran sentinel, who had been napping at his post, and had suffered his match to go out, returned the compliment by discharging his musket with the spark of a pipe borrowed from a comrade.   Governor Risingh accepted this as a courteous reply, and treated the fortress to a second salute ; well knowing its commander was apt to be marvelously delighted with these little ceremonials, considering them so many acts of homage paid to his greatness.   He then prepared to land with a military retinue of thirty men, a prodigious pageant in the wilderness.

And now took place a terrible rummage and racket in Fort Casimir, to receive such a visitor in proper style, and to make an imposing appearance.   The main guard was turned out as soon as possible, equipped to the best advantage in the few suits of regimentals, which had to do duty by turns with the whole garrison.   One tall, lank fellow appeared in a little man's coat, with the buttons between his shoulders ; the skirts scarce covering his bottom ; his hands hanging like spades out of the sleeves ; and the coat linked in front by worsted loops made out of a pair of red garters.   Another had a cocked hat stuck on the back of his head, and decorated with a bunch of cock's-tails ; a third had a pair of rusty gaiters hanging about his heels—while a fourth, a little duck-legged fellow, was equipped in a pair of the general's cast-off breeches, which he held up with one hand while he grasped his firelock with the other.   The rest were accoutred in similar style, excepting three ragamuffins without shirts, and with but a pair and a half of breeches between them, wherefore they were sent to the black hole, to keep them out of sight, that they might not disgrace the fortress.

His men being thus gallantly arrayed—those who lacked muskets shouldering spades and pickaxes, and every man being ordered to tuck in his shirt-tail and pull up his brogues—General Van Poffenburgh first took a sturdy draught of foaming ale, which, like the magnanimous More of More-hall,* was his invariable practice on all great occasions; this done, he put himself at their head, and issued forth from his castle, like a mighty giant, just refreshed with wine. But when the two heroes met, then began a scene of warlike parade that beggars all description. The shrewd Risingh, who had grown gray much before his time, in consequence of his craftiness, saw at one glance the ruling passion of the great Van Poffenburgh, and humored him in all his valorous fantasies.

Their detachments were accordingly drawn up in front of each other; they carried arms and they presented arms; they gave the standing salute and the passing salute; they rolled their drums, they flourished their fifes, and they waved their colors; they faced to the left, and they faced to the right, and they faced to the right about; they wheeled forward, and they wheeled backward, and they wheeled into *echellon*; they marched and they countermarched, by grand divisions, by single divisions, and by subdivisions; by platoons, by sections, and by files; in quick

---

* " ———————— as soon as he rose,
　　To make him strong and mighty,
　　He drank by the tale, six pots of ale,
　　And a quart of aqua vitæ."
　　　　　　　　　　　Dragon of Wantley.

time, in slow time, and in no time at all; for, having gone through all the evolutions of two great armies, including the eighteen manœuvres of Dundas; having exhausted all that they could recollect or imagine of military tactics, including sundry strange and irregular evolutions, the like of which were never seen before nor since, excepting among certain of our newly-raised militia, the two commanders and their respective troops came at length to a dead halt, completely exhausted by the toils of war. Never did two valiant train-band captains, or two bus-kined theatric heroes, in the renowned tragedies of Pizarro, Tom Thumb, or any other heroical and fighting tragedy, marshal their gallows-looking, duck-legged, heavy-heeled myrmidons with more glory and self-admiration.

These military compliments being finished, General Van Poffenburgh escorted his illustrious visitor, with great ceremony, into the fort; attended him throughout the fortifications; showed him the horn-works, crown-works, half-moons, and various other outworks, or rather the places were they ought to be erected, and where they might be erected if he pleased; plainly demonstrating that it was a place of "great capability," and though at present but a little redoubt, yet that it was evidently a formidable for-tress, in embryo. This survey over, he next had the whole gar-rison put under arms, exercised, and reviewed; and concluded by ordering the three bridewell birds to be hauled out of the black hole, brought up to the halberds, and soundly flogged, for the amusement of his visitor, and to convince him that he was a great disciplinarian.

The cunning Risingh, while he pretended to be struck dumb outright with the puissance of the great Van Poffenburgh, took silent note of the incompetency of his garrison, of which he gave a wink to his trusty followers, who tipped each other the wink, and laughed most obstreperously—in their sleeves.

The inspection, review, and flogging being concluded, the party adjourned to the table; for among his other great qualities, the general was remarkably addicted to huge carousals, and in one afternoon's campaign would leave more dead men on the field than he ever did in the whole course of his military career. Many bulletins of these bloodless victories do still remain on record; and the whole province was once thrown in amaze by the return of one of his campaigns; wherein it was stated, that though, like Captain Bobadil, he had only twenty men to back him, yet in the short space of six months he had conquered and utterly annihilated sixty oxen, ninety hogs, one hundred sheep, ten thousand cabbages, one thousand bushels of potatoes, one hundred and fifty kilderkins of small beer, two thousand seven hundred and thirty-five pipes, seventy-eight pounds of sugar-plums, and forty bars of iron, besides sundry small meats, game, poultry, and garden-stuff:—an achievement unparalleled since the days of Pantagruel and his all-devouring army, and which showed that it was only necessary to let Van Poffenburgh and his garrison loose in an enemy's country, and in a little while they would breed a famine, and starve all the inhabitants.

No sooner, therefore, had the general received intimation of the visit of Governor Risingh, than he ordered a great dinner to be prepared; and privately sent out a detachment of his most experienced veterans, to rob all the hen-roosts in the neighborhood, and lay the pigsties under contribution;—a service which they discharged with such zeal and promptitude, that the garrison table groaned under the weight of their spoils.

I wish, with all my heart, my readers could see the valiant

Van Poffenburgh, as he presided at the head of the banquet; it was a sight worth beholding:—there he sat, in his greatest glory surrounded by his soldiers, like that famous wine-bibber, Alexander, whose thirsty virtues he did most ably imitate—telling astounding stories of his hair-breadth adventures and heroic exploits; at which, though all his auditors knew them to be incontinent lies and outrageous gasconadoes, yet did they cast up their eyes in admiration, and utter many interjections of astonishment. Nor could the general pronounce any thing that bore the remotest resemblance to a joke, but the stout Risingh would strike his brawny fist upon the table till every glass rattled again, throw himself back in the chair, utter gigantic peals of laughter, and swear most horribly it was the best joke he ever heard in his life.—Thus all was rout and revelry and hideous carousal within Fort Casimir, and so lustily did Van Poffenburgh ply the bottle, that in less than four short hours he made himself and his whole garrison, who all sedulously emulated the deeds of their chieftain, dead drunk, with singing songs, quaffing bumpers, and drinking patriotic toasts, none of which but was as long as a Welsh pedi gree or a plea in chancery.

No sooner did things come to this pass, than Risingh and his Swedes, who had cunningly kept themselves sober, rose on their entertainers, tied them neck and heels, and took formal possession of the fort, and all its dependencies, in the name of Queen Christina of Sweden; administering at the same time an oath of alle giance to all the Dutch soldiers who could be made sober enough to swallow it. Risingh then put the fortifications in order, appointed his discreet and vigilant friend Suen Schüte, otherwise called Skytte, a tall, wind-dried, water-drinking Swede, to the command, and departed, bearing with him this truly amiable garrison and its puissant commander; who, when brought to himself by a sound drubbing, bore no little resemblance to a "deboshed fish," or bloated sea-monster, caught upon dry land.

The transportation of the garrison was done to prevent the transmission of intelligence to New-Amsterdam; for much as the cunning Risingh exulted in his stratagem, yet did he dread the vengeance of the sturdy Peter Stuyvesant; whose name spread as much terror in the neighborhood as did whilom that of the unconquerable Scanderbeg among his scurvy enemies the Turks.

14*

CHAPTER III.

SHOWING HOW PROFOUND SECRETS ARE OFTEN BROUGHT TO
LIGHT; WITH THE PROCEEDINGS OF PETER THE HEAD-
STRONG WHEN HE HEARD OF THE MISFORTUNES OF GEN-
ERAL VAN POFFENBURGH.

WHOEVER first described common fame, or rumor, as belonging
to the sager sex, was a very owl for shrewdness. She has in
truth certain feminine qualities to an astonishing degree; particularly that benevolent anxiety to take care of the affairs of others,
which keeps her continually hunting after secrets, and gadding
about proclaiming them. Whatever is done openly and in the
face of the world, she takes but transient notice of; but whenever
a transaction is done in a corner, and attempted to be shrouded
in mystery, then her goddess-ship is at her wits' end to find it
out, and takes a most mischievous and lady-like pleasure in publishing it to the world.

It is this truly feminine propensity which induces her continually to be prying into the cabinets of princes, listening at the
key-holes of senate-chambers, and peering through chinks and
crannies, when our worthy congress are sitting with closed doors,
deliberating between a dozen excellent modes of ruining the
nation. It is this which makes her so baneful to all wary

statesmen and intriguing commanders—such a stumbling-block
to private negotiations and secret expeditions; betraying them
by means and instruments which never would have been thought
of by any but a female head.

Thus it was in the case of the affair of Fort Casimir. No
doubt the cunning Risingh imagined, that, by securing the garrison, he should for a long time prevent the history of its fate from
reaching the ears of the gallant Stuyvesant; but his exploit was
blown to the world when he least expected; and by one of the
last beings he would ever have suspected of enlisting as trumpeter to the wide-mouthed deity.

This was one Dirk Schuiler (or Skulker), a kind of hanger-
on to the garrison, who seemed to belong to nobody, and in a manner to be self-outlawed. He was one of those vagabond cosmo-
polites who shark about the world, as if they had no right or
business in it, and who infest the skirts of society like poachers
and interlopers. Every garrison and country village has one or
more scape-goats of this kind, whose life is a kind of enigma,
whose existence is without motive, who comes from the Lord
knows where, who lives the Lord knows how, and who seems
created for no other earthly purpose but to keep up the ancient
and honorable order of idleness. This vagrant philosopher was
supposed to have some Indian blood in his veins, which was
manifested by a certain Indian complexion and cast of countenance; but more especially by his propensities and habits. He
was a tall, lank fellow, swift of foot, and long-winded. He was
generally equipped in a half Indian dress, with belt, leggings,
and moccasons. His hair hung in straight gallows locks about
his ears, and added not a little to his sharking demeanor. It is
an old remark, that persons of Indian mixture are half civilized,

half savage, and half devil—a third half being provided for
their particular convenience. It is for similar reasons, and probably with equal truth, that the backwoodsmen of Kentucky are
styled half man, half horse, and half alligator, by the settlers
on the Mississippi, and held accordingly in great respect and
abhorrence.

The above character may have presented itself to the garrison
as applicable to Dirk Schuiler, whom they familiarly dubbed Gallows Dirk. Certain it is, he acknowledged allegiance to no one
—was an utter enemy to work, holding it in no manner of estimation—but lounging about the fort, depending upon chance for
a subsistence, getting drunk whenever he could get liquor, and
stealing whatever he could lay his hands on. Every day or two
he was sure to get a sound rib-roasting for some of his misde-
meanors; which, however, as it broke no bones, he made very
light of, and scrupled not to repeat the offence whenever another
opportunity presented. Sometimes, in consequence of some flagrant villany, he would abscond from the garrison, and be absent
for a month at a time; skulking about the woods and swamps,
with a long fowling-piece on his shoulder, lying in ambush for
game—or squatting himself down on the edge of a pond catching
fish for hours together, and bearing no little resemblance to that
notable bird of the crane family, ycleped the Mudpoke. When
he thought his crimes had been forgotten or forgiven, he would
sneak back to the fort with a bundle of skins, or a load of poultry,
which, perchance, he had stolen, and would exchange them for
liquor, with which having well soaked his carcass, he would lie in
the sun and enjoy all the luxurious indolence of that swinish philosopher Diogenes. He was the terror of all the farm-yards in
the country, into which he made fearful inroads; and sometimes

he would make his sudden appearance in the garrison at day-
break, with the whole neighborhood at his heels; like the scoundrel thief of a fox, detected in his maraudings and hunted to his
hole. Such was this Dirk Schuiler; and from the total indifference he showed to the world and its concerns, and from his truly
Indian stoicism and taciturnity, no one would ever have dreamt
that he would have been the publisher of the treachery of Risingh.

When the carousal was going on, which proved so fatal to the
brave Poffenburgh and his watchful garrison, Dirk skulked about
from room to room, being a kind of privileged vagrant, or useless
hound, whom nobody noticed. But though a fellow of few words,
yet, like your taciturn people, his eyes and ears were always open,
and in the course of his prowlings he overheard the whole plot
of the Swedes. Dirk immediately settled in his own mind how
he should turn the matter to his own advantage. He played the
perfect jack-of-both-sides—that is to say, he made a prize of
every thing that came in his reach, robbed both parties, stuck the
copper-bound cocked hat of the puissant Van Poffenburgh on his
head, whipped a huge pair of Risingh's jack-boots under his arms,
and took to his heels, just before the catastrophe and confusion at
the garrison.

Finding himself completely dislodged from his haunt in this
quarter, he directed his flight towards his native place, New-
Amsterdam, whence he had formerly been obliged to abscond precipitately, in consequence of misfortune in business—that is to
say, having been detected in the act of sheep-stealing. After
wandering many days in the woods, toiling through swamps, ford-
ing brooks, swimming various rivers, and encountering a world
of hardships that would have killed any other being but an Indian,
a backwoodsman, or the devil, he at length arrived, half-famished.

and lank as a starved weasel, at Communipaw, where he stole a
canoe, and paddled over to New-Amsterdam. Immediately on
landing, he repaired to Governor Stuyvesant, and in more words
than he had ever spoken before in the whole course of his life,
gave an account of the disastrous affair.

On receiving these direful tidings, the valiant Peter started
from his seat—dashed the pipe he was smoking against the back
of the chimney—thrust a prodigious quid of tobacco into his left
cheek—pulled up his galligaskins, and strode up and down the
room, humming, as was customary with him when in a passion, a
hideous northwest ditty. But, as I have before shown, he was not
a man to vent his spleen in idle vaporing. His first measure,
after the paroxysm of wrath had subsided, was to stump up stairs
to a huge wooden chest, which served as his armory, from whence
he drew forth that identical suit of regimentals described in the
preceding chapter. In these portentous habiliments he arrayed
himself, like Achilles in the armor of Vulcan, maintaining all the
while an appalling silence, knitting his brows, and drawing his
breath through his clinched teeth. Being hastily equipped, he
strode down into the parlor and jerked down his trusty sword from
over the fireplace, where it was usually suspended; but before
he girded it on his thigh, he drew it from its scabbard, and as his
eye coursed along the rusty blade, a grim smile stole over his iron
visage—it was the first smile that had visited his countenance for
five long weeks; but every one who beheld it prophesied that
there would soon be warm work in the province!

Thus armed at all points, with grisly war depicted in each
feature, his very cocked hat assuming an air of uncommon defiance, he instantly put himself upon the alert, and dispatched Antony Van Corlear hither and thither, this way and that way,

through all the muddy streets and crooked lanes of the city, summoning by sound of trumpet his trusty peers to assemble in instant council.—This done, by way of expediting matters, according to the custom of people in a hurry, he kept in continual bustle, shifting from chair to chair, popping his head out of every window, and stumping up and down stairs with his wooden leg in such brisk and incessant motion, that, as we are informed by an authentic historian of the times, the continual clatter bore no small resemblance to the music of a cooper hooping a flour-barrel.

A summons so peremptory, and from a man of the governor's mettle, was not to be trifled with: the sages forthwith repaired to the council-chamber, seated themselves with the utmost tranquillity, and lighting their long pipes, gazed with unruffled composure on his excellency and his regimentals; being, as all counsellors should be, not easily flustered, nor taken by surprise. The governor, looking around for a moment with a lofty and soldier-like air, and resting one hand on the pommel of his sword, and flinging the other forth in a free and spirited manner, addressed them in a short but soul-stirring harangue.

I am extremely sorry that I have not the advantages of Livy, Thucydides, Plutarch, and others of my predecessors, who were furnished, as I am told, with the speeches of all their heroes, taken down in short hand by the most accurate stenographers of the time; whereby they were enabled wonderfully to enrich their histories, and delight their readers with sublime strains of eloquence. Not having such important auxiliaries, I cannot possibly pronounce what was the tenor of Governor Stuyvesant's speech. I am bold, however, to say, from the tenor of his character, that he did not wrap his rugged subject in silks and

ermines, and other sickly trickeries of phrase; but spoke forth
like a man of nerve and vigor, who scorned to shrink in words
from those dangers which he stood ready to encounter in very
deed. This much is certain, that he concluded by announcing his
determination to lead on his troops in person, and rout these costard-monger Swedes from their usurped quarters at Fort Casimir.
To this hardy resolution, such of his council as were awake gave
their usual signal of concurrence; and as to the rest, who had
fallen asleep about the middle of the harangue (their " usual custom in the afternoon"), they made not the least objection.

And now was seen in the fair city of New-Amsterdam a prodigious bustle and preparation for iron war. Recruiting parties
marched hither and thither, calling lustily upon all the scrubs,
the runagates, and tatterdemalions of the Manhattoes and its
vicinity, who had any ambition of sixpence a day, and immortal
fame into the bargain, to enlist in the cause of glory:—for I
would have you note that your warlike heroes who trudge in the
rear of conquerors are generally of that illustrious class of gentlemen, who are equal candidates for the army or the bridewell—
the halberds or the whipping-post—for whom Dame Fortune has
cast an even die, whether they shall make their exit by the sword
or the halter—and whose deaths shall, at all events, be a lofty
example to their countrymen.

But, notwithstanding all this martial rout and invitation, the
ranks of honor were but scantily supplied; so averse were the
peaceful burghers of New-Amsterdam from enlisting in foreign
broils, or stirring beyond that home, which rounded all their
earthly ideas. Upon beholding this, the great Peter, whose noble
heart was all on fire with war and sweet revenge, determined to
wait no longer for the tardy assistance of these oily citizens, but

to muster up his merry men of the Hudson, who, brought up among woods, and wilds, and savage beasts, like our yeomen of Kentucky, delighted in nothing so much as desperate adventures and perilous expeditions through the wilderness. Thus resolving, he ordered his trusty squire Antony Van Corlear to have his state galley prepared and duly victualed; which being performed, he attended public service at the great church of St. Nicholas, like a true and pious governor; and then leaving peremptory orders with his council to have the chivalry of the Manhattoes marshaled out and appointed against his return, departed upon his recruiting voyage, up the waters of the Hudson.

CHAPTER IV.

Now did the soft breezes of the south steal sweetly over the face of nature, tempering the panting heats of summer into genial and prolific warmth; when that miracle of hardihood and chivalric virtue, the dauntless Peter Stuyvesant, spread his canvas to the wind, and departed from the fair island of Manna-hata. The galley in which he embarked was sumptuously adorned with pendants and streamers of gorgeous dyes, which fluttered gayly in the wind, or drooped their ends into the bosom of the stream. The bow and poop of this majestic vessel were gallantly bedight, after the rarest Dutch fashion, with figures of little pursy Cupids with periwigs on their heads, and bearing in their hands garlands of flowers, the like of which are not to be found in any book of botany; being the matchless flowers which flourished in the golden age, and exist no longer, unless it be in the imaginations of ingenious carvers of wood and discolorers of canvas.

Thus rarely decorated, in style befitting the puissant potentate of the Manhattoes, did the galley of Peter Stuyvesant launch forth upon the bosom of the lordly Hudson, which, as it rolled its broad waves to the ocean, seemed to pause for a while and swell with pride, as if conscious of the illustrious burthen it sustained.

But trust me, gentlefolk, far other was the scene presented to the contemplation of the crew from that which may be witnessed at this degenerate day. Wildness and savage majesty reigned on the borders of this mighty river—the hand of cultivation had not as yet laid low the dark forest, and tamed the features of the landscape—nor had the frequent sail of commerce broken in upon the profound and awful solitude of ages. Here and there might be seen a rude wigwam perched among the cliffs of the mountains with its curling column of smoke mounting in the transparent atmosphere—but so loftily situated that the whoopings of the savage children, gamboling on the margin of the dizzy heights, fell almost as faintly on the ear as do the notes of the lark, when lost in the azure vault of heaven. Now and then, from the beetling brow of some precipice, the wild deer would look timidly down upon the splendid pageant as it passed below; and then, tossing his antlers in the air, would bound away into the thickets of the forest.

Through such scenes did the stately vessel of Peter Stuyvesant pass. Now did they skirt the bases of the rocky heights of Jersey, which spring up like everlasting walls, reaching from the waves unto the heavens, and were fashioned, if tradition may be believed, in times long past, by the mighty spirit Manetho, to protect his favorite abodes from the unhallowed eyes of mortals. Now did they career it gayly across the vast expanse of Tappan Bay, whose wide-extended shores present a variety of delectable scenery—here the bold promontory, crowned with embowering trees, advancing into the bay—there the long woodland slope,

sweeping up from the shore in rich luxuriance, and terminating in
the upland precipice—while at a distance a long waving line of
rocky heights threw their gigantic shades across the water.   Now
would they pass where some modest little interval, opening among
these stupendous scenes, yet retreating as it were for protection into
the embraces of the neighboring mountains, displayed a rural paradise, fraught with sweet and pastoral beauties; the velvet-tufted
lawn—the bushy copse—the tinkling rivulet, stealing through the
fresh and vivid verdure—on whose banks was situated some little
Indian village, or, peradventure, the rude cabin of some solitary
hunter.

The different periods of the revolving day seemed each, with
cunning magic, to diffuse a different charm over the scene.   Now
would the jovial sun break gloriously from the east, blazing from
the summits of the hills, and sparkling the landscape with a
thousand dewy gems; while along the borders of the river were
seen heavy masses of mist, which, like midnight caitiffs, disturbed
at his approach, made a sluggish retreat, rolling in sullen reluc-
tance up the mountains.   At such times all was brightness, and
life, and gayety—the atmosphere was of an indescribable pure
ness and transparency—the birds broke forth in wanton madrigals,
and the freshening breezes wafted the vessel merrily on her
course.   But when the sun sunk amid a flood of glory in the
west, mantling the heavens and the earth with a thousand gorgeous dyes—then all was calm, and silent, and magnificent.   The
late swelling sail hung lifelessly against the mast—the seaman, with
folded arms, leaned against the shrouds, lost in that involuntary
musing which the sober grandeur of nature commands in the
rudest of her children.   The vast bosom of the Hudson was like
an unruffled mirror, reflecting the golden splendor of the heavens

excepting that now and then a bark canoe would steal across its surface, filled with painted savages, whose gay feathers glared brightly, as perchance a lingering ray of the setting sun gleamed upon them from the western mountains.

But when the hour of twilight spread its majestic mists around, then did the face of nature assume a thousand fugitive charms, which to the worthy heart that seeks enjoyment in the glorious works of its Maker are inexpressibly captivating. The mellow dubious light that prevailed just served to tinge with illusive colors the softened features of the scenery. The deceived but delighted eye sought vainly to discern in the broad masses of shade, the separating line between the land and water; or to distinguish the fading objects that seemed sinking into chaos. Now did the busy fancy supply the feebleness of vision, producing with industrious craft a fairy creation of her own. Under her plastic wand the barren rocks frowned upon the watery waste, in the semblance of lofty towers, and high embattled castles—trees assumed the direful forms of mighty giants, and the inaccessible summits of the mountains seemed peopled with a thousand shadowy beings.

Now broke forth from the shores the notes of an innumerable variety of insects, which filled the air with a strange but not inharmonious concert—while ever and anon was heard the melancholy plaint of the Whip-poor-will, who, perched on some lone tree, wearied the ear of night with his incessant moanings. The mind, soothed into a hallowed melancholy, listened with pensive stillness to catch and distinguish each sound that vaguely echoed from the shore—now and then startled perchance by the whoop of some straggling savage, or by the dreary howl of a wolf, stealing forth upon his nightly prowlings.

Thus happily did they pursue their course, until they entered upon those awful defiles denominated THE HIGHLANDS, where it would seem that the gigantic Titans had erst waged their impious war with heaven, piling up cliffs on cliffs, and hurling vast masses of rock in wild confusion. But in sooth very different is the history of these cloud-capt mountains.—These in ancient days, before the Hudson poured its waters from the lakes, formed one vast prison, within whose rocky bosom the omnipotent Manetho confined the rebellious spirits who repined at his control. Here, bound in adamantine chains, or jammed in rifted pines, or crushed by ponderous rocks, they groaned for many an age.—At length the conquering Hudson, in its career towards the ocean, burst open their prison-house, rolling its tide triumphantly through the stupendous ruins.

Still, however, do many of them lurk about their old abodes; and these it is, according to venerable legends, that cause the echoes which resound throughout these awful solitudes; which are nothing but their angry clamors when any noise disturbs the profoundness of their repose.—For when the elements are agitated by tempest, when the winds are up and the thunder rolls, then horrible is the yelling and howling of these troubled spirits, making the mountains to rebellow with their hideous uproar; for at such times it is said that they think the great Manetho is returning once more to plunge them in gloomy caverns, and renew their intolerable captivity.

But all these fair and glorious scenes were lost upon the gallant Stuyvesant; naught occupied his mind but thoughts of iron war, and proud anticipations of hardy deeds of arms. Neither did his honest crew trouble their heads with any romantic speculations of the kind. The pilot at the helm quietly smoked his pipe, thinking of nothing either past, present, or to come—those of his comrades who were not industriously smoking under the hatches were listening with open mouths to Antony Van Corlear; who, seated on the windlass, was relating to them the marvelous history of those myriads of fireflies, that sparkled like gems and spangles upon the dusky robe of night. These, according to tradition, were originally a race of pestilent sempiternous beldames, who peopled these parts long before the memory of man; being of that abominated race emphatically called *brimstones;* and who, for their innumerable sins against the children of men, and to furnish an awful warning to the beauteous sex, were doomed to infest the earth in the shape of these threatening and terrible little bugs; enduring the internal torments of that fire, which they formerly carried in their hearts and breathed forth in their words; but now are sentenced to bear about for ever—in their tails !

And now I am going to tell a fact, which I doubt much my readers will hesitate to believe; but if they do, they are welcome not to believe a word in this whole history—for nothing which it contains is more true. It must be known then that the nose of Antony the Trumpeter was of a very lusty size, strutting boldly from his countenance like a mountain of Golconda; being sumptuously bedecked with rubies and other precious stones—the true regalia of a king of good fellows, which jolly Bacchus grants to all who bouse it heartily at the flagon. Now thus it happened, that bright and early in the morning, the good Antony, having washed his burly visage, was leaning over the quarter railing of the galley, contemplating it in the glassy wave below.—Just at this moment the illustrious sun, breaking in all his splendor from behind a high bluff of the highlands, did dart one of his most

potent beams full upon the refulgent nose of the sounder of brass
—the reflection of which shot straightway down, hissing hot, into
the water, and killed a mighty sturgeon that was sporting beside
the vessel! This huge monster being with infinite labor hoisted
on board, furnished a luxurious repast to all the crew, being
accounted of excellent flavor, excepting about the wound, where
it smacked a little of brimstone—and this, on my veracity, was
the first time that ever sturgeon was eaten in these parts by
Christian people.*

When this astonishing miracle came to be made known to
Peter Stuyvesant, and that he tasted of the unknown fish, he, as
may well be supposed, marveled exceedingly; and as a monument thereof, he gave the name of *Antony's Nose* to a stout promontory in the neighborhood—and it has continued to be called
Antony's Nose ever since that time.

But hold: whither am I wandering? By the mass, if I
attempt to accompany the good Peter Stuyvesant on this voyage,
I shall never make an end; for never was there a voyage so
fraught with marvelous incidents, nor a river so abounding with
transcendant beauties, worthy of being severally recorded. Even
now I have it on the point of my pen to relate how his crew were
most horribly frightened, on going on shore above the highlands,
by a gang of merry roistering devils, frisking and curveting on a
flat rock, which projected into the river—and which is called the
Duyvel's Dans-Kamer to this very day.—But no! Diedrich

---

* The learned Hans Megapolonsis, treating of the country about Albany,
in a letter which was written sometime after the settlement thereof, says,
" There is in the river great plenty of sturgeon, which we Christians do not
make use of, but the Indians eat them greedily."

Knickerbocker—it becomes thee not to idle thus in thy historic wayfaring.

Recollect that while dwelling with the fond garrulity of age over these fairy scenes, endeared to thee by the recollections of thy youth, and the charms of a thousand legendary tales, which beguiled the simple ear of thy childhood; recollect that thou art trifling with those fleeting moments which should be devoted to loftier themes.—Is not Time—relentless Time! shaking, with palsied hand, his almost exhausted hour-glass before thee?—hasten then to pursue thy weary task, lest the last sands be run ere thou hast finished thy history of the Manhattoes.

Let us, then, commit the dauntless Peter, his brave galley, and his loyal crew, to the protection of the blessed St. Nicholas; who, I have no doubt, will prosper him in his voyage, while we await his return at the great city of New-Amsterdam.

15

CHAPTER V.

WHILE thus the enterprising Peter was coasting, with flowing
sail, up the shores of the lordly Hudson, and arousing all the
phlegmatic little Dutch settlements upon its borders, a great and
puissant concourse of warriors was assembling at the city of New-
Amsterdam.   And here that invaluable fragment of antiquity, the
Stuyvesant manuscript, is more than commonly particular; by
which means I am enabled to record the illustrious host that encamped itself in the public square in front of the fort, at present
denominated the Bowling Green.

In the centre, then, was pitched the tent of the men of battle
of the Manhattoes, who being the inmates of the metropolis, composed the lifeguards of the governor.   These were commanded
by the valiant Stoffel Brinkerhoof, who whilom had acquired such
immortal fame at Oyster Bay—they displayed as a standard a
beaver *rampant* on a field of orange; being the arms of the

province, and denoting the persevering industry and the amphibious origin of the Nederlanders.*

On their right hand might be seen the vassals of that renowned
Mynheer, Michael Paw,† who lorded it over the fair regions of
ancient Pavonia, and the lands away south, even unto the Navesink mountains,‡ and was moreover patroon of Gibbet Island.
His standard was borne by his trusty squire, Cornelius Van
Vorst; consisting of a huge oyster *recumbent* upon a sea-green
field; being the armorial bearings of his favorite metropolis,
Communipaw. He brought to the camp a stout force of warriors,
heavily armed, being each clad in ten pair of linsey-woolsey
breeches, and overshadowed by broad-brimmed beavers, with
short pipes twisted in their hatbands. These were the men who
vegetated in the mud along the shores of Pavonia; being of the
race of genuine copperheads, and were fabled to have sprung
from oysters.

At a little distance was encamped the tribe of warriors who
came from the neighborhood of Hell-gate. These were com-

* This was likewise the grea seal of the New-Netherlands, as may still be
seen in ancient records.

† Besides what is related in the Stuyvesant MS. I have found mention
made of this illustrious patroon in another manuscript, which says : " De Heer
(or the squire) Michael Paw, a Dutch subject, about 10th Aug. 1630, by deed
purchased Staten-Island. N. B. The same Michael Paw had what the Dutch
call a colonie at Pavonia, on the Jersey shore, opposite New-York, and his
overseer in 1636 was named Corns. Van Vorst—a person of the same name
in 1769, owned Pawles Hook, and a large farm at Pavonia, and is a lineal descendant from Van Vorst."

‡ So called from the Navesink tribe of Indians that inhabited these parts—
at present they are erroneously denominated the Neversink, or Neversunk
mountains.

manded by the Suy Dams, and the Van Dams, incontinent hard
swearers, as their names betoken—they were terrible looking
fellows, clad in broad-skirted gaberdines, of that curious colored
cloth called thunder and lightning—and bore as a standard three
Devil's darning-needles, *volant*, in a flame-colored field.

Hard by was the tent of the men of battle from the marshy
borders of the Waale-Boght* and the country thereabouts—these
were of a sour aspect, by reason that they lived on crabs, which
abound in these parts. They were the first institutors of that
honorable order of knighthood, called *Fly-market shirks*, and if
tradition speak true, did likewise introduce the far-famed step in
dancing, called " double trouble." They were commanded by
the fearless Jacobus Varra Vanger, and had, moreover, a jolly
band of Breuckelen† ferry-men, who performed a brave concerto
on conch shells.

But I refrain from pursuing this minute description, which
goes on to describe the warriors of Bloemen-dael, and Wee-hawk,
and Hoboken, and sundry other places, well known in history and
song—for now do the notes of martial music alarm the people of
New-Amsterdam, sounding afar from beyond the walls of the city.
But this alarm was in a little while relieved, for lo, from the
midst of a vast cloud of dust, they recognized the brimstone-colored breeches and splendid silver leg of Peter Stuyvesant, glaring
in the sunbeams ; and beheld him approaching at the head of a
formidable army, which he had mustered along the banks of the
Hudson. And here the excellent but anonymous writer of the
Stuyvesant manuscript breaks out into a brave and glorious de-

* Since corrupted into the *Wallabout* ; the bay where the Navy-Yard is
situated.

† Now spelt Brooklyn.

scription of the forces, as they defiled through the principal gate of the city, that stood by the head of Wall-street.

First of all came the Van Bummels, who inhabit the pleasant borders of the Bronx : these were short fat men, wearing exceeding large trunk-breeches, and were renowned for feats of the trencher—they were the first inventors of suppawn or mush and milk.—Close in their rear marched the Van Vlotens, of Kaatskill, horrible quaffers of new cider, and arrant braggarts in their liquor.—After them came the Van Pelts of Groodt Esopus, dextrous horsemen, mounted upon goodly switch-tailed steeds of the Esopus breed—these were mighty hunters of minks and muskrats, whence came the word *Peltry.*—Then the Van Nests of Kinderhoeck, valiant robbers of birds' nests, as their name denotes ; to these, if report may be believed, are we indebted for the invention of slap-jacks, or buckwheat cakes.—Then the Van Higginbottoms, of Wapping's creek ; these came armed with ferules and birchen rods, being a race of schoolmasters, who first discovered the marvelous sympathy between the seat of honor and the seat of intellect—and that the shortest way to get knowledge into the head was to hammer it into the bottom.—Then the Van Grolls, of Anthony's Nose, who carried their liquor in fair round little pottles, by reason they could not bouse it out of their canteens, having such rare long noses.—Then the Gardeniers, of Hudson and thereabouts, distinguished by many triumphant feats, such as robbing watermelon patches, smoking rabbits out of their holes, and the like, and by being great lovers of roasted pigs' tails ; these were the ancestors of the renowned congressman of that name.—Then the Van Hoesens, of Sing-Sing, great choristers and players upon the jewsharp ; these marched two and two, singing the great song of St. Nicholas.—Then the Couenho-

vens, of Sleepy Hollow ; these gave birth to a jolly race of publicans, who first discovered the magic artifice of conjuring a quart
of wine into a pint bottle.—Then the Van Kortlandts, who lived
on the wild banks of the Croton, and were great killers of wild
ducks, being much spoken of for their skill in shooting with the
long bow.—Then the Van Bunschotens, of Nyack and Kakiat,
who were the first that did ever kick with the left foot ; they were
gallant bush-whackers and hunters of racoons by moonlight.—
Then the Van Winkles, of Haerlem, potent suckers of eggs,
and noted for running of horses, and running up of scores at
taverns ; they were the first that ever winked with both eyes at
once.—Lastly came the KNICKERBOCKERS, of the great town of
Scaghtikoke, where the folk lay stones upon the houses in windy
weather, lest they should be blown away. These derive their
name, as some say, from *Knicker*, to shake, and *Beker*, a goblet,
indicating thereby that they were sturdy toss-pots of yore ; but,
in truth, it was derived from *Knicker*, to nod, and *Boeken*, books ;
plainly meaning that they were great nodders or dozers over
books—from them did descend the writer of this history.

Such was the legion of sturdy bush-beaters that poured in at
the grand gate of New-Amsterdam ; the Stuyvesant manuscript
indeed speaks of many more, whose names I omit to mention,
seeing that it behooves me to hasten to matters of greater moment.
Nothing could surpass the joy and martial pride of the lion-hearted
Peter as he reviewed this mighty host of warriors, and he determined no longer to defer the gratification of his much-wished-for
revenge, upon the scoundrel Swedes at Fort Casimir.

But before I hasten to record those unmatchable events, which
will be found in the sequel of this faithful history, let me pause
to notice the fate of Jacobus Van Poffenburgh, the discomfited

commander-in-chief of the armies of the New-Netherlands. Such is the inherent uncharitableness of human nature, that scarcely did the news become public of his deplorable discomfiture at Fort Casimir, than a thousand scurvy rumors were set afloat in New-Amsterdam, wherein it was insinuated, that he had in reality a treacherous understanding with the Swedish commander; that he had long been in the practice of privately communicating with the Swedes; together with divers hints about "secret service money."—To all which deadly charges I do not give a jot more credit than I think they deserve.

Certain it is, that the general vindicated his character by the most vehement oaths and protestations, and put every man out of the ranks of honor who dared to doubt his integrity. Moreover, on returning to New-Amsterdam, he paraded up and down the streets with a crew of hard swearers at his heels—sturdy bottle companions, whom he gorged and fattened, and who were ready to bolster him through all the courts of justice—heroes of his own kidney, fierce-whiskered, broad-shouldered, colbrand-looking swaggerers—not one of whom but looked as though he could eat up an ox, and pick his teeth with the horns. These lifeguard men quarreled all his quarrels, were ready to fight all his battles, and scowled at every man that turned up his nose at the general, as though they would devour him alive. Their conversation was interspersed with oaths like minute-guns, and every bombastic rhodomontade was rounded off by a thundering execration, like a patriotic toast honored with a discharge of artillery.

All these valorous vaporings had a considerable effect in convincing certain profound sages, who began to think the general a hero, of unmatchable loftiness and magnanimity of soul; particularly as he was continually protesting *on the honor of a soldier*

—a marvelously high-sounding asseveration. Nay, one of the members of the council went so far as to propose they should immortalize him by an imperishable statue of plaster of Paris.

But the vigilant Peter the Headstrong was not thus to be deceived. Sending privately for the commander-in-chief of all the armies, and having heard all his story, garnished with the customary pious oaths, protestations, and ejaculations—" Harkee, comrade," cried he, " though by your own account you are the most brave, upright, and honorable man in the whole province, yet do you lie under the misfortune of being damnably traduced, and immeasurably despised. Now, though it is certainly hard to punish a man for his misfortunes, and though it is very possible you are totally innocent of the crimes laid to your charge; yet as heaven, doubtless for some wise purpose, sees fit at present to withhold all proofs of your innocence, far be it from me to counteract its sovereign will. Beside, I cannot consent to venture my armies with a commander whom they despise, nor to trust the welfare of my people to a champion whom they distrust. Retire therefore, my friend, from the irksome toils and cares of public life, with this comforting reflection—that if guilty, you are but enjoying your just reward—and if innocent, you are not the first great and good man who has most wrongfully been slandered and maltreated in this wicked world—doubtless to be better treated in a better world, where there shall be neither error, calumny, nor persecution. In the meantime let me never see your face again, for I have a horrible antipathy to the countenances of unfortunate great men like yourself."

CHAPTER VI.

IN WHICH THE AUTHOR DISCOURSES VERY INGENUOUSLY OF HIMSELF—AFTER WHICH IS TO BE FOUND MUCH INTERESTING HISTORY ABOUT PETER THE HEADSTRONG AND HIS FOLLOWERS.

As my readers and myself are about entering on as many perils as ever a confederacy of meddlesome knights-errant willfully ran their heads into, it is meet that, like those hardy adventurers, we should join hands, bury all differences, and swear to stand by one another, in weal or woe, to the end of the enterprise. My readers must doubtless perceive how completely I have altered my tone and deportment since we first set out together. I warrant they then thought me a crabbed, cynical, impertinent little son of a Dutchman; for I scarcely ever gave them a civil word, nor so much as touched my beaver, when I had occasion to address them. But as we jogged along together on the high road of my history, I gradually began to relax, to grow more courteous, and occasionally to enter into familiar discourse, until at length I came to conceive a most social, companionable kind of regard for them. This is just my way—I am always a little cold and reserved at first, particularly to people whom I neither know nor care for, and am only to be completely won by long intimacy.

Besides, why should I have been sociable to the crowd of how-d'ye-do acquaintances that flocked around me at my first appearance? Many were merely attracted by a new face; and having stared me full in the title-page, walked off without saying a word; while others lingered yawningly through the preface, and, having gratified their short-lived curiosity, soon dropped off one by one. But, more especially to try their mettle, I had recourse to an expedient, similar to one which we are told was used by that peerless flower of chivalry, King Arthur; who, before he admitted any knight to his intimacy, first required that he should show himself superior to danger or hardships, by encountering unheard-of mishaps, slaying some dozen giants, vanquishing wicked enchanters, not to say a word of dwarfs, hippogriffs, and fiery dragons. On a similar principle did I cunningly lead my readers, at the first sally, into two or three knotty chapters, where they were most wofully belabored and buffeted, by a host of pagan philosophers and infidel writers. Though naturally a very grave man, yet could I scarce refrain from smiling outright at seeing the utter confusion and dismay of my valiant cavaliers. Some dropped down dead (asleep) on the field; others threw down my book in the middle of the first chapter, took to their heels, and never ceased scampering until they had fairly run it out of sight; when they stopped to take breath, to tell their friends what troubles they had undergone, and to warn all others from venturing on so thankless an expedition. Every page thinned my ranks more and more; and of the vast multitude that first set out, but a comparatively few made shift to survive, in exceedingly battered condition, through the five introductory chapters.

What, then! would you have had me take such sunshine,

faint-hearted recreants to my bosom at our first acquaintance?
No—no; I reserved my friendship for those who deserved it, for
those who undauntedly bore me company, in despite of difficulties,
dangers and fatigues. And now, as to those who adhere to me at
present, I take them affectionately by the hand.—Worthy and
thrice-beloved readers! brave and well-tried comrades! who have
faithfully followed my footsteps through all my wanderings—I
salute you from my heart—I pledge myself to stand by you to
the last; and to conduct you (so Heaven speed this trusty
weapon which I now hold between my fingers) triumphantly to
the end of this our stupendous undertaking.

But, hark! while we are thus talking, the city of New-
Amsterdam is in a bustle. The host of warriors encamped in
the Bowling Green are striking their tents; the brazen trumpet
of Antony Van Corlear makes the welkin to resound with portentous clangor—the drums beat—the standards of the Manhattoes, of Hell-gate, and of Michael Paw, wave proudly in the air.
And now behold where the mariners are busily employed, hoisting
the sails of yon topsail schooner, and those clump-built sloops,
which are to waft the army of the Nederlanders to gather immortal honors on the Delaware!

The entire population of the city, man, woman, and child,
turned out to behold the chivalry of New-Amsterdam, as it paraded
the streets previous to embarkation. Many a handkerchief was
waved out of the windows; many a fair nose was blown in
melodious sorrow on the mournful occasion. The grief of the
fair dames and beauteous damsels of Granada could not have
been more vociferous on the banishment of the gallant tribe of
Abencerrages, than was that of the kind-hearted fair ones of
New-Amsterdam on the departure of their intrepid warriors.

Every love-sick maiden fondly crammed the pockets of her hero with gingerbread and doughnuts—many a copper ring was exchanged, and crooked sixpence broken, in pledge of eternal constancy—and there remain extant to this day some love-verses written on that occasion, sufficiently crabbed and incomprehensible to confound the whole universe.

But it was a moving sight to see the buxom lasses, how they hung about the doughty Antony Van Corlear—for he was a jolly, rosy-faced, lusty bachelor, fond of his joke, and withal a desperate rogue among the women. Fain would they have kept him to comfort them while the army was away ; for besides what I have said of him, it is no more than justice to add, that he was a kind-hearted soul, noted for his benevolent attentions in comforting disconsolate wives during the absence of their husbands— and this made him to be very much regarded by the honest burghers of the city. But nothing could keep the valiant Antony from following the heels of the old governor, whom he loved as he did his very soul—so embracing all the young vrouws, and giving every one of them that had good teeth and rosy lips a dozen hearty smacks, he departed loaded with their kind wishes.

Nor was the departure of the gallant Peter among the least causes of public distress. Though the old governor was by no means indulgent to the follies and waywardness of his subjects, yet somehow or other he had become strangely popular among the people. There is something so captivating in personal bravery, that, with the common mass of mankind, it takes the lead of most other merits. The simple folk of New-Amsterdam looked upon Peter Stuyvesant as a prodigy of valor. His wooden leg, that trophy of his martial encounters, was regarded with reverence and admiration. Every old burgher had a budget of miraculous stories to tell about the exploits of Hardkoppig Piet, wherewith he regaled his children of a long winter night; and on which he dwelt with as much delight and exaggeration, as do our honest country yeomen on the hardy adventures of old General Putnam (or, as he is familiarly termed, *Old Put*) during our glorious revolution. Not an individual but verily believed the old governor was a match for Beelzebub himself; and there was even a story told, with great mystery, and under the rose, of his having shot the devil with a silver bullet one dark stormy night, as he was sailing in a canoe through Hell-gate—but this I do not record as being an absolute fact. Perish the man who would let fall a drop to discolor the pure stream of history!

Certain it is, not an old woman in New-Amsterdam but considered Peter Stuyvesant as a tower of strength, and rested satisfied that the public welfare was secure, so long as he was in the city. It is not surprising, then, that they looked upon his departure as a sore affliction. With heavy hearts they draggled at the heels of his troop, as they marched down to the river side to embark. The governor from the stern of his schooner gave a short but truly patriarchal address to his citizens, wherein he recommended them to comport like loyal and peaceable subjects—to go to church regularly on Sundays, and to mind their business all the week besides. That the women should be dutiful and affectionate to their husbands—looking after nobody's concerns but their own; eschewing all gossipings, and morning gaddings—and carrying short tongues and long petticoats. That the men should abstain from intermeddling in public concerns, intrusting the cares of government to the officers appointed to support them—staying at home, like good citizens, making money for themselves, and getting children for the benefit of their country. That the

burgomasters should look well to the public interest—not op-
pressing the poor nor indulging the rich—not tasking their ingenuity to devise new laws, but faithfully enforcing those which were
already made—rather bending their attention to prevent evil than
to punish it; ever recollecting that civil magistrates should consider themselves more as guardians of public morals than rat-
catchers employed to entrap public delinquents.   Finally, he
exhorted them, one and all, high and low, rich and poor, to
conduct themselves *as well as they could,* assuring them that if
they faithfully and conscientiously complied with this golden rule,
there was no danger but that they would all conduct themselves
well enough.   This done, he gave them a paternal benediction;
the sturdy Antony sounded a most loving farewell with his trumpet, the jolly crews put up a shout of triumph, and the invincible
armada swept off proudly down the bay.

The good people of New-Amsterdam crowded down to the
Battery—that blest resort, from whence so many a tender prayer
has been wafted, so many a fair hand waved, so many a tearful
look been cast by love-sick damsel, after the lessening bark, bearing her adventurous swain to distant climes!—Here the populace
watched with straining eyes the gallant squadron, as it slowly
floated down the bay, and when the intervening land at the
Narrows shut it from their sight, gradually dispersed with silent
tongues and downcast countenances.

A heavy gloom hung over the late bustling city—the honest
burghers smoked their pipes in profound thoughtfulness, casting
many a wistful look to the weather-cock on the church of St.
Nicholas; and all the old women, having no longer the presence
of Peter Stuyvesant to hearten them, gathered their children home,
and barricaded the doors and windows every evening at sundown.

In the meanwhile the armada of the sturdy Peter proceeded prosperously on its voyage, and after encountering about as many storms, and water-spouts, and whales, and other horrors and phenomena, as generally befall adventurous landsmen in perilous voyages of the kind; and after undergoing a severe scouring from that deplorable and unpitied malady called sea-sickness, the whole squadron arrived safely in the Delaware.

Without so much as dropping anchor and giving his wearied ships time to breathe, after laboring so long on the ocean, the intrepid Peter pursued his course up the Delaware, and made a sudden appearance before Fort Casimir. Having summoned the astonished garrison by a terrific blast from the trumpet of the long-winded Van Corlear, he demanded, in a tone of thunder, an instant surrender of the fort. To this demand, Suen Skytte, the wind-dried commandant, replied in a shrill whiffling voice, which, by reason of his extreme spareness, sounded like the wind whistling through a broken bellows—"that he had no very strong reason for refusing, except that the demand was particularly disagreeable, as he had been ordered to maintain his post to the last extremity." He requested time, therefore, to consult with Governor Risingh, and proposed a truce for that purpose.

The choleric Peter, indignant at having his rightful fort so treacherously taken from him, and thus pertinaciously withheld, refused the proposed armistice, and swore by the pipe of St. Nicholas, which, like the sacred fire, was never extinguished, that unless the fort were surrendered in ten minutes, he would incontinently storm the works, make all the garrison run the gauntlet, and split their scoundrel of a commander like a pickled shad. To give this menace the greater effect, he drew forth his trusty sword, and shook it at them with such a fierce and vigorous motion, that doubtless, if it had not been exceeding rusty, it would have lightened terror into the eyes and hearts of the enĕ-my. He then ordered his men to bring a broadside to bear upon the fort, consisting of two swivels, three muskets, a long duck fowling-piece, and two brace of horse-pistols.

In the meantime the sturdy Van Corlear marshaled all his forces, and commenced his warlike operations. Distending his cheeks like a very Boreas, he kept up a most horrific twanging of his trumpet—the lusty choristers of Sing-Sing broke forth into a hideous song of battle—the warriors of Breuckelen and the Wallabout blew a potent and astounding blast on their conch shells, altogether forming as outrageous a concerto as though five thousand French fiddlers were displaying their skill in a modern overture.

Whether the formidable front of war thus suddenly presented smote the garrison with sore dismay—or whether the concluding terms of the summons, which mentioned that he should surrender "at discretion," were mistaken by Suen Skytte, who, though a Swede was a very considerate, easy-tempered man—as a compli-ment to his discretion, I will not take upon me to say; certain it is he found it impossible to resist so courteous a demand. Ac-cordingly, in the very nick of time, just as the cabin-boy had gone after a coal of fire, to discharge the swivel, a chamade was beat on the rampart by the only drum in the garrison, to the no small satisfaction of both parties; who, notwithstanding their great stomach for fighting, had full as good an inclination to eat a quiet dinner as to exchange black eyes and bloody noses.

Thus did this impregnable fortress once more return to the domination of their High Mightinesses; Skytte and his garrison of twenty men were allowed to march out with the honors of war, and the victorious Peter, who was as generous as brave, permitted them to keep possession of all their arms and ammunition—the same on inspection being found totally unfit for service, having long rusted in the magazine of the fortress, even before it was wrested by the Swedes from the windy Van Poffenburgh. But I must not omit to mention, that the governor was so well pleased with the service of his faithful squire Van Corlear, in the reduction of this great fortress, that he made him on the spot lord of a goodly domain in the vicinity of New-Amsterdam—which goes by the name of Corlear's Hook unto this very day.

The unexampled liberality of Peter Stuyvesant towards the Swedes, occasioned great surprise in the city of New-Amsterdam—nay, certain factious individuals, who had been enlightened by political meetings in the days of William the Testy, but who had not dared to indulge their meddlesome habits under the eye of their present ruler, now, emboldened by his absence, gave vent to their censures in the street. Murmurs were heard in the very council-chamber of New-Amsterdam; and there is no knowing whether they might not have broken out into downright speeches and invectives, had not Peter Stuyvesant privately sent home his walking-staff, to be laid as a mace on the table of the council-chamber, in the midst of his counsellors; who, like wise men, took the hint, and for ever after held their peace.

CHAPTER VII.

LIKE as a mighty alderman, when at a corporation feast the first spoonful of turtle-soup salutes his palate, feels his appetite but tenfold quickened, and redoubles his vigorous attacks upon the tureen ; while his projecting eyes roll greedily round, devouring every thing at table—so did the mettlesome Peter Stuyvesant feel that hunger for martial glory, which raged within his bowels, inflamed by the capture of Fort Casimir, and nothing could allay it but the conquest of all New-Sweden. No sooner, therefore, had he secured his conquest, than he stumped resolutely on, flushed with success, to gather fresh laurels at Fort Christina.*

This was the grand Swedish post, established on a small river (or, as it is improperly termed, creek) of the same name ; and here that crafty governor Jan Risingh lay grimly drawn up, like a gray-bearded spider in the citadel of his web.

But before we hurry into the direful scenes which must attend

---

* At present a flourishing town, called Christiana, or Christeen, about thirty-seven miles from Philadelphia, on the post-road to Baltimore.

the meeting of two such potent chieftains, it is advisable to pause for a moment, and hold a kind of warlike council. Battles should not be rushed into precipitately by the historian and his readers, any more than by the general and his soldiers. The great commanders of antiquity never engaged the enemy without previously preparing the minds of their followers by animating harangues ; spiriting them up to heroic deeds, assuring them of the protection of the gods, and inspiring them with a confidence in the prowess of their leaders. So the historian should awaken the attention and enlist the passions of his readers ; and having set them all on fire with the importance of his subject, he should put himself at their head, flourish his pen, and lead them on to the thickest of the fight.

An illustrious example of this rule may be seen in that mirror of historians the immortal Thucydides. Having arrived at the breaking out of the Peloponnesian war, one of his commentators observes that " he sounds the charge in all the disposition and spirit of Homer. He catalogues the allies on both sides. He awakens our expectations, and fast engages our attention. All mankind are concerned in the important point now going to be decided. Endeavors are made to disclose futurity. Heaven itself is interested in the dispute. The earth totters, and nature seems to labor with the great event. This is his solemn, sublime manner of setting out. Thus he magnifies a war between two, as Rapin styles them, petty states ; and thus artfully he supports a little subject by treating it in a great and noble method."

In like manner, having conducted my readers into the very teeth of peril—having followed the adventurous Peter and his band into foreign regions—surrounded by foes, and stunned by the horrid din of arms—at this important moment, while darkness and doubt hang o'er each coming chapter, I hold it meet to harangue them, and prepare them for the events that are to follow.

And here I would premise one great advantage which, as historian, I possess over my reader; and this it is, that though I cannot save the life of my favorite hero, nor absolutely col tradict the event of a battle (both which liberties, though often taken by the French writers of the present reign, I hold to be utterly unworthy of a scrupulous historian), yet I can now and then make him bestow on his enemy a sturdy back stroke sufficient to fell a giant; though, in honest truth, he may never have done any thing of the kind—or I can drive his antagonist clear round and round the field, as did Homer make that fine fellow Hector scamper like a poltroon round the walls cf Troy; for which, if ever they have encountered one another in the Elysian fields, I'll warrant the prince of poets has had to make the most humble apology.

I am aware that many conscientious readers will be ready to cry out "foul play!" whenever I render a little assistance to my hero—but I consider it one of those privileges exercised by historians of all ages—and one which has never been disputed. An historian is, in fact, as it were, bound in honor to stand by his hero—the fame of the latter is intrusted to his hands, and it is his duty to do the best by it he can. Never was there a general, an admiral, or any other commander, who, in giving an account of any battle he had fought, did not sorely belabor the enemy; and I have no doubt that, had my heroes written the history of their own achievements, they would have dealt much harder blows than any that I shall recount. Standing forth, therefore, as the guardian of their fame, it behooves me to do them the same justice they would have done themselves; and if I happen to be a little hard upon the Swedes, I give free leave to any of their descendants, who may write a history of the State of Delaware, to take fair retaliation, and belabor Peter Stuyvesant as hard as they please.

Therefore stand by for broken heads and bloody noses!—My pen hath long itched for a battle—siege after siege have I carried on without blows or bloodshed; but now I have at length got a chance, and I vow to Heaven and St. Nicholas, that, let the chronicles of the times say what they please, neither Sallust, Livy, Tacitus, Polybius, nor any other historian, did ever record a fiercer fight than that in which my valiant chieftains are now about to engage.

And you, oh most excellent readers, whom, for your faithful adherence, I could cherish in the warmest corner of my heart— be not uneasy—trust the fate of our favorite Stuyvesant with me —for by the rood, come what may, I'll stick by Hardkoppig Piet to the last. I'll make him drive about these losels vile, as did the renowned Launcelot of the Lake a herd of recreant Cornish knights—and if he does fall, let me never draw my pen to fight another battle in behalf of a brave man, if I don't make these lubberly Swedes pay for it.

No sooner had Peter Stuyvesant arrived before Fort Christina than he proceeded without delay to intrench himself, and immediately on running his first parallel, dispatched Antony Van Corlear to summon the fortress to surrender. Van Corlear was received with all due formality, hoodwinked at the portal, and conducted through a pestiferous smell of salt fish and onions to the citadel, a substantial hut built of pine logs. His eyes were here uncovered, and he found himself in the august presence of Governor Risingh. This chieftain, as I have before noted, was a very

giantly man; and was clad in a coarse blue coat, strapped round
the waist with a leathern belt, which caused the enormous skirts
and pockets to set off with a very warlike sweep.   His ponderous
legs were cased in a pair of foxy-colored jack-boots, and he was
straddling in the attitude of the Colossus of Rhodes, before a bit
of broken looking-glass, shaving himself with a villanously dull
razor.   This afflicting operation caused him to make a series of
horrible grimaces, which heightened exceedingly the grisly terrors
of his visage.   On Antony Van Corlear's being announced, the
grim commander paused for a moment, in the midst of one of his
most hard-favored contortions, and after eyeing him askance over
the shoulder, with a kind of snarling grin on his countenance,
resumed his labors at the glass.

This iron harvest being reaped, he turned once more to the
trumpeter, and demanded the purport of his errand.   Antony
Van Corlear delivered in a few words, being a kind of short-
hand speaker, a long message from his excellency, recounting the
whole history of the province, with a recapitulation of grievances, and enumeration of claims, and concluding with a peremptory demand of instant surrender; which done, he turned
aside, took his nose between his thumb and finger, and blew a
tremendous blast, not unlike the flourish of a trumpet of defiance
—which it had doubtless learned from a long and intimate neighborhood with that melodious instrument.

Governor Risingh heard him through, trumpet and all, but
with infinite impatience; leaning at times, as was his usual custom, on the pommel of his sword, and at times twirling a huge
steel watch-chain, or snapping his fingers.   Van Corlear having
finished, he bluntly replied, that Peter Stuyvesant and his summons might go to the d——l, whither he hoped to send him and

his crew of ragamuffins before supper-time. Then unsheathing his brass-hilted sword, and throwing away the scabbard—" 'Fore gad," quod he, " but I will not sheathe thee again until I make a scabbard of the smoke-dried leathern hide of this runagate Dutchman." Then having flung a fierce defiance in the teeth of his adversary, by the lips of his messenger, the latter was reconducted to the portal, with all the ceremonious civility due to the trumpeter, squire, and ambassador of so great a commander; and being again unblinded, was courteously dismissed with a tweak of the nose, to assist him in recollecting his message.

No sooner did the gallant Peter receive this insolent reply than he let fly a tremendous volley of red-hot execrations, which would infallibly have battered down the fortifications, and blown up the powder magazine about the ears of the fiery Swede, had not the ramparts been remarkably strong, and the magazine bomb-proof. Perceiving that the works withstood this terrific blast, and that it was utterly impossible (as it really was in those unphilosophic days) to carry on a war with words, he ordered his merry men all to prepare for an immediate assault. But here a strange murmur broke out among his troops, beginning with the tribe of the Van Bummels, those valiant trenchermen of the Bronx, and spreading from man to man, accompanied with certain mutinous looks and discontented murmurs. For once in his life, and only for once, did the great Peter turn pale, for he verily thought his warriors were going to falter in this hour of perilous trial, and thus to tarnish for ever the fame of the province of New-Netherlands.

But soon did he discover, to his great joy, that in this suspicion he deeply wronged this most undaunted army ; for the cause of this agitation and uneasiness simply was, that the hour of dinner was at hand, and it would have almost broken the hearts of these regular Dutch warriors to have broken in upon the invariable routine of their habits. Besides, it was an established rule among our ancestors always to fight upon a full stomach; and to this may be doubtless attributed the circumstance that they came to be so renowned in arms.

And now are the hearty men of the Manhattoes, and their no less hearty comrades, all lustily engaged under the trees, buffeting stoutly with the contents of their wallets, and taking such affectionate embraces of their canteens and pottles, as though they verily believed they were to be the last. And as I foresee we shall have hot work in a page or two, I advise my readers to do the same, for which purpose I will bring this chapter to a close ; giving them my word of honor, that no advantage shall be taken of this armistice to surprise, or in any wise molest, the honest Nederlanders, while at their vigorous repast.

CHAPTER VIII.

CONTAINING THE MOST HORRIBLE BATTLE EVER RECORDED
IN POETRY OR PROSE; WITH THE ADMIRABLE EXPLOITS
OF PETER THE HEADSTRONG.

"Now had the Dutchmen snatched a huge repast," and finding themselves wonderfully encouraged and animated thereby, prepared to take the field. Expectation, says the writer of the Stuyvesant manuscript—Expectation now stood on stilts. The world forgot to turn round, or rather stood still, that it might witness the affray; like a round-bellied alderman, watching the combat of two chivalrous flies upon his jerkin. The eyes of all mankind, as usual in such cases, were turned upon Fort Christina. The sun, like a little man in a crowd at a puppet-show, scampered about the heavens, popping his head here and there, and endeavoring to get a peep between the unmannerly clouds that obtruded themselves in his way. The historians filled their inkhorns—the poets went without their dinners, either that they might buy paper and goose-quills, or because they could not get any thing to eat—Antiquity scowled sulkily out of its grave, to see itself outdone—while even Posterity stood mute, gazing in gaping ecstasy of retrospection on the eventful field.

The immortal deities, who whilom had seen service at the

16

"affair" of Troy—now mounted their feather-bed clouds, and sailed over the plain, or mingled among the combatants in different disguises, all itching to have a finger in the pie. Jupiter sent off his thunderbolt to a noted coppersmith, to have it furbished up for the direful occasion. Venus vowed by her chastity to patronize the Swedes, and in semblance of a blear-eyed trull paraded the battlements of Fort Christina, accompanied by Diana, as a sergeant's widow, of cracked reputation. The noted bully, Mars, stuck two horse-pistols into his belt, shouldered a rusty firelock, and gallantly swaggered at their elbow, as a drunken corporal—while Apollo trudged in their rear, as a bandy-legged fifer, playing most villanously out of tune.

On the other side, the ox-eyed Juno, who had gained a pair of black eyes over night, in one of her curtain lectures with old Jupiter, displayed her haughty beauties on a baggage-wagon— Minerva, as a brawny gin-suttler, tucked up her skirts, brandished her fists, and swore most heroically, in exceeding bad Dutch, (having but lately studied the language,) by way of keeping up the spirits of the soldiers ; while Vulcan halted as a club-footed blacksmith, lately promoted to be a captain of militia. All was silent awe, or bustling preparation : war reared his horrid front, gnashed loud his iron fangs, and shook his direful crest of bristling bayonets.

And now the mighty chieftains marshaled out their hosts. Here stood stout Risingh, firm as a thousand rocks—incrusted with stockades, and intrenched to the chin in mud batteries. His valiant soldiery lined the breast-work in grim array, each having his mustachios fiercely greased, and his hair pomatumed back, and queued so stiffly, that he grinned above the ramparts like a grisly death's head.

There came on the intrepid Peter—his brows knit, his teeth set, his fists clenched, almost breathing forth volumes of smoke, so fierce was the fire that raged within his bosom. His faithful squire Van Corlear trudged valiantly at his heels, with his trumpet gorgeously bedecked with red and yellow ribands, the remembrances of his fair mistresses at the Manhattoes. Then came waddling on the sturdy chivalry of the Hudson. There were the Van Wycks, and the Van Dycks, and the Ten Eycks—the Van Nesses, the Van Tassels, the Van Grolls; the Van Hœsens, the Van Giesons, and the Van Blarcoms—the Van Warts, the Van Winkles, the Van Dams; the Van Pelts, the Van Rippers, and the Van Brunts. There were the Van Hornes, the Van Hooks, the Van Bunschotens; the Van Gelders, the Van Arsdales, and the Van Bummels; the Vander Belts, the Vander Hoofs, the Vander Voorts, the Vander Lyns, the Vander Pools, and the Vander Spiegles—there came the Hoffmans, the Hooghlands, the Hoppers, the Cloppers, the Ryckmans, the Dyckmans, the Hogebooms, the Rosebooms, the Oothouts, the Quackenbosses, the Roerbacks, the Garrebrantzes, the Bensons, the Brouwers, the Waldrons, the Onderdonks, the Varra Vangers, the Schermerhorns, the Stoutenburghs, the Brinkerhoffs, the Bontecous, the Knickerbockers, the Hockstrassers, the Ten Breecheses and the Tough Breecheses, with a host more of worthies, whose names are too crabbed to be written, or if they could be written, it would be impossible for man to utter—all fortified with a mighty dinner, and to use the words of a great Dutch poet,

"Brimful of wrath and cabbage."

For an instant the mighty Peter paused in the midst of his career, and mounting on a stump, addressed his troops in eloquent

Low Dutch, exhorting them to fight like *duyvels*, and assuring
them that if they conquered, they should get plenty of booty—if
they fell, they should be allowed the satisfaction, while dying, of
reflecting that it was in the service of their country—and after
they were dead, of seeing their names inscribed in the temple of
renown, and handed down, in company with all the other great
men of the year, for the admiration of posterity.—Finally, he
swore to them, on the word of a governor (and they knew him
too well to doubt it for a moment), that if he caught any mother's
son of them looking pale, or playing craven, he would curry his
hide till he made him run out of it like a snake in spring time.—
Then lugging out his trusty sabre, he brandished it three times
over his head, ordered Van Corlear to sound a charge, and shouting the words " St. Nicholas and the Manhattoes !" courageously
dashed forwards.   His warlike followers, who had employed the
interval in lighting their pipes, instantly stuck them into their
mouths, gave a furious puff, and charged gallantly, under cover
of the smoke.

The Swedish garrison, ordered by the cunning Risingh not to
fire until they could distinguish the whites of their assailants'
eyes, stood in horrid silence on the covert-way, until the eager
Dutchmen had ascended the glacis.   Then did they pour into them
such a tremendous volley, that the very hills quaked around, and
were terrified even unto an incontinence of water, insomuch that
certain springs burst forth from their sides, which continue to run
unto the present day.   Not a Dutchman but would have bitten
the dust beneath that dreadful fire, had not the protecting Minerva
kindly taken care that the Swedes should, one and all, observe
their usual custom of shutting their eyes and turning away their
heads at the moment of discharge.

The Swedes followed up their fire by leaping the counter-scarp, and falling tooth and nail upon the foe with furious outcries. And now might be seen prodigies of valor, unmatched in history or song. Here was the sturdy Stoffel Brinkerhoff brandishing his quarter-staff, like the giant Blanderon his oak tree (for he scorned to carry any other weapon), and drumming a horrific tune upon the hard heads of the Swedish soldiery. There were the Van Kortlandts, posted at a distance, like the Locrian archers of yore, and plying it most potently with the long-bow, for which they were so justly renowned. On a rising knoll were gathered the valiant men of Sing-Sing, assisting marvelously in the fight, by chanting the great song of St. Nicholas ; but as to the Garde-niers of Hudson, they were absent on a marauding party, laying waste the neighboring watermelon patches.

In a different part of the field were the Van Grolls of Anthony's Nose, struggling to get to the thickest of the fight, but horribly perplexed in a defile between two hills, by reason of the length of their noses. So also the Van Bunschotens of Nyack and Kakiat, so renowned for kicking with the left foot, were brought to a stand for want of wind, in consequence of the hearty dinner they had eaten, and would have been put to utter rout but for the arrival of a gallant corps of voltigeurs, composed of the Hoppers, who advanced nimbly to their assistance on one foot. Nor must I omit to mention the valiant achievements of Antony Van Corlear, who, for a good quarter of an hour, waged stubborn fight with a little pursy Swedish drummer ; whose hide he drummed most magnificently, and whom he would infalliby have annihilated on the spot, but that he had come into the battle with no other weapon but his trumpet.

But now the combat thickened.—On came the mighty Jacobus

Varra Vanger and the fighting men of the Wallabout ; after them
thundered the Van Pelts of Esopus, together with the Van Rippers and the Van Brunts, bearing down all before them—then the
Suy Dams, and the Van Dams, pressing forward with many a
blustering oath, at the head of the warriors of Hell-gate, clad in
their thunder and lightning gaberdines ; and lastly, the standard-
bearers and body-guards of Peter Stuyvesant, bearing the great
beaver of the Manhattoes.

And now commenced the horrid din, the desperate struggle,
the maddening ferocity, the frantic desperation, the confusion and
self-abandonment of war. Dutchman and Swede commingled,
tugged, panted, and blowed. The heavens were darkened with
a tempest of missives. Bang! went the guns—whack! went
the broad-swords—thump! went the cudgels—crash! went the
musket-stocks—blows—kicks—cuffs—scratches—black eyes and
bloody noses swelling the horrors of the scene! Thick thwack,
cut and hack, helter-skelter, higgledy-piggledy, hurly-burly, head
over heels, rough and tumble!—Dunder and blixum! swore the
Dutchmen—splitter and splutter! cried the Swedes—Storm the
works! shouted Hardkoppig Peter—Fire the mine! roared stout
Risingh—Tanta-ra-ra-ra! twanged the trumpet of Antony Van
Corlear—until all voice and sound became unintelligible—grunts
of pain, yells of fury, and shouts of triumph mingling in one
hideous clamor. The earth shook as if struck with a paralytic stroke
—trees shrunk aghast, and withered at the sight—rocks burrowed
in the ground like rabbits—and even Christina creek turned from
its course, and ran up a hill in breathless terror!

Long hung the contest doubtful, for though a heavy shower
of rain, sent by the " cloud-compelling Jove," in some measure
cooled their ardor, as doth a bucket of water thrown on a group

of fighting mastiffs, yet did they but pause for a moment, to return with tenfold fury to the charge. Just at this juncture a vast and dense column of smoke was seen slowly rolling toward the scene of battle. The combatants paused for a moment, gazing in mute astonishment until the wind, dispelling the murky cloud, revealed the flaunting banner of Michael Paw the Patroon of Communipaw. That valiant chieftain came fearlessly on at the head of a phalanx of oyster-fed Pavonians and a corps de reserve of the Van Arsdales and Van Bummels, who had remained behind to digest the enormous dinner they had eaten. These now trudged manfully forward, smoking their pipes with outrageous vigor, so as to raise the awful cloud that has been mentioned; but marching exceedingly slow, being short of leg, and of great rotundity in the belt.

And now the deities who watched over the fortunes of the Nederlanders having unthinkingly left the field and stepped into a neighboring tavern to refresh themselves with a pot of beer, a direful catastrophe had well nigh ensued. Scarce had the myrmidons of Michael Paw attained the front of battle, when the Swedes, instructed by the cunning Risingh, leveled a shower of blows full at their tobacco-pipes. Astounded at this assault, and dismayed at the havoc of their pipes, these ponderous warriors gave way, and like a drove of frightened elephants broke through the ranks of their own army. The little Hoppers were borne down in the surge: the sacred banner emblazoned with the gigantic oyster of Communipaw was trampled in the dirt: on blundered and thundered the heavy-sterned fugitives, the Swedes pressing on their rear and applying their feet *a parte poste* of the Van Arsdales and the Van Bummels with a vigor

that prodigiously accelerated their movements—nor did the renowned Michael Paw himself fail to receive divers grievous and
dishonorable visitations of shoe leather.

But what, oh Muse! was the rage of Peter Stuyvesant, when
from afar he saw his army giving way! In the transports of his
wrath he sent forth a roar, enough to shake the very hills.
The men of the Manhattoes plucked up new courage at the
sound; or rather, they rallied at the voice of their leader, of
whom they stood more in awe than of all the Swedes in Christendom. Without waiting for their aid, the daring Peter dashed
sword in hand into the thickest of the foe. Then might be seen
achievements worthy of the days of the giants. Wherever he
went, the enemy shrank before him; the Swedes fled to right
and left, or were driven, like dogs, into their own ditch; but, as
he pushed forward singly with headlong courage, the foe closed
behind and hung upon his rear. One aimed a blow full at his
heart; but the protecting power which watches over the great
and good turned aside the hostile blade and directed it to a side-
pocket, where reposed an enormous iron tobacco-box, endowed,
like the shield of Achilles, with supernatural powers, doubtless
from bearing the portrait of the blessed St. Nicholas. Peter
Stuyvesant turned like an angry bear upon the foe, and seizing
him as he fled, by an immeasurable queue, "Ah whoreson cater-
pillar," roared he, "here's what shall make worms' meat of thee!"
So saying, he whirled his sword and dealt a blow that would have
decapitated the varlet, but that the pitying steel struck short and
shaved the queue forever from his crown. At this moment an ar-
quebusier leveled his piece from a neighboring mound, with deadly
aim; but the watchful Minerva, who had just stopped to tie up

Darley Del.   Childs Sc.

her garter, seeing the peril of her favorite hero, sent old Boreas with his bellows, who, as the match descended to the pan, gave a blast that blew the priming from the touch-hole.

Thus waged the fight, when the stout Risingh, surveying the field from the top of a little ravelin, perceived his troops banged, beaten, and kicked by the invincible Peter. Drawing his falchion and uttering a thousand anathemas, ne strode down to the scene of combat with some such thundering strides as Jupiter is said by Hesiod to have taken, when he strode down the spheres to hurl his thunderbolts at the Titans.

When the rival heroes came face to face, each made a prodigious start in the style of a veteran stage champion. Then did they regard each other for a moment with the bitter aspect of two furious ram-cats on the point of a clapper-clawing. Then did they throw themselves into one attitude, then into another, striking their swords on the ground first on the right side, then on the left—at last at it they went, with incredible ferocity. Words cannot tell the prodigies of strength and valor displayed in this direful encounter—an encounter compared to which the far-famed battles of Ajax with Hector, of Æneas with Turnus, Orlando with Rodomont, Guy of Warwick with Colbrand the Dane, or of that renowned Welsh knight, Sir Owen of the Mountains, with the giant Guylon, were all gentle sports and holyday recreations. At length the valiant Peter, watching his opportunity, aimed a blow, enough to cleave his adversary to the very chine; but Risingh, nimbly raising his sword, warded it off so narrowly, that glancing on one side, it shaved away a huge canteen in which he carried his liquor; thence pursuing its trenchant course, it severed off a deep coat pocket, stored with bread and cheese—which provant rolling among the armies, occasioned a

16*

fearful scrambling between the Swedes and Dutchmen, and made
the general battle to wax ten times more furious than ever.

Enraged to see his military stores laid waste, the stout
Risingh, collecting all his forces, aimed a mighty blow full at the
hero's crest.   In vain did his fierce little cocked hat oppose its
course.   The biting steel clove through the stubborn ram beaver,
and would have cracked the crown of any one not endowed with
supernatural hardness of head; but the brittle weapon shivered
in pieces on the skull of Hardkoppig Piet, shedding a thousand
sparks, like beams of glory round his grizzly visage.

The good Peter reeled with the blow, and turning up his eyes
beheld a thousand suns, beside moons and stars, dancing about
the firmament—at length, missing his footing, by reason of his
wooden leg, down he came on his seat of honor with a crash which
shook the surrounding hills, and might have wrecked his frame,
had he not been received into a cushion softer than velvet, which
Providence or Minerva, or St. Nicholas, or some kindly cow had
benevolently prepared for his reception.

The furious Risingh, in despite of the maxim, cherished by
all true knights, that "fair play is a jewel," hastened to take
advantage of the hero's fall; but, as he stooped to give a fatal
blow, Peter Stuyvesant dealt him a thwack over the sconce
with his wooden leg, which set a chime of bells ringing triple bob
majors in his cerebellum.   The bewildered Swede staggered with
the blow, and the wary Peter seizing a pocket-pistol, which lay
hard by, discharged it full at the head of the reeling Risingh.
Let not my reader mistake ; it was not a murderous weapon loaded
with powder and ball; but a little sturdy stone pottle charged to
the muzzle with a double dram of true Dutch courage, which the
knowing Antony Van Corlear carried about him by way of re-

plenishing his valor; and which had dropped from his wallet during his furious encounter with the drummer. The hideous weapon sang through the air, and true to its course as was the fragment of a rock discharged at Hector by bully Ajax, encountered the head of the gigantic Swede with matchless violence.

This heaven-directed blow decided the battle. The ponderous pericranium of General Jan Risingh sank upon his breast; his knees tottered under him; a death-like torpor seized upon his frame, and he tumbled to the earth with such violence, that old Pluto started with affright, lest he should have broken through the roof of his infernal palace.

His fall was the signal of defeat and victory—the Swedes gave way—the Dutch pressed forward; the former took to their heels, the latter hotly pursued.—Some entered with them, pell-mell, through the sally-port—others stormed the bastion, and others scrambled over the curtain. Thus in a little while the fortress of Fort Christina, which, like another Troy, had stood a siege of full ten hours, was carried by assault, without the loss of a single man on either side. Victory, in the likeness of a gigantic ox-fly, sat perched upon the cocked hat of the gallant Stuyvesant, and it was declared, by all the writers whom he hired to write the history of his expedition, that on this memorable day he gained a sufficient quantity of glory to immortalize a dozen of the greatest heroes in Christendom!

CHAPTER IX.

THANKS to St. Nicholas, we have safely finished this tremendous battle: let us sit down, my worthy reader, and cool ourselves, for I am in a prodigious sweat and agitation—truly this fighting of battles is hot work! and if your great commanders did but know what trouble they give their historians, they would not have the conscience to achieve so many horrible victories. But methinks I hear my reader complain, that throughout this boasted battle there is not the least slaughter, nor a single individual maimed, if we except the unhappy Swede, who was shorn of his queue by the trenchant blade of Peter Stuyvesant; all which, he observes, is a great outrage on probability, and highly injurious to the interest of the narration.

This is certainly an objection of no little moment, but it arises entirely from the obscurity enveloping the remote periods of time about which I have undertaken to write. Thus, though doubtless, from the importance of the object, and the prowess of the parties concerned, there must have been terrible carnage, and prodigies of valor displayed before the walls of Christina, yet, notwithstanding that I have consulted every history, manuscript, and tradition, touching this memorable though long-forgotten battle, I cannot find mention made of a single man killed or wounded in the whole affair.

This is, without doubt, owing to the extreme modesty of our forefathers, who, unlike their descendants, were never prone to vaunt of their achievements; but it is a virtue which places their historian in a most embarrassing predicament; for, having promised my readers a hideous and unparalleled battle, and having worked them up into a warlike and bloodthirsty state of mind; to put them off without any havoc and slaughter would have been as bitter a disappointment as to summon a multitude of good people to attend an execution, and then cruelly balk them by a reprieve.

Had the fates only allowed me some half a score of dead men, I had been content; for I would have made them such heroes as abounded in the olden time, but whose race is now unfortunately extinct; any one of whom, if we may believe those authentic writers, the poets, could drive great armies like sheep before him, and conquer and desolate whole cities by his single arm.

But seeing that I had not a single life at my disposal, all that was left me was to make the most I could of my battle, by means of kicks, and cuffs, and bruises, and such like ignoble wounds. And here I cannot but compare my dilemma, in some sort, to that of the divine Milton, who, having arrayed with sublime preparation his immortal hosts against each other, is sadly put to it how to manage them, and how he shall make the end of his battle answer to the beginning; inasmuch as, being mere spirits, he cannot deal a mortal blow, nor even give a flesh wound to any

of his combatants.   For my part, the greatest difficulty I found
was, when I had once put my warriors in a passion, and let them
loose into the midst of the enemy, to keep them from doing
mischief.   Many a time had I to restrain the sturdy Peter from
cleaving a gigantic Swede to the very waistband, or spitting half
a dozen little fellows on his sword, like so many sparrows.   And
when I had set some hundred of missives flying in the air, I did
not dare to suffer one of them to reach the ground, lest it should
have put an end to some unlucky Dutchman.

The reader cannot conceive how mortifying it is to a writer
thus in a manner to have his hands tied, and how many tempting
opportunities I had to wink at, where I might have made as fine
a death-blow as any recorded in history or song.

From my own experience I begin to doubt most potently of
the authenticity of many of Homer's stories.   I verily believe,
that when he had once launched one of his favorite heroes among
a crowd of the enemy, he cut down many an honest fellow,
without any authority for so doing, excepting that he presented a
fair mark—and that often a poor fellow was sent to grim Pluto's
domains, merely because he had a name that would give a sounding turn to a period.   But I disclaim all such unprincipled liberties—let me but have truth and the law on my side, and no man
would fight harder than myself—but since the various records I
consulted did not warrant it, I had too much conscience to kill a
single soldier.—By St. Nicholas, but it would have been a pretty
piece of business!   My enemies, the critics, who I foresee will
be ready enough to lay any crime they can discover at my door,
might have charged me with murder outright—and I should have
esteemed myself lucky to escape with no harsher verdict than
manslaughter!

And now, gentle reader, that we are tranquilly sitting down here, smoking our pipes, permit me to indulge in a melancholy reflection which at this moment passes across my mind.—How vain, how fleeting, how uncertain are all those gaudy bubbles after which we are panting and toiling in this world of fair delusions! The wealth which the miser has amassed with so many weary days, so many sleepless nights, a spendthrift heir may squander away in joyless prodigality;—the noblest monuments which pride has ever reared to perpetuate a name, the hand of time will shortly tumble into ruins—and even the brightest laurels, gained by feats of arms, may wither, and be for ever blighted by the chilling neglect of mankind.—"How many illustrious heroes," says the good Boëtius, "who were once the pride and glory of the age, hath the silence of historians buried in eternal oblivion!" And this it was that induced the Spartans, when they went to battle, solemnly to sacrifice to the Muses, supplicating that their achievements might be worthily recorded. Had not Homer tuned his lofty lyre, observes the elegant Cicero, the valor of Achilles had remained unsung. And such too, after all the toils and perils he had braved, after all the gallant actions he had achieved, such too had nearly been the fate of the chivalric Peter Stuyvesant, but that I fortunately stepped in and engraved his name on the indelible tablet of history, just as the caitiff Time was silently brushing it away forever!

The more I reflect, the more I am astonished at the important character of the historian. He is the sovereign censor, to decide upon the renown or infamy of his fellow-men. He is the patron of kings and conquerors, on whom it depends whether they shall live in after-ages, or be forgotten as were their ancestors before them. The tyrant may oppress while the object of his tyranny

exists; but the historian possesses superior might, for his power
extends even beyond the grave. The shades of departed and
long-forgotten heroes anxiously bend down from above, while
he writes, watching each movement of his pen, whether it shall
pass by their names with neglect, or inscribe them on the death-
less pages of renown. Even the drop of ink which hangs trem
bling on his pen, which he may either dash upon the floor, or
waste in idle scrawlings—that very drop, which to him is not
worth the twentieth part of a farthing, may be of incalculable
value to some departed worthy—may elevate half a score, in one
moment, to immortality, who would have given worlds, had they
possessed them, to ensure the glorious meed.

Let not my readers imagine, however, that I am indulging in
vainglorious boastings, or am anxious to blazon forth the importance of my tribe. On the contrary, I shrink when I reflect on
the awful responsibility we historians assume—I shudder to think
what direful commotions and calamities we occasion in the world
—I swear to thee, honest reader, as I am a man, I weep at the
very idea! Why, let me ask, are so many illustrious men daily
tearing themselves away from the embraces of their families—
slighting the smiles of beauty—despising the allurements of fortune, and exposing themselves to the miseries of war?—Why are
kings desolating empires, and depopulating whole countries? In
short, what induces all great men, of all ages and countries, to
commit so many victories and misdeeds, and inflict so many miseries upon mankind and upon themselves, but the mere hope that
some historian will kindly take them into notice, and admit them
into a corner of his volume? For, in short, the mighty object of
all their toils, their hardships, and privations, is nothing but
immortal fame—and what is immortal fame?——·why, half a

page of dirty paper!——alas! alas! how humiliating the idea—
that the renown of so great a man as Peter Stuyvesant should
depend upon the pen of so little a man as Diedrich Knickerbocker!

And now, having refreshed ourselves after the fatigues and
perils of the field, it behooves us to return once more to the scene
of conflict, and inquire what were the results of this renowned
conquest. The fortress of Christina being the fair metropolis,
and in a manner the key to New-Sweden, its capture was speedily
followed by the entire subjugation of the province. This was not
a little promoted by the gallant and courteous deportment of the
chivalric Peter. Though a man terrible in battle, yet in the hour
of victory was he endued with a spirit generous, merciful, and
humane. He vaunted not over his enemies, nor did he make
defeat more galling by unmanly insults; for like that mirror of
knightly virtue, the renowned Paladin Orlando, he was more
anxious to do great actions than to talk of them after they were
done. He put no man to death; ordered no houses to be burnt
down; permitted no ravages to be perpetrated on the property of
the vanquished; and even gave one of his bravest officers a severe
admonishment with his walking staff, for having been detected in
the act of sacking a hen-roost.

He moreover issued a proclamation, inviting the inhabitants
to submit to the authority of their High Mightinesses; but
declaring, with unexampled clemency, that whoever refused should
be lodged at the public expense, in a goodly castle provided for
the purpose, and have an armed retinue to wait on them in the
bargain. In consequence of these beneficent terms, about thirty
Swedes stepped manfully forward and took the oath of allegiance;
in reward for which they were graciously permitted to remain on

the banks of the Delaware, where their descendants reside at this
very day. I am told, however, by divers observant travelers, that
they have never been able to get over the chap-fallen looks of
their ancestors; but that they still do strangely transmit from
father to son manifest marks of the sound drubbing given them
by the sturdy Amsterdammers.

The whole country of New-Sweden, having thus yielded to
the arms of the triumphant Peter, was reduced to a colony
called South River, and placed under the superintendence of a
lieutenant-governor; subject to the control of the supreme government of New-Amsterdam. This great dignitary was called
Mynheer William Beekman, or rather *Beck*-man, who derived his
surname, as did Ovidius Naso of yore, from the lordly dimensions of his nose, which projected from the centre of his countenance, like the beak of a parrot. He was the great progenitor
of the tribe of the Beekmans, one of the most ancient and honorable families of the province; the members of which do gratefully
commemorate the origin of their dignity; not as your noble families in England would do, by having a glowing proboscis emblazoned in their escutcheon; but by one and all wearing a right
goodly nose, stuck in the very middle of their faces.

Thus was this perilous enterprise gloriously terminated, with
the loss of only two men,—Wolfert Van Horne, a tall spare man,
who was knocked overboard by the boom of a sloop in a flaw of
wind; and fat Brom Van Bummel, who was suddenly carried off
by an indigestion; both, however, were immortalized, as having
bravely fallen in the service of their country. True it is, Peter
Stuyvesant had one of his limbs terribly fractured in the act of
storming the fortress; but as it was fortunately his wooden leg,
the wound was promptly and effectually healed.

And now nothing remains to this branch of my history but to mention that this immaculate hero, and his victorious army, returned joyously to the Manhattoes; where they made a solemn and triumphant entry, bearing with them the conquered Risingh, and the remnant of his battered crew, who had refused allegiance; for it appears that the gigantic Swede had only fallen into a swoon, at the end of the battle, from which he was speedily restored by a wholesome tweak of the nose.

These captive heroes were lodged, according to the promise of the governor, at the public expense, in a fair and spacious castle; being the prison of state, of which Stoffel Brinkerhoff, the immortal conqueror of Oyster Bay, was appointed governor; and which has ever since remained in the possession of his descendants.*

It was a pleasant and goodly sight to witness the joy of the people of New-Amsterdam, at beholding their warriors once more return from this war in the wilderness. The old women thronged round Antony Van Corlear, who gave the whole history of the campaign with matchless accuracy; saving that he took the credit of fighting the whole battle himself, and especially of vanquishing the stout Risingh; which he considered himself as clearly entitled to, seeing that it was effected by his own stone pottle.

The schoolmasters throughout the town gave holiday to their little urchins,—who followed in droves after the drums, with paper caps on their heads, and sticks in their breeches, thus taking the first lesson in the art of war. As to the sturdy

---

* This castle, though very much altered and modernized, is still in being, and stands at the corner of Pearl-street, facing Coentie's slip.

rabble, they thronged at the heels of Peter Stuyvesant wherever he went, waving their greasy hats in the air, and shouting
" Hardkoppig Piet for ever !"

It was indeed a day of roaring rout and jubilee. A huge
dinner was prepared at the Stadthouse in honor of the conquerors, where were assembled in one glorious constellation the
great and little luminaries of New-Amsterdam.   There were
the lordly Schout and his obsequious deputy—the burgomasters
with their officious schepens at their elbows—the subaltern
officers at the elbows of the schepens, and so on down to the
lowest hanger-on of police : every tag having his rag at his side,
to finish his pipe, drink off his heel-taps, and laugh at his flights
of immortal dullness. In short—for a city feast is a city feast
all the world over, and has been a city feast ever since the
creation—the dinner went off much the same as do our great
corporation junketings and fourth of July banquets. Loads of
fish, flesh, and fowl were devoured, oceans of liquor drunk,
thousands of pipes smoked, and many a dull joke honored with
much obstreperous fat-sided laughter.

I must not omit to mention, that to this far-famed victory
Peter Stuyvesant was indebted for another of his many titles
—for so hugely delighted were the honest burghers with his
achievements, that they unanimously honored him with the name
of *Pieter de Groodt*, that is to say Peter the Great; or, as it
was translated into English by the people of New-Amsterdam,
for the benefit of their New England visitors, *Piet de pig*—an
appellation which he maintained even unto the day of his death.

BOOK VII.

CONTAINING THE THIRD PART OF THE REIGN OF PETER THE HEADSTRONG—HIS TROUBLES WITH THE BRITISH NATION, AND THE DECLINE AND FALL OF THE DUTCH DYNASTY

CHAPTER I.

HOW PETER STUYVESANT RELIEVED THE SOVEREIGN PEOPLE FROM THE BURTHEN OF TAKING CARE OF THE NATION; WITH SUNDRY PARTICULARS OF HIS CONDUCT IN TIME OF PEACE, AND OF THE RISE OF A GREAT DUTCH ARISTOCRACY

THE history of the reign of Peter Stuyvesant furnishes an edifying picture of the cares and vexations inseparable from sovereignty, and a solemn warning to all who are ambitious of attaining the seat of honor. Though returning in triumph and crowned with victory, his exultation was checked on observing the abuses which had sprung up in New-Amsterdam during his short absence. His walking-staff, which he had sent home to act as his vicegerent, had, it is true, kept his council-chamber in order; the counsellors eyeing it with awe, as it lay in grim repose upon the table, and smoking their pipes in silence; but its control extended not out of doors.

The populace unfortunately had had too much their own way under the slack though fitful reign of William the Testy; and though upon the accession of Peter Stuyvesant they had felt, with the instinctive perception which mobs as well as cattle possess, that the reins of government had passed into stronger hands, yet could they not help fretting and chafing and champing upon the bit, in restive silence.

Scarcely, therefore, had he departed on his expedition against the Swedes, than the old factions of William Kieft's reign had again thrust their heads above water. Pot-house meetings were again held to "discuss the state of the nation," where cobblers, tinkers, and tailors, the self-dubbed "friends of the people," once more felt themselves inspired with the gift of legislation, and undertook to lecture on every movement of government.

Now, as Peter Stuyvesant had a singular inclination to govern the province by his individual will, his first move, on his return, was to put a stop to this gratuitous legislation. Accordingly, one evening, when an inspired cobbler was holding forth to an assemblage of the kind, the intrepid Peter suddenly made his appearance, with his ominous walking-staff in his hand, and a countenance sufficient to petrify a mill-stone. The whole meeting was thrown into confusion—the orator stood aghast, with open mouth and trembling knees, while "horror! tyranny! liberty! rights! taxes! death! destruction!" and a host of other patriotic phrases were bolted forth before he had time to close his lips. Peter took no notice of the skulking throng, but strode up to the brawling bully-ruffian, and pulling out a huge silver watch, which might have served in times of yore as a town-clock, and which is still retained by his descendants as a family curiosity, requested the orator to mend it, and set it going. The orator humbly confessed it was utterly out of his power, as he was unacquainted with the nature of its construction. "Nay, but," said Peter, "try your ingenuity, man: you see all the springs and wheels, and how easily the clumsiest hand may stop it, and pull it to pieces; and why should it not be equally easy to regulate as to stop it?" The orator declared that his trade was wholly different—that he was a poor cobbler, and had never meddled with a watch in his life—that there were men skilled in the art, whose business it was to attend to those matters; but for his part, he should only mar the workmanship and put the whole in confusion——"Why, harkee, master of mine," cried Peter, turning suddenly upon him, with a countenance that almost petrified the patcher of shoes into a perfect lapstone—"dost thou pretend to meddle with the movements of government—to regulate, and correct, and patch, and cobble a complicated machine, the principles of which are above thy comprehension, and its simplest operations too subtle for thy understanding, when thou canst not correct a trifling error in a common piece of mechanism, the whole mystery of which is open to thy inspection?—Hence with thee to the leather and stone, which are emblems of thy head; cobble thy shoes, and confine thyself to the vocation for which Heaven has fitted thee—but," elevating his voice until it made the welkin ring, "if ever I catch thee, or any of thy tribe, meddling again with affairs of government, by St. Nicholas, but I'll have every mother's bastard of ye flay'd alive, and your hides stretched for drum-heads, that ye may thenceforth make a noise to some purpose!"

This threat, and the tremendous voice in which it was uttered, caused the whole multitude to quake with fear. The hair of the

orator rose on his head like his own swine's bristles, and not a
knight of the thimble present but his heart died within him, and
he felt as though he could have verily escaped through the eye
of a needle.   The assembly dispersed in silent consternation ; the
pseudo statesmen who had hitherto undertaken to regulate public
affairs, were now fain to stay at home, hold their tongues, and
take care of their families ; and party feuds died away to such a
degree, that many thriving keepers of taverns and dram-shops
were utterly ruined for want of business.   But though this measure produced the desired effect in putting an extinguisher on the
new lights just brightening up : yet did it tend to injure the popularity of the Great Peter with the thinking part of the community :
that is to say, that part which think for others instead of for themselves ; or, in other words, who attend to every body's business but
their own.   These accused the old governor of being highly aristocratical, and in truth there seems to have been some ground for
such an accusation ; for he carried himself with a lofty soldier-
like air, and was somewhat particular in his dress, appearing,
when not in uniform, in rich apparel of the antique flaundrish
cut, and was especially noted for having his sound leg (which was
a very comely one) always arrayed in a red stocking and high-
heeled shoe.

Justice he often dispensed in the primitive patriarchal way,
seated on the " stoep " before his door, under the shade of a great
button-wood tree ; but all visits of form and state were received
with something of court ceremony in the best parlor ; where
Antony the Trumpeter officiated as high chamberlain.   On public
occasions he appeared with great pomp of equipage, and always
rode to church in a yellow wagon with flaming red wheels.

These symptoms of state and ceremony, as we have hinted,

were much caviled at by the thinking (and talking) part of the
community. They had been accustomed to find easy access to
their former governors, and in particular had lived on terms of
extreme intimacy with William the Testy, and they accused Peter
Stuyvesant of assuming too much dignity and reserve, and of
wrapping himself in mystery. Others, however, have pretended
to discover in all this a shrewd policy on the part of the old governor. It is certainly of the first importance, say they, that a
country should be governed by wise men: but then it is almost
equally important that the people should think them wise; for
this belief alone can produce willing subordination. To keep up,
however, this desirable confidence in rulers, the people should be
allowed to see as little of them as possible. It is the mystery
which envelopes great men, that gives them half their greatness.
There is a kind of superstitious reverence for office which leads
us to exaggerate the merits of the occupant; and to suppose that
he must be wiser than common men. He, however, who gains
access to cabinets, soon finds out by what foolishness the world is
governed. He finds that there is quackery in legislation as in
every thing else; that rulers have their whims and errors as well
as other men, and are not so wonderfully superior as he had imagined, since even he may occasionally confute them in argument.
Thus awe subsides into confidence, confidence inspires familiarity, and familiarity produces contempt. Such was the case,
say they, with William the Testy. By making himself too easy
of access he enabled every scrub-politician to measure wits with
him, and to find out the true dimensions not only of his person
but of his mind: and thus it was that, by being familiarly scanned, he was discovered to be a very little man. Peter Stuyvesant, on the contrary, say they, by conducting himself with dignity

17

and loftiness, was looked up to with great reverence. As he never gave his reasons for any thing he did, the public gave him credit for very profound ones; every movement, however intrinsically unimportant, was a matter of speculation; and his very red stockings excited some respect, as being different from the stock- ings of other men.

Another charge against Peter Stuyvesant was that he had a great leaning in favor of the patricians: and indeed in his time rose many of those mighty Dutch families which have taken such vigorous root, and branched out so luxuriantly in our State. Some, to be sure, were of earlier date, such as the Van Kortlandts, the Van Zandts, the Ten Broecks, the Harden Broecks, and others of Pavonian renown, who gloried in the title of " Discoverers," from having been engaged in the nautical expedition from Communi- paw, in which they so heroically braved the terrors of Hell-gate and Buttermilk-channel, and discovered a site for New-Amsterdam.

Others claimed to themselves the appellation of Conquerors, from their gallant achievements in New-Sweden and their victory over the Yankees at Oyster Bay. Such was that list of warlike worthies heretofore enumerated, beginning with the Van Wycks, the Van Dycks, and the Ten Eycks, and extending to the Rut- gers, the Bensons, the Brinkerhoffs, and the Schermerhorns; a roll equal to the Doomsday Book of William the Conqueror, and establishing the heroic origin of many an ancient aristocratical Dutch family. These, after all, are the only legitimate nobility and lords of the soil; these are the real " beavers of the Man- hattoes;" and much does it grieve me in modern days to see them elbowed aside by foreign invaders, and more especially by those ingenious people, " the Sons of the Pilgrims;" who out-bargain them in the market, out-speculate them on the exchange, out-top them in fortune, and run up mushroom palaces so high, that the tallest Dutch family mansion has not wind enough left for its weather-cock.

In the proud days of **Peter Stuyvesant**, however, the good old Dutch aristocracy loomed out in all its grandeur. The burly burgher, in round-crowned flaundrish hat with brim of vast circumference; in portly gabardine and bulbous multiplicity of breeches, sat on his "stoep" and smoked his pipe in lordly silence, nor did it ever enter his brain that the active, restless Yankee, whom he saw through his half-shut eyes worrying about in dog-day heat, ever intent on the main chance, was one day to usurp control over these goodly Dutch domains. Already, however, the races regarded each other with disparaging eye. The Yankees sneeringly spoke of the round-crowned burghers of the Manhattoes as the "Copper-heads;" while the latter, glorying in their own nether rotundity, and observing the slack galligaskins of their rivals, flapping like an empty sail against the mast, retorted upon them with the opprobrious appellation of "Platter-breeches.'

CHAPTER II.

HOW PETER STUYVESANT LABORED TO CIVILIZE THE COMMU-
NITY—HOW HE WAS A GREAT PROMOTER OF HOLYDAYS—
HOW HE INSTITUTED KISSING ON NEW-YEAR'S DAY—HOW
HE DISTRIBUTED FIDDLES THROUGHOUT THE NEW-NETH-
ERLANDS—HOW HE VENTURED TO REFORM THE LADIES'
PETTICOATS, AND HOW HE CAUGHT A TARTAR.

FROM what I have recounted in the foregoing chapter I would
not have it imagined that the great Peter was a tyrannical
potentate, ruling with a rod of iron. On the contrary, where
the dignity of office permitted he abounded in generosity and
condescension. If he refused the brawling multitude the right
of misrule, he at least endeavored to rule them in righteousness.
To spread abundance in the land, he obliged the bakers to give
thirteen loaves to the dozen—a golden rule which remains a
monument of his beneficence. So far from indulging in unreasonable austerity, he delighted to see the poor and the laboring
man rejoice; and for this purpose he was a great promoter of
holydays. Under his reign there was a great cracking of eggs
at Paas or Easter; Whitsuntide or Pinxter also flourished in all
its bloom; and never were stockings better filled on the eve of
the blessed St. Nicholas.

New-year's day, however, was his favorite festival, and was ushered in by the ringing of bells and firing of guns. On that genial day the fountains of hospitality were broken up, and the whole community was deluged with cherry-brandy, true Hollands, and mulled cider; every house was a temple to the jolly god; and many a provident vagabond got drunk out of pure economy, taking in liquor enough gratis to serve him half a year afterwards.

The great assemblage, however, was at the governor's house, whither repaired all the burghers of New-Amsterdam with their wives and daughters, pranked out in their best attire. On this occasion the good Peter was devoutly observant of the pious Dutch rite of kissing the women-kind for a happy new-year; and it is traditional that Antony the Trumpeter, who acted as gentleman usher, took toll of all who were young and handsome, as they passed through the antechamber. This venerable custom, thus happily introduced, was followed with such zeal by high and low, that on new-year's day, during the reign of Peter Stuyvesant, New-Amsterdam was the most thoroughly be-kissed community in all Christendom.

Another great measure of Peter Stuyvesant for public improvement was the distribution of fiddles throughout the land. These were placed in the hands of veteran negroes, who were dispatched as missionaries to every part of the province. This measure, it is said, was first suggested by Antony the Trumpeter; and the effect was marvelous. Instead of those "indignation meetings" set on foot in the time of William the Testy, where men met together to rail at public abuses, groan over the evils of the times, and make each other miserable, there were joyous gatherings of the two sexes to dance and make merry. Now

were instituted "quilting bees," and "husking bees," and other
rural assemblages, where, under the inspiring influence of the
fiddle, toil was enlivened by gayety and followed up by the dance.
"Raising bees" also were frequent, where houses sprang up at
the wagging of the fiddle-stick, as the walls of Thebes sprang up
of yore to the sound of the lyre of Amphion.

Jolly autumn, which pours its treasures over hill and dale,
was in those days a season for the lifting of the heel as well as
the heart; labor came dancing in the train of abundance, and
frolic prevailed throughout the land. Happy days! when the
yeomanry of the Nieuw-Nederlands were merry rather than
wise; and when the notes of the fiddle, those harbingers of good
humor and good will, resounded at the close of the day from
every hamlet along the Hudson!

Nor was it in rural communities alone that Peter Stuyvesant
introduced his favorite engine of civilization. Under his rule the
fiddle acquired that potent sway in New-Amsterdam which it
has ever since retained. Weekly assemblages were held, not in
heated ball-rooms at midnight hours, but on Saturday afternoons,
by the golden light of the sun, on the green lawn of the battery;
with Antony the Trumpeter for master of ceremonies. Here
would the good Peter take his seat under the spreading trees,
among the old burghers and their wives, and watch the mazes
of the dance. Here would he smoke his pipe, crack his joke,
and forget the rugged toils of war, in the sweet oblivious
festivities of peace, giving a nod of approbation to those of the
young men who shuffled and kicked most vigorously; and, now
and then a hearty smack, in all honesty of soul, to the buxom
lass who held out longest, and tired down every competitor;
infallible proof of her being the best dancer.

Once it is true the harmony of these meetings was in danger of interruption. A young belle just returned from a visit to Holland, who of course led the fashions, made her appearance in not more than half a dozen petticoats, and these of alarming shortness. A whisper and a flutter ran through the assembly. The young men of course were lost in admiration, but the old ladies were shocked in the extreme, especially those who had marriageable daughters; the young ladies blushed and felt excessively for the " poor thing," and even the governor himself appeared to be in some kind of perturbation.

To complete the confusion of the good folks she undertook, in the course of a jig, to describe some figures in algebra taught her by a dancing-master at Rotterdam. Unfortunately, at the highest flourish of her feet some vagabond zephyr obtruded his services, and a display of the graces took place, at which all the ladies present were thrown into great consternation; several grave country members were not a little moved, and the good Peter Stuyvesant himself was grievously scandalized.

The shortness of the female dresses, which had continued in fashion ever since the days of William Kieft, had long offended his eye; and though extremely averse to meddling with the pet-ticoats of the ladies, yet he immediately recommended that every one should be furnished with a flounce to the bottom. He like-wise ordered that the ladies, and indeed the gentlemen, should use no other step in dancing than " shuffle and turn," and " double trouble;" and forbade, under pain of his high displeasure, any young lady thenceforth to attempt what was termed " exhibiting the graces."

These were the only restrictions he ever imposed upon the sex, and these were considered by them as tyrannical oppressions, and resisted with that becoming spirit manifested by the gentle sex whenever their privileges are invaded. In fact, Antony Van Corlear, who, as has been shown, was a sagacious man, experienced in the ways of women, took a private occasion to intimate to the governor that a conspiracy was forming among the young vrouws of New-Amsterdam; and that, if the matter were pushed any further, there was danger of their leaving off petticoats altogether; whereupon the good Peter shrugged his shoulders, dropped the subject, and ever after suffered the women to wear their petticoats and cut their capers as high as they pleased; a privilege which they have jealously maintained in the Manhattoes unto the present day.

CHAPTER III.

HOW TROUBLES THICKEN ON THE PROVINCE—HOW IT IS
THREATENED BY THE HELDERBERGERS, THE MERRYLAND-
ERS, AND THE GIANTS OF THE SUSQUEHANNA.

IN the last two chapters I have regaled the reader with a delectable picture of the good Peter and his metropolis during an interval of peace. It was, however, but a bit of blue sky in a stormy
day; the clouds are again gathering up from all points of the
compass, and, if I am not mistaken in my forebodings, we shall
have rattling weather in the ensuing chapters.

It is with some communities as it is with certain meddlesome
individuals; they have a wonderful facility at getting into scrapes,
and I have always remarked that those are most prone to get in
who have the least talent at getting out again. This is doubtless
owing to the excessive valor of those states; for I have likewise
noticed that this rampant quality is always most frothy and fussy
where most confined; which accounts for its vaporing so ama-
zingly in little states, little men and ugly little women more especially.

Such is the case with this little province of the Nieuw-Nederlands; which, by its exceeding valor, has already drawn upon
itself a host of enemies; has had fighting enough to satisfy a pro-
17*

vince twice its size; and is in a fair way of becoming an exceedingly forlorn, well-belabored, and woe-begone little province. All
which was providentially ordered to give interest and sublimity
to this pathetic history.

The first interruption to the halcyon quiet of Peter Stuyvesant was caused by hostile intelligence from the old belligerent
nest of Rensellaerstein. Killian, the lordly patroon of Rensellaerwick, was again in the field, at the head of his myrmidons of
the Helderberg; seeking to annex the whole of the Kaats-kill
mountains to his domains. The Indian tribes of these mountains
had likewise taken up the hatchet and menaced the venerable
Dutch settlement of Esopus.

Fain would I entertain the reader with the triumphant campaign of Peter Stuyvesant in the haunted regions of those mountains; but that I hold all Indian conflicts to be mere barbaric
brawls, unworthy of the pen which has recorded the classic war
of Fort Christina; and as to these Helderberg commotions, they
are among the flatulencies which from time to time afflict the
bowels of this ancient province, as with a wind-colic, and which I
deem it seemly and decent to pass over in silence.

The next storm of trouble was from the south. Scarcely had
the worthy Mynheer Beekman got warm in the seat of authority
on the South River, than enemies began to spring up all around
him. Hard by was a formidable race of savages inhabiting the
gentle region watered by the Susquehanna, of whom the following mention is made by Master Hariot in his excellent history:

"The Susquesahanocks are a giantly people, strange in proportion, behavior and attire—their voice sounding from them as
out of a cave. Their tobacco-pipes were three quarters of a yard
long; carved at the great end with a bird, beare, or other device.

sufficient to beat out the brains of a horse. The calfe of one of their legges measured three quarters of a yard about; the rest of the limbs proportionable."*

These gigantic savages and smokers caused no little disquiet in the mind of Mynheer Beekman, threatening to cause a famine of tobacco in the land; but his most formidable enemy was the roaring, roystering English colony of Maryland, or as it was anciently written Merryland; so called because the inhabitants, not having the fear of the Lord before their eyes, were prone to make merry and get fuddled with mint-julep and apple-toddy. They were, moreover, great horse-racers and cock-fighters; mighty wrestlers and jumpers, and enormous consumers of hoe-cake and bacon. They lay claim to be the first inventors of those recondite beverages, cock-tail, stone-fence, and sherry cobbler, and to have discovered the gastronomical merits of terrapins, soft crabs, and canvas-back ducks.

This rantipole colony, founded by Lord Baltimore, a British nobleman, was managed by his agent, a swaggering Englishman, commonly called Fendall; that is to say, "offend all," a name given him for his bullying propensities. These were seen in a message to Mynheer Beekman, threatening him, unless he immediately swore allegiance to Lord Baltimore as the rightful lord of the soil, to come at the head of the roaring boys of Merryland and the giants of the Susquehanna, and sweep him and his Nederlanders out of the country.

The trusty sword of Peter Stuyvesant almost leaped from its scabbard, when he received missives from Mynheer Beekman, informing him of the swaggering menaces of the bully Fendall;

* Hariot's Journal, Purch. Pilgrims.

and as to the giantly warriors of the Susquehanna, nothing would have more delighted him than a bout, hand to hand, with half a score of them; having never encountered a giant in the whole course of his campaigns, unless we may consider the stout Risingh as such—and he was but a little one.

Nothing prevented his marching instantly to the South River and enacting scenes still more glorious than those of Fort Christina, but the necessity of first putting a stop to the increasing aggressions and inroads of the Yankees, so as not to leave an enemy in his rear; but he wrote to Mynheer Beekman to keep up a bold front and stout heart, promising, as soon as he had settled affairs in the east, that he would hasten to the south with his burly warriors of the Hudson, to lower the crests of the giants, and mar the merriment of the Merrylanders.

CHAPTER IV

To explain the apparently sudden movement of Peter Stuyvesant against the crafty men of the East Country, I would observe that, during his campaigns on the South River, and in the enchanted regions of the Catskill Mountains, the twelve tribes of the East had been more than usually active in prosecuting their subtle scheme for the subjugation of the Nieuw-Nederlands.

Independent of the incessant maraudings among hen-roosts and squattings along the border, invading armies would penetrate, from time to time, into the very heart of the country. As their prototypes of yore went forth into the land of Canaan, with their wives and their children, their men-servants and their maid-servants, their flocks and herds, to settle themselves down in the land and possess it; so these chosen people of modern days would progress through the country in patriarchal style; conducting carts and wagons laden with household furniture, with women and children piled on top, and pots and kettles dangling beneath. At the tail of these vehicles would stalk a crew of long-limbed, lank-sided varlets, with axes on their shoulders and packs on their backs, resolutely bent upon " locating" themselves, as they termed

it, and improving the country. These were the most dangerous
kind of invaders. It is true they were guilty of no overt acts of
hostility; but it was notorious that, wherever they got a footing,
the honest Dutchmen gradually disappeared, retiring slowly as do
the Indians before the white men; being in some way or other
talked and chaffered, and bargained and swapped, and, in plain
English, elbowed out of all those rich bottoms and fertile nooks
in which our Dutch yeomanry are prone to nestle themselves.

Peter Stuyvesant was at length roused to this kind of war in
disguise, by which the Yankees were craftily aiming to subjugate
his dominions. He was a man easily taken in, it is true, as all
great-hearted men are apt to be; but if he once found it out, his
wrath was terrible. He now threw diplomacy to the dogs; determined to appear no more by ambassadors, but to repair in
person to the great council of the Amphyctions, bearing the sword
in one hand and the olive branch in the other; and giving them
their choice of sincere and honest peace, or open and iron war.

His privy councillors were astonished and dismayed when he
announced his determination. For once they ventured to remon-
strate, setting forth the rashness of venturing his sacred person
in the midst of a strange and barbarous people. They might as
well have tried to turn a rusty weather-cock with a broken-winded
bellows. In the fiery heart of the iron-headed Peter sat en-
throned the five kinds of courage described by Aristotle, and had
the philosopher enumerated five hundred more, I verily believe
he would have possessed them all. As to that better part of
valor called discretion, it was too cold-blooded a virtue for his
tropical temperament.

Summoning, therefore, to his presence his trusty follower,
Antony Van Corlear, he commanded him to hold himself in readi-

ness to accompany him the following morning on this his hazardous enterprise. Now Antony the Trumpeter was by this time a
little stricken in years, yet by dint of keeping up a good heart,
and having never known care or sorrow (having never been married), he was still a hearty, jocund, rubicund, gamesome wag, and
of great capacity in the doublet. This last was ascribed to his
living a jolly life on those domains at the Hook, which Peter
Stuyvesant had granted to him for his gallantry at Fort Casimir.

Be this as it may, there was nothing that more delighted Antony than this command of the great Peter, for he could have
followed the stout-hearted old governor to the world's end, with
love and loyalty—and he moreover still remembered the frolick-
ing, and dancing, and bundling, and other disports of the east
country, and entertained dainty recollection of numerous kind
and buxom lasses, whom he longed exceedingly again to encounter.

Thus then did this mirror of hardihood set forth, with no
other attendant but his trumpeter, upon one of the most perilous
enterprises ever recorded in the annals of knight-errantry.—For
a single warrior to venture openly among a whole nation of foes
—but, above all, for a plain downright Dutchman to think of ne-
gotiating with the whole council of New-England!—never was
there known a more desperate undertaking!—Ever since I have
entered upon the chronicles of this peerless but hitherto uncele-
brated chieftain, has he kept me in a state of incessant action and
anxiety with the toils and dangers he is constantly encountering—
Oh! for a chapter of the tranquil reign of Wouter Van Twiller,
that I might repose on it as on a feather bed!

Is it not enough, Peter Stuyvesant, that I have once already
rescued thee from the machinations of these terrible Amphicty-

ons, by bringing the powers of witchcraft to thine aid?—Is it not
enough, that I have followed thee undaunted, like a guardian
spirit, into the midst of the horrid battle of Fort Christina?—
That I have been put incessantly to my trumps to keep thee safe
and sound—now warding off with my single pen the shower of
dastard blows that fell upon thy rear—now narrowly shielding
thee from a deadly thrust, by a mere tobacco-box—now casing
thy dauntless skull with adamant, when even thy stubborn ram
beaver failed to resist the sword of the stout Risingh—and now,
not merely bringing thee off alive, but triumphant, from the
clutches of the gigantic Swede, by the desperate means of a paltry stone pottle?—Is not all this enough, but must thou still be
plunging into new difficulties, and hazarding in headlong enterprises thyself, thy trumpeter, and thy historian?

And now the ruddy-faced Aurora, like a buxom chambermaid, draws aside the sable curtains of the night, and out bounces
from his bed the jolly red-haired Phœbus, startled at being caught
so late in the embraces of Dame Thetis. With many a stable-
boy oath he harnesses his brazen-footed steeds, and whips, and
lashes, and splashes up the firmament, like a loitering coachman,
half an hour behind his time. And now behold that imp of
fame and prowess, the headstrong Peter, bestriding a raw-boned,
switch-tailed charger, gallantly arrayed in full regimentals, and
bracing on his thigh that trusty brass-hilted sword, which had
wrought such fearful deeds on the banks of the Delaware.

Behold hard after him his doughty trumpeter, Van Corlear,
mounted on a broken-winded, wall-eyed, calico mare; his stone
pottle, which had laid low the mighty Risingh, slung under his
arm; and his trumpet displayed vauntingly in his right hand,
decorated with a gorgeous banner, on which is emblazoned the

great beaver of the Manhattoes. See them proudly issuing out of the city gate, like an iron-clad hero of yore, with his faithful squire at his heels; the populace following with their eyes, and shouting many a parting wish and hearty cheering—Farewell, Hardkoppig Piet! Farewell, honest Antony!—Pleasant be your wayfaring—prosperous your return! The stoutest hero that ever drew a sword, and the worthiest trumpeter that ever trod shoe-leather!

Legends are lamentably silent about the events that befell our adventurers in this their adventurous travel, excepting the Stuyvesant manuscript, which gives the substance of a pleasant little heroic poem, written on the occasion by Dominie Ægidius Luyck,* who appears to have been the poet-laureat of New-Amsterdam. This inestimable manuscript assures us, that it was a rare spectacle to behold the great Peter and his loyal follower hailing the morning sun, and rejoicing in the clear countenance of nature, as they pranced it through the pastoral scenes of Bloemen Dael; which, in those days, was a sweet and rural valley, beautified with many a bright wild-flower, refreshed by many a pure streamlet, and enlivened here and there by a delectable little Dutch cottage, sheltered under some sloping hill, and almost buried in embowering trees.

Now did they enter upon the confines of Connecticut, where they encountered many grievous difficulties and perils. At one place they were assailed by a troop of country squires and militia colonels, who, mounted on goodly steeds, hung upon their rear for several miles, harassing them exceedingly with guesses and

* This Luyck was moreover rector of the Latin School in Nieuw-Nederlands, 1663. There are two pieces addressed to Ægidius Luyck in D. Selyn's MSS. of poesies, upon his marriage with Judith Isendoorn. Old MS.

questions, more especially the worthy Peter, whose silver-chased
leg excited not a little marvel.   At another place, hard by the
renowned town of Stamford, they were set upon by a great and
mighty legion of church deacons, who imperiously demanded of
them five shillings, for traveling on Sunday, and threatened to
carry them captive to a neighboring church, whose steeple peered
above the trees; but these the valiant Peter put to rout with
little difficulty, insomuch that they bestrode their canes and gal-
loped off in horrible confusion, leaving their cocked hats behind
in the hurry of their flight.   But not so easily did he escape from
the hands of a crafty man of Pyquag; who, with undaunted
perseverance, and repeated onsets, fairly bargained him out of
his goodly switch-tailed charger, leaving in place thereof a villanous, foundered Narraganset pacer.

   But, maugre all these hardships, they pursued their journey
cheerily along the course of the soft flowing Connecticut, whose
gentle waves, says the song, roll through many a fertile vale and
sunny plain ; now reflecting the lofty spires of the bustling city,
and now the rural beauties of the humble hamlet ; now echoing
with the busy hum of commerce, and now with the cheerful song
of the peasant.

   At every town would Peter Stuyvesant, who was noted for
warlike punctilio, order the sturdy Antony to sound a courteous
salutation ; though the manuscript observes, that the inhabitants
were thrown into great dismay when they heard of his approach
For the fame of his incomparable achievements on the Delaware
had spread throughout the east country, and they dreaded lest
he had come to take vengeance on their manifold transgressions.

   But the good Peter rode through these towns with a smiling
aspect ; waving his hand with inexpressible majesty and con-

deseension ; for he verily believed that the old clothes which these ingenious people had thrust into their broken windows, and the festoons of dried apples and peaches which ornamented the fronts of their houses, were so many decorations in honor of his approach ; as it was the custom in the days of chivalry to compliment renowned heroes by sumptuous displays of tapestry and gorgeous furniture. The women crowded to the doors to gaze upon him as he passed, so much does prowess in arms delight the gentle sex. The little children, too, ran after him in troops, staring with wonder at his regimentals, his brimstone breeches, and the silver garniture of his wooden leg. Nor must I omit to mention the joy which many strapping wenches betrayed at beholding the jovial Van Corlear, who had whilom delighted them so much with his trumpet, when he bore the great Peter's challenge to the Amphictyons. The kind-hearted Antony alighted from his calico mare, and kissed them all with infinite loving-kindness—and was right pleased to see a crew of little trumpeters crowding round him for his blessing ; each of whom he patted on the head, bade him be a good boy, and gave him a penny to buy molasses candy.

CHAPTER V.

Now so it happened that while the great and good Peter Stuyvesant, followed by his trusty squire, was making his chivalric progress through the east country, a dark and direful scheme of war against his beloved province, was forming in that nursery of monstrous projects, the British Cabinet.

This, we are confidently informed, was the result of the secret instigations of the great council of the league; who, finding themselves totally incompetent to vie in arms with the heavy-sterned warriors of the Manhattoes and their iron-headed commander, sent emissaries to the British government, setting forth in eloquent language the wonders and delights of this delicious little Dutch Canaan, and imploring that a force might be sent out to invade it by sea, while they should co-operate by land.

These emissaries arrived at a critical juncture, just as the British Lion was beginning to bristle up his mane and wag his tail; for we are assured by the anonymous writer of the Stuyvesant manuscript, that the astounding victory of Peter Stuyvesant at Fort Christina, had resounded throughout Europe; and his annexation of the territory of New-Sweden had awakened the jealousy of the British cabinet for their wild lands at the south. This jealousy was brought to a head by the representations of Lord Baltimore, who declared that the territory thus annexed, lay within the lands granted to him by the British crown, and he claimed to be protected in his rights. Lord Sterling, another British subject, claimed the whole of Nassau or Long Island, once the Ophir of William the Testy, but now the kitchen-garden of the Manhattoes, which he declared to be British territory by the right of discovery, but unjustly usurped by the Nederlanders.

The result of all these rumors and representations was a sudden zeal on the part of his majesty Charles the Second, for the safety and well-being of his transatlantic possessions, and especially for the recovery of the New-Netherlands, which Yankee logic had, somehow or other, proved to be a continuity of the territory taken possession of for the British crown by the Pilgrims, when they landed on Plymouth rock, fugitives from British oppression. All this goodly land, thus wrongfully held by the Dutchmen, he presented, in a fit of affection, to his brother the Duke of York: a donation truly royal, since none but great sovereigns have a right to give away what does not belong to them. That this munificent gift might not be merely nominal, his majesty ordered that an armament should be straightway dispatched to invade the city of New-Amsterdam by land and water, and put his brother in complete possession of the premises.

Thus critically situated are the affairs of the New-Nederlanders. While the honest burghers are smoking their pipes in sober security, and the privy councillors are snoring in the council chamber; while Peter the Headstrong is undauntedly making his way through the east country in the confident hope by honest words and manly deeds to bring the grand council to terms, a hostile fleet is sweeping like a thunder cloud across the Atlantic, soon to rattle a storm of war about the ears of the dozing Nederlanders, and to put the mettle of their governor to the trial.

But come what may, I here pledge my veracity, that in all warlike conflicts and doubtful perplexities, he will ever acquit himself like a gallant, noble-minded, obstinate old cavalier.—Forward then to the charge! Shine out, propitious stars, on the renowned city of the Manhattoes; and the blessing of St. Nicholas go with thee—honest Peter Stuyvesant.

CHAPTER VI.

GREAT nations resemble great men in this particular, that their
greatness is seldom known until they get in trouble ; adversity,
therefore, has been wisely denominated the ordeal of true greatness, which, like gold, can never receive its real estimation until
it has passed through the furnace. In proportion, therefore, as a
nation, a community, or an individual (possessing the inherent
quality of greatness) is involved in perils and misfortunes, in proportion does it rise in grandeur—and even when sinking under
calamity, makes, like a house on fire, a more glorious display than
ever it did in the fairest period of its prosperity.

The vast empire of China, though teeming with population
and imbibing and concentrating the wealth of nations, has vegetated through a succession of drowsy ages ; and were it not for
its internal revolution, and the subversion of its ancient government by the Tartars, might have presented nothing but a dull
detail of monotonous prosperity. Pompeii and Herculaneum
might have passed into oblivion, with a herd of their contemporaries, had they not been fortunately overwhelmed by a volcano.

The renowned city of Troy acquired celebrity only from its ten years' distress, and final conflagration—Paris rose in importance by the plots and massacres which ended in the exaltation of Napoleon—and even the mighty London has skulked through the records of time, celebrated for nothing of moment excepting the plague, the great fire, and Guy Faux's gunpowder plot! Thus cities and empires creep along, enlarging in silent obscurity, until they burst forth in some tremendous calamity—and snatch, as it were, immortality from the explosion!

The above principle being admitted, my reader will plainly perceive that the city of New-Amsterdam and its dependent province are on the high road to greatness. Dangers and hostilities threaten from every side, and it is really a matter of astonishment, how so small a state has been able, in so short a time, to entangle itself in so many difficulties. Ever since the province was first taken by the nose, at the Fort of Good Hope, in the tranquil days of Wouter Van Twiller, has it been gradually increasing in historic importance; and never could it have had a more appropriate chieftain to conduct it to the pinnacle of grandeur than Peter Stuyvesant.

This truly headstrong hero having successfully effected his daring progress through the east country, girded up his loins as he approached Boston, and prepared for the grand onslaught with the Amphictyons, which was to be the crowning achievement of the campaign. Throwing Antony Van Corlear, who, with his calico mare, formed his escort and army, a little in the advance, and bidding him be of stout heart and great wind; he placed himself firmly in his saddle, cocked his hat more fiercely over his left eye, summoned all the heroism of his soul into his countenance, and, with one arm akimbo, the hand resting on the pommel of his sword, rode into the great metropolis of the league, Antony sounding his trumpet before him in a manner to electrify the whole community.

Never was there such a stir in Boston as on this occasion; never such a hurrying hither and thither about the streets; such popping of heads out of windows; such gathering of knots in market-places. Peter Stuyvesant was a straightforward man, and prone to do every thing above board. He would have ridden at once to the great council-house of the league and sounded a parley; but the grand council knew the mettlesome hero they had to deal with, and were not for doing things in a hurry. On the contrary they sent forth deputations to meet him on the way; to receive him in a style befitting the great potentate of the Manhattoes, and to multiply all kinds of honors, and ceremonies, and formalities, and other courteous impediments in his path. Solemn banquets were accordingly given him, equal to thanksgiving feasts. Complimentary speeches were made him, wherein he was entertained with the surpassing virtues, long sufferings, and achievements of the Pilgrim Fathers; and it is even said he was treated to a sight of Plymouth Rock, that great corner-stone of Yankee empire.

I will not detain my readers by recounting the endless devices by which time was wasted, and obstacles and delays multiplied to the infinite annoyance of the impatient Peter. Neither will I fatigue them by dwelling on his negotiations with the grand council, when he at length brought them to business. Suffice it to say, it was like most other diplomatic negotiations; a great deal was said and very little done; one conversation led to another; one conference begot misunderstandings which it took a dozen conferences to explain, at the end of which both parties found

18

themselves just where they had begun, but ten times less likely to come to an agreement.

In the midst of these perplexities which bewildered the brain and incensed the ire of honest Peter, he received private intelligence of the dark conspiracy matured in the British cabinet, with the astounding fact that a British squadron was already on the way to invade New-Amsterdam by sea; and that the grand council of Amphictyons, while thus beguiling him with subtleties, were actually prepared to co-operate by land!

Oh! how did the sturdy old warrior rage and roar, when he found himself thus entrapped, like a lion in the hunter's toil! Now did he draw his trusty sword, and determine to break in upon the council of the Amphictyons and put every mother's son of them to death. Now did he resolve to fight his way throughout all the regions of the east, and to lay waste Connecticut river!

Gallant, but unfortunate Peter! Did I not enter with sad forebodings on this ill-starred expedition? Did I not tremble when I saw thee, with no other counselor than thine own head; no other armor but an honest tongue, a spotless conscience, and a rusty sword; no other protector but St. Nicholas, and no other attendant but a trumpeter—did I not tremble when I beheld thee thus sally forth to contend with all the knowing powers of New England?

It was a long time before the kind-hearted expostulations of Antony Van Corlear, aided by the soothing melody of his trumpet, could lower the spirits of Peter Stuyvesant from their warlike and vindictive tone, and prevent his making widows and orphans of half the population of Boston. With great difficulty, he was prevailed upon to bottle up his wrath for the present; to conceal from the council his knowledge of their machinations, and by effecting his escape, to be able to arrive in time for the salvation of the Manhattoes.

The latter suggestion awakened a new ray of hope in his bosom; he forthwith dispatched a secret message to his councilors at New-Amsterdam, apprising them of their danger, and commanding them to put the city in a posture of defence; promising to come as soon as possible to their assistance. This done, he felt marvelously relieved, rose slowly, shook himself like a rhinoceros, and issued forth from his den, in much the same manner as Giant Despair is described to have issued from Doubting Castle, in the chivalric history of the Pilgrim's Progress.

And now much does it grieve me that I must leave the gallant Peter in this imminent jeopardy; but it behooves us to hurry back and see what is going on at New-Amsterdam, for greatly do I fear that city is already in a turmoil. Such was ever the fate of Peter Stuyvesant; while doing one thing with heart and soul, he was too apt to leave every thing else at sixes and sevens. While, like a potentate of yore, he was absent attending to those things in person which in modern days are trusted to generals and ambassadors, his little territory at home was sure to get in an uproar;—all which was owing to that uncommon strength of intellect, which induced him to trust to nobody but himself, and which had acquired him the renowned appellation of Peter the Headstrong.

CHAPTER VII.

THERE is no sight more truly interesting to a philosopher than a community, where every individual has a voice in public affairs; where every individual considers himself the Atlas of the nation; and where every individual thinks it his duty to bestir himself for the good of his country—I say, there is nothing more inter-esting to a philosopher than such a community in a sudden bustle of war. Such clamor of tongues—such patriotic bawling—such running hither and thither—every body in a hurry—every body in trouble—every body in the way, and every body interrupting his neighbor—who is busily employed in doing nothing! It is like witnessing a great fire, where the whole community are agog—some dragging about empty engines—others scampering with full buckets, and spilling the contents into their neighbor's boots—and others ringing the church bells all night, by way of putting out the fire. Little firemen—like sturdy little knights storming a breach, clambering up and down scaling-ladders, and bawling through tin trumpets, by way of directing the attack.— Here a fellow, in his great zeal to save the property of the unfortunate, catches up an anonymous chamber utensil, and gallants it off with an air of as much self-importance as if he had rescued a pot of money—there another throws looking-glasses and china out of the window, to save them from the flames—whilst those who can do nothing else run up and down the streets, keeping up an incessant cry of *Fire! Fire! Fire!*

"When the news arrived at Sinope," says Lucian—though I own the story is rather trite—"that Philip was about to attack them, the inhabitants were thrown into a violent alarm. Some ran to furbish up their arms ; others rolled stones to build up the walls—every body, in short, was employed, and every body in the way of his neighbor. Diogenes alone could find nothing to do—whereupon, not to be idle when the welfare of his country was at stake, he tucked up his robe, and fell to rolling his tub with might and main up and down the Gymnasium." In like manner did every mother's son in the patriotic community of New-Amsterdam, on receiving the missives of Peter Stuyvesant, busy himself most mightily in putting things in confusion, and assisting the general uproar. "Every man"—saith the Stuyvesant manuscript—"flew to arms !"—by which is meant, that not one of ou· honest Dutch citizens would venture to church or to market without an old-fashioned spit of a sword dangling at his side, and a long Dutch fowling-piece on his shoulder—nor would he go out of a night without a lantern ; nor turn a corner without first peeping cautiously round, lest he should come unawares upon a British army :—and we are informed that Stoffel Brinkerhoff, who was considered by the old women almost as brave a man as the governor himself, actually had two one-pound swivels mount-ed in his entry, one pointing out at the front door, and the other at the back.

But the most strenuous measure resorted to on this awful occasion, and one which has since been found of wonderful efficacy, was to assemble popular meetings. These brawling convocations, I have already shown, were extremely offensive to Peter Stuyvesant; but as this was a moment of unusual agitation and as the old governor was not present to repress them, they broke out with intolerable violence. Hither, therefore, the orators and politicians repaired; striving who should bawl loudest, and exceed the others in hyperbolical bursts of patriotism, and in resolutions to uphold and defend the government. In these sage meetings it was resolved that they were the most enlightened, the most dignified, the most formidable, and the most ancient community upon the face of the earth. This resolution being carried unanimously, another was immediately proposed—whether it were not possible and politic to exterminate Great Britain? upon which sixty-nine members spoke in the affirmative, and only one arose to suggest some doubts—who, as a punishment for his treasonable presumption, was immediately seized by the mob, and tarred and feathered—which punishment being equivalent to the Tarpeian Rock, he was afterwards considered as an outcast from society, and his opinion went for nothing. The question, therefore, being unanimously carried in the affirmative, it was recommended to the grand council to pass it into a law; which was accordingly done. By this measure the hearts of the people at large were wonderfully encouraged, and they waxed exceeding choleric and valorous. Indeed, the first paroxysm of alarm having in some measure subsided—the old women having buried all the money they could lay their hands on, and their husbands daily getting fuddled with what was left—the community began even to stand on the offensive. Songs were manufactured in Low Dutch and sung about the streets, wherein the English were most wofully beaten, and shown no quarter; and popular addresses were made, wherein it was proved to a certainty that the fate of Old England depended upon the will cf the New-Amsterdammers.

Finally, to strike a violent blow at the very vitals of Great Britain, a multitude of the wiser inhabitants assembled, and having purchased all the British manufactures they could find, they made thereof a huge bonfire; and, in the patriotic glow of the moment, every man present, who had a hat or breeches of English workmanship, pulled it off, and threw it into the flames—to the irreparable detriment, loss, and ruin, of the English manufacturers. In commemoration of this great exploit, they erected a pole on the spot, with a device on the top intended to represent the province of Nieuw-Nederlands destroying Great Britain, under the similitude of an Eagle picking the little Island of Old England out of the globe; but either through the unskillfulness of the sculptor, or his ill-timed waggery, it bore a striking resemblance to a goose, vainly striving to get hold of a dumpling.

CHAPTER VIII.

IT will need but little penetration in any one conversant with the
ways of that wise but windy potentate, the sovereign people, to
discover that notwithstanding all the warlike bluster and bustle
of the last chapter, the city of New-Amsterdam was not a whit
more prepared for war than before. The privy councilors of
Peter Stuyvesant were aware of this; and, having received his
private orders to put the city in an immediate posture of defence,
they called a meeting of the oldest and richest burghers to assist
them with their wisdom. These were that order of citizens commonly termed "men of the greatest weight in the community;"
their weight being estimated by the heaviness of their heads and
of their purses. Their wisdom in fact is apt to be of a ponderous kind, and to hang like a millstone round the neck of the community.

Two things were unanimously determined in this assembly of
venerables: First, that the city required to be put in a state of
defence; and Second, that, as the danger was imminent, there
should be no time lost: which points being settled, they fell to

making long speeches and belaboring one another in endless and
intemperate disputes. For about this time was this unhappy city
first visited by that talking endemic, so prevalent in this country,
and which so invariably evinces itself, wherever a number of
wise men assemble together; breaking out in long, windy speeches;
caused, as physicians suppose, by the foul air which is ever generated in a crowd. Now it was, moreover, that they first introduced the ingenious method of measuring the merits of an
harangue by the hour-glass; he being considered the ablest orator
who spoke longest on a question. For which excellent invention,
it is recorded, we are indebted to the same profound Dutch critic
who judged of books by their size.

This sudden passion for endless harangues, so little consonant
with the customary gravity and taciturnity of our sage forefathers,
was supposed by certain philosophers to have been imbibed, together
with divers others barbarous propensities, from their savage neighbors; who were peculiarly noted for *long talks* and *council fires*,
and never undertook any affair of the least importance, without
previous debates and harangues among their chiefs and *old men*.
But the real cause was, that the people, in electing their representatives to the grand council, were particular in choosing them
for their talents at talking, without inquiring whether they possessed the more rare, difficult, and ofttimes important talent of
holding their tongues. The consequence was, that this deliberative body was composed of the most loquacious men in the community. As they considered themselves placed there to talk,
every man concluded that his duty to his constituents, and, what
is more, his popularity with them, required that he should
harangue on every subject, whether he understood it or not.
There was an ancient mode of burying a chieftain, by every sol-

18*

dier throwing his shield full of earth on the corpse, until a mighty mound was formed; so whenever a question was brought forward in this assembly, every member pressing forward to throw on his quantum of wisdom, the subject was quickly buried under a mountain of words.

We are told, that disciples on entering the school of Pythagoras, were for two years enjoined silence, and forbidden either to ask questions, or make remarks. After they had thus acquired the inestimable art of holding their tongues, they were gradually permitted to make inquiries, and finally to communicate their own opinions.

With what a beneficial effect could this wise regulation of Pythagoras be introduced in modern legislative bodies—and how wonderfully would it have tended to expedite business in the grand council of the Manhattoes!

At this perilous juncture the fatal word economy, the stumbling-block of William the Testy, had been once more set afloat, according to which the cheapest plan of defence was insisted upon as the best; it being deemed a great stroke of policy in furnishing powder to economize in ball.

Thus did dame Wisdom (whom the wags of antiquity have humorously personified as a woman) seem to take a mischievous pleasure in jilting the venerable councilors of New-Amsterdam. To add to the confusion, the old factions of Short Pipes and Long Pipes, which had been almost strangled by the herculean grasp of Peter Stuyvesant, now sprang up with tenfold vigor. Whatever was proposed by a Short Pipe was opposed by the whole tribe of Long Pipes, who, like true partisans, deemed it their first duty to effect the downfall of their rivals; their second to elevate themselves, and their third, to consult the public good;

though many left the third consideration out of question altogether.

In this great collision of hard heads it is astonishing the number of projects that were struck out; projects which threw the wind-mill system of William the Testy completely in the background. These were almost uniformly opposed by the "men of the greatest weight in the community!" your weighty men, though slow to devise, being always great at "negativing." Among these were a set of fat, self-important old burghers, who smoked their pipes, and said nothing except to negative every plan of defence proposed. These were that class of "conservatives," who, having amassed a fortune, button up their pockets, shut their mouths, sink, as it were, into themselves, and pass the rest of their lives in the indwelling beatitude of conscious wealth; as some phlegmatic oyster, having swallowed a pearl, closes its shell, sinks in the mud, and devotes the rest of its life to the conservation of its treasure. Every plan of defence seemed to these worthy old gentlemen pregnant with ruin. An armed force was a legion of locusts, preying upon the public property—to fit out a naval armament was to throw their money into the sea—to build fortifications was to bury it in the dirt. In short, they settled it as a sovereign maxim, so long as their pockets were full, no matter how much they were drubbed.—A kick left no scar—a broken head cured itself—but an empty purse was of all maladies the slowest to heal, and one in which nature did nothing for the patient.

Thus did this venerable assembly of sages lavish away that time which the urgency of affairs rendered invaluable, in empty brawls and long-winded speeches, without ever agreeing, except on the point with which they started, namely, that there was no time to be lost, and delay was ruinous.   At length, St. Nicholas taking compassion on their distracted situation, and anxious to preserve them from anarchy, so ordered, that in the midst of one of their most noisy debates on the subject of fortification and de- fence, when they had nearly fallen to loggerheads in consequence of not being able to convince each other, the question was happily settled by the sudden entrance of a messenger, who informed them that a hostile fleet had arrived, and was actually advancing up the bay .

CHAPTER IX.

IN WHICH THE TROUBLES OF NEW-AMSTERDAM APPEAR TO
THICKEN—SHOWING THE BRAVERY, IN TIME OF PERIL, OF
A PEOPLE WHO DEFEND THEMSELVES BY RESOLUTIONS.

LIKE as an assemblage of belligerent cats, gibbering and cater-
wauling; eyeing one another with hideous grimaces and contortions; spitting in each other's faces, and on the point of a general
clapper-clawing, are suddenly put to scampering rout and confusion by the appearance of a house-dog; so was the no less vociferous council of New-Amsterdam amazed, astounded, and totally
dispersed, by the sudden arrival of the enemy. Every member
waddled home as fast as his short legs could carry him, wheezing as
he went with corpulency and terror. Arrived at his castle, he barricadoed the street-door, and buried himself in the cider-cellar,
without venturing to peep out, lest he should have his head carried off by a cannon ball.

The sovereign people crowded into the market-place, herding
together with the instinct of sheep, who seek safety in each other's
company, when the shepherd and his dog are absent, and the
wolf is prowling round the fold. Far from finding relief, however, they only increased each other's terrors. Each man looked
ruefully in his neighbor's face, in search of encouragement, but

only found in its wobegone lineaments a confirmation of his own
dismay. Not a word now was to be heard of conquering Great
Britain, not a whisper about the sovereign virtues of economy—
while the old women heightened the general gloom by clamor-
ously bewailing their fate, and calling for protection on St. Nicholas
and Peter Stuyvesant.

Oh, how did they bewail the absence of the lion-hearted
Peter!—and how did they long for the comforting presence
of Antony Van Corlear! Indeed a gloomy uncertainty hung
over the fate of these adventurous heroes. Day after day had
elapsed since the alarming message from the governor, without
bringing any further tidings of his safety. Many a fearful conjecture was hazarded as to what had befallen him and his loyal
squire. Had they not been devoured alive by the cannibals of
Marblehead and Cape Cod?—Had they not been put to the question by the great council of Amphictyons?—Had they not been
smothered in onions by the terrible men of Pyquag?—In the
midst of this consternation and perplexity, when horror, like a
mighty nightmare, sat brooding upon the litttle, fat, plethoric city
of New-Amsterdam, the ears of the multitude were suddenly
startled by the distant soun? of a trumpet—it approached—it
grew louder and louder—and now it resounded at the city gate.
The public could not be mistaken in the well-known sound—a
shout of joy burst from their lips, as the gallant Peter, covered
with dust, and followed by his faithful trumpeter, came galloping
into the market-place.

The first transports of the populace having subsided, they
gathered round the honest Antony, as he dismounted, overwhelming him with greetings and congratulations. In breathless
accents he related to them the marvelous adventures through

which the old governor and himself had gone, in making their escape from the clutches of the terrible Amphictyons. But though the Stuyvesant manuscript, with its customary minuteness where any thing touching the great Peter is concerned, is very particular as to the incidents of this masterly retreat, the state of the public affairs will not allow me to indulge in a full recital thereof. Let it suffice to say, that, while Peter Stuyvesant was anxiously revolving in his mind how he could make good his escape with honor and dignity, certain of the ships sent out for the conquest of the Manhattoes touched at the eastern ports to obtain supplies, and to call on the grand council of the league for its promised co-operation. Upon hearing of this, the vigilant Peter, perceiving that a moment's delay were fatal, made a secret and precipitate decampment; though much did it grieve his lofty soul to be obliged to turn his back even upon a nation of foes. Many hair-breadth 'scapes and divers perilous mishaps did they sustain, as they scoured, without sound of trumpet, through the fair regions of the east. Already was the country in an uproar with hostile preparation, and they were obliged to take a large circuit in their flight, lurking along through the woody mountains of the Devil's backbone; whence the valiant Peter sallied forth one day like a lion, and put to rout a whole legion of squatters, consisting of three generations of a prolific family, who were already on their way to take possession of some corner of the New-Netherlands. Nay, the faithful Antony had great difficulty, at sundry times, to prevent him, in the excess of his wrath, from descending down from the mountains, and falling, sword in hand, upon certain of the border-towns, who were marshaling forth their draggle-tailed militia.

The first movement of the governor, on reaching his dwelling, was to mount the roof, whence he contemplated with rueful
aspect the hostile squadron. This had already come to anchor
in the bay, and consisted of two stout frigates, having on board,
as John Josselyn, gent., informs us, " three hundred valiant redcoats." Having taken this survey, he sat himself down and
wrote an epistle to the commander, demanding the reason of his
anchoring in the harbor without obtaining previous permission
so to do. This letter was couched in the most dignified and
courteous terms, though I have it from undoubted authority that
his teeth were clinched, and he had a bitter sardonic grin upon
his visage all the while he wrote. Having dispatched his letter,
the grim Peter stumped to and fro about the town with a most
war-betokening countenance, his hands thrust into his breeches
pockets, and whistling a Low Dutch psalm-tune, which bore no
small resemblance to the music of a northeast wind, when a
storm is brewing. The very dogs as they eyed him skulked
away in dismay; while all the old and ugly women of New-
Amsterdam ran howling at his heels, imploring him to save them
from murder, robbery, and pitiless ravishment !

The reply of Colonel Nichols, who commanded the invaders,
was couched in terms of equal courtesy with the letter of the
governor; declaring the right and title of his British Majesty to
the province; where he affirmed the Dutch to be mere interlopers; and demanding that the town, forts, etc., should be forthwith rendered into his majesty's obedience and protection; prom
ising, at the same time, life, liberty, estate, and free trade, to
every Dutch denizen who should readily submit to his majesty's
government.

Peter Stuyvesant read over this friendly epistle with some

such harmony of aspect as we may suppose a crusty farmer reads
the loving letter of John Stiles, warning him of an action of
ejectment. He was not, however, to be taken by surprise; but,
thrusting the summons into his breeches pocket, stalked three
times across the room, took a pinch of snuff with great vehemence, and then, loftily waving his hand, promised to send an
answer the next morning. He now summoned a general meeting
of his privy councilors and burgomasters, not to ask their advice,
for, confident in his own strong head, he needed no man's counsel,
but apparently to give them a piece of his mind on their late
craven conduct.

His orders being duly promulgated, it was a piteous sight to
behold the late valiant burgomasters, who had demolished the
whole British empire in their harangues, peeping ruefully out of
their hiding places; crawling cautiously forth; dodging through
narrow lanes and alleys; starting at every little dog that barked;
mistaking lamp-posts for British grenadiers; and, in the excess
of their panic, metamorphosing pumps into formidable soldiers,
leveling blunderbusses at their bosoms! Having, however, in
despite of numerous perils and difficulties of the kind, arrived
safe, without the loss of a single man, at the hall of assembly,
they took their seats, and awaited in fearful silence the arrival of
the governor. In a few moments the wooden leg of the intrepid
Peter was heard in regular and stout-hearted thumps upon the
staircase. He entered the chamber, arrayed in full suit of regimentals, and carrying his trusty toledo, not girded on his thigh,
but tucked under his arm. As the governor never equipped
himself in this portentous manner unless something of martial
nature were working within his pericranium, his council regarded
him ruefully, as if they saw fire and sword in his iron coun-

tenance, and forgot to light their pipes in breathless sus-
pense.

His first words were, to rate his council soundly for having
wasted in idle debate and party feud the time which should have
been devoted to putting the city in a state of defence. He was
particularly indignant at those brawlers who had disgraced the
councils of the province by empty bickerings and scurrilous
invectives against an absent enemy. He now called upon them
to make good their words by deeds, as the enemy they had defied
and derided was at the gate. Finally, he informed them of the
summons he had received to surrender, but concluded by swearing to defend the province as long as Heaven was on his side and
he had a wooden leg to stand upon; which warlike sentence he
emphasized by a thwack with the flat of his sword upon the table,
that quite electrified his auditors.

The privy councilors, who had long since been brought into
as perfect discipline as were ever the soldiers of the great Frede-
rick, knew there was no use in saying a word—so lighted their
pipes, and smoked away in silence, like fat and discreet councilors.
But the burgomasters, being inflated with considerable importance
and self-sufficiency, acquired at popular meetings, were not so
easily satisfied. Mustering up fresh spirit, when they found there
was some chance of escaping from their present jeopardy without
the disagreeable alternative of fighting, they requested a copy of
the summons to surrender, that they might show it to a general
meeting of the people.

So insolent and mutinous a request would have been enough
to have roused the gorge of the tranquil Van Twiller himself—
what then must have been its effect upon the great Stuyvesant,
who was not only a Dutchman, a governor, and a valiant wooden-

legged soldier to boot, but withal a man of the most stomachful
and gunpowder disposition ? He burst forth into a blaze of indignation,—swore not a mother's son of them should see a syllable
of it—that as to their advice or concurrence, he did not care a
whiff of tobacco for either—that they might go home, and go to
bed like old women ; for he was determined to defend the colony
himself, without the assistance of them or their adherents ! So
saying, he tucked his sword under his arm, cocked his hat upon
his head, and girding up his loins, stumped indignantly out of the
council-chamber—every body making room for him as he passed.

No sooner was he gone than the busy burgomasters called a
public meeting in front of the Stadt-house, where they appointed
as chairman one Dofue Roerback, formerly a meddlesome member of the cabinet during the reign of William the Testy, but
kicked out of office by Peter Stuyvesant on taking the reins of
government. He was, withal, a mighty gingerbread baker in the
land, and reverenced by the populace as a man of dark knowledge, seeing that he was the first to imprint New-Year cakes
with the mysterious hieroglyphics of the Cock and Breeches, and
such like magical devices.

This burgomaster, who still chewed the cud of ill-will against
Peter Stuyvesant, addressed the multitude in what is called a
patriotic speech, informing them of the courteous summons which
the governor had received, to surrender ; of his refusal to comply
therewith, and of his denying the public even a sight of the summons, which doubtless contained conditions highly to the honoi
and advantage of the province.

He then proceeded to speak of his Excellency in high-sounding terms of vituperation, suited to the dignity of his station ; com-
paring him to Nero, Caligula, and other flagrant great men of

yore; assuring the people that the history of the world did not contain a despotic outrage equal to the present. That it would be recorded in letters of fire, on the blood-stained tablet of history! That ages would roll back with sudden horror when they came to view it! That the womb of time (by the way, your orators and writers take strange liberties with the womb of time, though some would fain have us believe that time is an old gentleman)—that the womb of time, pregnant as it was with direful horrors, would never produce a parallel enormity!—with a variety of other heart-rending, soul-stirring tropes and figures, which I cannot enumerate; neither, indeed, need I, for they were of the kind which even to the present day form the style of popular harangues and patriotic orations, and may be classed in rhetoric under the general title of RIGMAROLE.

The result of this speech of the inspired burgomaster, was a memorial addressed to the governor, remonstrating in good round terms on his conduct. It was proposed that Dofue Roerback himself should be the bearer of this memorial, but this he warily declined, having no inclination of coming again within kicking distance of his Excellency. Who did deliver it has never been named in history, in which neglect he has suffered grievous wrong; seeing that he was equally worthy of blazon with him perpetuated in Scottish song and story by the surname of Bell-the-cat. All we know of the fate of this memorial is, that it was used by the grim Peter to light his pipe; which, from the vehemence with which he smoked it, was evidently any thing but a pipe of peace.

CHAPTER X.

Now did the high-minded Pieter de Groodt shower down a pannier
load of maledictions upon his burgomasters for a set of self-willed,
obstinate, factious varlets, who would neither be convinced nor
persuaded. Nor did he omit to bestow some left-handed compliments upon the sovereign people, as a herd of poltroons, who had no
relish for the glorious hardships and illustrious misadventures of
battle—but would rather stay at home, and eat and sleep in ignoble ease, than fight in a ditch for immortality and a broken head.

Resolutely bent, however, upon defending his beloved city,
in despite even of itself, he called unto him his trusty Van Corlear, who was his right-hand man in all times of emergency.
Him did he adjure to take his war-denouncing trumpet, and
mounting his horse, to beat up the country night and day—
sounding the alarm along the pastoral borders of the Bronx—
startling the wild solitudes of Croton—arousing the rugged yeomanry of Weehawk and Hoboken—the mighty men of battle of
Tappan Bay—and the brave boys of Tarry-Town, Petticoat-

Lane, and Sleepy-Hollow—charging them one and all to sling their powder-horns, shoulder their fowling-pieces, and march merrily down to the Manhattoes.

Now there was nothing in all the world, the divine sex excepted, that Antony Van Corlear loved better than errands of this kind. So just stopping to take a lusty dinner, and bracing to his side his junk bottle, well charged with heart-inspiring Hollands, he issued jollily from the city gate, which looked out upon what is at present called Broadway; sounding a farewell strain, that rung in sprightly echoes through the winding streets of New-Amsterdam—Alas! never more were they to be gladdened by the melody of their favorite trumpeter!

It was a dark and stormy night when the good Antony arrived at the creek (sagely denominated Haerlem *river*) which separates the island of Manna-hata from the mainland. The wind was high, the elements were in an uproar, and no Charon could be found to ferry the adventurous sounder of brass across the water. For a short time he vapored like an impatient ghost upon the brink, and then bethinking himself of the urgency of his errand took a hearty embrace of his stone bottle, swore most valorously that he would swim across in spite of the devil! (Spyt den Duyvel,) and daringly plunged into the stream. Luckless Antony! scarce had he buffeted half-way over, when he was observed to struggle violently, as if battling with the spirit of the waters—instinctively he put his trumpet to his mouth, and giving a vehement blast—sank forever to the bottom!

The clangor of his trumpet, like that of the ivory horn of the renowned Paladin Orlando, when expiring in the glorious field of Roncesvalles, rang far and wide through the country, alarming the neighbors round, who hurried in amazement to the spot.

Here an old Dutch burgher, famed for his veracity, and who had been a witness of the fact, related to them the melancholy affair; with the fearful addition (to which I am slow of giving belief) that he saw the duyvel, in the shape of a huge moss-bonker, seize the sturdy Antony by the leg, and drag him beneath the waves. Certain it is, the place, with the adjoining promontory, which projects into the Hudson, has been called *Spyt den Duyvel* ever since—the ghost of the unfortunate Antony still haunts the surrounding solitudes, and his trumpet has often been heard by the neighbors, of a stormy night, mingling with the howling of the blast. Nobody ever attempts to swim across the creek after dark; on the contrary, a bridge has been built to guard against such melancholy accidents in future—and as to moss-bonkers, they are held in such abhorrence, that no true Dutchman will admit them to his table, who loves good fish and hates the devil.

Such was the end of Antony Van Corlear—a man deserving of a better fate. He lived roundly and soundly, like a true and jolly bachelor, until the day of his death; but though he was never married, yet did he leave behind some two or three dozen children, in different parts of the country—fine, chubby, brawling, flatulent little urchins; from whom, if legends speak true, (and they are not apt to lie,) did descend the innumerable race of editors, who people and defend this country, and who are bountifully paid by the people for keeping up a constant alarm—and making them miserable. It is hinted, too, that in his various expeditions into the East he did much towards promoting the population of the country; in proof of which is adduced the notorious propensity of the people of those parts to sound their own trumpet.

As some way-worn pilgrim, when the tempest whistles through his locks and night is gathering round, beholds his faithful dog, the companion and solace of his journeying, stretched lifeless at his feet, so did the generous-hearted hero of the Manhattoes contemplate the untimely end of Antony Van Corlear. He had been the faithful attendant of his footsteps; he had charmed him in many a weary hour by his honest gayety and the martial melody of his trumpet, and had followed him with unflinching loyalty and affection through many a scene of direful peril and mishap. He was gone forever! and that, too, at a moment when every mongrel cur was skulking from his side. This—Peter Stuyvesant—was the moment to try thy fortitude; and this was the moment when thou didst indeed shine forth—Peter *the Headstrong!*

The glare of day had long dispelled the horrors of the stormy night; still all was dull and gloomy. The late jovial Apollo hid his face behind lugubrious clouds, peeping out now and then for an instant, as if anxious, yet fearful, to see what was going on in his favorite city. This was the eventful morning when the great Peter was to give his reply to the summons of the invaders. Already was he closeted with his privy council, sitting in grim state, brooding over the fate of his favorite trumpeter, and anon boiling with indignation as the insolence of his recreant burgomasters flashed upon his mind. While in this state of irritation, a courier arrived in all haste from Winthrop, the subtle governor of Connecticut, counseling him, in the most affectionate and disinterested manner, to surrender the province, and magnifying the dangers and calamities to which a refusal would subject him.— What a moment was this to intrude officious advice upon a man who never took advice in his whole life!—The fiery old governor strode up and down the chamber with a vehemence that made the bosoms of his councilors to quake with awe—railing at his unlucky fate, that thus made him the constant butt of factious subjects, and jesuitical advisers.

Just at this ill-chosen juncture, the officious burgomasters, who had heard of the arrival of mysterious dispatches, came marching in a body into the room, with a legion of schepens and toad-eaters at their heels, and abruptly demanded a perusal of the letter. This was too much for the spleen of Peter Stuyvesant. He tore the letter in a thousand pieces—threw it in the face of the nearest burgomaster—broke his pipe over the head of the next—hurled his spitting-box at an unlucky schepen, who was just retreating out at the door, and finally prorogued the whole meeting *sine die*, by kicking them down stairs with his wooden leg.

As soon as the burgomasters could recover from their confusion and had time to breathe, they called a public meeting, where they related at full length, and with appropriate coloring and exaggeration, the despotic and vindictive deportment of the governor; declaring that, for their own parts, they did not value a straw the being kicked, cuffed, and mauled by the timber toe of his excellency, but that they felt for the dignity of the sovereign people, thus rudely insulted by the outrage committed on the seat of honor of their representatives. The latter part of the harangue came home at once to that delicacy of feeling, and jealous pride of character, vested in all true mobs; who, though they may bear injuries without a murmur, yet are marvelously jealous of their sovereign dignity—and there is no knowing to what act of resentment they might have been provoked, had they not been somewhat more afraid of their sturdy old governor than they were of St. Nicholas the English—or the d——l himself.

19

CHAPTER XI.

THERE is something exceedingly sublime and melancholy in the
spectacle which the present crisis of our history presents. An
illustrious and venerable little city—the metropolis of a vast
extent of uninhabited country—garrisoned by a doughty host of
orators, chairmen, committee-men, burgomasters, schepens, and
old women—governed by a determined and strong-headed warrior, and fortified by mud batteries, palisadoes, and resolutions—
blockaded by sea, beleaguered by land, and threatened with direful desolation from without; while its very vitals are torn with
internal faction and commotion! Never did historic pen record
a page of more complicated distress, unless it be the strife that
distracted the Israelites during the siege of Jerusalem—where
discordant parties were cutting each other's throats, at the moment when the victorious legions of Titus had toppled down their
bulwarks, and were carrying fire and sword into the very sanctum sanctorum of the temple.

Governor Stuyvesant having triumphantly put his grand
council to the rout, and delivered himself from a multitude of

impertinent advisers, dispatched a categorical reply to the commanders of the invading squadron; wherein he asserted the right and title of their High Mightinesses the Lords States General to the province of New-Netherlands, and trusting in the righteousness of his cause, set the whole British nation at defiance!

My anxiety to extricate my readers and myself from these disastrous scenes prevents me from giving the whole of this gallant letter, which concluded in these manly and affectionate terms:

"As touching the threats in your conclusion, we have nothing to answer, only that we fear nothing but what God (who is as just as merciful) shall lay upon us; all things being in his gracious disposal, and we may as well be preserved by him with small forces as by a great army; which makes us to wish you all happiness and prosperity, and recommend you to his protection.— My lords, your thrice humble and affectionate servant and friend,

"P. STUYVESANT."

Thus having thrown his gauntlet, the brave Peter stuck a pair of horse-pistols in his belt, girded an immense powder-horn on his side—thrust his sound leg into a Hessian boot, and clapping his fierce little war-hat on the top of his head—paraded up and down in front of his house, determined to defend his beloved city to the last.

While all these struggles and dissensions were prevailing in the unhappy city of New-Amsterdam, and while its worthy but ill-starred governor was framing the above-quoted letter, the English commanders did not remain idle. They had agents secretly employed to foment the fears and clamors of the populace; and moreover circulated far and wide, through the adjacent country, a proclamation, repeating the terms they had already held out in their summons to surrender, at the same time beguiling the simple Nederlanders with the most crafty and conciliating professions. They promised that every man who voluntarily submitted to the authority of his British Majesty should retain peaceful possession of his house, his vrouw, and his cabbage-garden. That he should be suffered to smoke his pipe, speak Dutch, wear as many breeches as he pleased, and import bricks, tiles, and stone jugs from Holland, instead of manufacturing them on the spot. That he should on no account be compelled to learn the English language, nor eat codfish on Saturdays, nor keep accounts in any other way than by casting them up on his fingers, and chalking them down upon the crown of his hat; as is observed among the Dutch yeomanry at the present day. That every man should be allowed quietly to inherit his father's hat, coat, shoe-buckles, pipe, and every other personal appendage; and that no man should be obliged to conform to any improvements, inventions, or any other modern innovations; but, on the contrary, should be permitted to build his house, follow his trade, manage his farm, rear his hogs, and educate his children, precisely as his ancestors had done before him from time immemorial. Finally, that he should have all the benefits of free trade, and should not be required to acknowledge any other saint in the calendar than St. Nicholas, who should thenceforward, as before, be considered the tutelar saint of the city.

These terms, as may be supposed, appeared very satisfactory to the people, who had a great disposition to enjoy their property unmolested, and a most singular aversion to engage in a contest, where they could gain little more than honor and broken heads— the first of which they held in philosophic indifference, the latter in utter detestation. By these insidious means, therefore, did the English succeed in alienating the confidence and affections of the populace from their gallant old governor, whom they considered as obstinately bent upon running them into hideous misadventures; and did not hesitate to speak their minds freely, and abuse him most heartily—behind his back.

Like as a mighty grampus, when assailed and buffeted by roaring waves and brawling surges, still keeps on an undeviating course, rising above the boisterous billows, spouting and blowing as he emerges—so did the inflexible Peter pursue, unwavering, his determined career, and rise, contemptuous, above the clamors of the rabble.

But when the British warriors found that he set their power at defiance, they dispatched recruiting officers to Jamaica and Jericho, and Nineveh, and Quag, and Patchog, and all those towns on Long Island which had been subdued of yore by Stoffel Brink-erhoff; stirring up the progeny of Preserved Fish, and Determined Cock, and those other New-England squatters, to assail the city of New-Amsterdam by land; while the hostile ships prepared for an assault by water.

The streets of New-Amsterdam now presented a scene of wild dismay and consternation. In vain did Peter Stuyvesant order the citizens to arm and assemble on the battery. Blank terror reigned over the community. The whole party of Short Pipes in the course of a single night had changed into arrant old women—a metamorphosis only to be paralleled by the prodigies recorded by Livy as having happened at Rome at the approach of Hannibal, when statues sweated in pure affright, goats were converted into sheep, and cocks, turning into hens, ran cackling about the street.

Thus baffled in all attempts to put the city in a state of defence; blockaded from without; tormented from within, and menaced with a Yankee invasion, even the stiff-necked will of Peter Stuyvesant for once gave way, and in spite of his mighty heart, which swelled in his throat until it nearly choked him, he consented to a treaty of surrender.

Words cannot express the transports of the populace, on receiving this intelligence ; had they obtained a conquest over their enemies, they could not have indulged greater delight.   The streets resounded with their congratulations—they extolled their governor as the father and deliverer of his country—they crowded to his house to testify their gratitude, and were ten times more noisy in their plaudits than when he returned, with victory perched upon his beaver, from the glorious capture of Fort Christina.—But the indignant Peter shut his doors and windows, and took refuge in the innermost recesses of his mansion, that he might not hear the ignoble rejoicings of the rabble.

Commissioners were now appointed on both sides and a capitulation was speedily arranged; all that was wanting to ratify it was that it should be signed by the governor.   When the commissioners waited upon him for this purpose they were received with grim and bitter courtesy.   His warlike accoutrements were laid aside—an old Indian night-gown was wrapped about his rugged limbs, a red night-cap overshadowed his frowning brow, an iron-gray beard of three days' growth gave additional grimness to his visage.   Thrice did he seize a worn-out stump of a pen, and essay to sign the loathome paper—thrice did he clinch his teeth, and make a horrible countenance, as though a dose of rhubarb, senna, and ipecacuanha, had been offered to his lips ; at length, dashing it from him, he seized his brass-hilted sword, and jerking it from the scabbard, swore by St. Nicholas, to sooner die than yield to any power under heaven.

For two whole days did he persist in this magnanimous resolution, during which his house was besieged by the rabble, and menaces and clamorous revilings exhausted to no purpose. And now another course was adopted to soothe, if possible, his mighty ire. A procession was formed by the burgomasters and schepens, followed by the populace, to bear the capitulation in state to the governor's dwelling. They found the castle strongly barricadoed, and the old hero in full regimentals, with his cocked hat on his head, posted with a blunderbuss at the garret window.

There was something in this formidable position that struck even the ignoble vulgar with awe and admiration. The brawling multitude could not but reflect with self-abasement upon their own pusillanimous conduct, when they beheld their hardy but deserted old governor, thus faithful to his post, like a forlorn hope, and fully prepared to defend his ungrateful city to the last. These compunctions, however, were soon overwhelmed by the recurring tide of public apprehension. The populace arranged themselves before the house, taking off their hats with most respectful humility—Burgomaster Roerback, who was of that popular class of orators described by Sallust, as being "talkative rather than eloquent," stepped forth and addressed the governor in a speech of three hours' length, detailing, in the most pathetic terms, the calamitous situation of the province, and urging him in a constant repetition of the same arguments and words to sign the capitulation.

The mighty Peter eyed him from his garret window in grim silence—now and then his eye would glance over the surrounding rabble, and an indignant grin, like that of an angry mastiff, would mark his iron visage. But though a man of most undaunted mettle—though he had a heart as big as an ox, and a head that would have set adamant to scorn—yet after all he was a mere mortal. Wearied out by these repeated oppositions, and this eternal haranguing, and perceiving that unless he complied, the inhabitants would follow their own inclination, or rather their fears, without waiting for his consent; or, what was still worse, the Yankees would have time to pour in their forces and claim a share in the conquest, he testily ordered them to hand up the paper. It was accordingly hoisted to him on the end of a pole, and having scrawled his name at the bottom of it, he anathematized them all for a set of cowardly, mutinous, degenerate poltroons—threw the capitulation at their heads, slammed down the window, and was heard stumping down stairs with vehement indignation. The rabble incontinently took to their heels; even the burgomasters were not slow in evacuating the premises, fearing lest the sturdy Peter might issue from his den, and greet them with some unwelcome testimonial of his displeasure.

Within three hours after the surrender, a legion of British beef-fed warriors poured into New-Amsterdam, taking possession of the fort and batteries. And now might be heard, from all quarters, the sound of hammers made by the old Dutch burghers, in nailing up their doors and windows, to protect their vrouws from these fierce barbarians, whom they contemplated in silent sullenness from the garret windows as they paraded through the streets.

Thus did Colonel Richard Nichols, the commander of the British forces, enter into quiet possession of the conquered realm as *locum tenens* for the Duke of York. The victory was attended with no other outrage than that of changing the name of the

province and its metropolis, which thenceforth were denominated
NEW-YORK, and so have continued to be called unto the present
day. The inhabitants, according to treaty, were allowed to maintain quiet possession of their property; but so inveterately did
they retain their abhorrence of the British nation, that in a
private meeting of the leading citizens, it was unanimously determined never to ask any of their conquerors to dinner.

NOTE.

Modern historians assert that when tne New-Netherlands were thus overrun
by the British, as Spain in ancient days by the Saracens, a resolute band
refused to bend the neck to the invader. Led by one Garret Van Horne, a
valorous and gigantic Dutchman, they crossed the bay and buried themselves
among the marshes and cabbage-gardens of Communipaw ; as did Pelayo and
his followers among the mountains of Asturias. Here their descendants have
remained ever since, keeping themselves apart, like seed corn, to repeople the
city with the genuine breed whenever it shall be effectually recovered from its
intruders. It is said the genuine descendants of the Nederlanders who inhabit
New-York, still look with longing eyes to the green marshes of ancient Pavonia,
as did the conquered Spaniards of yore to the stern mountains of Asturias,
considering these the regions whence deliverance is to come.

19*

CHAPTER XII.

CONTAINING THE DIGNIFIED RETIREMENT, AND MORTAL SUR-
RENDER OF PETER THE HEADSTRONG.

THUS then have I concluded this great historical enterprise; but
before I lay aside my weary pen, there yet remains to be performed one pious duty. If among the variety of readers who
may peruse this book, there should haply be found any of those
souls of true nobility, which glow with celestial fire at the history
of the generous and the brave, they will doubtless be anxious
to know the fate of the gallant Peter Stuyvesant. To gratify
one such sterling heart of gold I would go more lengths than to
instruct the cold-blooded curiosity of a whole fraternity of philosophers.

No sooner had that high-mettled cavalier signed the articles
of capitulation, than, determined not to witness the humiliation
of his favorite city, he turned his back on its walls and made a
growling retreat to his *bouwery*, or country-seat, which was
situated about two miles off; where he passed the remainder of
his days in patriarchal retirement. There he enjoyed that tranquillity of mind, which he had never known amid the distracting
cares of government; and tasted the sweets of absolute and

uncontrolled authority, which his factious subjects had so often dashed with the bitterness of opposition.

No persuasions could ever induce him to revisit the city—on the contrary, he would always have his great arm-chair placed with its back to the windows which looked in that direction; until a thick grove of trees planted by his own hand grew up and formed a screen that effectually excluded it from the prospect. He railed continually at the degenerate innovations and improvements introduced by the conquerors—forbade a word of their detested language to be spoken in his family, a prohibition readily obeyed, since none of the household could speak any thing but Dutch—and even ordered a fine avenue to be cut down in front of his house because it consisted of English cherry-trees.

The same incessant vigilance, which blazed forth when he had a vast province under his care, now showed itself with equal vigor, though in narrower limits. He patrolled with unceasing watchfulness the boundaries of his little territory; repelled every encroachment with intrepid promptness; punished every vagrant depredation upon his orchard or his farm-yard with inflexible severity; and conducted every stray hog or cow in triumph to the pound. But to the indigent neighbor, the friendless stranger, or the weary wanderer, his spacious doors were ever open, and his capacious fire-place, that emblem of his own warm and generous heart, had always a corner to receive and cherish them. There was an exception to this, I must confess, in case the ill-starred applicant were an Englishman or a Yankee; to whom, though he might extend the hand of assistance, he could never be brought to yield the rites of hospitality. Nay, if peradventure some straggling merchant of the east should stop at his door, with his cart-load of tin ware or wooden bowls, the fiery Peter would issue forth like a giant from his castle, and make such a furious clattering among his pots and kettles, that the vender of " *notions*" was fain to betake himself to instant flight.

His suit of regimentals, worn threadbare by the brush, were carefully hung up in the state bed-chamber, and regularly aired the first fair day of every month; and his cocked hat and trusty sword were suspended in grim repose over the parlor mantel-piece, forming supporters to a full-length portrait of the renowned admiral Von Tromp. In his domestic empire he maintained strict discipline, and a well-organized despotic government; but though his own will was the supreme law, yet the good of his subjects was his constant object. He watched over, not merely their immediate comforts, but their morals, and their ultimate welfare; for he gave them abundance of excellent admonition, nor could any of them complain, that, when occasion required, he was by any means niggardly in bestowing wholesome correction.

The good old Dutch festivals, those periodical demonstrations of an overflowing heart and a thankful spirit, which are falling into sad disuse among my fellow-citizens, were faithfully observed in the mansion of Governor Stuyvesant. New-year was truly a day of open-handed liberality, of jocund revelry, and warm-hearted congratulation, when the bosom swelled with genial good-fellowship, and the plenteous table was attended with an unceremonious freedom, and honest broad-mouthed merriment, unknown in these days of degeneracy and refinement. Paas and Pinxter were scrupulously observed throughout his dominions; nor was the day of St. Nicholas suffered to pass by, without making presents, hanging the stocking in the chimney, and complying with all its other ceremonies.

Once a-year, on the first day of April, he used to array himself in full regimentals, being the anniversary of his triumphal entry into New-Amsterdam, after the conquest of New-Sweden. This was always a kind of saturnalia among the domestics, when they considered themselves at liberty, in some measure, to say and do what they pleased; for on this day their master was always observed to unbend, and become exceeding pleasant and jocose, sending the old gray-headed negroes on April-fools errands for pigeons' milk; not one of whom but allowed himself to be taken in, and humored his old master's jokes, as became a faithful and well-disciplined dependant. Thus did he reign, happily and peacefully on his own land—injuring no man—envying no man—molested by no outward strifes; perplexed by no internal commotions—and the mighty monarchs of the earth, who were vainly seeking to maintain peace, and promote the welfare of mankind, by war and desolation, would have done well to have made a voyage to the little island of Manna-hata, and learned a lesson in government from the domestic economy of Peter Stuyvesant.

In process of time, however, the old governor, like all other children of mortality, began to exhibit evident tokens of decay. Like an aged oak, which, though it long has braved the fury of the elements, and still retains its gigantic proportions, begins to shake and groan with every blast—so was it with the gallant Peter; for though he still bore the port and semblance of what he was, in the days of his hardihood and chivalry, yet did age and infirmity begin to sap the vigor of his frame—but his heart, that unconquerable citadel, still triumphed unsubdued. With matchless avidity would he listen to every article of intelligence concerning the battles between the English and Dutch—still would his pulse beat high, whenever he heard of the victories of

De Ruyter—and his countenance lower, and his eyebrows knit, when fortune turned in favor of the English. At length, as on a certain day he had just smoked his fifth pipe, and was napping after dinner, in his arm-chair, conquering the whole British nation in his dreams, he was suddenly aroused by a ringing of bells, rattling of drums, and roaring of cannon, that put all his blood in a ferment. But when he learnt that these rejoicings were in honor of a great victory obtained by the combined English and French fleets over the brave De Ruyter, and the younger Von Tromp, it went so much to his heart, that he took to his bed, and, in less than three days, was brought to death's door, by a violent cholera morbus! Even in this extremity he still displayed the unconquerable spirit of Peter *the Headstrong*; holding out to the last gasp, with inflexible obstinacy, against a whole army of old women who were bent upon driving the enemy out of his bowels, in the true Dutch mode of defence, by inundation.

While he thus lay, lingering on the verge of dissolution, news was brought him, that the brave de Ruyter had made good his retreat, with little loss, and meant once more to meet the enemy in battle. The closing eye of the old warrior kindled with martial fire at the words—he partly raised himself in bed—clinched his withered hand, as if he felt within his gripe that sword which waved in triumph before the walls of Fort Christina, and giving a grim smile of exultation, sank back upon his pillow, and expired.

Thus died Peter Stuyvesant, a valiant soldier—a loyal subject—an upright governor, and an honest Dutchman—who wanted only a few empires to desolate, to have been immortalized as a hero !

His funeral obsequies were celebrated with the utmost grandeur and solemnity. The town was perfectly emptied of its inhabitants, who crowded in throngs to pay the last sad honors to their good old governor. All his sterling qualities rushed in full tide upon their recollection, while the memory of his foibles and his faults had expired with him. The ancient burghers contended who should have the privilege of bearing the pall; the populace strove who should walk nearest to the bier, and the melancholy procession was closed by a number of gray-headed negroes, who had wintered and summered in the household of their departed master for the greater part of a century.

With sad and gloomy countenances, the multitude gathered round the grave. They dwelt with mournful hearts on the sturdy virtues, the signal services, and the gallant exploits of the brave old worthy. They recalled, with secret upbraidings, their own factious oppositions to his government; and many an ancient burgher, whose phlegmatic features had never been known to relax, nor his eyes to moisten, was now observed to puff a pensive pipe, and the big drop to steal down his cheek; while he muttered, with affectionate accent, and melancholy shake of the head—" Well, den!—Hardkoppig Peter ben gone at last!"

His remains were deposited in the family vault, under a chapel which he had piously erected on his estate, and dedicated to St Nicholas—and which stood on the identical spot at present occupied by St. Mark's church, where his tombstone is still to be seen. His estate, or *bouwery*, as it was called, has ever continued in the possession of his descendants, who, by the uniform integrity of their conduct, and their strict adherence to the customs and manners that prevailed in the *"good old times,"* have proved themselves worthy of their illustrious ancestor. Many a time and oft has the farm been haunted at night by enterprising money-diggers, in quest of pots of gold, said to have been buried by the old governor—though I cannot learn that any of them have ever been enriched by their researches—and who is there, among my native-born fellow-citizens, that does not remember when, in the mischievous days of his boyhood, he conceived it a great exploit to rob " Stuyvesant's orchard" on a holiday afternoon?

At this strong-hold of the family may still be seen certain memorials of the immortal Peter. His full-length portrait frowns in martial terrors from the parlor wall—his cocked hat and sword still hang up in the best bedroom—his brimstone-colored breeches were for a long while suspended in the hall, until some years since they occasioned a dispute between a new-married couple—and his silver-mounted wooden leg is still treasured up in the store-room, as an invaluable relique.

CHAPTER XIII.

THE AUTHOR'S REFLECTIONS UPON WHAT HAS BEEN SAID.

AMONG the numerous events, which are each in their turn the most direful and melancholy of all possible occurrences, in your interesting and authentic history, there is none that occasions such deep and heart-rending grief as the decline and fall of your renowned and mighty empires. Where is the reader who can contemplate without emotion the disastrous events by which the great dynasties of the world have been extinguished? While wandering, in imagination, among the gigantic ruins of states and empires, and marking the tremendous convulsions that wrought their overthrow, the bosom of the melancholy inquirer swells with sympathy commensurate to the surrounding desolation. Kingdoms, principalities, and powers, have each had their rise, their progress, and their downfall—each in its turn has swayed a potent sceptre—each has returned to its primeval nothingness. And thus did it fare with the empire of their High Mightinesses, at the Manhattoes, under the peaceful reign of Walter the Doubter —the fretful reign of William the Testy, and the chivalric reign of Peter the Headstrong.

Its history is fruitful of instruction, and worthy of being pondered over attentively, for it is by thus raking among the ashes of departed greatness, that the sparks of true knowledge are to be found, and the lamp of wisdom illuminated. Let then the reign of Walter the Doubter warn against yielding to that sleek, contented security, and that overweening fondness for comfort and repose, which are produced by a state of prosperity and peace. These tend to unnerve a nation; to destroy its pride of character; to render it patient of insult; deaf to the calls of honor and of justice; and cause it to cling to peace, like the sluggard to his pillow, at the expense of every valuable duty and consideration. Such supineness insures the very evil from which it shrinks. One right yielded up produces the usurpation of a second; one encroachment passively suffered makes way for another; and the nation which thus, through a doting love of peace, has sacrificed honor and interest, will at length have to fight for existence.

Let the disastrous reign of William the Testy serve as a salutary warning against that fitful, feverish mode of legislation, which acts without system; depends on shifts and projects, and trusts to lucky contingencies. Which hesitates, and wavers, and at length decides with the rashness of ignorance and imbecility. Which stoops for popularity by courting the prejudices and flattering the arrogance, rather than commanding the respect of the rabble. Which seeks safety in a multitude of counselors, and distracts itself by a variety of contradictory schemes and opinions. Which mistakes procrastination for wariness—hurry for decision—parsimony for economy—bustle for business, and vaporing for valor. Which is violent in council—sanguine in expectation, precipitate in action, and feeble in execution. Which undertakes enterprises without forethought—enters upon them without preparation—conducts them without energy, and ends them in confusion and defeat.

Let the reign of the good Stuyvesant show the effects of vigor and decision, even when destitute of cool judgment, and surrounded by perplexities. Let it show how frankness, probity, and high-souled courage will command respect, and secure honor, even where success is unattainable. But at the same time, let it caution against a too ready reliance on the good faith of others, and a too honest confidence in the loving professions of powerful neighbors, who are most friendly when they most mean to betray. Let it teach a judicious attention to the opinions and wishes of the many, who, in times of peril, must be soothed and led, or apprehension will overpower the deference to authority.

Let the empty wordiness of his factious subjects; their intemperate harangues; their violent "resolutions;" their hectorings against an absent enemy, and their pusillanimity on his approach, teach us to distrust and despise those clamorous patriots, whose courage dwells but in the tongue. Let them serve as a lesson to repress that insolence of speech, destitute of real force, which too often breaks forth in popular bodies, and bespeaks the vanity rather than the spirit of a nation. Let them caution us against vaunting too much of our own power and prowess, and reviling a noble enemy. True gallantry of soul would always lead us to treat a foe with courtesy and proud punctilio; a contrary conduct but takes from the merit of victory, and renders defeat doubly disgraceful.

But I cease to dwell on the stores of excellent examples to be drawn from the ancient chronicles of the Manhattoes. He who reads attentively will discover the threads of gold which run throughout the web of history, and are invisible to the dull eye of ignorance. But, before I conclude, let me point out a solemn warning, furnished in the subtle chain of events by which the capture of Fort Casimir has produced the present convulsions of our globe.

Attend then, gentle reader, to this plain deduction, which, if thou art a king, an emperor, or other powerful potentate, I advise thee to treasure up in thy heart—though little expectation have I that my work will fall into such hands, for well I know the care of crafty ministers, to keep all grave and edifying books of the kind out of the way of unhappy monarchs—lest peradventure they should read them and learn wisdom.

By the treacherous surprisal of Fort Casimir, then, did the crafty Swedes enjoy a transient triumph; but drew upon their heads the vengeance of Peter Stuyvesant, who wrested all New-Sweden from their hands. By the conquest of New-Sweden, Peter Stuyvesant aroused the claims of Lord Baltimore, who appealed to the Cabinet of Great Britain; who subdued the whole province of New-Netherlands. By this great achievement the whole extent of North America, from Nova Scotia to the Floridas, was rendered one entire dependency upon the British crown.— But mark the consequence: the hitherto scattered colonies being thus consolidated, and having no rival colonies to check or keep them in awe, waxed great and powerful, and finally becoming too strong for the mother country, were enabled to shake off its bonds, and by a glorious revolution became an independent empire. But the chain of effects stopped not here; the successful revolution in America produced the sanguinary revolution in France; which produced the puissant Bonaparte; who produced the French despotism; which has thrown the whole world in confusion!—Thus have these great powers been successively punished for their ill-starred conquests—and thus, as I asserted, have all the present convulsions, revolutions, and disasters that overwhelm mankind, originated in the capture of the little Fort Casimir, as recorded in this eventful history.

And now, worthy reader, ere I take a sad farewell—which, alas! must be for ever—willingly would I part in cordial fellowship, and bespeak thy kind-hearted remembrance. That I have not written a better history of the days of the patriarchs is not my fault—had any other person written one as good, I should not have attempted it at all. That many will hereafter spring up and surpass me in excellence, I have very little doubt, and still less care; well knowing that, when the great Christovallo Colon (who is vulgarly called Columbus) had once stood his egg upon its end, every one at table could stand his up a thousand times more dextrously.—Should any reader find matter of offence in this history, I should heartily grieve, though I would on no account question his penetration by telling him he was mistaken—his good nature by telling him he was captious—or his pure conscience by telling him he was startled at a shadow.—Surely when so ingenious in finding offence where none was intended, it were a thousand pities he should not be suffered to enjoy the benefit of his discovery.

I have too high an opinion of the understanding of my fellow-citizens, to think of yielding them instruction, and I covet too much their good will, to forfeit it by giving them good advice. I am none of those cynics who despise the world, because it desspises them—on the contrary, though but low in its regard, I look up to it with the most perfect good nature, and my only sorrow is, that it does not prove itself more worthy of the unbounded love I bear it.

If, however, in this my historic production—the scanty fruit of a long and laborious life—I have failed to gratify the dainty palate of the age, I can only lament my misfortune—for it is too late in the season for me even to hope to repair it. Already has withering age showered his sterile snows upon my brow; in a little while, and this genial warmth which still lingers around my heart, and throbs—worthy reader—throbs kindly towards thyself. will be chilled for ever. Haply this frail compound of dust, which while alive may have given birth to naught but unprofitable weeds, may form a humble sod of the valley, whence may spring many a sweet wild flower, to adorn my beloved island of Manna-hata!

THE END.